The Wisdom Of The Old Cities

Fritz Lerch

The Wisdom Of The Old Cities

By Fritz Lerch

Copyright 2016 Fritz Lerch

ISBN 978-0-692-79188-2

First Edition 11/21/2016

I'm writing this book for a number of reasons. The most singular reason is to provide a clear milepost for future people to understand that we did understand what was happening in the US and the world; we understood what the future could portend if a series of events took place. The second reason I am writing this book is to get a better understanding of my own intellectual acuity and philosophic thought. The third reason is to suggest a course forward to keep America and the world from entering into a second Dark Age of greater barbarity, pestilence, Orwellian surveillance and war than the first Dark Age.

Currently, we have a beggardly negro named Barrack Hussein Obama in the White House of the United States, whose highest calling in life appears to be to dance down the line in Soul Train like a simian in the throes of extreme cocaine intoxication while wearing platform shoes. Barry Obama from all know information is the progeny of misogynist rape, were Barry Obama a professional wrestler he would be hailed as coming from whereabouts unknown. Barry Obama's father resembles some anti-imperialist African Chieftain who could be enjoying a lightly sautéed human heart with Idi Amin on the veranda. His mother was some kind of flower child who from all outward appearances was utterly confused about the edicts of society and civilization, and hence open to the sexual predations of this Nubian beast.

Barry Obama brought with him to the White House an androgynous wife (Michelle Obama), who appears to have stored enough water in her rear flank to make it through the dry season. Michelle Obama is currently the odds on favorite to Christian the transgender bathroom in the White House. Barry Obama has allegedly fathered two girl children with this ebony hippopotamus, Michelle Obama, discounting rumors of his penchant for interracial homosexual fellatio. Barry Obama's right hand man is a carpet bagging negro heretic named Eric Holder, who Barry Obama had to personally baptize at the altar of political correctness. This administration has all of the integrity of some dastardly negro driving around in a twenty year old Chevrolet with 12 old copies of the TV guide glued together in the place usually reserved for the back window of the vehicle. The unofficial motto of this administration is Barry Obama empowering black thugs since 2008. The initial glee of the liberal cannon fodder at the second coming of this negro messiah is starting to wear off as they come to the realization, already known by the wise, that anything the black man has touched in governance is destined to be made worse.

CURRENT STATE ENCAPSULATED

Philosophically when we say that civilization is headed for destruction what do we mean. Is the whole civilization to be vanquished like Rome or Babylon or is the civilization destined to become a second class power like happened to Britain over the last 120 years. The British Empire ruled the world for a few hundred years based upon coffee, tea, tobacco, spices, opium and an extremely disciplined military. The US has basically followed a similar strategy except the trade products have changed to oil, tropical fruits, gmo crops, pharmaceuticals, heroin and cheaply manufactured goods from China. We are headed down the same road as Britain in the 1890's which will eventually cause the US to become a second class power and a realigning of the world. What causes civilizations to decay is it the rotting of governmental, religious and economic institutions or is it the decay of the peoples themselves or some symbiotic combination of all of these elements. I believe that there is a symbiotic relationship between all of these elements. As they are all prognosticators of the overall health of the civilization, they should be taken as a whole. Unfortunately, the tendency of any form of government is for its most self destructive traits to grow and not its most effective traits.

Let's look for a minute at what has happened in this country since the 1970's to produce such a general malaise. Why does everyone in society walk around with a frown on their face, even the wealthy? The answer lies in what has happened in the last forty years in this country. Demographically, we are becoming a less white country. We have been taking many minorities into this country from inferior cultures and nation states, in particular Mexico. This creates conflict because these people come from vastly inferior cultures and do not understand such complex topics as food poisoning by bacteria. These people that we are getting are so inferior, they do not even want these people in Mexico. We are an aging population and we will have less able workers who will be supporting an aging population of baby boomers. The reason that we have fewer workers is due to the declining birthrate caused in large part by a flawed tax system, however this is a global phenomenon as Europe and Japan are experiencing the same effect and are subject to the same type of political forces. This declining birth rate is largely a result of putting the tax burden on the middle class of countries. This aging population puts a greater strain on our medical services and other healthcare institutions. Based on real dollars there will be a decline in real income, the spending power of your money will decrease as the true value of the dollar is subject to market forces which we no longer have the power to control due to the lack of physical precious metals and the increased financial power of countries like India, China and Russia. There will be a decrease of highly skilled blue collar workers as jobs are outsourced and the knowledge and training with these jobs will leave also. Women are surpassing men in educational achievement; this will create a society that is militarily vulnerable as politics will be influenced more by emotional decisions and less by logic and quantitative measures. Large metropolitan areas have outpaced the growth in smaller metros and non metros for the last 35 years, this will create a more powerful political base in the cities which tend to be far more liberal and bureaucratically difficult to do business in than rural or the suburban areas. The growth of these mega cities will test our roadway infrastructure and educational systems as well as the water and sewage treatment facilities. There are a few important trends emerging: the browning of America, intermarriage increasing, college graduates living with their parents until a later age due to lack of employment opportunities and the cost of living, access to foreign markets for manufacturing, and the power of large corporations to control the macro economic infrastructure in the world and manipulate these markets to their advantage. People back in the 1970's would go to food, music and art festivals on the weekends and enjoy themselves. It did not matter what kind of car you drove, what your job was, what your GPA was in graduate school or where you came from. We do not have events like this anymore for a number of reasons. A great many people are lacking the personal discipline as a result of the way that they were raised to enjoy themselves at such a gathering. The feminist have espoused this ideology that women don't need a family or men, and that being a mother comes second to their career and themselves, family time is a waste of time. This feminist nonsense has been utilized very effectively to also act as a dogma for career women to not have kids and has played a role in the declining birth rate. We have become a society where individuals have a myopic focus only on themselves. This has been catalyzed by the long hours that people work in companies, many companies that I've worked for act like you are asking for a kidney if you ask for 4 days off. Why do we tolerate these things in our own society? We tolerate them because the populace has largely been programmed to believe that this is part of the new way. Should we shut down the factories for 6 weeks like in the socialized countries of Europe?- no. We should have a better work personal life balance in this country. I noticed that I got sucked up into this cycle myself and I had to really consider what life is about.

I will go through the institutions and topics contained in this book briefly and designate the root cause with each and then I will break these down and address each in more detailed manner and note the overlap between them. In the final analysis, I shall wrap all of these topics together and chart a course forward. These topics I believe are largely responsible for the mediocre state of the country as well as at the loci of many international problems.

Current State-American Business Model

The heart of the current US quagmire is the result of the corruption between business and government. Large international companies provide a corrupt conduit for a managed currency pipe line to politicians. This creates a skewed economic system that is fortified by peck sniff politicians such as McCain, McConnell, Reid, Schumer, Boxer and many other boodlers, jacklegs and grafters not listed. A marketplace has been created whereby large corporations are the final arbiters of their own laws and regulations which benefit them and stifle the competitiveness and innovation of small and medium companies in the marketplace. One of the most singular ways that this stifling takes place is by putting an onerous and expensive process in place that these small companies have to meet, in order to comply with governmental rules and regulations. Innovation is the defining weapon of competitive strategy for the US economy. We have the capabilities to innovate products better and faster than any country on the face of the earth, or any nation state in history and this is the competitive advantage which the US currently enjoys in business. Even though we control this innovation, we many times fail to manufacture these innovative products in our country and hence do not reap the full economic benefits of this competitive advantage. These onerous laws and regulations also stifle innovation.

The current business climate in the US is being dominated by fewer and fewer large international corporations. Large companies such as Google, Apple, and Microsoft are the gatekeepers of technology and basically have the say of what technologies get introduced to the public, and hence control the conscious realty created in this business environment. The only buffer on this theory is the veto power by the military and intelligence community of not letting certain high tech manufacturing secrets into the hands of our enemies.

The most singular destructive effect of this current corruption in this insidious economic and governmental laced monolith is that innovation which has been the driving force behind the US economy for the last 35 years and will continue to be so for at least the next 30 years has been stifled and controlled. This control has stopped the innovation of products in alternative energy, medicine and transportation; deeply entrenched business interest have robbed the American public of a better society where man is less dependent upon the government for resources. When we are dealing with technology in particular, smaller companies have the capabilities of creating greater innovations in a shorter period of time than large corporation. The most singular elements inside of larger corporations which stifle creativity are bureaucracy, petty jealousy, control of society, the rewards of patents and superior technologies from a monetary perspective.

Current State-Technological Revolution

We are entering into a new technologically revolutionary business cycle which has an ominous start. The last two business cycles can be instructive to look at, to gain a better under standing of the current problems that confront us and the gargantuan shifts in governance, business and culture.

The period between 1980-1992 can be characterized as laying the foundation for a prosperous economy, and coming out of a slight depression in the 1970's. The American voters wisely decided that a peanut agrarinanist from Georgia was lacking herculaneum leadership skills and not the mortal to be at the pinnacle of this economic cycle. This time period was characterized by the military industrial complex being the main driver of the economic machine and technological development in the arms race against the former Soviet Union.

The aspect of this period that is most singular in terms of control of assets and the cultural identity is people in business and government and the cultural identity that they created. The business leaders of this time period were born in the 1910's-1940's. These leaders were raised thinking that America was the greatest country, and during this period of their lives the country was the greatest. These leaders had an extremely powerful patriotic streak and this is reflected in the way that their money was invested. These individuals invested heavily in US industries and believed in the economic and innovative superiority of US industry. These large investors and magnates placed a high value on educational achievement, individual merit and the rule of law was respected. These people prided themselves on being part of the establishment. This old money aristocracy was centered on the financial centers of the East Coast even though their tentacles extended into the Midwestern, Southern and Western business centers domestically. These families are part of financial empires that were bulwarks of American industry such as Carnegie, Rockefeller and JP Morgan. These families set the political and economic agenda of the country and had since the beginning of the 20th century. Even though these individuals allowed some creeping liberalism in the governments of the East Coast in the form of gun control, affirmative action, high taxation and other measures. They were largely conservative stalwarts when it came to solid conservative economic principles and the movement of resources, who were largely not lured into foolish chicanery which runs contrary to the rules of biology.

The concept of trickle down economics was a valid concept during this time period, because these stalwarts of industry were plowing their earnings back into these companies and into the United States. In order to have trickle down be a viable economic concept, you have to have those who have large amounts of capital, have a nationalist streak and belief in the country, economic prospects and faith in the national currency. This time period was also characterized by job security, a strong family unit, male dominated society, innovation, recognition of individual achievement irregardless of personal designation and very little pandering to extreme liberalism.

The second economic cycle that we need to look at is the period from 1992-present. In the US, during this period large movements of capital were moved from the blue blood centers of the East Coast and to a lesser extent the Midwest to the West Coast and the South West of the US. The movement of this economic and political power took place because the East Coast did not have a friendly environment from a labor and tax perspective for the coming technological revolution. The East Coast and the Midwest had the intellectual capital and the land and clean water to fire the technologically revolution. However, there were two issues which totally halted the technological boom from happening on the East Coast and Midwest: The politicians were plugged into a paradigm which could not have allowed them to give these companies free land, water and lower taxes. This is the explanation of the tangible assets. The unions were also a problem, as they would have been unable to bend their principles for this technological revolution, another paradigm centered issue. These East Coast politicians lacked a sense of vision in understanding how this technological revolution was going to impact every aspect of life in America in the short and long term and the potential monetary windfall which was behind this revolution. They would rather stay with a failed economic system and paradigm rather than change and do what was best for their constituents, such is the mindset of radical liberals.

Executives of companies and capital investors do not like uncertainties and the West Coast had an economic environment where many of these issues were removed from the table. In terms of intangible assets, the people on the East Coast lacked the technological vision to make this happen. They were incapable of seeing the way in which these innovations were going to fundamentally change the way that people lived their lives.

The East Coast of the United States had been the economic and cultural center of the US since the 1920's and perhaps earlier. The wealthy magnates and their families from the East Coast basically dictated the agenda for the entire country at the macro level. The fundamental problem is that the political machines used a game plan in these cities that was economically successful for many years, however the nature of the economy was different and had changed in many different ways, namely the speed at which business is done and the embracing of new technologies. Some of the political machines in these cities had decided that it would be a good idea to impose a tax on people pay checks just for the privilege of going to work in these cities. The mayors of some of these cities have no clue about what is discussed when they talk about new locales for the location of a company or barriers to entry in the marketplace.

What developed in many of these cities in particular: NYC, Philadelphia, Boston, Baltimore, Detroit, Chicago, St Louis and Cleveland was this symbiotic relationship between politicians, union leaders and business men. This relationship involves money being paid from the businesses to union leaders in order to ensure that a certain level of work is done and to grease the political wheels. The union bosses give the politician a blanket union vote and they pass money onto the politicians who in turn give it to community organizers and religious hacks. This is a compact synthesis of how trickle down economics works in the Democratic machine. The bright side of this is that the individuals in business became sick of this parasitic machine taking the money out of the pockets of share holders and had decided to do something about it. That is a key factor in why the West Coast enjoyed this technological economic boom.

It is important to take a quick sojourn and examine the conscious world of union goons to examine on the micro level; the mind set which reeked economic destruction on these cities. Unions were recognized by Marx and Lenin as the perfect conduits through which to dump their pipeline of communism on unsuspecting rubes. They also realized that these union dues could be used to fund their apocalyptic political theories. The clearest theory of this use of unions to push a communist agenda is the teachers unions. The blue collar unions are no better, but more covert about their aims. These undistinguished union members are characterized by voting a straight democratic ticket irregardless of who is running and what they stand for, these members opinions are formed by shop stewards who think for them and also because these blue collar imbeciles are wholly incapable of higher level thought. These members are totally clueless about the actual political forces that actually drive their union. Many of the union members greatest intellectual achievement is passing the GED in their first three tries and managing to stuff their swollen guts into their elegant satin Teamster jackets. Unionist are convinced that it is their god given right or some political decree of which they have no knowledge of, that they are entitled to be paid $20/hr, full medical coverage and three weeks of paid vacation irregardless of the financial solvency of their employer. Unions absolutely love people who have these intellectual shortcomings and beliefs because they are pliable parts of the unthinking union money machine. They strike when they are told, vote for who they are told and have no higher thought than what if the town's football team trades their star quarterback. They are incapable of understanding the most rudimentary economic arguments and they completely fail to understand why cities that have been run by union supported Democrats have no manufacturing base in them anymore. This is one of the great mysteries of the universe which confounds these brigands particularly after a case of old Milwaukee and a few burnt bratwursts. They think that the root cause of this economic nihilism can be traced to people trying to take their rights away. They could not even entertain the thought that perhaps businesses don't want to deal with the union stranglehold. The most singular problems with these unions are that they fail to see that we are in the middle of a major technological transformation in civilization. Union membership is going to be lost because the only way that the US can remain competitive in manufacturing is to replace the human elements with machines. This has two important ramifications. One is that we are going to have a permanent lower class of unemployable and untrainable double digit IQ workers and the second implication is that jobs inside of factories are going to require a much higher level of technology training from maintenance and from the managers. This topic will be discussed in greater detail later in the book. What large companies and the politically corrupt, are doing right now so that they can resist the capital investment in this equipment, is they are flooding the marketing with cheap third world laborers who possess no familiarity with the wonderful conveniences of modern plumbing ie:Mexicans, Dominicans and Puerto Ricans. The catalyst to this capital investment is the overlords who are pushing the $15 an hour minimum wage; the real goal behind raising the minimum wage is to force companies to \make large investments in capital equipment which will replace US manufacturing workers and create a financial windfall in the form of a new industry which designs and manufactures this equipment. There are dueling financial interests at the top between those that own the current manufacturing companies and don't want to lay out the capital for these machines, and those who are pushing for the rise in wages so that they can develop this new automated manufacturing industry and makes the machines for this technological boom. This is really a battle between the old world and the new world from a technological paradigm. The socialist protesters who are pushing for this raising of the minimum wage have no idea what the real agenda behind this is. They falsely believe that this is their golden opportunity to get even with the bully boys of capitalism and put up a solid victory for the proletariat. The government does not want these workers replaced too quickly as this will create chaos in society as this is such a major paradigm shift for mankind.

We also have the wrong philosophical mindset at upper management in manufacturing. The mindset of many company owners and senior management is that we are making a profit therefore we are successful and are operating the company correctly. There is a difference between making a profit and doing things with the best strategic tools. That you are running a profitable company does not by any standard entail that your company is running at anything approaching maximum efficiency. This is a point that is missed and not understood by many in US business. It is necessary to be process oriented in order to build long term sustainable results oriented companies. When companies become focused on short term profits and are not process oriented the results can be disastrous. This phenomenon has shown itself in the United States in the auto industry, stereo and TV manufacturing and the production of high grade steel. These were all industries inside of the US which were making sizable profits in recent times and had no vision to take a look at continuous improvements in their processes, methods and material. This lackadaisical attitude that correlated profit with proper methodology caused all of these industries to be partially or totally wiped out in the US by foreign competition, primarily by the Japanese who were looking to continuously improve their manufacturing methods and ultimately the quality of their products. Further evidence of this phenomenon can be found in the DOW 30 industrial average of 1896, the DOW 30 still exists but every single entity on the list in 1896 has disappeared. Currently, we have a system in the US where a great many people are basically worked to death and their wages are set, so that they barely have enough to keep themselves from drowning in financial debt which will eventually cause these individuals to be removed from society. This is largely a factor of the weakness of the dollar as a form of currency, greed at the upper levels of management, and degenerate trade negotiation. After Nixon pulled the US off the gold standard on August 15, 1971, thirty five dollars purchased one ounce of gold; the dollar now requires roughly one thousand three hundred and sixty dollars to purchase that one ounce of gold. We endured immediate inflation and malfeasance in the handling of government money after the divesting of the gold standard. This allowed the bureaucrats in DC to spend money which they did not have, and thus allowed them to basically have an open ended credit card. It also allowed virtually unimpeded spending on the military industrial complex and on social programs which made demasculized Democrats appear as though their sleeplessness was the result of the sufferings of the disenfranchised.

This high tech revolution has brought with it a windfall in other forms of power which are engendered by control of large amounts of assets and portions of the economy. The people that developed these high tech companies were primarily born between 1950-1970. These individuals hold a very different set of values from the staid class of earlier economies. These individuals have very little allegiance to the United States and this is reflected in their overseas manufacturing, investment overseas and in non dollar dominated assets. They are driven by a collectivist mentality, politically correct ideology (which is a soft form of tyranny) and a dislike of European heritage and achievement. Whereas the previous leaders played football and baseball in their free time these gynandrous men played video games and Dungeon and Dragons. The people on these high tech companies on the West Coast have been utilizing their new found financial power to push their own political agenda namely: transgender and gay minority status, hate crime laws and censorship, tyranny by technology and gun control.

The culture inside of these technology companies also reflects a new approach to business. We went from having a business culture where the achievements and failures of an individual are recognized to being a corporate culture where there is a collectivist effort. Namely no personal recognition for achievements, individuals aren't fired by one person they are fired by a panel. The current business climate has undergone a major shift in the last 20-30 years. This has been driven by the collectivist mentality that has become part of the culture of many of these companies. This mentality entails an understanding that nobody takes individual credit for their actions. If the entire group is in on the decision then we can not single out one person. This is part of the process of the destruction of the individual identity and a move towards a socialist economy. This logic can be seen in the way people are fired, they are not just fired by one person they are fired by a panel of 5 or 6 people. What this collectivist system does is usurp personal accountability and responsibility from any one person in the system. In this way, individual achievement or failure is not recognized. This pantheon presents the question of how people are recognized and promoted in these companies, if we are no longer operating on a merit system. The individuals in these companies have this sort of hierarchy without positions of responsibility, because at the bottom of the matter this is a reflection of the owner's personality and cowardice in accepting personal responsibility in business matters. The managers or individual operators are ultimately not responsible for what happens in these facilities. I would propose that individuals who are being promoted are going along with the political, social and cultural programming that is at the base of many of these companies. This is a furtherance of the political agenda from the upper echelons of these companies by utilizing economic control over people's paychecks to drive a political agenda. Namely, if you want a job a you are going to like our political agenda and by god you had better be one of the loudest clappers when the chairman of the board announces his affirmative action agenda for the year or you are going to find yourself on the miscreant list. This is a system based on uniformity to a sort of totalitarian ideology and has been practiced in many governmental agencies and inside of unions. This is the same type of culture that we see inside of colleges and universities where the power of peer pressure and the threat of poor marks are brought to bear on anyone who does not go along with the political program. This type of political correctness is a political philosophy which indoctrinates people to police and inform on others and it ultimately creates a society where you can not trust anyone. A society where no one is trusted has no cohesion and is hence able to be easily controlled by those in governance. This political correctness is used to stigmatize anyone who does not agree with the program, and the controllers will make the person appear as if they have mental issues for not going along with the program.

In business, the people who rise to the top are not always the smartest or best strategic thinkers. This problem, which has impeded business progress in the US, is basically a form of jealously whereby those who are skilled and intelligent are hated inside of companies and those who are mouth breathing yes men are promoted. There is a class of business professionals that will never rise much past middle management because of their intelligence and moral turpitude. For some, they do not understand why these people do not go past middle management. The real reason that they will never go higher is that they are extremely dangerous individuals and they are gifted with the intellect to close down a company either by being an over achiever, whistle blower or through other legal channels. The people that are holding these people down may not even realize why they are doing it, but they realize that there is something strange about these people. Their fellow co-workers may notice that these people are strange or even think that they are homosexuals.

An important thing to remember about business, is that most people are gutless cowards who protect their own turf and could care less if your family enjoys Christmas dinner at the homeless center. If you do not believe me take a look around your office and ask yourself how many of these people would you like to be in a military bunker with firing at the enemies on a foreign battlefield. The company that does not promote the strongest managers, fields a management team of mediocrity and will eventually fail in the marketplace. When an individual has greater intelligence and a better business skill set than all or almost all of the people that they work with, it is time to start their own company. If you do not start your own company you will continue to run up against two issues. One you will create jealously in your co-workers and boss who you will have far higher intellect than, and two you will have to sit and watch people make strategic decisions that you know are not the best way to do things and you will have to keep your mouth shut.

      In furtherance of our breakdown of the current business culture and issues within this technological revolution, let's look at the difference between the blue collar peasants and white collar people. The principle ability that separates these two groups is the ability to retain capital. By this, I mean that there are plenty of blue collar people in the skilled trades who earn six figure salaries. Even though these individuals have these high salaries they are incapable of retaining any of the money because they generally spend it on important things such as a $60,000 Harley-Davidson model diesel trucks with all of the extra accruements that the dealership has, or buy an $80,000 boat for a lake which they visit three times per year. From this nugacious dispensing of capital, the peasant (blue collar) class will always languish at the bottom of society aside from the fact that they have different clothes, vernacular and ideas about society this is where they will languish. The white collar class can put themselves at the top of the pyramid because they have the capability of understanding such concepts as the time value of money by investing in assets which almost always guaranteed a return, and the upgrading of equipment that they already have. There is a large intelligence, sensory variation and logical thinking gap between these two groups. The peasant class does not have the capability to taste the difference between world class chocolate from the North of Germany and Hershey's. Hershey's is the only anchor against which they have to judge chocolate. The same test can be applied to their beer. The peasant class will sit and drink Bud Light wholly unaware that they are probably drinking the worst beer in the world in terms of taste and craft. That's why when you are dealing with the general public you buy commodity quality products because most of the worker ants in any country are wholly incapable of differentiating between handmade goods of the best raw ingredients and items from the dent discount cart at the front of the grocery. In terms of the blue collar and peasant class, the intellectual base of this class is best seen in their humor and frequent topics of discussion.

Blue collar humor centers primarily around two topics, using the toilet and putting out disinformation on sexual activity. If you have heard a verbal exchange on these topics from these individuals it will be readily apparent that they understand neither of these topics on a high intellectual level, and in fact both topics are an intellectual mystery to them. However, that does not stop them from conveying information to others that they work with about the consistency color and texture of their latest dealings with feces. I also do not preclude them from putting out their sexual misinformation about such luminary topics as pregnancy, menstruation and venereal disease: obtaining sexual information from the first stall in the restroom of the nearest interstate truck stop is not the most staid information source. Women should take heed as well and not garner their information on gynecological matters from Frieda the Mexican woman in the packing department.

Affirmative action is another insidious bulwark of this warped West Coast agenda although its roots can be traced back much further to early communist movements in the US. Businesses have been forced into affirmative action by the philosophical destruction of the legal system by parasitic elements. Affirmative action is an insanity predicated upon the belief that the incapable can function capably if only given sufficient opportunity. Affirmative action further rests upon the absurd notion that the bestowal of third world genetics into the workplace of a first world country and the placement of these calumnious individuals into positions of management somehow enhances the company. This affirmative action aberration is nonsense, because the false supposition at the heart of this practice is putting individuals into positions that fundamentally lack the mental faculties and effectuation   to complete the job in a productive manner over the more qualified candidates somehow makes the company more effective. This policy promotes mediocrity over merit. This liberal nonsense puts US companies at a disadvantage in the world economic centers because we are not taking our best troops out to the battle. Taking an unqualified Indian who has been wearing the same pair of defiled grey pants everyday for a year and putting him into the upper rungs of engineering or management is an unwise decision and puts the company at a disadvantage. One of the greatest ironies of this affirmative action hoax is that these liberal high tech companies in Silicon Valley are not themselves subjected to this affirmative action poppycock, they do not have databanks of negro programmers creating their latest breakthroughs. They know damn well that putting negroes in key positions in their companies will destroy them, but this does not preclude them from forcing this apocalyptic agenda on others. Affirmative action ignores the innate human differences that exist within the human race and the strongest candidate should always be placed in the position or a weak link is intentionally being created in the management chain.

Technological Revolution And The Future Of The US And Europe

The Europeans have been cowered into socialism through the horrors of war. They have suffered so much that they have bought into this horrible system which has totally stifled creativity for a number of reasons: there is no monetary incentive to invent anything, socialism encourages conformity and not thinking outside of the box, socialism stifles people by pigeonholing them and socialism brings with it white slavery for a portion of the population. This socialist ideology is completely anathema to me and the culture in which I grew up. Socialism is largely to blame for the declining white birth rate in Europe and the US. Socialism does not invest in the middle class the means to create a family. Educated white people care about the way that their kids are going to be raised and educated. The underclass has no problem at all with sending their kids to the worst sort of schools. These are the considerations that go through a white mans head when he is planning on starting a family. Do you think the notion of educational integrity, which a negroe's child will get in elementary school, is a thought that has ever entered into any negroes head when he is disrobed and about to enter into coitus. Socialism is never voluntary it is always administered by force, because no people would voluntarily walk the road of socialism. The first victim of socialism is always personal initiative and thus innovation. However, this ideology seems to be a developing paradigm in many business institutions. There are underhanded communist who are pushing the same ideologies, under this political funnel which emanates from the upper echelons of these high tech companies on the West Coast, and in schools. This ideology manifests itself in the form of giving awards to everyone and disengaging the achievements of the individual. This is a dangerous ideology because this ideology is based upon the belief that everyone is equal in talent and ability and should therefore be paid and treated equally. This is creeping incremental socialism, which is quite perilous because one day you wake up and realize you country has changed so much that it is lost. Individuals that are pushing for an end to achievement tests in order to gain university admissions are of the same left wing school. How are colleges supposed to ascertain without the same quantitative measurement tool the abilities of a diverse student population? It is a given that being intellectually endowed is not the sole criterion for success. However, in a vigorous academic environment if you are fundamentally lacking the mental faculties to be competitive, then you will fail in your mission as a student at that institution.

There is a technological revolution that we are in right now; this will change not only the face of business but the nature of mankind's relation to work. We are reaching a point where all manual labor by man will become obsolete. Man will be largely replaced by machine. This is the only way that the US will have a competitive manufacturing base in the future against countries like China and India with low cost labor. The most unskilled laborers are about to become a permanent burden on the US society and what will happen to them is not going to be very pleasant; they are going to be permanently unemployable and hence a burden on society. Before the industrialists buy these machines, they will cut these workers salaries to below survivable wages and these employees will basically be worked to death. The women will also be working and this will not allow them to procreate and eventually this will end up destroying the white working class.

The coming changes in business and medicine are going to be directed so that they have a eugenic effect. The lower and middle class is not going to be granted access to the advances in medicine, without this access there will be eugenic effects upon these people .The reason that they will not be granted access is because their net output for society is far greater than there net input. There are going to be such advances in technology in manufacturing and other low skill set jobs that a means will have to be found to get rid of these people. The people especially on the bottom are going to become obsolete. Where we might have 30 people on a production line now, with upcoming technology we may only have 4 people on the whole line and these people will be trained for more technical jobs. This creates a few dilemmas for civilization, one we have approximately 200 million people in the US due to their low IQ's and motivational issues will be unable to be trained for this new economy. There will be fewer people in the country so our consumer goods marketplace will shrink considerably. The end game behind raising the minimum wage is to force companies to put their capital into this equipment. It is not in the government's interest to have this technological revolution happen quickly because that will displace a great many people quickly and cause a major disturbance to the economy and society. We have the technology for this equipment now; it is just being introduced slowly. Agricultural workers, waitresses, law enforcement, and factory workers will eventually be almost totally replaced by robots. Imagine a police force that is run with robots by four men behind computer terminals, this is the future. Governments and oligarchs have traditionally dealt with this kind of excess workforce in a number of ways. One, they have started a massive war. Two, they have instituted massive public works-infrastructure jobs which work people to death and three they have utilized biological and chemical agents to rid society of these people. These permanently unemployable individuals will be dealt with at the end of the next paragraph in the manner that I believe is most likely for them to experience.

The other important change that is about to come upon society is the advances in medicine. We will be able to grow human organs from a few sampled cells and insert them back into humans.

Many people are hailing this as great, however if the reprobates who are life long welfare recipients believe that they are going to enjoy this sustaining medical treatment they are sadly mistaken. When this technology first comes out it will be cost prohibitive for most hospitals. The hospitals in cities whose primary client are minorities and the poor will not have access to this. There is no one in society except some Democratic politicians who relies on block votes, that wants to see some old barnyard negro live to be 150 years old. The repercussions of this new medical technology are going to be multifaceted: the super wealthy will have access to these technologies and may become immortal, the poor will be allowed to die and there will be a point at which the two different groups will start to evolve differently. There will be a clean out of humanity before these technologies are rolled out. The usual methods that the oligarchs have utilized to clean out humanity are: wars, plagues, designed famines, economic destruction and biological and chemical poisoning. Due to the large removal that the oligarchs will deem as necessary, I believe that the most likely scenario will be a calamitous war. The important thing to remember is that this is not science fiction at some far distant point in time; this is the apex upon which humanity currently rests.

The eugenics problem can be pushed even further once we have the capabilities of DNA modification and designer babies. Once the intelligence code is cracked you are going to have a totally different stratified society. There will be a point in mankind where it will be decided whether or not to go forth with these super humans and what will happen will be like what happened in the evolutionary chain from Cro-Magnon to Homo-Sapiens when both of these species of humans inhabited Europe simultaneously except that there will be a quantum leap in human potential in genetically manufactured man. These capabilities are being developed now and they may already be done in secret labs around the world. What if the new humans ban together and decide that the old humans are a problem and decide to genocide them, these are moral questions that we will have to grapple with.

There is also the geographic shift of people who are retiring, many individuals who had successful careers in some states are incapable of staying in those locales. The reason for this is that the property taxes and other imposed expenses are too high. This is particularly acute in the states of California, New York, New Jersey, Massachusetts, Maryland and Illinois. The people that leave these states not only leave physically and sell their homes; they will bring their assets with them to their new locale. This is a trend which can have massive repercussions inside of the United States as well as internationally.

The US and parts of Europe are undergoing a massive financial upheaval and this will eventually lead to war and the destruction of the current society The resulting financial system will be contingent on which side wins the war. I will write specifically about the US, but the principle can just as easily be applied to Europe. War has a different dynamic for the different classes. The aristocratic class is emotionally unaffected by war because their blood shall not be spilled because they are not in a dangerous area of the conflict. The aristocratic blood is about 30 miles from the center of action where they are certain to have ready access to 15 year old scotch should they face a delayed delivery of a lorry load of fresh booze. The middle class and the lower class are the ones who physically fight wars; in order for these classes to mobilize, it is necessary through the use of propaganda to create a reality for these classes which creates a sense of urgency and fear of a godless enemy among these people. This notion relies upon the fact that a majority of these individuals are incapable of certain levels of logic and ascertaining what is actually going on in a theatre of war from incomplete information. In order to maintain this charade, the media is utilized to attack anyone who dare disagree with the story line being created. The clearest present example of this is the unmitigated attack that the media makes upon anyone who dares criticize the venerable Johnny McCain; even questioning something that he says inside the space of your own mind is blasphemous in the world of the mainstream US media.

For the aristocracy, war is an economic opportunity which ensures that they gain control of valuable assets or others individual freedoms. Propaganda from recent wars has been propagated by John McCain, Norman Schwarzkopf, George Bush Jr, Bill Kristol and Harry Reid. A prime example of a recent propagandist (ie: professionall bullshitter backed up by the mainstream media) is John McCain's hornswoggling of the American public into the first Gulf War. Amongst older Americans, McCain represents some type of patriotic sounding board, and he exploited this status to call for war. McCain did everything he could on TV to convince grandmas in Ohio that bearded hordes of unwashed Arabic men were coming to rape them and sell their daughters in foreign slave markets if Sad am Hussein was not immediately removed. The whole thing was a complete lie sold to the bamboozled American public. Sad am Hussein was accepting payment for OPEC oil in currency other than US dollars which was a threat to the US dollar, but this argument was far too involute for the American public to comprehend. We simply created a problem which the unsophisticated American public could understand in the form of a large mustached Muslim Cretan who had poisonous gas and it wasn't from a rotten kebab he had eaten.

    The current political situation facing America has been created by the masses of the great unwashed who vote, yet have no idea what the prime lending rate, Constitution, Bill Of Rights, petrodollars or the Magna Carta actually mean. For many of these men, I am surprised that urinating in a porcelain bowl a foot and half below their waste is not a daunting task. Some of these women, I am sure are equally confounded by the laws of biology which act upon their bodies every 28 days in the form of the man with the red suitcase. One only need travel to the vegetable section of the local Wal-Mart to get a field scientist eye view of these brigands and their offspring to grasp an understanding of the destructive racial and reproductive forces which destroyed the Roman Empire and currently threaten America.. In the United States, the current dysgenic problem has been created by unchecked immigration of swine from countries; like Mexico, Jamaica, Panama, and Puerto Rico and anywhere in the Middle East and Africa. The problem with the people from all of these countries is that they all have low double digit IQ's on average and they have no understanding of the concept of inalienable rights and do not support these rights when they come to the US. These people hail from civilizations where there is a low level form of tribal war lordship. The most singular problem that these individual create in a modern western democracy is that when enough of them get here; we go from being a first world country similar to a country like Switzerland, and we start moving towards a country like Brazil. Where you have a large mass of uncontrollable brown communist swine on the bottom that need the firm boot of a brutal military on their neck to keep them from stealing food, this is how police states start getting created and the rights of the citizenry start becoming usurped one brick at a time. Politicians can use the behavior of the third world cur mongers as a solid reason to take away the rights of whites also. This is precisely what happened in the Patriot Act.

 The situation currently in Europe is different from America in that you have the far left bringing in the radical scum of the Muslim world in to the EU to destroy the countries genetically, societally and culturally. The far left and jihadi's both hate white western culture and in this sense they seek the same aims. The whitest countries with the strongest cultures (ie: Germany, the Scandinavian countries, and Hungary) are the ones the cultural Marxist in Brussels most seek to eradicate. The problem with this strategy is that the leftist who are bringing in this rabble will eventually be attacked themselves. The Europeans are currently at the cross roads of a grave fork in the road, elements in the populace, military and police will either instigate armed revolt against the heavy hand of these culture destroyers in Brussels or their countries and genetic material will be lost forever. One notable difference between the US and Europe is that the Europeans have been disarmed and are at the absolute mercy of these Muslim swine. The patriots in the US still have guns and this is why it is soo vital to preserve this right, as it is always better to die a free man with a gun in your hand rather than live as a disarmed slave. The left seeks to ban private gun ownership, but the wise know that gun control is the road to tyranny. One only need take a long hard look at Europe right now to understand the foresight of America's founders and the grave importance of private gun ownership. The other situation that I see in Europe right now is that there is such a divide between the nationalist and the EU lap dogs that these countries would be unable to defend themselves from an outside attack. In Germany for instance, the government could not arm Germans from the former Eastern Block and some elements in Bayern because they would be risking an internal revolution if they instituted a military draft.

THE FIVE GREATEST MISTAKES IN THE HISTORY OF THE COUNTRY

I think it would be instructional for me to list and systematically analyze the greatest mistakes that have been made in the history of this country and analyze the ill effects that we are still suffering with today. 1. Integrating the public schools 2. Not returning the blacks to Africa after the Civil War 3. Not militarily sacking and destroying the country of Mexico 4. Not controlling the rise of the military industrial complex 5.Allowing bad entities to take control philosophically of the media, legal system, education system and finances in this country and to create a false consciousness.

Integrating The Public Schools

How in a forty year period did our school systems slip soo far, when we spend more on a per student basis than almost any country in the world. Well there were a number of seismic changes that this educational system was forced too absorb and the combination of these changes ground the learning process and the operational aspects of this system to a halt. This destruction was instituted by bureaucrats whose political ideology included pushing forth not only an insane multicultural communist agenda but of destroying the entire system. The hubris of these bureaucratic swine was such that they tried to forcefully convince a large portion of the public that their ideas were the only ones that had any merit, and that they were the only ones capable of implementing this virtuous program upon the educational system. These suppositions have no foundation in practice or theory. When these nacine communists could not foist these multicultural ideas on the public through propaganda, they utilized the courts to usurp the will of the general public as they did in <u>Brown vs. The Board of Education.</u>

    I was in school at North Glendale Grade School in the St. Louis metropolitan area when this court ordered insanity of school integration was foisted on the local community from unseen legal robes. My grade school had almost no negroes in the entire school, so these bureaucrats searched for the most squalid negroes they could find in order that my family and the other children at my school may drink from the well of cultural enrichment. When the bright yellow school buses came from the sacred land of Meacham Park housing project nobody knew what was going to emerge from those buses, until the buses pulled to a halt in front of North Glendale School. The bus driver unceremoniously opened the door of the first school bus and the acrid smell of violence, failure, disease, mental ineptitude, death, lack of personal hygiene, lack of self restraint, prison, and unkempt apes in trousers emanated from the door of that bus. What the liberals in the news media and their allies in government had been hailing as one of the greatest achievements in the history of our country now stood on the backdoor of my school. Strangely enough the elite boarding schools of the East Coast where the liberal elites send their kids to school were strangely untouched by this destructive phenomenon of desegregation.

    I quickly realized that the negro is especially skilled at the destruction of the learning process inside of the classroom. It takes only a single or few wayward negroes to totally destroy the learning process for all of the students in the classroom. This was a phenomenon which I observed first hand in my own local school and my parents swiftly identified this trend also. After only one semester of these tameless negro hordes, my father decided to place myself and my sister in a private institution of learning where we were no longer allowed to enjoy the wonders of a multicultural institution and instead were able to erect an economic fence around ourselves which isolated us from the internecine disease of liberal progressivism in the educational system. These negroes created massive backlogs in the punitive system in the schools from their barbarous behavior, to the point where some of the negroes should have been immortalized by having their names and faces bronzed on a bench outside of the principal's office.

The idea of placing low double digit IQ negroes in the same classroom with white students who are largely college bound has no basis in sound logic. The only thing that desegregation proved was the inferiority of the negro intellectually and from a moral-behavioral standpoint. While some liberals may have falsely believed that the negro was going to somehow obtain some of the white mans educational magic, this failed to happen. The educational failure of these negroes caused other changes to transpire within the educational context. This multicultural educational system then stopped tracking students. For those of you who were born after the advent of remote controls, I shall briefly surmise the practice of tracking in the schools. The underlying premise for tracking students is that students of like minded IQ's and capabilities should be placed in classrooms of similar students. This ensures that the students could be intellectually pushed at a level where they can absorb the maximum amount of material without being constrained by the feeble minded or overwhelmed by material that is too complex. This system also ensures a fairly uniform product is produced in all of these tracks. The assignment of tracks was ascertained by IQ tests administered at the schools. The IQ test created a quagmire in the multicultural educational community. These IQ test were almost uniformly stratified along racial lines, and no matter how much the multiculturalists tried to alter these test, the results they were obtaining were still uniform. What ended up happening was the schools scrapped the IQ tests, and they also did away with the tracking. This enabled borderline retarded negroes to display their paltry grasp of Euclidean geometry to individuals in the same class who were headed to the Ivy League. The system further digressed from this point, and the multiculturalists decided that the curriculums in schools should be watered down particularly in the hard sciences and mathematics. This ensured that that these ennoble savages would not feel bad about themselves because they had received poor marks. Never mind, the fact that this would put budding engineers, inventors and scientist at a major advantage against the rest of the world. The most singular problem with this sort of learning structure is that it creates an environment where the vast majority of students are not getting anywhere close to realizing their intellectual potential. The highest capability students are held down by the imbeciles in the class who are wholly incapable of gaining a grasp of the simplest mathematical and verbal concepts; and the imbeciles are overwhelmed by individuals who are capable of doing simple mathematical transactions without using their fingers. One nonsensical argument posited by these multiculturalists was that the IQ test was racist because it was designed primarily by Caucasians. This test design argument fails the logic test because if high IQ negroes had designed the test, the results would be the same. I love the fact that the liberals attempted to blame the IQ test designers for the abject failure of these negroes, like there is a secret test design lab somewhere and doctors are sitting around a table with beads of sweat running down their brows brainstorming about ways to stifle negroes on the test they are designing for the upcoming academic year. This type of insane thinking, allows one to see inside of the deluded mind of a liberal and how they always are trying to create a victim mentality and blame someone else for the genetic short comings of negroes. The negroes should have support groups similar in format to AA meetings where they can confess their abject intellectual failures to other sympathetic negroes. Some negroe named Janeer could start the meeting by saying yeah I dun thought I were pretty smart, and then I got my IQ test scores back and got a 74, I know that was racist I just know it. Competition in academics is healthy and brings out the best intellectually in students. However, having a 60 point IQ difference in a classroom is not only unhealthy it is down right insane. The division of tracks almost uniformly ends in whites and Asians being in the first and second tracks and negroes and their allies in track four. This may be the basis for a theory as to how all of the negroe constituents of any city seem to have an acquantance with each other.

    The educational system has numerous issues, however to boil it down into one sentence we can say that we need to develop an unbiased educational system that ensures that the individual creates the maximum value for society with the least educational waste possible. American negros have been a problem because they have been totally inassimilable into an educational system that is designed for college bound whites and this unassimalibility costs society billions of dollars yearly. However, there is a political body in this country that is wholly incapable of looking at the negro population from an unbiased perspective. The legacy of the desegregation of the schools is that three generations of white students had their primary school educational process either partially or totally destroyed by these unruly negro hordes.

The school districts have now re-segregated many of the schools because this theory of desegregation was such an absolutely nihilistic liberal policy. The worst part of this is that there are liberals in the news and other quarters who still act as if this was a major step forward for our civilization, even though there is compelling evidence about the abject destruction this policy caused. The public education system also has no competition which means that there is a virtual monopoly in public education, allowing these liberals to administer a second class intellectual education but a first class course in politically correct programming. What the politicians should be feverishly pushing is a school system whereby families can be issued vouchers for each of their students in a local school. These vouchers could be used for private schooling of their children and should represent the full sum of money that would be going to the public school. The money from these vouchers should be pulled directly from the local public school budget in this way; these unaccountable bureaucratic swine are hit directly in their pocket book and must compete for their students or lose their own livelihood. These vouchers would not only create accountability in the system it would force the public schools to be run as centers of higher learning and not indoctrination centers for political correctness. The cost of private schools would also be driven down as they would be allowed to grow their student body and through economies of scale could lower their tuition. The Democratic Party and the totalitarian teachers unions are totally opposed to any type of system which has any type of built in competitive mechanism. A perfect analogy of this is a town with only one shop, this shop can basically choose what they want to charge and serve their customers a product which may or may not meet their quality requirements. The shop keeper does not care, because the customer does not have a choice in purchasing any other goods. This is how the public education system works in the US at the K-12 level. Politicians need to lead and not be worried about what a few goons in the teachers union who read Marx on the commode care about what they are going to do. The private education system is better because it operates in the pantheon of the free market. While the private school education system does have a few issues like the parasites, who like to hang around boarding schools, so that they can rub shoulders with individuals about five steps up the social ladder from themselves. These parasitic social-climber individuals like to engage in conversations with the mothers of these wealthy offspring and act as though they have a very busy schedule but somehow may be able to tutor their kids in calculus; the truth of the matter is these parasites would give their left arm just to get a whiff of some of the Barron's of Wall Street's flatulence or be allowed to clean bugs from a dirty corner of their garage.

Our collegiate system is one of the key factors which keeps the US from sliding into an educational abyss. The reason for this is that the collegiate system is based upon an admittance system which uses standardized tests to select students. These standardized tests are basically variations of IQ tests, furthermore in this system the best generally rise to the top. However, there has been a move to implement affirmative action in admissions which is un-American because it allows unqualified candidates into slots which should be given to the best and the brightest. Another thing that gives the US college system a competitive advantage is the way that we look at business, we do not offer the European view that studying business is primarily a focus of economic principles. We utilize cutting edge techniques and skill sets when we train our business students, and we also have greater resources for research at the university level.

Not Repatriating The Negroes Back To Africa After The Civil War

The blacks were kept in this country and not shipped back to Africa after the Civil War, primarily by the forces of wealthy business men. These are the same forces that we see today bringing 3rd world immigrants and other such swine in the country to drive down wages and destroy the middle class. The negro needs the white man far more than we need them. We offer the negro electricity, modern pharmaceuticals, a fair legal system, satellites, automobiles, the internet, modern sewage treatment and a safe food supply among other things. There is no where in the world where the negroe is self sufficient; the unseen hand of the white man is always upon his back. The fundamental problem with the negro is that he has no place in a white society and he is bound by his IQ, moral inferiority and work ethic to be part of a permanent underclass. Could you imagine a vineyard in Napa Valley being started and producing a top wine, from some negro with a beaded hair weave and a half cocked smile. Indulge me even more and imagine a likeness of this negro on the label of the wine and the vineyard being named Chateau du Toquan. This image and name of this vineyard would radiate nothing short of the black genius in viticulture and the ancient art of wine fermentation in hand hewn oak barrels. No black has started any successful top vineyard in the world and they are not about to now. The negroe wholly lacks the faculties and discipline to produce something like Belgian beer or hand carved crystal. The negro has been imbibed with the intellectual faculties and skin pigments to conduct his business on the estate of the whites. Occasionally there are negroes who do not fit this mold, they are in possession of greater intelligence however these are rare specimens and almost universally have been endowed by white genes as a result of the moral shortcoming of a white ancestor.

In the United States currently, we have a rather dire situation in our major metropolitan areas as concerns negroes. Principally, the Democratic Party has figured out that they can keep a stranglehold on power and enjoy the graces of a black voting block, simply by telling these negroes that they will be fed and watered on a regular basis, and will be permitted to occasionally partake of a small amount of marijuana, can of Vienna Sausages and a barbecued turkey neck. The logic capabilities of these negroes are so infantilisimal that they can not figure out how this case of Ebonics déjà vu keeps transpiring. Some of the poltroons in the Democratic and Republican parties actually let these beggarly negroes make demands upon them and their offices and acquiesce. What cowardly and corrupt men we have become to let our former slaves dictate the economic, political and legal structures by which we are going to live our lives.

The negro has a racial survival instinct in politics, namely that he will covet his own people politically even when he knows that this politician or sheriff is wholly incapable of performing the duties of the job. The negroes would vote for Obama again if he defecated in front of the White House and ate it on live TV, this is how bought into this paradigm they are. Unfortunately for the negroe, his survival instinct in politics quite frequently has a dysgenic effect upon him and is the harbinger of economic calamity. There is a political body which I refer to as snake eyes; this is the phenomenon where you have a black sheriff and a black mayor. Snakes eyes is the irrefutable way to completely and totally destroy a city and all of its institutions Once snake eyes is established the first effect will be a spike in the crime rate, the negroe lacks the moral turpitude to deal with his own people in a fair and even handed way. The negro sheriff will roll out a great deal of crime fighting programs and act like his department is right on the edge of turning the corner on this crime wave but it will never happen as long as the sheriff is black. Businesses will leave the city as the crime escalates and the new mayor asks for bribes from successful business owners. The mayor and the city council will offset the economic downfall by putting a city tax on payroll for all companies; an economic stroke of genius which all economists from Keynesians to free market communists think is a good idea. The school system will rot as the new mayor slides some well heeled negroes in to key positions within the educational system. Eventually there will be riots, the negroes will go out and burn some of the economic lexicons of the black community: hair weave shops, Korean convenience stores which sell crack pipes, the local cash checking store, liquor stores with a fine menu of malt liquor and some fat negroes bbq shop.

What the negro fails to realize is that the narcotics pyramid is headed at the top by the super rich who trace their history of narcotics trade back to at least the time of the Chinese opium wars. Currently, rogue elements of the CIA, mafia and military and highly placed politicians at the state and federal level are the apex administrators of this pyramid. The middle of the pyramid is stocked by ex-military and mercenary elements who unload the goods and bring them into cities for distribution. The black community is the conduit through which most of these narcotics are passed at the lowest level on the street. An executive decision was made to sacrifice the soul of the black community to the profits of the narcotics trade. The negro community was intentionally constructed in the following format for the narcotics trade: a large number were intentionally placed on government assistance in the inner cities and were given enough money to live but not enough to thrive, if these negroes wanted more money there are few economic opportunities other than the street level drug trade. You now have the perfect sales force. The higher the level of violence the better it is for those at the top, as violence is congruent with greater profits. The negroes have been strategically placed in the center of these cities for amicable access to these drugs. The Democratic Politicians have no intentions whatsoever of stopping these open air drug markets as these narcotics peddlers are the core constituency of their voting base. This is a matrix that once the negro is under its spell there is no way out. Furthermore, the negro on negro violence which is largely a product of the competition in the drug trade has a slightly eugenic effect and does serve to keep the negroe population at bay. A tool that is used by those at the top of the pyramid to always keep these people on unsteady footing is to occasionally dump some bad dope on the street (either tainted or super powerful and kill off a few junkies) this is a very similar strategy to what we see employed in the Middle East whenever a stable government happens to emerge. The only difference in the Middle East is that a bomb is used in a red flag project. The reason that this strategy looks familiar is that it is developed from the same group of people. The CIA and other rogue elements use this untraceable money to fund many of their secret wars and purchase untraceable arms. There are a few negroes who have taken a step back to see the matrix, however it is always difficult to see the trees from the forest.

The negro fortunately has his own separate religious institutions, so he has not sodden the whites mans church or temple yet. The current problem with religious organizations is this issue of parasitic multiculturalism; I am talking about the Protestant and Catholic Churches. These religious institutions have both come under attack by elements that have aimed to entrench themselves within and destroy the religious orders with this politically correct program from the inside out. This was most recently seen in the Southern Baptist convention putting a negro in the president's chair in the organization. What transpired in this instance was a series of white guilt issues, which evinced the top leadership at the Southern Baptist Convention to engage in this calumnious decision, that they should place a self righteous negro at some position of power within the organization. This is a textbook case of creeping political correctness that has destroyed soo many other institutions. Putting any negro in charge of anything important is never a good idea, because there is always a white that is far more capable. Pope Francis is clearly a Chavanista aligned politically with a communist ideology which seeks to destroy Europe through Muslim immigration. The Catholic Church has fought for over a 1000 years to keep this Muslim scum from soiling the sacred land in Europe. If the leadership of the Catholic Church continues on this road of white genocide, I believe that you will eventually have a schism inside of the church. What some of these religious parishioners fail to realize is, that they have been ideologically programmed into a socialist Christianity that will eventually destroy their church. One should always be wary of those who would follow leaders, even religious leaders if it is clearly not in the best interest of their race. Deeply religious people have never invented anything scientifically because they do not have some corridors of the brain open to receive such ideas. When I was growing up the churches were divided along racial lines. The blacks had one church, the Irish, Italians and Germans each had their own and everybody enjoyed worshipping with their own ethnic group.

No white man wants to go into the lord's house and sit down in the pews with his family next to some ghoulish negro wearing a bright orange suit who smells like a fresh cut lime. These negroes like to sit in the pews with goofy macabre smiles on their faces, belaying an evil glimmer in the corner of their eye. This ivory smile conceals the dream like scenes of the anal rape of your 14 year old daughter and wife dancing the boogie woogie shuffle in this coolie's simian brain. These negroes always have an obese wife who sweats gallons of sudoriferous mammie juice on your freshly laundered suit and yells I've got the power in your ear for two hours. If the power makes someone smell like that then I don't want it. However, the cultural Marxist which have inflicted our religious institutions think that you should be forcibly inculcated in this Marxist dribble even in the Lord's House.

The fundamental danger of minorities to civilization is not only represented by their numbers and their ability to affect the political body. The greatest danger of minorities is their inability to grasp the philosophical precepts upon which the Declaration of Independence, the Constitution and the Bill of Rights are based on and apply these natural born rights to man in this country. The minds of the Orientals, negroes and mixed race Latino's are so far detached in their thinking from Europeans that it is impossible for them to apply ideas of justice and human rights in the same manner as the European/American model. The greatest threat to the civilization known as the United States is that these minorities will become a majority if the current trend continues. Though the republic may be based on the same documents, the application of the laws and governmental institutions will fail to be even handed or run properly. Could you imagine the local county health department being run entirely by negroes or how about the CDC. The ideas embedded in these founding documents are as foreign to the minority as the idea of being reincarnated into a beetle or rat is to a Western European. In India some of these ideas are embedded philosophically in ancient transcripts and modern society, this is why I distinguished the Orientals from the rest of the Asians. The negroes are the least likely to be reasoned with through an outlining of logic. The negroe is an idler who has no investment in improving himself, the European man far above the negro is an explorer and inventor. The average negro, is wholly incapable of venturing to a foreign land or doing field research, he barely has the faculties to explore the corridors of his mail box to see if his welfare check is there. The negroes in the United States would be living in a mud hut and cooking on dung bricks were it not for the genius and drive of Europeans.

Negroes should be treated like dangerous farm animals and kept in their pens. This is the policy that should be followed in our cities, we will leave some food and water for these violent swine but under no circumstances should they be allowed to leave this area, which would be like letting a bull out of his pen. One or two areas of the city should be designated as living areas for these creatures, in that format they are easy to control and allowed to corrupt and destroy only a very limited area. Anywhere in the world that the black man lives violence and disease follow him like his own shadow, this is one of the most concise and singular statements about the black race. The Obama Administration has done everything that they can to destroy white living spaces; however their most specious tool has been building federal housing projects in middle of white middle class neighbor hoods. This insures that the white folks get to enjoy the cultural enrichment that these blackened swine bring to the table when they wake at 11:00am in the morning step out the taxpayer funded front door with their winter hat on and start smelling the air like some mountain gorilla looking for his first bug and banana meal of the day. These building are never placed in gated mansion areas because the super wealthy and even the liberals have no oculation about what happens when these reprobates are placed in close proximity to their living and breeding quarters. The housing of negroes in any neighborhood housing project is like incubating a parasitic horde of violent malfeasors ready for the call to riot by so called black leaders or the local Democratic official.

NOT SACKING MEXICO MILITARILY WHEN WE HAD THE CHANCE

Except by warfare is it possible to go into another country as an outside group and conquer the people if you do not speak their language. The concise answer is yes, this is the legacy of our not dealing with these vulturous swine in Mexico in a decisive military manner. We had the opportunity in the Mexican-American war to sack Mexico and seize their land and assets which we should have done. Instead a decision was made against the proponents of the All of Mexico Movement, to pay reparations to Mexico and allow these genetic Indian train wrecks to ripen into a cancer on the face of Uncle Sam. Mexico not only has oil and fertile ground it is the principal producer of silver in the world. One can clearly see from the example of South Africa or Israel what happens when you have a population of savages outside the gates of your country and they are not dealt with in a definitive matter. The Mexican genetics would have lowered the IQ of the US and this was recognized by the political body at the time had we accepted these Indian genetics into our gene pool, therefore there were only two ways with which to deal with the population of Mexico. They could have been genocided back into the sands from which they came or the population could have been pushed out of the territory. Leaving Mexico to its present course was a terrible decision as this land of hepatitis and tamale flatulence has now become a country of 140 million plus breeding maggots. Mexico is a parasitic country which utilizes the US as its chief dumping zone for illegal drugs; this insures just enough monetary flow to keep Mexico from having a communist insurgency emanating from Chiapas. Through these transactions for drugs, wealth is being permanently siphoned from the US and put into Mexico. Mexicans come to the US illegally and send money back to Mexico on which no payroll taxes are deducted, this gives greedy employers cheap labor but it also helps bring the end of the government social security Ponzi scheme a day closer to collapse. The Mexicans drain further money from our country in the cost of housing these animals in our penal institutions and in attempting to train their piglets in our educational institutions.

Mexico lost a great deal of its territories through armed conflict with the US. The impetus of these defeats was superior technology, battlefield tactics and ultimately intellectual and genetic superiority. The Mexicans have no ambiguities that the European –Americans are far superior to them intellectually, morally and genetically and they harbor an absolute hatred of us for it. Immigration can be beneficial to a society in that it allows a superior society to effect a brain drain and bring the greatest scientific and cultural talents into a superior civilization. This phenomenon can be observed with a nation state as well. Thus great minds are drawn to areas of a country where there skills will be appreciated and they can be monetarily compensated in the greatest manner. However this is not the only symbiotic effect of the groupings of these stratified individuals, they also enjoy the companionship, camaraderie and ability to be sounding boards for those of a similar skill set in like industries. This is why places like Silicon Valley and Austin Texas act as magnets for technology gurus and why places such as Greenwich Village and Sedona Arizona and soho act as magnets for artists. These places not only offer abundance for these individuals there is also a sense of community and it allows these skilled people to take a look at others in the same field and try and push the boundaries further for themselves and not stay in the same place. These areas become incubators for new technology and artistic movements which develop a healthy competition for innovation, whether these ideas have buoyancy in the marketplace is another thing. What the Mexicans genetics are doing is steering the average workforce IQ in the US back toward the intellect of the Cro-Magnon, and this effect acts contrary to the intellectual evolvement of civilization and the reaching of human potential.

Immigration should be looked at as an opportunity to select individuals from around the world who can help strengthen the areas of civilization upon which we are weak or can help us develop new sets of skills which do not exist in our current civilization. Immigration as used by the business and ruling elite is a force which can propel society in two directions. Society can move towards creating a higher society which moves towards a civilization like they have in Switzerland where there is great emphasis on the intellectual value of the individual and a development of a complex skill set that is very specialized and used to produce unique products. In this society, a far greater emphasis is placed on the quality of the individual over the quantity. In this society individual freedoms are quite high as Switzerland has the freeist gun right laws in Europe and this society is largely racially homogenous even though Switzerland has different languages, there is a high degree of clear nation identity in this country. This society will have a low crime rate as those with low IQs will largely be bred out of this country, and those that remain will be gainfully employed and their propagation will be held in check by their monetary compensation for their skill set. The other direction that society can go in is the destructive trajectory that the US is currently on.

We are moving toward a civilization which resembles Brazil; we are starting to have a class of ruling oligarchs on the top and a massive brown communist mass of peasants on the bottom, with every Mexican or other third worlder that enters this country the IQ of the labor pool slips. In this respect, this is an attack on the high paying jobs that require a complex skill set. This also moves us closer to being a civilization where the military is used to control the population and hence a militarization of the police forces and erosion of civil rights. Employers are going to put their companies in settings where the labor pool matches the necessary skill set for the work. A key point to remember is that very few Mexicans have ever been hired for their intellectual capabilities.

Failure To Control The Growth Of The Military Industrial Complex

The rise of the military industrial complex was warned of by President Eisenhower in 1954. The Vietnam War was when this steep military spending phenomenon really took off, the US military spending as a percentage of GDP continued to accelerate even as the GDP itself went up. One of the greatest known effects of war is that the bankers make money hand over fist as wars are expensive business. In medieval Europe, leaders would borrow money from usurers; today we still do the same thing which puts our democracy increasingly at the mercy of bankers. When Nixon pulled us off the gold standard, this fiat currency matter was made worse because this allowed the bankers to create money out of thin air, with nothing backing it up of any value. This financial power then allowed the banking industry in the US to exert a greater deal of control over their industry regulations contrary to the interest of the people and institutions in the US. The US economy led by these cowardly neocons represented by Bill Kristol John McCain, Glenn Beck, Mitch McConnell, Paul Wolfowitz, Michael Chertoff, The Bush Family and Paul Ryan preceded to start running the democracy into a chasm of unextractable debt. This warmongering has led us into an economy where it is contingent for the US to be in a constant state of war, the problem is that this road leads to a complete and total collapse of the dollar fiat currency and hence the US economy. This can be stopped right now if the will exists to stop it, however the current poltroons in government do not have the intestinal fortitude to stop it. This further creates the dilemma of politicians going out with nefarious propaganda and convincing the general public that the latest boogeyman is the greatest threat that the country has faced since the Spanish flu. My favorite repeated scene in this theatre of the absurd is when some politician gets on a Sunday talking heads show and says that he has a great deal of trust in the American public. What he means is that he beliefs that the American public is going to buy his latest pile of fresh manure at a fair price, which is the conscious realty created by him and his henchmen in the news industry. One of the most singular problems in the military industrial complex is the fact that since the Korean War the politicians have attempted to run the wars from Washington DC. The most glaring example of this was the Vietnam War. War should be a nihilistic force when used, and if you are going to go into war then you should be prepared to die yourself in the worst way possible. This is what war is, it is not some sanitized drone game, civilians are going to die and you can't be concerned about them if you are truly going to war. The US propagandist have created a large pile of bogeymen from the yellow gooks in Vietnam and Korea, to the communist Russians who don't want to practice religion, to North African warlords who wear restaurant table cloths, to tropical women with large shoe collections, to Central American dictators with pock marked faces and cocaine addictions, to communist dictators who smoke cigars and like baseball, to fat

African dictators who look like hotel valets and have a bunch of self awarded military medals, and finally to Middle Eastern dictators with big mustaches who gas people, most Americans have never fucking heard of and don't care about. The real question is how many of these people were really threats to vital American interests and did we deal with the real threats in a decisive manner militarily?

Allowing Bad Interests To Philosophically Insert Themselves Into The Legal System, Media And Finances

The philosophical underpinnings of our legal system have been bent through the courts making law and judicial stacking as well as a system that is crafted so that the legal professionals in the system are able to extract the maximum amount of financial gains. T he legal system has been recently utilized to legislate from the bench in favor of this nonsense known as gay marriage. When these leftist have failed because the population will not accept their ideas in a democratic election; they have taken to finding sympathetic judges to push forth their political agenda against the will of the people and against the principle of legislating from the bench which the forefathers of this country intended to never transpire. The legal system in the US has become a money machine which distributes money to trial lawyers who are the vanguard of pushing this nihilistic socialist agenda. Through the use of such things as discrimination lawsuits, companies are financially blackmailed into acquiescing to the demands of these rogue legal elements whether they are guilty of discrimination against minorities or not. It is a better financial risk to settle with these communist beggars than face the prospect of going to trial and paying fifty times as much. Whether the company is guilty or not is one of the lowest factors in the equation. Our legal system needs to be barricaded against these frivolous lawsuits which do not ultimately involve questions of the law, and these minority reprobates need to accept the fact that they were terminated for having poor performance at work. We also need to have caps on lawsuits as this will lower the insurance cost for individuals and companies. The legal system and its outcomes should not be a guiding force for business and it operation within certain localities.

  The mainstream media in the US is controlled by a small number of individuals who have interlocking interests with the boards of directors of these large international companies. This is the NWO and I will explain briefly how they operate and why they represent a danger to all free men in the world. Lets first look at how the mainstream media is utilized in order to create consciousness and control the American public. These same principles are utilized in every country to control the unthinking masses. The mainstream media creates consciousness by covering stories that support the world view that they want the public to believe this is the conscious reality, let's look at the Ferguson shooting in Missouri of Michael Brown as a prime example. The reality is that very few white officers shoot black men, in comparison to the number of blacks that kill their own people on a daily basis. The mainstream media does not want to deal with facts, what they want to do is try to create a story line wherein, we have many racist officers who are going out and looking to shoot young blacks. They are trying to create the false reality in the public conscious that these police officers are straightening up their ties in the mirror in the morning, and saying I am going to shoot some really down and out negro today whether he deserves it or not. This is the false narrative that the mainstream media is creating. The mainstream media should be asking Michael Brown's parents how they managed to raise such an unworthy swine in this country, and how in so few years under their guidance Michael Brown became such a violent felon. The media will also use outright lies in the propaganda such as hands up don't shoot which never occurred in reality, but if you keep repeating the same lie to enough stupid people, eventually they will start to believe it. This type of propaganda is based on building upon hatred and jealousies that already find themselves buried in the average negroes cavernous skull. It is just like training a dog for schutzhund, you are building up the animals natural prey instincts. Then the string pullers will hire rent a mob protestors and present this on the TV news even though it may only be a few protesters, like this is a major issue with millions of people backing this cause when in reality it is a couple of wayward swine who when actually questioned have no grasp of the issues involved. The media will then elicit legal advice from uneducated negro women on the streets who are more than willing to give their interpretation of statutory law to the media. The media gives these swine credence by putting them on the national news. The media continues to bait these people more and more until a violent episode happen, like in the case of Black Lives Matter terrorists urging the murder of upright police officers. This is the short term goal of these string pullers because as the violence and chaos escalates, this creates a situation where the public will be begging for someone to save them. However, in order to save the general public their rights will have to be taken away, and they will incrementally be positioned into a tyrannical society and government. This is the ultimate goal of the string pullers to enslave the people and have complete control over the banking systems and resources of the country. This is the stage that we are at, at this point in time in America we are sitting upon the precipice of going one way or the other. 9/11 Which I believe was a red flag event, only helped aid the process along, as it set the stage for the government to suspend habeas corpus under a wide legal definition and it also authorized a suspicion of the 14th amendment and massive surveillance in the country to the point where every electronic communication and phone call was being recorded. How convenient it was that members of the Bush administration just happened to have financial relationships with companies which provided full body scanners for airports and other equipment to this Orwellian surveillance state, a complete coincidence I am sure. Let's take away their rights and make a buck out of doing it. The news media is utilized at every point to create the belief that suspending the constitution is the only reasonable thing to do in order to solve this problem and keep order. This is complete nonsense; your rights should never be given up to the authoritarian gangsters.

The Homosexual Problem

Homosexuals have been around since the beginning of man and with few exceptions they have been the worst case of idiocy in the sexual world. The reason that they are despised from the most backward tribes to the most modern societies is that they have been eternal pariahs of disease. Liberals will defend this aberrant behavior because the facts don't matter, what matters is the emotional appeal of the argument. The problem with the homosexuals is that the sexual acts that they engage in have repercussions beyond themselves. Currently homosexuals cost society in the inflated rate of venereal disease and the economic impact upon the medical and insurance industries. Homosexuality is also anti-civilization because this deviative union is incapable of producing offspring. I do not care if homosexuals engage in these acts, if some fruitcake wants to put another adult fruitcake on the receiving end of his stink hammer that is his business. The homosexuals have even invaded the senate; Barney Frank is a former member of the senate whose index finger has the permanent odor of some other man's rectum permanently engrained in it

The fundamental problem is that the homosexual lobby has political aims and is seeking minority status for these sexual reprobates. This minority status is already causing legal issues in states which have created non-discrimination laws against homosexuals. These issues should have been clearly seen by politicians and these ridiculous laws should not have been unjudicially forced on businesses and the public. These fruitcakes have taken page one out of the negro victim handbook and are claiming when they get fired, that it is solely because of the enjoyment they take from despoiling the fruits of another mans anus not because of their job performance. Furthermore, I do not want some fruitcake cooking my cheeseburger after he has just been shoving his fist up some other fruitcake named Larry's ass and acting out the first scene in some kind of queer thespian theatre. In conclusion, homosexuals, lesbians, transsexuals and other sexually confused blackguard who engage in this unchaste business are free to do so but this does grant them the right to strong arm the public into accepting them or granting them minority status. The last two great civilizations to accept this aberrant behavior were the Romans and Greeks, and it contributed to their moral destruction. What many in these radical homosexual political organizations or any radical left organization do not realize, is that these are the only people that will tolerate them socially.

Deterioration Of The Small Farm Erosion of Property Rights

There has been an unholy coalition between agribusiness, international banks, ruling oligarchs, UN agendist and grocery interests to destroy small farms in the US since the 1970's.

Agribusiness seeks to destroy the small farms for a number of reasons. The most singular and financially compelling is that they wish to force these farms to use gmo seeds and the accompanying farming methods. These companies have utilized the courts to force compliance through lawsuits involving accidental germination of non-GMO fields. These companies have also tried to control the labeling of their products through aggressive lobbying and corruption of the political process by financially fueling politicians, this process has been highly effective in the US but has created great difficulties in other countries. If there is nothing wrong with GMO foods then these companies should not be opposed to having their food labeled as such. GMO farming is unsustainable and the gains made from production by using these products is offset by the destruction of beneficial bacteria, the pollution of water resources, the effects upon human dna and the rest period for fields using this farming method. The other more odious aspect is the lack of long term studies on GMO food and lack of objective scientific studies which are non industry funded. The agribusiness has set the cost of butchering animals and the vaccination requirements so high that the cost are prohibitive if you are not running an extremely large feed lot. Through legislation and control of the slaughterhouses the industry has totally destroyed the model of profitability for small live stock keepers. The control of vast amounts of livestock on a single property is much more dangerous from a disease perspective than a smaller farm where the farmer has more direct knowledge of his animals and their health condition.

    The destruction of the small farm is tied into a larger agenda and more issues namely the federal government owning large swaths of land, water rights, energy control and mineral rights. The controllers do not want micro farms and have tried to pen legislation against them for a number of reasons; the most singular is self reliance. As technology continues to increase, this will make the concept of living off the grid and producing your own water a reality with low cost water, energy and filtering your own sewage an effective and viable concept. The controllers want you in metro areas and reliant upon them and their cronies for food, water, electricity and sewage requirements, this aligns pretty closely with UN

Agenda 21. This is a form of control and I believe that water will be the next major battlefield which is used in an attempt to control the populace. This allows them much greater control over the food supply and life as water is the essence of all life. All of this is directly related to those in government trying to usurp personal freedoms through backdoor deals with those in big-ag. The state governments have been lobbied by the agribusiness and large grocers such as Safeway, Publix and Wal-Mart to produce legislation which attempt to maximize their profits through the enactment of arduous agricultural laws. This results in higher food costs for the consumer and variation in food products. Local politicians need to stand up and push back against these industries, the rights of land owners need to be expanded not shrunk. People should not need to go through endless paperwork and applications to cut down a few trees on their property or do a little bit of row crop farming. Who in the hell decided that it would be a good idea to throw someone in jail and fine them for collecting rain water in a barrel off of their pipes. What the hell kind of tyrannical bureaucrat came up with this crap?

Unholy Swine In Our Midst

There are a few lesions on the cultural body which I should direct your attention to. My favorite is peoples whose only disability seems to be an entire lack of knowledge about nutrition and who seem to lack any discipline whatsoever at the dinner table. The individuals are usually able to secure themselves some type of disability benefit for some wasting disease related to their squalid diet, and the fact that the TV remote control has enabled these sloth's to remain stationary in lazy boy chairs for extended periods of time. Unfortunately the hardened bureaucrats in the disability office are forced into the issuance of benefits (i.e. your tax dollars) to these monstrosities of a biped. One can usually observe these swine on a motorized cart in the meat section of the grocery stuffing about 5\3lb packages of mixed pork sausage into their cart. These swine roll around the store and release their poisononous cutaneous musk into the air on any unlucky passerby who happens to stray down an isle to close to the excretion zones of one of their blowholes. The brain synapses of the swine have difficulty firing properly due to the unprocessed fat from Moon Pies and corn dogs which clog their neural pathways making the most rudimentary functions difficult. We even have some celebrity sloth's who while not physically disabled are certainly gluttonous swine of the first class; Michael Moore, Rosie O'Donnell and Sally

Struthers, any of these three could be used as secret military weapons in the destruction of the enemies food supply in war.

 The most intriguing aspect of these individuals is the almost miraculous recovery these individuals make when free samples of food are being offered in the store. These Cretans rise from their swine cart like some great swan taking to flight and walk rapidly over to the free food. Furthermore, these swine enjoy blocking the entrance of markets by hoisting their posterior bloat onto one of the swine carts at the front of the store in the most encumbering way for any other shoppers. They terrorize every department in the store by asking for something that is not visible to the eye, knowing that there is some government bureaucrat or ACLU lawyer who will who will come down upon the company if they feel that this swine has been inconvenienced in the least. These swine are a close relative of the male who has walked with a cane since his early 20's though he has no apparent medical affliction. These individuals walk with a limp as though they had been shot on some foreign soil bravely defending old glory. They refer to ladies as women folk and enjoying using that cane to poke embers in the camp fire or for knocking on doors of potential donors. However, these cur mongers never were in a war and they never were shot and furthermore their legs are in perfect working order. They will continue this slapstick charade because some government employee is foolish enough to pad his benefit wallet every month at our expense. A close relative of this ner-do-well is the obese white trash woman who wears a Harley Davidson shirt, looks like she drinks vodka straight out of the bottle, has 2 inch thick bifocals, and utilizes corporal discipline on her kids in the automotive section of Kmart. When she eats, she goes to the drive thru window of KFC and orders a bucket of chicken, 2 small cole slaws and 2 small containers of mashed potatoes. She proceeds to eat all of the chicken in the bucket herself and gives her three kids the cole slaw and potatoes. Should her kids have the audaciousness to ask for a piece of chicken she invokes the power of god and says the good lord gave you something to eat and you should be grateful for that.

Nascar People

I grew up in the South and I don't like NASCAR but I do like the mini races. The main reason that I don't like NASCAR is because of the people that go to the races. NASCAR is basically 100,000 drunken auto mechanics cheering for a car crash. The fans of NASCAR like reading these magazines about the cars and gleaming a few technical details. They then go to their blue collar job armed with this sacred technical automobile knowledge looking to prey on the young workers or the intellectually weak. What they do is find someone at work who is a few IQ points lower than themselves and present this technical data to the unsuspecting mark and thereby ingratiate themselves as some type of technical opinion leader when then are technical questions that should arise which deal with the torque or horsepower of a vehicle. In this aspect, modern man has not evolved from villagers asking the local witchdoctor important questions. These blue collar heliolaters cement themselves as lauded idolaters on NASCAR technical capabilities among the uninformed working class. Should these brigands not have the answer to a technical question they need only excuse themselves to go to the commode where they have concealed their racing magazines in the middle of the newspaper.

The American Negro

The American negro is a petty, villainous beast who fails to produce an output anywhere close to the input required to keep him live. The American negro should be thought of as a cross between a small child and a billy goat, and they should be handled as such. Namely the negro should be kept in a confined and preferably fenced in area of the city, and kept watered and fed. The difference between a goat and a negro is that one can not be certain as to when the negro is going to attack. The negro is the poster child for rape, aggravated assault and carjacking as these are crimes which are the hallmarks of the negro, and statistically the hallmark of his criminal calling. The European man far above the negro is an explorer and inventor. The average negroe is wholly incapable of even exploring his kitchen to see if he has German cockroaches in the putrefying dishes in his sink.

One interesting behavior of the negro is that they enjoy blocking things off as it gives them a sense of power and makes them feel good about themselves. Namely the negro likes to take his bag and other belonging and position himself next to the coffee machine so that no one else can use the equipment. One of the other favorite power plays of the negro is to go into a restaurant and ask the waitress for five times as much as the usual customer and then leave a paltry tip. Negroes are notoriously bad tippers even if they are professional athletes. Negroes are excellent financiers and their money power comes by taking a huge roll of one dollar bills and placing a twenty on the outside. The negro enjoys adorning his twenty year old Buick, with some stolen golf course green carpet on his dashboard, playboy key locks on the door and a pungent cherry air freshener on his mirror; this gives the modern negro male a sense of pride in himself and his family history while concealing the vile odor of his personal musk. The negro also likes to take three times as long in the grocery line as any other race and then take the opportunity with a captive audience to complain about their check. There are few things in this world more loathsome than some old negro woman bellowing from the back of the grocery line about the progression of the cue. The negro also enjoys talking much louder than anybody else as this signals his strength to the other tribe members. One of the favorite activities of the negro is to find an obese white woman as a sexual concubine. The negro will then move in with her and proceed to take as much as he is allowed. One need not ponder too deeply who will be responsible for the grocery bill when these two are in the checkout line at the grocery. The American negro should never have anything new built in his neighborhood at tax payer's expense, as this is just something new for the local negroes to destroy. The negro has no idea what it means to appreciate and take care of something. The negro lives in a matriarchical society because most male negroes are incapable of running anything that resembles a properly functioning household. The female negro is often left alone to care for her negro children as the male negro is frequently incapable of dealing with the responsibility that comes with being a father either from a financial perspective or from a parenting perspective. A great many negroes in the US are traumatized for life from spending the first four years of their life staring at the bulbous posterior of an obese negro woman in their infancy. This impacts many of the male negroes on a deeply sub-conscious level in their selection of a mating partner whereby they associate enormous posteriors on women with the security that they found in their early infant years and the fertility of their partner. The American negro undermines the rights of whites and Asians in the US because the sole purpose of gun control in cities is to keep negros from killing one another, even those these laws always fail. Unfortunately, the local news like to engage in obstufication as regards the negro and his nefarious activities. The producers of news segments think they are doing the local negro community some favors by not putting the race of the perpetrators into criminal stories. Let's think about that for a minute, if we have a suspect that is 6 foot 2 and weighs two hundred and fifty pounds and no racial description is given how in the hell are we going to locate this Cretan. The recent ploy of the negroes is to go on TV and complain about not getting any respect from authorities. The only respect that the negro has earned is the respect of the criminal community as a violent beast and idoler. Black leadership may not appreciate this surmisal but is black leadership not an oxymoron.

Hate Speech Laws And The Threat That They Represent To Society

Hate speech laws are a form of political censorship by the left utilized to stop free discussion of topics and from halting the public from knowing the truth about topics. The reason behind these kingmakers' efforts is to stop the truth in that this interferes with the reality that they are trying to create. As hate speech laws are an enslavement of our free speech rights, they must be fought tooth and nail, and we should never give into any of these statutes or laws. Many European countries have these hate speech laws like the UK Incitement To Racial Hatred Law, and as we can see in the application of this law, it is an almost exact duplicate in application of the hate crime laws in the US. Namely, these laws are only utilized against whites and are never used against anyone of color particularly blacks, even if in the commission of their crime they are shouting racial obscenities at the whites as they are attacked. The agenda behind these laws is to silence white critics of the policies of the king makers behind the scenes; these king makers want to be the sole entities in charge of creating the public conscious and do not want their power impeded. However, with the advent of the internet and the access of the minions to cameras, and the capability of broadcasting to millions at little to no charge this capability is greatly impacted. Political correctness is a transitory point for the passage of hate crime laws and ultimately control of the political discourse within a society. Political correctness is the far left trying to dictate their agenda to the rest of the country by being the thought police on which topics are acceptable for humor. Trying to control what types of humor are acceptable is a form of control censorship which seeks to reshapes peoples beliefs system; the ultimate goal behind this is to implement some sort of political programming so that they can control peoples thought. One of the lefts favorite topics is to portray anyone who disagrees with this nonsense as a Nazi or in some way psychologically deranged, this was a favorite trick of the Russian communist to control the people and dictate consciousness. This is also the springboard from which the left will try and launch hate speech laws. One of the greatest problems with hate speech laws are, who exactly defines what hate speech is, a number of faceless bureaucrats who live in ivory towers behind closed doors? The founders of the United States realized that the most egregious speech needed to be protected under the law that is why they put it as the First Amendment in the Constitution. These swine are not only out to censor people they are out to destroy the Constitution and that is why they should be regarded as a clear and present dangers to the United States and all free men. Evidence of this incremental censorship is the humor of the mid and late 1980's from comics such as Sam Kennison and Eddie Murphy, both of these guys had funny routines which involved a lot of gay humor and this was what the mainstream companies put out then and was promoted by the biggest names in the business. The routines these guys did at that time would never ever get play on cable TV now. This is a perfect example of the creeping censorship in our society. I particularly like it when some of these NYC butt sniffers such as Barbara Walters starts talking about the dreaded N word, a word so horrible she can't even say it lest one of her tits fall off and her left kidney stop operating for 23 days. This is truly a theatre of the absurd because everyday in this country millions of blacks call each other niggers and millions of whites use the word too. Its almost like these media Cretans are cowering in some dark corner during the inquisition. We have free speech in the US currently, the EU has no free speech, let's use it to expose and destroy these vermin in our midst.

The Education System

The most singular problem in our education system is the paradigm that you need a college education in order to be successful. The public school system was designed for white middle class kids whom are college bound. Trying to have kids with IQ's in the mid 80's do calculus is a complete and total waste of resources and a doomed recipe for failure and waste. Education needs to maximize the value of the individual to society. The greatest waste in the education system is that money is not being directed into the classroom. The teachers are not being paid this money because it is being wasted on a bureaucracy in the school. We do not need three assistant principles in the schools; we need a much flatter management structure. We also do not need to purchase new textbooks every 2 years because the author has added five pages to the index. We should look at utilizing computers and technology to cut down on the cost of textbooks. The other problem with the education system is that there is no competition, because unions and politicians do not want money taken away from these useless bureaucracies. If you are sending your kids to a public school you should be able to take the tuition from that public school and apply it to the educational school of your choice. The school system has been controlled from within by the far left who value social justice nonsense over results oriented education. The bureaucracy in these schools just looks at the student body as a head count and does not care whether they are actually learning or not. This is a really singular point; these bureaucrats are solely concerned with keeping up their enrollment numbers and getting their federal money. Whether little Jimmy knows his times tables when he is a sophomore in high school is way down the line in the importance ladder to these bureaucrats. This is the absolute wrong way to think about the education system. We should have trade schools where many of our students should go after middle school, trying to push many of these double digit IQer's through a college preparatory curriculum is nothing short of insanity. If the public had any idea about what was going on in many of our classrooms in terms of waste and the lack of learning they would be appalled.

    The college system has become intellectually watered down as the federal government has been releasing more and more money for school loans. This had had a multi pronged effect- the schools have been raising their tuitions at many times the rate of inflation, the students are getting into perpetual debt to the US government, and the curriculums are getting watered down in order to allow more students to engage in this usury who may have historically lacked the intellectual faculties to be in the college system. Colleges have started to utilize the internet to siphon more money from students who are otherwise unable to come to the campus through their online degree programs.

Graduate schools have also begun watering down their programs and accepting students who really have no business in graduate school and would not have been allowed to enter traditional programs 30 years ago. Social justice should not be the goal of the college education system; this cheapens the value of a degree for those who have earned it through a rigorous program.

TAXES

There are numerous problems with tax structure in the US but the gravest is the loopholes that allow major corporations to pay little or no taxes through the chicanery of highly paid accountants. The small or medium size companies which cannot afford these accountants are then forced to pay an uneven share of their taxes. The tax rate needs to be lowered and a flat tax needs to be imposed on corporate entities. In terms of the private tax rate, a structure should be imposed which has a positive eugenic effect on the civilization. Namely individuals with high IQ's should be should be given tax breaks to have kids. This will insulate civilization to some degree against the universally destructive effect of some of these bottom feeders out breeding those on top and destroying the civilization intellectually and morally. This also ensures against undesirable minorities breeding too much as they will be monetarily disensentivazed to have kids. There needs to be direct and harsh effects for the mentally and morally inferior when they are unable to control their breeding, this breeding has taken many a civilization down and currently stands as one of the greatest threats in the US. The lower and upper classes of any society will always have the same amount of kids because their economic situation will not change. The size and quality of the middle class of any society are what serve as the true gauge of any civilization.

Marriage and Relationship

The woman that a man keeps company with says a lot about him. A great man may look for a relationship with a woman who is markedly less intelligent than them; this usually assumes that this woman will not be in possession of the faculties to see through his falsehoods and nonsensical stories. Usually men make their decision on a subconscious level and do not fully understand what they are doing; if men do not realize it they are able to rationalize the decision to themselves. When a man chooses a woman below his IQ level she is almost certainly lower on the social ladder than himself. This is why it is best to pick someone with a similar IQ and cultural background as you. The lower IQ people are intrigued by the basest of entertainment such as reality TV programs, graphic bathroom humor and projects that do not have a long time requirement and little or no planning, video games, temporary swimming pools where people in cut offs swim who haven't been to a dentist in the last three presidential administrations, bbq's where a mutt dog is fed hamburgers until he vomits, people who eat Vienna sausages directly out of the can, aficionados of professional wrestling and radio contests that entail driving your vehicle from place to place looking for clues. A man who marries a high IQ woman is comfortable in his own intellect and not afraid to have his ideas challenged by a high IQ woman. This contrasts to the blue collar greaser mechanic that tells his wife that he is the head of the household because he lacks the capabilities of engaging in the basest philosophical debate after having consumed 8 cans of cold Ham's beer, or the fundamentalist Christian, who wears a suit with a retractable key chain on his three prong belt. The head of the house hold should be clear, anyone who has to produce primary or secondary research to bolster their claims of being the head of the household, is most likely not the captain of the boat. If you have to convince your woman that you are in fact the head of the household then you are not. A more intelligent woman is less likely to wander from a relationship for a number of reasons The primary reason is that woman who are of a higher iq are less likely to display behavior driven by the base sexual traits. These traits are more closely associated with wild animals, and in general the lower your IQ the more driven you will be by the need for sex. People of lower intelligence generally do not have much patience when it comes to challenging relationships. A woman that you are in a relationship with will almost never reveal her true breadth of knowledge about phalluses; this allows the unperceptive to keep the myth alive that they in fact have the best medieval battering ram between your legs that their partner has ever had the pleasure of making acquaintance with. Women who are lower culturally and are considered white trash should not be considered marriage material under any circumstances. The reason for this is that the behavior patterns that they exhibit are unacceptable in civilized society and they should be properly viewed as the human refuse that they are, as the king makers have their bloodlines so do the peasants of the manor.

Radical Religious Politics

Countries with the most radicalized religious populations become this way because the personal moral character of the people in the civilization is so low, excellent examples of this are countries like Saudi Arabia in the Middle East or some of the Northern Indian States. Most of these regimes have little to do with religion, a great deal of this is this religious front is used as a form of tyranny where the laws can be quickly shifted to meet the needs of the state in any situation. I was born in St. Louis, but graduated from high school in Louisville, Kentucky. I consider myself to be a Southerner and my moms family roots go deep into the South. While I spent a great deal of time in the South I also lived in other parts of the country and this time away, and then going back to the South caused me to objectively reflect upon the economic conditions in the South and what caused this to take place. The largest roadblock to the South moving forward and advancing economically is the fundamentalist Christians which have engrained themselves in the Southern political body. These politicians lack any sort of vision and have no original ideas. They also are focused on the wrong ideas. We are almost 20 trillion dollars in debt and these charlatans are focused on abortion like it is the most important issue facing the country. Abortion is something that I am fundamentally opposed to as it is the destruction of a living organism, however abortion should also be looked at as a means of controlling and ultimately eliminating undesirable minorities from the population along with taxation and education programs. While opposed to abortion in principle, I believe that it is the women's decision and that these anti-abortionists are engaged in the same type of politics that the left likes, namely trying to control other peoples behavior. The South of the US is endowed with tremendously arable land, clean water and excellent weather for farming and could have become the fertile crescent of North America; however the politicians in the south of the US have failed the people and businesses that could have benefited from this economic windfall. The South has also never developed from an educational standpoint and while there are a few excellent universities in the South they are lacking in comparison to other parts of the country. The South has been largely left behind in the technological boom. The Civil War had extremely dysgenic effects upon the South and this was further compounded by a political movement in the North to punish the South economically. However the South has done damage to themselves through governance. The South has also suffered greatly from the corruption of local politicians who fear losing control of their small fiefdom and as such have stifled the flow of capital and development into their areas. In concluding, we should note that the South of the United States has failed to develop economically and culturally as a result of a symbiotic relationship between the vision lacking fundamentalist Christians and the petty corrupt local politicians, sometimes who are the same person.

The Penal System

The penal system in the United States should be a place where convicted criminals are kept from society until they have served their crimes. Instead what the penal system has become is a cash machine for housing prisoners, somebody figured out that a lot of money could be made by housing prisoners and building the jails as a private entity and then charging the states for this. This was never what our penal system was meant to become. What has happened is that so many prisoners are being housed that they are bankrupting the states primarily for drug offenses. The corporations that build and house these prisoners are the chief opponents to marijuana legalization because they realize that their money will be derailed if people are no longer prosecuted for marijuana offenses. The sheriff's offices have also become a major opponent of legalization as their money train would also be derailed by the lack of seized goods auctions. Nobody wants their money train cut off and they don't care if it is good for the economy or not.

Let's take a quick look at what transpired in the War on Drugs over the last 36 years. This was started by Reagan but the true king pin behind it was Bush SR. What the war on drugs did in many cases was imprison people for possession of small amounts of drugs who were otherwise productive citizens. The affect of the war on drugs was to drive up the price of drugs and hence put more money in the hands of the mafia and rogue governmental agents in the CIA and other departments who were bringing drugs into the country. I personally believe that marijuana should be legalized because what is transpiring right now is drug money is leaving the country and going to places like Mexico, Columbia and Thailand. What this does economically is permanently remove wealth from the US. It is not in the utility of casual drug user in the US to keep these despotic regimes afloat. Let's rejuvenate the small farms and produce our own marijuana and produce new jobs and industries. You have many ancillary industries that can accompany the marijuana industry namely: security work, trimming and processing of marijuana, production of green house products, marijuana retail outlets and production of marijuana paraphernalia. I do not think that legalizing marijuana is going to make society any better; however having marijuana illegal has not stopped people from accessing and smoking the product. This legalization of marijuana would allow states to free up space for violent criminals and lower the administrative costs of the penal system.

The penal system should not only be utilized to isolate violent criminals from society, it should be used to generate a positive cash flow. Namely prisons should seek to be self sufficient and produce their own food through prison labor. The prisoners should be retrained for other jobs and be allowed to do work at below market pay so a positive cash flow is created for the prison.

There is one aspect of the penal and judicial system that I do not believe is just. This is the handling of cases where major financial damage is caused to the country like the housing bubble or the Bernie Madoff scandal. I believe that we should have the death penalty for people who cause massive financial damage to this country which has a criminal intent to it, this is a treasonous activity. I believe the adjudication of whether or not to use the death penalty should be by a panel of 10 people from all walks of government and political beliefs, but if 7 out of 10 are in favor of death, then an execution is called for. Furthermore, if we are going to have the death penalty then it should be utilized in a timely manner and none of this sitting on death row for 20 years crap. Prisoners should be allowed one appeal to be heard within 6 months of conviction. The prisoner should be shot with a 9 man firing squad as this is the cheapest and most effective method of execution. How is it that some of these executions cost hundreds of thousands of dollars? As I believe in equal rights, if I were the governor of any state I would immediately execute the people on death row starting with the men first and finish it off with the women. Keeping these cold blooded murderers alive is unjust to the victim's families and a waste of tax payer's money.

Dangerous Trends For The Economy

There are many dangerous trends which can have calamitous economic results for the US. We could be facing a type of brain drain whereby highly skilled individuals take their capital and set up manufacturing facilities overseas and ship there goods back to the US. Currently, there are many large companies that do this however I believe that this is going to be an emerging trend among under 40 entrepreneurs in start ups and medium size businesses. This trend will be driven by onerous laws and regulations within the US and what the net effect of this will be is transference of intellectual and monetary capital out of the US and into countries where there money is treated well.

A disturbing trend that I see emerging is the large amount amounts of debt that college students are piling up. This coupled with the fact that banks have put onerous capital outlays on housing loans is going to create a really economically damaging trend in the US. You are going to have two generations of housing age individuals who are going to be unable to own a house until they are in their 50's. This will collapse the housing market in the US, irregardless of how much the institutional investors try to prop it up. The other trends that will be associated with this debt are a decimation of the long term durable goods markets (in particular automobiles.), individuals will buy used products and make repairs to the products that they have.

Alternative energies such as cold fusion and solar are becoming viable concepts and the US and British are no longer going to be able to stifle this technology. The implications of this are quite radical to society and the banking system. This will allow individuals to become less controlled through energy as they have access to super low cost technologies, the petrol dollar will no longer exist and a different paradigm will have to be created. Oil is still being utilized as an energy source for a few reasons: Trillions of dollars are being made by a small handful of powerful business men who own politicians, if oil is no longer used the OPEC petrol-dollars will come flooding back into the US and crash the dollar. Israeli and Saudi Arabia will no longer be important countries and will take about 20 steps down the ladder in terms of their power and worth to the US and other western countries –these two countries will also affect the military industrial complex as they will no longer have the funds to purchase our weaponry. The Middle East will most likely devolve into something resembling current sub-Saharan Africa and not a word will be spoken on the nightly network news about the "troubles" in the Middle East. This is coming in the next 20 years and there is no hope of suppression as so many countries are doing research on these technologies.

  Baby Boomers retiring and moving outside of the US to live. There are many countries in the world now which offer access to healthcare on par with the US and are far cheaper to live in. If enough of these individuals sell their houses and live out their retirement years in these countries this could have a huge affect on the US economy in terms of consumer spending and the housing market in some locales. This trend is already happening and many people are moving to Costa Rica, Ecuador and Chile. The individuals that are doing this are high net worth individuals . This trend is also related to record numbers of US citizens giving up their citizenship. Many of these people worked abroad and do not want to pay the insane double taxation on foreign earned assets and face jail time so they simply renounce their citizenship.

    The rising cost of health care in this country, this is a dynamic of numerous things. First, insured tax payers are picking up the bills for 20 million illegal aliens in this country, my solution to this is to keep these illegals after they are healed up in work camps until they have paid off their bill at minimum wage pay. The second issue is that the US citizens are paying outrageously high drug prices in our own country; we are funding the research for the entire world. This needs to stop; if these other countries can't pay for these drugs then they will not have the privilege of using them. The hospitals jack up the the prices and get ready to corn hole Uncle Sam every time the government is paying the bill. The general public needs to have more open access to drugs that are now prescriptions. What I mean by this is that adults over the age of 18 should have access to anti-biotic and other low level drugs without seeing a doctor, the individual would have to sign a form saying they take full legal responsibility. This would shave billions off of heath care cost, when you have a nasal infection you do not need to spend a $150 for a doctor's visit this is a waste of patient's money, doctor's time, fuel and work hours lost. We need to stop the federal government from throwing out drugs that are past the expiration date but are still fully potent. This costs taxpayers millions of dollars every year particularly in the Veterans Administration.

We need to initially charge Mexicans $20 per car when they come into the US to spread their VD, flatulence, and bloody awful mariachi music and criminality. This will help offset the financial wounds that these swine inflict upon the US monetarily every year in terms of their: hospital cost, childhood education, penal system housing, welfare, credit card fraud, narcotics crime, and drunk driving. This should start as a test point, if $20 does not cover the cost of these illegals then raise it to $50 or $100; these swine need to be held responsible for the economic damage that they inflict upon this country.

We need to give people on welfare 2 months to get a job. If they fail to get a job we need to put them into work in order to keep receiving benefits. If we used these people to pick the crops, we could kill two birds with one stone and get rid of the illegal aliens. I can guarantee you with 100% certainty that after a week of picking crops many of these rust a bouts would find gainful employment in their chosen trade.

The United Nations And Other Internationalist Organizations

The only good thing about the United Nations is that it is located in New York and this allows us to keep an eye on these cutthroats, dictators, cannibals, despots, buggerers, terrorist, brigands, toxic polluters, and French drunkards. The purpose of the UN is for the US and other western powers to utilize foreign aid in order to black mail other countries into voting our way when a despotic CIA coup backfires and the people who we thought were our friends in Burundi turned out to not be such good acquaintances. This somehow creates this bullshit image for the American people that the United States is some great moral entity second only to Jesus and the Buddha. We should close the UN down and cut these Cretans off financially. The US needs to look after our own internal interest first, before we look after other nations. NATO, The Council On Foreign Relations and the other bullshit clubs need to be done away with, the US taxpayer should not be funding the military defense for Lichtenstein. The latest rounds of nonsense wars in the Middle East was predicated upon President Bush making some claim that the United Nations said their were human rights violations in Iraq, as if this was an iron clad case for war. There are probably human rights violations going on in the first bathroom stall at gay night clubs all across America. The US military is not the world's police force, neither are we a private security force for the oil industry.

Black Lives Matter

Black Lives Matters is a terrorist organization most likely funded by George Soros and emanating from the brains of the neighbors of this strong arm robber and law enforcement assaulter Michael Brown. These hapless negroes know as the progenitors of this offspring, instead of being embarrassed about raising such a rabid violent beast get on TV after this swine was shot and demand justice. Justice was done, they should be glad he died in such a short non-suffering manner. It would have been more just if this obese water buffalo had been publically flogged to death as a deterrent to the beggarly negro knaves of his neighborhood. This Black Lives Matter terrorist organization then proceeded with the help of their communist allies in the media to produce this false narrative that this violent criminal had his hands up and said don't shoot. Nothing could be further from the truth. Michael Brown's hands were used as deadly weapons in his attacking of the store clerk during his strong arm robbery and his rabid, violent attack on law enforcement. The greatest irony of Black Lives Matters is that they are producing this narrative that officers are out killing thousands of negroes a day, when the truth of the matter is that a black mans worst enemy stares at him in the mirror everyday. This propaganda has no basis in realty and the news media figures that are pandering to this false narrative should be forced to share their homes with two other black families for a year. I can guarantee you with 100% certainty that these civilization destroyers would be singing quite a different tune. Imagine for a moment if Wolf Blitzer had a few negro families sharing his abode with him, he'd probably have everything that he owned misappropriated including his $200 beard trimmer. Black Lives Matter has intentionally egged others on to acts of violence and should be considered a terrorist organization and those who provided the financing for these violent swine should have all of their assets seized and be tried by a secret military tribunal and shot at dawn after conviction. The Charlotte police detectives need only do their due diligence on these people and trace their backers and hold them financially responsible for the carnage, when the string pullers get personally affected this nonsense will stop.

Thoughts On Politicians And The Republican Party

The Republican Party has become hijacked by neocons and their allies, the fundamentalist Christians. The keystone of the neocon agenda is the continued growth of the military industrial complex, keeping the US in a constant state of war, support of Zionism, open borders and export of US manufacturing to other countries. The result of this agenda is the US being in debt twenty trillion dollars, a debased manufacturing state, cities and other institutions destroyed by minorities, difficulty in negotiating with the rest of the world, declining white birth rates and a Republican Party that is full of corrupt small men with no sense of racial identity or interest in preservation of western ideals and emboldened negroes who have learned that they only need start a small riot to get politicians to acquiesce to whatever they demand. One of the major players in this is the duplicitous weasel John McCain who stands as the poster boy for term limits. He was shot down by the Vietcong, tortured and brainwashed. I truly believe that he has done more damage to this country than almost any other individual in recent times and that he was returned to this country in order to destroy it. They say that a mans family is a representative of him. Well John McCain's wife appears to be a lush with a monopoly on Budweiser products in the city of Phoenix, who has used this monopoly power to finance little Johnnies political career. His daughter is a fat pig party girl in Scottsdale who gets on the talk shows and clearly demonstrates that her brain has the analytical capability of a broken parking meter. Johnnie's son has been struck with the worst case of Jungle fever that the Arizona medical community has ever seen. McCain himself has rolled out the welcome mat for millions of illegals in Arizona and Johnny takes his orders from the inbred Mormon horse thief's in Mesa, Arizona and people in the military industrial complex who think nothing of running the US into the ground financially. The perfect scenario which illustrates what a scurfy chamber pot this swine is; was when he spoke out against a bill that would have allowed wine and liquor to be delivered by mail into residences in Arizona. He spoke out against this bill and portrayed himself as protecting the youth from the vileness of liquor, however the truth is that this swine was protecting his wife's monopoly. He didn't care if the youth got sloppy drunk but by god they were going to do it on our Budweiser products. Johnny should have spent a little more time around the house and then maybe the country and his family would not have been so screwed up. Mitch McConnell is another parasite in the Republican Party who is a knavish representative of the caricature of the corrupt Southern politician. He lavishes getting in front of the camera with his turkey gobbler neck, glasses, and positing some enormous lies upon the American people where he portrays himself as the last defender of liberty in this country. One can almost smell the vapors of 15 year old scotch bellowing from his mouth and nasal apparitions as he speaks on TV. Mitch McConnell is incapable of stopping a poodle from defecating on the hinterlands of his property, much the less of saving a civilization from financial and cultural ruin. His ineffectuality as a leader makes him more qualified to be the head custodian at a struggling church in an economically challenged neighborhood than the progenitor of a strong nationalistic political movement. Paul Ryan is a true traitor inside of the gates. He is an ardent champion of one world government and trade deals which seek to subjugate and destroy the white working class of the United States. Paul Ryan strikes me as the sort of bloke who doesn't trim his finger nails for long periods of time so that his thumb nail may become an edged scythe and plowshare utilized to scratch his rectum and clear the caverns of his nose after airplane trips to humid climates. Lyndsey Graham is another parasite who the mainstream media like to portray on TV as representative of the conservatives. Lyndsey Graham looks like he is about two beers away from being in the third stall at a truck stop in Kansas engaged in unnatural acts with a long haul trucker. He is a professional mommy's boy wimp who should be wearing a white suit and working in an antique store on St. Charles Street.

The Republican Party needs to be almost totally cleaned out. The Republicans have wielded a great deal of power in the last 25 years however they have put out a terrible agenda. The Republicans should have pushed for a nationwide concealed gun permit. They should have deported the animals back to Mexico and mined the border on Mexico's expense tab. They should have put forth tax and education bills which would have had a positive eugenic effect upon the country. They should have put a permanent nail in the nonsense of affirmative action. They should have stopped socialized health care. They should have charged the oil industry to use our military as their personal defense force. They should have used the oil revenues from Iraq to pay off the US debt. They should have taken away all funding for the Department of Education. They should have drowned Castro in the sea and finally they should have executed Jonathan Pollard and Sandy Berger. This is a partially list of what the Republican Party should have accomplished over the last 25 years but they have failed on almost every front. The Republicans should have stopped apologizing to communist and traitors and started acting like men and not some sophomores that are intimidated by a group of guys on the football team. Make no mistake about it many of these Republicans like McConnell, McCain, Ryan, Cruz, Mark Levin, Glenn Beck and others are traitors inside of the gates, I will say a good word for Newt Gingrich as he did balance the budget and lay the economic framework for the technology boom to transpire in the 1990's. However, the Republican Party is totally without the vision and leadership of a Newt Gingrich at present time.

Genocide Of Whites In The US And Europe

The current barrage of these rogue scavengers from the Middle East in Europe is clearly an orchestrated effort by the string pullers to cause white genocide in Europe. The reason for this is that all of these invaders seem to be armed with a clear set of instructions about what to do and where to go. There is absolutely no good reason on god's clear earth to allow the scum from the Muslim world to set foot on the sacred soil of Europe. The European mind and land has served as the basis for almost all that we have in the sciences and engineering. Some women are bad drivers but this does not entitle the women in Middle East to not drive cars. You can almost see a bunch of these unshaven Arabs watch a car drive by with a woman behind the wheel and start chasing it while yelling stop you bitch you can't drive, this is a true theatre of the absurd but this goes on in the Middle East as accepted norms. This Middle Eastern and North African scum have already shown their capabilities in raping women from infancy to old age, for this reason the Muslim should be looked at as having more in common with the Cro-Magnons than with modern man. The final conclusion about the Muslims is that they should not be allowed to travel outside of their countries into other cultures, and will hence eventually implode upon themselves.

The genocide of the whites in the US is more insidious. However, I will outline how the thinking of the European and this lack of procreation has similar parallels in the US. The whites in the US are the main generators of wealth and the greatest holders of knowledge and civilization in the US. A white man can be distinguished from the lesser minorities by a few behaviors in his breeding patterns. A white man will want his child to attend the best grade schools possible. A lesser minority will have kids and either not care about the local school or such deep thoughts will not even enter his frontal lobe when confronted by the specter of instant sexual gratification. A white man will be concerned about his present and future economic situation and job outlook; a lesser minority will put his stink hammer into the chamber of vd without any thought whatsoever to his current or future employment prospects. This is a dangerous blight to any society as it ensures a permanent underclass of unworthy, swarthy minorities who lack sexual restraint and are only concerned with immediate sexual gratification and violence. The need for instant gratification is also representative of the mindset of a mugger who has no impulse control. The whites are also being pushed out of economic opportunities by affirmative action in particular the hiring of black owned businesses. If these black owned business were run so proficiently you can be assured that people would be knocking on their doors. Blacks usually assemble something that does not work properly and then a white owned business has to come in and fix the problem these hornswoggling negro jockeys have created. You can almost see these negro foremen twitching their unmuzzled mustaches, getting in their cars, and driving away after they constructed a building where the toilet sewers run into the hand washing sinks. Feminism has also been a communist political movement to poison the intellectual wells of women into thinking that having children is not important and that your career should be first. There are many sorry women who have bought into this political ideology who are now in their 40's and 50' and are quite sorry that they did not have kids. One only need look at one of the leaders of this movement such as Andrea Dworkin, to get an idea of the kind of filth that is involved in this movement. If one pays careful attention to some of these feminist dykes you can see the cheese smellers. These are dykes who look like they always have a rotten piece of limburger cheese under their nose: these would include Ellen Degeneres, Rosie O'Donnell and Andrea Dworkin. However, Andrea Dworkin and Rosie O'Donnell fall into what I classify as the barn door dyke because their hind quarters are so rotund the only type of trouser that they can find for themselves are either purple or green corduroys. Not even the most despicable negro in heat would have sex with Andre Dworkin or Rosie so, they have to try and bring the rest of the world into their level of misery and ruin many young girls lives and slow the pro-creation of the white race in America and worldwide. The churches have been losing their moral authority and have been impugned as they have been infected with the cancer of multiculturalism. This has turned many people against the leaders inside of their own church. As churchgoers generally have larger families, this trend has affected the numbers of white families having kids. Through the political movements of the Democratic Party, there has been a procreation situation set up for the wrong people namely negroes and their allies in the inner cities. The proper way to think of this is a farmer getting ready to fertilize his fields and instead of fertilizing the healthy plants the manure is only put on the weeds in the peripheries of the fields. This is the affect that welfare has on those who do not deserve its' merit. Abortion has also had a destructive affect upon young women because they have learned to use it as a form of birth control instead of being responsible for their sexual activities. The end result of this that women can be haunted by health issues down the road and will be morally haunted their lives thinking of that baby. While I am generally opposed to abortion except in cases of rape or genetic diseases. I do not think that this is an issue that the government should be involved in and it should be a moral decision of the woman. The encouragement of homosexuality also causes the birth rate to decline as it encourages a lifestyle from a quantitative perspective which does not bolster the numbers of whites in the country. The successive waves of immigrants also serve to dilute the whites in the US, with those in government considering Mexicans white in the census however when it comes to affirmative action or government contracts that is a different story. Where these

Mexican scoundrels are given contracts, they are unmeritous of these contracts, let me reiterate again the importance of the role government should play in a sculpted society for optimum genetics. The tax structure and the opportunity for secondary education should be optimized to create the maximum number of high IQ and capable individuals. Propping up the weak has never helped in any society and its practice should be brought to a stand still in the US. I would like to differentiate between helping a desirous worthy person in the Christian sense and elevating human manure to an exalted state as we have done with Barry Obama. There has also been a defeminization of men, and young men have to be told by somebody in the education system what that strange protrusion is between their legs. Our young men wear tight jeans and androgynous shirts, drink energy drinks and they look like someone who might get passed around by a bunch of old corrupt licentious faggots like a rag doll. God forbid if these men should ever have to take up arms and defend the country against a hostile military force. In concluding, this topic there has been a compelling strategy put forth by the string pullers in order to marginalize and ultimately destroy the white populations and the principle reason for this is that whites will fight harder and are more capable of waging warfare than anybody else and the string pullers know this. The greatest example of this in recent history is the British Empire enslaving the Chinese and Indians with a relatively small handful of British soldiers

Popular Movies And Television

The news has clearly been used to create a false consciousness for the public. However, the sitcoms and movies have also been utilized as a tool to try and alter the opinions of the whites in America against their own interests. There has been a push in movies to portray it as being acceptable to engage in misogynistic relationships. The negroe has been exemplified as morally superior and the hero of the movie. When being bombarded with these false images and trying to reshape someone's belief system by telling these same lies over and over again through the media of film; this insidious propaganda has the affect of altering people's perception even from what they believe to know is true in the real world. The true racial realty of the world will never be shown to you from the fantasy land of Hollywood or the local newscasts. The closest that you will ever get to the truth from Hollywood is some of the old films like on The Waterfront or Serpico.

The way forward is quite daunting as there are great odds stacked against us and the enemy is well funded and entrenched within the business and governmental system. The two most important tools are virtually free and very effective. The first is organization. It is absolutely important to become involved in organizations that are already fighting against the Orwellian tyranny and get yourself into a position of leadership within these organizations to keep the proper agenda from being usurped by ngo infiltrators and spooks within the intelligence communities who seek to destroy these political movements from within. Fine examples of these types of organizations are the NRA, Gun Owners of America, The American Policy Center, American Land Rights Association, prepping groups, conservative religious groups that are both protestant and catholic conservative, veterans organizations, the first amendment lobby, and conservative pod cast groups. The second thing that can be done is to utilize the internet and the alternative media to make the public aware of what is going, who is doing it and why. The string pullers are really starting to fear the internet because these people are like a bunch of cockroaches who do not want any light shone on them. They have operated in the darkness for a long time and the last thing that they want is for a sizable portion of the American public to be made aware of what they are doing because they know that their agenda will be met with enormous force. The alternative media has started to evolve and become what I knew that their true potential was. They are doing this by taking control of these news stories in a timely manner and refuting the propaganda, which sometimes entails completing all of the factual information about a story. A few great web sites and people have been doing this namely: The Daily Stormer, American Renaissance, Red Ice Radio, Bill Engdahl, The Drudge Report, David Icke, John Rappaport, Pat Buchanan, Jeff Rinse, Paul Craig Roberts, James Edwards, Stefan Molyneux, Radox, Sheeple, John B Wells and Caravan to Midnight, and Colin Flaherty. An alternative point of view is being presented without the liberal bias and what really separates these people from the mainstream news is that they are filling in the factual spaces that have been left off by the main stream media. The people that run these websites and pod casts are doing a great service to freemen the world over. However what the alt-right has recently started doing which the leftist controllers hate, is they have started using their own playbook against them and these communist infiltrators are fuming. The alt right is publishing the addresses and private information about these swine online and they are fuming because there is nothing that they can do about it. The alt right is continuing to develop their technological capabilities through people such as Vox Day and others in America and Europe and they are starting to get exposed through hacks for the lying scoundrels they are and some of the real reasons for military actions in places like Libya are coming to the attention of the American public. These people are being shown to be the absolute war mongering parasitic representatives of the new world order that they are. Hopefully as the alt right becomes more influential, we will be able to tap into financing from sympathetic patriots in the business and entertainment industries because there are way more of us than the string pullers. Black Lives Matters activist and LBGT demoniacs have been portrayed by the mainstream media as the majority of Americas and perfectly normal people with a legitimate reason to protest. My response to this is that only a lunatic would want their 10 year old daughter to go use the restroom next to some 47 year old computer programmer with a beard and dress.

    The alternative right has to tap into the economic potential of certain industries by working to control these industries. I would recommend the micro farm and organic farming industries. These require a small capital outlay and they are industries with a small amount of regulation in many states. Furthermore this entails self reliance and it gives us some degree of control over a healthy food supply. It will allow like minded whites to feed their family non-GMO food which will ensure the production of healthy children. Let the negroes and their allies enjoy GMO food that is sprayed with wax and dna altering pesticides. Furthermore, we can open small grocery stores which will control the food supply from producer to end consumer while at the same time taking money out of internationalist pocket like the people who run Wal-Mart, and hate and are out to take advantage of the American workforce. Research the food laws in your state and find out what they are, you will be surprised to see how tilted the table is for giant grocers that is why there are very few flea markets even in the South of the US. These giant grocers and their allies like Wal-Mart, Publix, Safeway, Kroger, Monsanto and ADM have all quietly been lobbying your representatives to get their own laws passed and they have done everything that they can in many states like Florida to try and completely and totally wipe out the micro farming business and ancillary markets. Do your research and talk to the general public, most people are on our side and they do not want to go to Wal-Mart and eat this Frankenstein food produced on mega unsafe farms where they fly helicopters to even get a view of the property because these places are so massive. Start your own farm and print up stickers that say support your local farm and put your logo on there, give these stickers away this is free advertising and helps forward our agenda.

Utilize the internet in less time consuming ways get on Yahoo or other comments sections and challenge these uncouth communist cowards with fact and not emotional arguments. The last thing that any liberal wants to get into is a situation where their point of view is challenged with objective facts. A perfect example of this is the Black Lives Matters protestors, this baboon stench does not want to acknowledge the fact that blacks kill far more blacks than whites do, they are their own worst enemy.

Thoughts on Current Events

Hillary Clinton-Hillary Clinton is a pathological evil woman who has a bloodthirsty drive for absolute power. She is fundamentally driven by a communist ideology and seeks to exert as much control over you as possible. She is an open borders internationalist who is owned by large banking interest, she cares about no one but her self. She looks like a cross between Chairman Mao and a space alien from a B grade science fiction movie when she wears her robot suits, but make no mistake she is extremely dangerous. There is a massive pile of dead bodies behind her and her husband including many of the state troopers that were Bill's personal bodyguards. The Clintons are absolutely ruthless people that will use any means necessary both legal and illegal to thwart any blows against Billy's copulation tour or their political control. Think about what Hillary Clinton has done in Benghazi, where she sat there and watched our ambassador and troops get slaughtered in cold blood when she could have called in drone air strikes or Blackhawk helicopters and they could have unloaded their payload within 15 minutes and stopped this slaughter. The Clinton foundation is a type of slush fund for foreign despots who want anything done. Hillary has masqueraded as a charitable fundraiser for the down trodden when the truth of the matter is that she is a money changer that needs to be driven from the temple. Hillary has acted like she cares a great deal for these Haitians but the truth of the matter is that Hillary would not even let one of these black swine put a buff and shine on Billy's barber pole.

Donald Trump-Donald Trump has been a real estate magnet and casino owner. His personal politics were little known until he got into the presidential race. He was largely pilloried by the talking heads on TV until the Lego fanatic and watermelon head Jeb Bush, booger eating, internationalist maniac Ted Cruz, the man with the homosexual mouth Marco Rubio, and the I'm from Ohio and I can piss my name in the snow Jon Kasich were repudiated at the polls by an unchaste public who thoroughly rejected the Republican neo-conservative anti-American platform. Donald Trump was able to tap into populist issues such as trade, our costly defense policy, our failed trade negotiations which destroyed the blue collar class, our open borders and the animals which have invaded our schools with disease eliminated in the last mid-century, affirmative action and the ownership of politicians by special interest. These elites in the Republican Party lived in such ivory towers that they were totally out of touch with the outrage and contempt that the American public had for their ideas and policies. Donald Trump connected in a serious way with those that had been forgotten in this country. He was saying all of the right things and this in turn brought out record crowds not seen in recent times to political rallies; he was also bringing Democrats in blue collar jobs to his side to vote for him. Bad things can be said about Donald Trump, but the guy does know how to generate money, which is totally lacking in the current politicians at the federal level.

Mitt Romney-Mitt Romney was put forward as the presidential candidate in 2012. Mitt Romney is a Wall Street insider. However this was not his biggest problem. The fact that he was an inbred Mormon cult leader was the real problem with him. The Catholics, Evangelicals, Jews, negroes and other minorities absolutely hate the Mormons. The American public did not want a man who is involved with a cult in the foremost political position in the free world. The question that needs to be asked of the Republican Party was what in the hell were they thinking putting up a Mormon for the top office, were they intentionally throwing the election or was this the greatest political blunder of the last 50 years.

Diane Feinstein- Is a liberal parasite from California who has used her position in office to influence business for her husbands dealings with California. She is an internationalist with no allegiance to the country and she should be dealt with as such. She is totally opposed to the second amendment and if she had her way, would confiscate every gun in this country. She is one of the principal architects of the current Orwellian surveillance state, and looks at the NSA whistle blowers as traitors. She is only watching out for herself. She is the worst form of civilization destroyer. If there were any justice in this country Diane Feinstein would be tried and convicted as a traitor and suffer DBN. Death by negroes, in the form of being raped to death by any NBA team.

Chuck Schumer-Is one of the foremost proponents of gun control he has absolutely no respect for the constitution of the US. He is the absolute perfect representation of an individual who has no respect for anything that the forefathers of this country stood for. He is a corrupt internationalist who seeks to usurp personal freedoms and place the US population in a hellish surveillance state that the Stasi would be quite jealous of. If there were any justice he would be tried as a traitor, convicted, buried in the dirt up to his head and have his head physically beaten from his body with a four iron. This is just deserts for these traitors.

The Way Forward

Now I shall go through each point I have raised in this book and the solution to it. The US federal government has been systematically growing and becoming more tyrannical and unreasoning. This is a trend which is also starting to envelop the state and local governments as well. This is an issue which defies political parties and it is a trend that needs to be reversed. We can see some of the states starting to break from the maniacal grip of this growing bureaucracy; this is starting to happen in the form of states flouting the federal marijuana laws. Even though these states are technically violating federal marijuana laws they are able to operate these businesses free of the federal government and this is enheartening because the states decided that they are not going to follow these laws, and there has been no push back from the federal government. This is a key point because the thing that these federal bureaucrats most fear is the politicians from the governor level in a state pushing back against the federal government in a strong manner and backing it with force or civil disobedience. The reason that they fear this is because this creates a quagmire for the federal government ; they can either let the state do this and secede some of their power or they can go in and use force and allow the general public to see that they are actually living in a form of tyranny which is the last thing that they want revealed. The federal government has used their purse strings as a means of forcing compliance with their agenda, the politicians at the state level need to focus on ways to push back against the federal government without hurting the state economically. I believe as time goes by we will see a balkanization of states in the US which form economic blocks and are economically connected, this will create a more decentralized form of government in the US and hence the federal government will have less control over how people use their property and personal freedoms. The next battleground for the federal government is going to be the control of water and states water rights. We will have extremely low cost alternative fuels for our houses so this will cause the string pullers to look for alternative means to control the populations. Water is the essence of life and we must not allow bureaucrats in DC or internationalist organizations to control these assets. The power of water is the much greater than the product itself, it gives those who control it the means to create famines and control the food supply as well. The most important thing that individuals can do is make information available to as many people as possible because information is power and most of the public is on our side they just do not know what is truly going on. Our politicians need to be vetted, by this I mean we need to back people who are strong constitutionalist and men of character who are willing to die for what they believe in. A website needs to be created which really digs into the political leanings of these Cretans and alerts need to be sent out when these swine vote against the interests of the people. Take a good hard look at the current leaders of the Republican Party and ask yourself if you believe any of those men would be willing to die for any of the ideas embedded in the constitution, clearly the answer is no. However, we need to start out at the local level and vet these politicians on issues like land use, gun rights, water rights, gmo labeling, affirmative action, immigration, programming in our schools, timely execution of those convicted of murder, and school choice vouchers. Where do your local politicians really stand, are they truly supporters of individuals rights and constitutionalist or are they cowardly party men who are comfortable with their position in life and do not want to rock the boat. We need men of action, we are nearing a point of no return if these corrupt jack legs continue their course we are going to have a complete breakdown of society in the US and a civil war which will totally tear apart the country and destroy important genetic material. We need politicians who are going to stand up for their states rights and form balkanized blocks with other states where the federal government has way overstepped their bounds on issues whether it be land rights or education. These federal opposition forces need to draws a clear line of demarcation in the sand.

    The business culture in the US is changed through two conduits. The first is ensuring that undergraduate and graduate business programs are studying Maasaki Imai and Deming. I went to a top 50 graduate business school and Maasaki Imai was only mentioned in passing. The US business community ignored Deming when he came up with his original points of business and ways to improve quality control so he took them to Japan and they embraced him and basically totally wiped out a few our industries, operational programs need to be implemented within these large companies to change the way that management thinks. The individuals or managers that are incapable or unwilling to change need to be removed from the equation because they are making the company less competitive and there is an expense associated with keeping those people in the companies. We need a flat tax structure which closes the loopholes for these companies. A 10% corporate tax is reasonable and will draw capital to the United States. These large international companies are not paying their fair share and they need to step up to the plate. The most egregious example of this was GE which had over 14 billion dollars in profit, and payed not one penny in taxes. I am a capitalist; however capitalism needs to have checks and balances. Bankers and other business men who cause a large amount of financial damage to the country should be treated as traitors and if found guilty executed.

    Affirmative action is an egregious practice that needs to be totally driven out of the United States operationally, legally and statistically. This practice puts us at a major disadvantage in comparison to the rest of the world and it is un-American. A similar problem exists in our elementary schools, the negro scholars are calling for Ebonics and specialized African curriculums. This is great, lets work on further desegregating the schools and allow the negroes to teach themselves if they think that they are so capable let them have a school with all black teachers and administrators. I am quite certain that this will be the very breeding grounds for many a Rhodes Scholar and some of the great thinkers of the western world. We should not offer the negro any assistance because they hate us and most of them would cut our throats given half a chance. Let these ignominious swine live in the world they are capable of creating, and let them be destroyed by their own people who are their greatest enemy.

The immigration situation in Europe has a very clear simple solution. This Muslim dysentery needs to be forcibly repatriated to where they came from. If they do not want to leave voluntarily and cause a great deal of trouble they should be shot on sight and shoveled into compactors like the dung that they are. The borders of Europe need to be sealed with troops and armed patriots and any of these Mohammedan beasts that set foot on the hallow ground of Europe deserve nothing short of 135 grains of lead between the eyes. These scum represent the greatest threat ever to the current cradle of civilization. If this kingmaker Erdogan should ever threaten Western Europe again with releasing more of these rodents, he should be told in no uncertain terms that if he does that again Turkey will be made Christian by a nihilistic supernatural military force and he will pray for a swift death. The internationalist in

Belgium need to be repudiated, they are in the processing of trying to ethnically cleanse Europe of whites; the Europeans either need to stiffen up and take back their countries by force or they will be destroyed by internationalist and their street force Muslim swine. The first step for these countries is to break away from the EU and then they need to regain control of their currency, as long as the EU holds the purse strings they are doomed.

The immigration situation in America is just as dire as regards the Mexicans. Any Mexican illegal in this country should be rounded up and implanted with a micro chip for tracking, then summarily deported with instructions in Spanish not to return without the proper papers. The border with Mexico needs to be mined and the US military needs to be placed on the border with Blackhawk helicopters with stingers missiles and gatling guns, in order to take back sovereignty of the border from the Mexican Military/drug cartels. If the Mexican military fires on our military again with weapons giving these drug mules cover, the closest Mexican town should be carpet bombed to the point where not one twig is left standing. Mexicans have been incrementally destroying the US cities starting with Los Angeles, Tucson, El Paso, Fresno, Albuquerque and Phoenix. The Mexicans absolutely hate whites and our civilization because they know that we are far superior to them by any measure. No Mexican has ever been responsible for any important scientific invention and they never will be, they are a derelict group of injuns with a few drops of Spanish blood. It is time to put an end to this and take our country back, we have no duty whatsoever to support the country of Mexico and all aid should be stopped immediately and focused on important issues in the US like building infrastructure.

Metropolitan areas should be safe areas where people can walk around and enjoy life and conduct business free of the spontaneous negro riots and other violent negro criminality which is a common daily facet of many cities. Why is Washington DC the capitol of the country a black hellhole unfit to walk after dark, should the capital of our country not be a place that all Americans can be proud of. Police need to be put back on foot and bicycle patrols where the crime is. There needs to be a zero tolerance of violent crime from negroes, if it becomes necessary to grease a few of them to get the message out then so be it. If the negroes act like rioters after one of their clan gets justifiably shot, treat them as such and open up on them with a few bursts of live rounds. When a negroe sees the guy standing next to him have his head removed courtesy of a 500 grain boat tail, it may cause him to ponder his own existence for a moment. The negro is not in a position to ask for anything. The negro will accept what we give to him and be grateful. If the situation was reversed the negro would certainly not give you anything. One only need take a good look at South Africa currently to see what will happen if the whites in America do not dig in and fight back against this tyranny.

The issue with the religious institutions getting attacked by the corrosion of socialism is certainly quite disheartening. There are two ways to deal with this problem. The first solution is to find like minded individuals within the confines of your religious institution and sit down and talk with your local religious leaders and tell them that you have serious reservations about these policies. This will produce a couple of different scenarios. One your religious leader may acknowledge your claims and support them and communicate to you that he has passed these upstairs through the proper channels. The second scenario is that your religious leader will attempt to use doctrine to support this destructive policy. If your leader is really opposed to your beliefs you may want to try and find a more conservative religious institution or you could opt for the second action which is to simply leave your church and worship in private.

The military industrial complex presents us with a complex quagmire, because we want to maintain a strong national defense this allows us to impose our will on countries economically and ensures the safe transport of our goods in the air and sea. However, our military forces currently are not optimally suited for the needs of the United State and we have some enormous inefficiencies created through our poor uses of resources. The first problem with the military is that we have too many bases in too many countries and many of these are not strategic areas that we need to have military capital. The second problem is that we are providing the defensive forces for countries such as Japan and Germany which are fully well capable of defending themselves and we are not receiving any financial compensation for this. In actuality, when our troops are buying goods in those other countries they are displacing capital from the US. There is a political element inside of the US that wants to control the German people and keep a permanent occupation force there, but the world is a different place and we need to move away from this way of thinking. The research that is done by the US military industrial complex has yielded some incredible technologies which have consumer applications and in this respect research and development is an important piece for the US to maintain military and economic dominance. However the cost of single unit planes and military systems has gone through the roof. We need to try and have much better cost controls on our items for a number of reasons-this is draining off too much money from the American economy and the more expensive our goods are the less likely it will be that our allies will be able to purchase them. Single use items, like planes are very expensive because the technology has to be tested and used only once because it is new, this is a very expensive system but for some cutting edge technologies this is the only way to do it. The military needs to be pulled out of these communist social experiments like women in combat and unfit minorities in positions of leadership. The military is not the place to engage in social experiments. Our military in its' past form has been shown to be an effective and unequaled fighting force in modern combat. The formula that we have for our forces should not be tinkered with in the name of progressive socialist policies. The US defense department needs to have their military bases planted for a lexicon which represents the current threat and we need to cut down our spending as a percentage of out GDP.

The legal system in the US needs to get back to the philosophical intentions of the founding fathers. We do not need slipshod interpretations of the second amendment and other founding documents in this country. The founding fathers of this country I can assure you with a high degree of certainty never intended for there to be a handgun ban in Chicago and New York City or hate speech laws. These legal trends where subversive infiltrator have tried to push their political agendas through non –customary channels such as the appeals courts were never intended to happen by the founding fathers. What I am happy about seeing is individual citizens getting out and collecting enough signatures to get ballot measures on the voting block. This ensures that the grass roots groups can push things through that the political body is too cowardly or corrupt to perform even though these jack leg politicians know that it is the right thing to do. We need to create a greater awareness of who our judges are and what they stand for and this is a situation that is perfectly designed for an internet solution. Most people when they go to vote for judges have no idea who or what they are actually voting for.

    The homosexual political lobby which is agitating for minority status for homosexuals and their fellow back door trot needs to be repudiated in no uncertain terms. Two faggots pushing a turd back in forth in a swimming pool is not a family on an idyllic day playing with junior in the shallows of the pool. The political goals of these coital reprobates will only increase the cost of business and make it more difficult to fire unmeritous workers.

The hate speech lobby is a very dangerous political movement because their goal is to undermine free speech in this country and have their minions determine what are appropriate topics for discourse. Europe has already starting ascending this ladder, and anyone who thinks that someone should be thrown in jail for calling another person a name is no friend of liberty. They are in fact a small part of a budding tyranny. The anti-bullying campaign is an ally of this movement, and I am equally opposed to the anti-bullying campaign because that is how the real world works and you should get used to it in grade school. The anti-bullying campaign is made all the more ridiculous by the numerous spokesmen across the country who are almost universally fruitcakes with a lisp, who engage our youth by saying I was bullied in middle school and it made me feel bad about myself. Well let me tell you something if this butt pirate had already been made by the 7th grade and tormented, he was a real nancy boy who liked to watch the other boys undress in gym class. Who can blame the other students, nobody wants to disrobe in the locker room next to some pansy looking them up and down with a coat hanger erection you could hang a 10 lb weight on. The end goal of the bullying campaigns is to pollute the intellectual wells of our youth with socialist propaganda, it is really that simple.

The tax code needs to be totally redone. We have too many high worth individuals and companies who are effectively changing their tax rate to little or nothing through their use of highly paid accountants and lawyers. The most equitable system is a flat tax rate as this will have far less loopholes and is a much more equitable system.

The Middle East is a villainous hellhole of the very worst of the Muslim World. We should give these swine no aid. What we should in fact do is follow the Israeli policy and instigate conflicts between these various Muslim groups and sell both sides weapons to destroy each other. In this way we kill two birds with one stone, we profit from war and we have Arabs killing each other so that we don't have to. You could almost see Bebe Netanyahu negotiating with one of these cutthroats on his patio and trying to keep from smiling when he says it may be possible that I could procure you some weapons at that price, I will have to make a few calls but yes I believe that I can make it happen.

The penal system in the United States needs to be radically reformed. We need to legalize marijuana so that we can apply our finite resources to housing violent criminals and thieves in our penal institutions. The penal institutions need to also be forced into becoming self sufficient units as much as possible like some of the jails in the

South. The people who have been on the cash train of incarcerating people and seizing their assets are going to have to realize that this game is over and it is collapsing the economies of many states.

The debt that college students have run up poses a massive threat financially to the country. This coupled with the high unemployment has created massive default on these debts. What I would suggest is that we have these students engage in massive public works projects that would allow them to pay back some of their debt and put some money in their pockets. I believe the actual unemployment rate in this country is around 20% and this would also be a good way to help out some of these people as well. Our infrastructure is in quite a state of disrepair and this puts the US at a disadvantage from a business standpoint. This debt also creates a virtual slave class out of these people.

The US needs to exert its sovereignty on the international stage and this means that we need to stop being the worlds policemen. If the ebony scum in Somalia want to go and massacre 200,000 let them, we have no national interest in this type of conflict and do not need to become involved. We also need to uproot ourselves from internationalist organizations which do not have our best interest at heart such as the United

Nations and NATO, these two organizations are money sucking parasites on Uncle Sam. We no longer have the resources, nor is it prudent to try and interfere in regional conflicts in third world countries.

Black Lives Matters far from being a great humanitarian organization as being portrayed by the main stream media is the front for a rabid anti-police, anti-white agenda and a terrorist organization which should be banned and its financiers treated as traitors and arbiters of violent terrorism. The worst thing about this whole scenario is not one mainstream news outlets will post the quantitative figures which represent the realty of how many blacks are killed by blacks they selves as the negro says.

The Republican Party has unequivocally proven them selves to be largely corrupt internationalist who have no interest in fostering white nationalism in this country. There are a number of ways to deal with this political ungallantness. The first is to expose the activities of these brigands to the general public; if this should fail there are other tactics. One is to run against these people in races outside of cities in the rural areas and focus on moving towards the city. This is a strategy of infiltration from the country side in to the metropolitan areas. The second strategy is to run against these people as independents, even if you don't win you will keep these traitors inside the gate from ascending to power. These cut throats have no intention of following a proper agenda or ceding power to people that do. The third strategy is to get funding for a third party. However, the current system is so rigged for a two party system that it is quite difficult in any major races to get any traction and the American public has been very brainwashed upon this paradigm. The best way to deal with any corrupt politician is to shine a light on this cockroach and make the people aware of what they are doing, form your own news outlet or use platforms such as You tube to talk about what these politicians are doing at a local level. We have to utilize the new technologies more effectively than our enemies because the public is overwhelming on our side. Change should always be tried democratically, but if that fails and a breakdown of society is imminent other methods are reasonable and dictated by the circumstances.

  The K-12 education system in the US needs to be completely destroyed and rebuilt anew with the tools from the past which were successful. The schools need to be resegregated so that whites and Asians have an opportunity to maximize their educational potential. Students need to be tracked. A voucher system has to be initiated so that students can attend the school of their choosing, we can no longer accept this crap that the government passes off as the public school system. The vouchers will create competition and break the unproductive government monopoly. The Department of Education in Washington DC is a hive of liberals with the wrong ideas about education who have destroyed the public education system in the US. This institution needs to be permanently removed from the payroll and the employees need to go and try and sell their failed theories in the open marketplace. The same should apply for the EPA this is an organization which needs to be eliminated in its current format, and far from saving the environment it has become symbolic of the over reach of government. The schools are not communist indoctrination camps for installing political correctness into the unpolluted minds of our youth. These liberal professors and their failed ideology need to be routed out from the public schools and collegiate environments and trustworthy administrators need to be strategically placed to ensure that this communist cancer does not get a foothold in our educational institutions again. Remember that the only place communism has existed for the last 25 years is in the colleges and universities in the United States. The youth are our future and we owe them the right to an unbiased education and society or we are failed cowardly men.

In concluding let me write that free men in the United States and everywhere are getting fed up with the corrupt bankers and their allies trying to suck everything out of the economy and leave the populace in an inescapable debt. The people have patience right now, but if this NWO agenda continues to be pushed against the will of the people there will be a breaking point and we will have a revolution inside the US not unlike the French revolution where the greed of those who betrayed the people will consume them from the uncontrolled violence of the populace and these scoundrels and traitors will literally be torn limb from limb and have their heads beaten from their bodies with whatever implements are at hand. This is always the last stop on the train of greed and the civilization will revert into a short dark age if this happens and then a period of great prosperity. There are a few scenarios which I believe are the most likely to cause this: an absolute one day destruction of the stock market like the crash in 1929, a default on the dollar and a reevaluation for pennies on the dollar, a senate which goes and raids peoples pension funds to pay off the US debt, an emp attack used by the government against their own people or from a foreign government, a large red flag job in a major city involving nukes and blaming it on whoever happens to be the boogeyman of the week, an executive order where some maniac like Hillary

Clinton tries to forcibly seize guns from the general populace, a lack of access to funds in the banks, an intentional starting of a war with Russia or China or the placement of foreign troops on US soil and the authorization of these troops to use martial law on the populace. Any of these scenarios are possible for the complete unraveling of the United States as we know it or there may be a combination of multiple of these. Once this event occurs the American people will have their own night of the long knives. Just be prepared and let's pray that none of these things ever happen because these are all situations that we should not have to face in this country except for the forces of greed and evil which control our current government. Always remember that it is better to die a free man with a gun in your hands than live as an unarmed slave.

APHORISIMS

Some little kids do not realize how ugly their parents are

The older you get the more your chances of getting lucky decline someone once told me that by the time you are 42 your destiny is set in stone.

Democracy is a fine form of government as long as women, minorities and communists aren't allowed to vote.

Countries with the most radicalized religious populations became this way because the personal moral character of the people in these civilizations is so low; in many cases this relates to the male population.

The people are always the ones that actually solve problems, the politicians only serve to stand in the correct direction of the people

Anyone who truly believes that the negro is equal to the white man should be forced to live under the same roof and in the same neighborhood as negroes for 2 years time; he will then come to realize the truth.

The devil may be sitting next to you in the same pew in your church and you may not recognize him by his firm handshake and friendly manner.

Europeans are always like gasoline sitting on the floor once the proper match hits the old zeitgeists will appear if as by magic

Man can never break his ties to nature no matter how large the city or how many frappachinos and text messages he receives

The government really does not care what you do as long as they get their cut of the action.

www.ingramcontent.com/pod-product-compliance
Lightning Source LLC
Chambersburg PA
CBHW032124090426
42743CB00007B/459

Bleeding Red

A Red Sox Fan's Diary of the 2004 Season

Derek Catsam

VELLUM An imprint of New Academia Publishing, LLC
Washington, DC

Copyright © 2005 by Derek Catsam

First published by VELLUM/New Academia Publishing, 2005
Second edition, 2006

All rights reserved. No part of this book may be reproduced or transmitted in any form or by any means, electronic or mechanical, including photocopying, recording, or by any information storage and retrieval system.

Printed in the United States of America

Library of Congress Control Number: 2005932710
ISBN 0-9767042-6-9 paperback (alk. paper)

 An imprint of New Academia Publishing, LLC
P.O. Box 7420, Washington, DC 20038-7420
www.newacademia.com — info@newacademia.com

Cover photo: KRT/Chris Lee; Cover Design: NAP
Photos on pages viii, 261, and 267 by Jaime Aguila

*Dedicated to
Red Sox Nation
And everyone who knows what
October 27, 2004 meant.*

Contents

Introduction and Acknowledgments — ix

1. February: Anticipation — 1
2. March: In Like a Lion — 13
3. April: Let The Games Begin — 51
4. May: Keep It Rolling? — 95
5. June: The Race Is On — 107
6. July: The Dog Days Come Early — 127
7. August: Gut Check Time — 165
8. September: The Stretch Drive — 195
9. October: This Is The Year! (Is This The Year?) — 219
10. August 2005: Epilogue — 269

Introduction and Acknowledgments

Let me get it out of the way right now so you have some idea of the sort of pathetic wretch whose diary you are about to read: October 27, 2004 was the greatest day of my life. I've had a good go of it up to now, but that day and the night and days that followed were the pinnacle thus far.

For years I had thought about keeping a diary in which I followed my beloved Boston Red Sox through an entire season, from spring training through what I hoped would be the World Series. Every year I came up with reasons not to—the obvious commitment involved being chief among these. But 2004 felt different from almost the second we started thinking about baseball, which was as soon as we got out of bed and could face the world (and our hangovers) after Game 7 of the ALCS in October 2003. Once spring training approached, I decided to go for it.

But this is much more than just a chronicle of the 2004 season—indeed, the depth with which I cover various games varies from day to day, whim to whim. Some games I ignore, or miss out on entirely. Others I give a great deal of attention out of all proportion to their larger significance. *Bleeding Red* is ultimately about being a fan and what it means to be passionate and committed to a sports team, and how that affects our lives. It follows my own life through the 2004 season—from Charlottesville, Virginia, where I was on a fellowship for a semester, to Odessa, Texas where I took a new job as a college professor to Oxford, England, where I write this now. It finds me on trips to places such as Nashville and London, Washington, DC and Caretta, West Virginia.

Red Sox Nation is not a place on a map; it is located in the hearts of millions of people, with its soul on Yawkey Way in Boston. I am a Red Sox fan and this is part of my story. But if you are a fan (of any team in any sport, really, though Sox fans are privileged here) I hope that you will see some elements of yourself in this book. You may be more civilized than I am when it comes, say, to throwing beer bottles across your living room and kitchen after an especially egregious loss, or about how you refer to the dimwitted expectorating swamp trolls who root for the Yankees. You may have a healthier sense of perspective. You may be slightly less obsessed. But you may find that being a fan has certain universal contours that this book captures.

With the exception of editing for clarity and correcting obvious errors, the diary is as I wrote it. It is unflinching. I have not cleaned it up to make myself look better. I have not gone back to make my predictions look more sage or to change my judgments. I wrote the chapter titles as I wrote the diary, and the title metaphor, "Bleeding Red," comes not from Curt Schilling and his bloody sock, but rather it was the first thing I came up with in February 2004 to try to capture what the book would be about. Schill's warrior's heart simply makes the title all the more apt – it did not provide the inspiration. Over the course of the season my emotions changed thousands of times, often within the same hour, and I have tried as best I can to convey those emotions through the sometimes limiting format of a daily, or nearly so, diary. The October entries mark the highlights, of course, but the book chronicles the rhythms of a long, sometimes frustrating, sometimes infuriating, rarely dull team and at least one of its fans.

Although *Bleeding Red* was a labor of love, even in doing a project this personal one incurs debts. I owe many, probably more than I will acknowledge in this space. If you have ever rooted for a sports team, been to a game, known me, or walked upright, include yourself among the thanked.

But many people deserve particular attention. It all starts with Mom and Dad, of course. My uncles Nick and John Catsam nurtured my love of baseball from as early as I can remember, as did my late grandparents, Grammy and Papa, June and George Catsam. I had a kindred spirit in my stepfather, Fuzzy Wiggins, from my early teens. My brother Marcus endured it all.

Rob, the Thunderstick, followed this project more closely than anyone, and he appears throughout. Josh Pepin, Don Graves, Tom Bruscino, and others were there the whole way too. Tom and Don lose points for rooting for crappy teams from Cleveland, however. Mike Stark, Bill Elliott, Matt Dickens and Brendan O'Sullivan are Newport friends who are also brothers and Sox fans to varying degrees.

Dave Kane asked me to publish excerpts of the diary on Ephblog after I posted one of them on the History News Network blog Rebunk. It was at that point that the diary really took off. I appreciate every one of the readers of both blogs who commented, criticized, and argued throughout the summer and fall. My colleagues at Rebunk, Steve Tootle and the aforementioned Tom, indulged me. Suddenly there was an audience, and that audience drove my entries. You watched the birthing of parts of the first draft of this project. Now I hope you'll pay for the privilege of reading the final product.

My colleagues throughout 2004 and 2005 were incredibly supportive of a project that had very little to do with my regular work as a historian and professor. Nonetheless, they knew that I loved what I was doing in my free time even as I continued to plug away at writing my other works.

The Virginia Foundation for the Humanities in Charlottesville, The National Endowment for the Humanities Summer Institute at Ferrum College and Caretta, West Virginia, and the Rothermere American Institute at the University of Oxford provided me with time and opportunity to write and think, and they also served as the setting for the memoir of a year in the life of a fan. They deserve my ultimate praise. And I promise them that they will soon see the other work that I did during my tenure at their institutions blossom.

Early in the course of this project, I took my job at the University of Texas of the Permian Basin, in arid, wind swept Odessa, which is about as far from Yawkey Way in temperament and environment as a place in America possibly can be. I moved there in July, 2004. My colleagues at UTPB made me feel welcome. My history colleagues in particular welcomed me into their lives – Roland Spickermann, Diana Olien, Jay Tillapaugh, Lanita Akins, and the late Warren Gardner are among the greatest colleagues anyone has ever had.

Another history colleague, Jaime Aguila, his wife Holly, and their little boy, Ben (Go Red Sox!) allowed me to live in their house for a month while I searched for a place to live – while they were out of the country. Many entries for this diary were written there, and Jaime became one of the biggest supporters of my maniacal fandom. I'll be over in time for PTI, Jaime. Many of my colleagues even watched games with me, oftentimes at my home. Cecilio Ortiz and Josh Levy were most prominent among the non-historians who made mine a great place to be when sports were on, and even if the Sox lost, the presence of all of these folks made the losses bearable, the wins exquisite. Despite seeing me with my Sox on, they still claim to like me. That says a great deal about all of them, much of it good.

I want to thank Anna Lawton of New Academia Publishing and Vellum. She showed faith in this project and nurtured it from being a manuscript that I had given up hope of ever seeing the light of a bookshelf to an actual book with my name on the front. She guided it through the process, answering my innumerable dumb questions with grace and aplomb. Without her, this would still be sitting in one of the piles on my desk in Texas, and I would be plotting my revenge on Stephen King and Stewart O'Nan for parlaying their name recognition into a book superficially similar to but really very different from my own.

In addition to being a historian in my department, Jay Tillapaugh also is an able administrator at UTPB, and he helped me to find funds for this project's completion. Roland Spickermann, my area coordinator in history, Chris Stanley, chair of the Department of Humanities and Fine Arts, Lois Hale, Dean of the College of Arts & Sciences (and a native New Englander and Sox fan), Bill Fannin, VP for Academic Affairs, and David Watts, UTPB President also offered their support. Many academic administrators would have been reluctant to support a project that was not pure scholarship. They were not.

Ana Martinez probably bore more of my angst, especially of an ugly few days in October, than anyone. She learned what it means to be a Red Sox fan. More to the point, she learned what it is like to be with a Red Sox fan. She is my colleague, my friend, my partner, and my light. And hokey as it is, I want to thank the 2004 Boston

Red Sox. Being a fan is an act of unconditional love. You guys rewarded all of the years of suffering. Now all I ask is that you do it again this year.

1

February: Anticipation

Sunday, February 22, 2004

Spring training has begun. Pitchers and catchers have reported. The sour taste of Aaron Boone's late night home run to end the ALCS will linger forever, like Bucky Fucking Dent's home run off Mike Torrez and that cursed ground ball through Buckner's legs in 1986, but spring training represents a bit of a purging, and as always, even in cynical Red Sox Nation, hope springs eternal.

In what has to be an unprecedented phenomenon in the history of athletic competition, the rivalry between the Red Sox and the Yankees (let it be known that I used the term "Evil Empire" in an essay on the Sox a good two years before Larry Lucchino uttered it in 2002), already the most intense in all of sport, has become even more intense in the off-season. The Red Sox signing of Curt Schilling and Keith Foulke made theirs an incredibly productive Hot Stove Season as it was. But then in November rumors began to circulate that we might be about to trade for Alex Rodriguez, A-Rod, the consensus best player in baseball, for Manny Ramirez, our idiot savant hitter extraordinaire who comes with more baggage than US Airways. For the record, I was never very keen on the trade. I thought that giving up Manny and Nomar (whom we would have traded for Magglio Ordonez of the White Sox if the knights of the keyboards are to be believed) and taking on A-Rod's salary would not be worthwhile. Talks finally fell apart after several revivals. Tom Hicks, the Rangers' loose-lipped General Manager, declared A-Rod to be the Rangers captain in mid-January, promising Texas fans that he would be their starting shortstop indefinitely, and then promptly and stealthily he traded Rodriguez to the Yankees for Alfonso Soriano. Immediately the media whipped out the dual canards about the Curse of the Bambino (enough! Enough! A thousand times ENOUGH!) and about the tortured Red Sox fan, forgetting that many of us diehards are more than willing to go into the season against the Yankees with Pedro, Schilling, Lowe, Wakefield, and Foulke on the mound and Nomar, 'Tek, Manny and the rest of the Dirt Dogs who Cowboyed Up last year in the lineup.

Yup, spring training has begun. I couldn't be more excited. And in this memoir, we'll follow the Boston Red Sox, and in so doing, hopefully we'll explore the psyche and life of a Red Sox fan, an otherwise well-adjusted and successful individual who nonetheless has devoted way too much of his heart and soul to the Olde Towne Team.

Monday, February 23, 2004

It is such an enormous cliché, but there is something to the idea of hope springing eternal in the baseball fan's soul. I remember well being a little kid, and when the first thaws started to happen, sometimes as late as April (I did, after all, grow up in New Hampshire, where it has been said that there are nine months of winter and three months of rough sledding) I could not wait to get out and play baseball. Once I got to high school, track and field was by far my best sport, but from earliest memories, I was a baseball player and a baseball fan. For hours with just a glove and a ball I could entertain myself, pretending that I was Freddy Lynn in Center Field, catching balls that I tossed to myself from impossible angles off of our A-Frame house or off barn walls and roofs at my grandparents' and Dad's farm. Spring to me meant baseball. And baseball to me meant the Red Sox.

I don't really know how I became a Red Sox fan, except by some combination of nurture and nature. Being a native New Englander, the Sox were the logical choice, and the decision was certainly reinforced by my family, especially my uncles John and Nick, my Dad's brothers who were the big baseball fans (and players) in the family. I don't really know my first memories of the Red Sox, but they probably started to ferment sometime around the 1975 World Series. Carlton Fisk, of Game Six home run fame, was a local boy.

There were legendary stories of a home run he once hit at Newport's baseball field when he played Legion ball. In deepest deadest right-center field there was a tower for the football games back before our football field was at the high school. The tower was, at least in my child's mind, probably 500 feet from home plate, and it stood three stories. Center and especially right field stretched on for hundreds of feet, as the river that formed the natural left field border snaked off away from the outfield, leaving an endless expanse of ground when there wasn't storm fencing put up to make an outfield border. Apparently Fisk, a Vermont-born and New Hampshire-bred legion player from tiny nearby Charlestown, hit a home run that cleared the tower and crossed over the river. It is a Bunyanesque tale of strength and hitting prowess that is not less remarkable if it is apocryphal. Indeed, if it is apocryphal, I don't want to know. It is one of the received truths of my youth that would make me no better a person for knowing the facts if they debunk my conception.

In any case, nature or nurture, I became a Red Sox fan and by the time I was six or seven it was an unrequited love that would take hold of me and never let go. The hot stove league of the off-season always percolated, pregnant with possibility as new acquisitions could be. But when spring rolled around I would get myself into a baseball frenzy. My thousands of baseball cards would replace the football cards I dutifully and even passionately collected. Out would come my gloves and bats and balls. My neighborhood friends and I would put together our leagues of six teams (each represented by one player) that would keep us playing and fighting deep into the summer nights on the fields that abutted our dirt road in the woods. And when I was not playing baseball, I was soaking up everything I could about the Red Sox. The early 1980s were not good times for my team, but you'd have never known that from the way I predicted the league standings at the beginning of every season, placing the Red Sox first with the blind passion only a kid can muster.

Well, that's not true. I am more jaded, more cynical, more realistic these days. But that love has really not abated. That perhaps is why the rumors of a possible Curt Schilling calf injury made my heart jump this morning, especially after the confirmation of a Keith Foulke injury to the same body part in a drill yesterday. That is why I greet news of Manny showing up early and Pedro making it into camp today with all of the glee of a reunion among old friends. No, I still love the Red Sox. The difference between 2004 and 1984, however, is that when I make my predictions for the final standings in each league, and I place the Red Sox at the top of the American League East, the American League, the Majors, it won't simply be blind loyalty. Will it? I guess some compulsions never change, only the context within which those compulsions occur.

Tuesday, February 24, 2004

Today I write from Washington, a city that has been a central place in my life, the closest thing to home, really, for about four years now. I moved here with Katie, my then girlfriend the last year I actually lived in Ohio, where I was getting my history PhD at Ohio University. I lived here for two years, during which time Katie moved out, I started dating Rachel, and eventually met and fell in love with Katherine, the love of my life who broke up with me several months after I moved to Minnesota to take a job as a professor in 2002. During the year after I moved, I returned to DC often to be with Katherine through our breakup in April 2003. Since then I have still used Washington as something of a home base. I was a visiting scholar with the American Political Science Association's Centennial Center in January 2004, after which point I moved on to Charlottesville, where I am a fellow at the Virginia Foundation for the Humanities. I don't know too many people in C-Ville, so DC is still a touchstone, and in any case, I have been asked to fly to Texas to interview for a job at the University of Texas of the Permian Basin this weekend. I am miserably unhappy in Minnesota and things have fallen apart there for me personally and professionally anyway, so I am happy to have the option. I fly to Odessa-Midland tomorrow. Who knows—I may need to buy a bolo tie, alligator skin boots, and a ten gallon hat sometime soon. Such is the life of an academic—I don't get to choose where I am going to live, at least not for a long while, until fame, fortune, and a best seller (or a regular TV gig, a la Michael Beschloss) comes my way.

In any case, all of this just goes to show that for real fans, geography is almost irrelevant to being a fan of a team. Certainly geography—proximity—is a crucial aspect in what team most sports fans choose to support. The majority of my students in Minnesota were, not shockingly, Twins fans, just as most of the kids to whom I'll present a lecture on Thursday in the Lone Star State will be Rangers or Astros fans. What a weird idea—that there actually are Rangers or Astros fans. And while I wish that I could say that I had more important concerns, the fact is, whenever I have moved, and that has happened often in the past ten years, one of my main concerns has been how often I might be able to see Sox games, either live or on television. In an era of internet, following one's team is less problematic than it once was (thank God, or at least Al Gore—or so he'd like me to believe—for internet radio and Major League Baseball's $14.95 seasonal radio package). Nonetheless, the idea of being in West Texas and far, far, far away from Fenway Park sort of makes me sick to my stomach. The career goal was to be moving closer to New England, or at least the east coast, by now. Suffice it to say, the academic job market sucks. I need to write that bestseller soon.

Still, it feels good to be in familiar DC, with friends (and baseball fans—I am joining a fantasy league with buddies here. Let it be known now that there will be no Yankees on my team. No way am I putting myself in that potential conflict of interest scenario. God, the Yankees suck.) And it feels better to know that with each passing day more of the 2004 Sox are reporting to camp down in Fort Myers.

Wednesday, February 25, 2004

I write this from the 7th floor of the Eleganté Hotel in Odessa, Texas. My room overlooks the pool, and beyond that it overlooks, well, flat, scrub-brush-covered West Texas. I am not making any final decisions here, and I am thrilled that this place really seems to want me, but a positive decision will not come based on my being smitten with the landscape. On the flight in we came in over oilfields, which look vaguely like a series of long jump pits with dirt runways that lead to the side rather than the center of the pit. In the midst of that pit lie skeletal oil rigs, metal machines that look like prehistoric fossils from a future age. The landscape reminds me a bit of a duller South African veld; it reminds me of, well, West Texas as I imagined it from *Friday Night Lights*. Suffice it to say that

February

Friday Night Lights is probably not the Chamber of Commerce's ideal brochure for tourism to Odessa and its sister city Midland. I'm just guessing.

My guess is that there are not a lot of Sox fans in West Texas. Though at the restaurant tonight (I had serviceable baby back ribs; on the plus side Texans do like their meat.) one guy had a Sox hat on, probably more fashion accessory than fan's totem. Speaking of which, in this week's *The Hook*, one of Charlottesville's two alternative weeklies, there is an essay by a guy who went to Boston for a vacation with his girlfriend. He is not much of a baseball fan (which always brings to mind what Foghorn Leghorn says to Miss Priss about her dweebie little son who does not like the game—"There's something kind of eeeee-ewww about a boy who doesn't like baseball.") but he figures they ought to go to a Sox game. They can't get in to Fenway (on a nice summer's day? Just trying to walk up and get a ticket? No doubt, this guy isn't a fan, that's for sure.) But they enjoy the scene outside the park, and he buys a Sox hat. From there on, everywhere he goes in Charlottesville he makes friends. Let it be known—Sox fans, real Sox fans are everywhere. But that brings me back to my main point—they may be everywhere, but I doubt a lot of them are here in Odessa. Or in Midland. Nope, I'm going to need satellite if I end up here. Hell, Dallas and the closest team are nearly six hours away. Other than living abroad, have I ever lived anywhere in the US where I was six hours from Major League baseball? There is a minor league team here (an A's affiliate, I was told; I'll have to check) and big news has it that they have a popular minor league hockey team and are getting Arena Football. But no, baseball will require satellite. If I end up here. We'll have to see how tomorrow goes.

In any case, I was on planes most all day, so I have not gotten any new news on the Sox spring training. The A-Rod hangover seems to be subsiding. For the next few weeks we'll undoubtedly be seeing the media trying to fill space, talk about next year's potential free agents and their contract prospects (Nomar, Pedro, Lowe, Tek, Williamson, Ortiz and one of this year's new signees, Pokey Reese), and languid Florida games. Boston and Fort Myers are both a long damned way from Odessa, Texas.

Thursday, February 26, 2004

Well, let it be said that Texans like their sports, and West Texas is no exception. It may well be the rule. Today was a sports day in many ways. I went with Jaime, the chair of the search committee and a friendly young historian, and his wife to his son Ben's soccer practice and I even kicked a ball around for the whole time. We went on a tour of Midland and Odessa. I saw the Midland sports complex, including the minor league baseball team's digs (they are an A's AA affiliate called the Rockhounds—I see season tickets in my future if I end up in this area) and the adjacent Midland football stadium—high school football. West Texas. Damn. Then we saw Permian High, as well as taking a trip out to their home, Ratliffe Stadium. At the school is that giant sign that can be seen in *Friday Night Lights* showing their state, district, and other championships. Mojo fever! It is surreal to think of it as a real place after *Friday Night Lights*. In any case, I may not see a lot of Sox games live if I come out here, but I won't lack for sports, and there is always satellite television. Plus, Dallas and the Rangers is an hour flight, five or so hours by car.

The day has been devoted to the interview. They like me. They really, really like me. It's gone very well so far. We'll see how it ends up. West Texas. Rockhounds. Jackalopes (the local minor-league hockey team). Mojo. Oh my.

Friday, February 27, 2004

Yup, they definitely like me. Today went at least as well as yesterday, and if I may say, my classroom lecture on the "Road to *Brown*" was so well received that students were clamoring to talk to me, to encourage me to come to UTPB, to say "thanks." It was nice, and it clearly left an impression on the faculty. Indeed, one woman went to Roland Spickermann, one of the younger department members, and told him that my lecture made him want to be a teacher and she hopes she can be half as smart as me someday. Good for the ego. Not to mention good for the pocketbook. The department has sent their recommendation to hire me at the request of the VP for Academic Affairs. I'll probably have three days to decide. Suddenly I am going to be faced with both a great option—a decent job after the MSU fiasco but also a sudden decision whether or not to move to desolate, flat, bleak, huge, expansive, open, friendly West Texas. This is far afield from the Red Sox of course, but at the same time, a decision to move to West Texas would mean that I really would be watching what I hope will be this championship season from afar. Not that Odessa is much further from Boston than Mankato, Minnesota. But because of its vastness, it does feel pretty far removed.

The Sox only play in Texas once this year—April 30-May 2, which is not only rather early, but may be too early to coordinate a trip around, since I won't be ready to move out there, and I am highly unlikely to be able to get my stuff down there from Mankato.

Is one any less a fan as a result of distance? Surely proximity to a team, and as important, to a place where the passions are high and the talk is always of that team, where the local papers, newscasts, talk radio idiots, television, and of course advertisements all are wholly devoted to the team, matters. But I am certainly no less a fan now just because I don't live in New England any more than I love my Mom any less. This is always the case, but especially so in an age of internet, web radio, satellite television, and wall-to-wall Sportscenter/Baseball Tonight. No, I am no less a fan if I am in Odessa, Texas than if I am in Orleans, Massachusetts. Still, Odessa is a hell of a long way from Fenway.

Saturday, February 28, 2004

Today was supposed to be our fantasy league draft. I am not much of a fantasy league guy. In fact in my life I have only played fantasy football once and I have tried but never gotten through two fantasy baseball leagues. But I was asked to join with some friends, it seems like a good year to do it, and there is no harm in trying. It will help me keep more of an eye on other teams and players and should provide an added element of fun for the season. We could not pull it together, however, so we'll either automatically draft through the computer or else we'll have to find a future time. I had started to prepare for the draft. My only real ground rule—no Yankees. I do not want to be in a position where I actually have to want Derek Jeter to get an RBI at the end of a tie game. That will never happen, so if I am going to play I don't want guys on my team that I have to root against. One of my tendencies is to overrate Sox players. I get blinded by my passion for the Sox and my fondness for some of their players.

Spring training goes on. It seems to be on the slow side, which can actually be good. Controversy sells papers. It may not make for a good ball club. Yesterday the last player scheduled to report to camp, Reynoldo Garcia, a long shot to make the big league team, arrived in Fort Myers. He was held up by the annual right of spring known as "visa problems." It is an amazing yearly occurrence—these guys know for months they need to be in the US in February. The team has the resources of tens, and in the Sox's case, hundreds, of millions of dollars and access to any contacts they might need, and yet each year every team has guys who can't get to spring training because they don't have their visas in order. Meanwhile, the enigmatic Manny Ramirez seems jovial and upbeat, despite being put on waivers at the end of last year and on the trading block for A-Rod throughout the off-season. He drives us all nuts. He seems oblivious, he sometimes is clearly half-assing it out on the field, and yet there may be no better pure hitter in the game. He said there were no hard feelings about the off-season in a conversation with the media, but apparently from here on out he'll continue his policy of not talking to reporters.

As for the other two potential Sox malcontents: Jason Giambi, who shares an agent, Arm Tellem, with Nomar, was joking about Garciaparra joining him, A-Rod, and Jeter in the Yanks infield next season, when Nomar's contract will expire if the Sox cannot find a way to get a deal done in the next few months (and many of us hope weeks). The idea of Nomar in pinstripes just made me throw up in my mouth (to steal one of espn.com writer Bill Simmons' lines). Meanwhile, Pedro, whom Peter Gammons says looks poised to be dominant again, is also going into a walk year. (Peter Gammons is a first-rate reporter and for many is the face of the game, the conduit between fans and the game, but sometimes he is a caricature of himself and he does tend toward hyperbole for those who give him access; in other words, the most respected baseball journalist on the planet sometimes is a shill) Pedro has indicated that he wants a contract but that he'll be fine if he doesn't get one. Read: he knows Steinbrenner will be there with a checkbook open, ready to send a clear "Fuck You" to Boston. This can not happen. Nonetheless,

Pedro is in camp. He is not ready to throw in games—Bronson Arroyo, a guy many Sox fans, me included, think might be ready to enter the rotation as our regular fifth guy, is going to start the March 7 spring training game against the Yankees in the Empire's only visit to Boston's winter home. This will inevitably get Red Sox Nation into a worried game of speculation: is Pedro OK? This is a refrain that comes up every year. If Pedro struggles in a game: Is he alright? If he touches his shoulder: Is he alright? If he makes a funny face, if he bitches at the media, if he is late to the park, if it rains: Is Pedro alright. It is a tough thing to have the dreams of an entire people resting on one wispy man's right shoulder.

So these are prevailing story lines: The contracts of Nomar, Pedro, and to a lesser degree a handful of others; Pedro's health; weathering the storm of Manny being Manny. Meanwhile, the first exhibition comes on Thursday against the Twins, our Fort Myers neighbor. From that point on, the season opener against the Orioles will loom ever larger.

Sunday, February 29, 2004

I am back in Charlottesville. My friend and colleague (we have both been fellows for the last several months with the Foundation for the Defense of democracy, a Washington, DC-based anti-terrorism think tank, with which we went to Israel last May and June) Gerard Alexander, a UVA Poli-Sci professor, brought me down from his DC home. The weekend was great, very restful, and now I am ready for a week, or at least a few days, here in Charlottesville where I desperately need to get work done.

With each passing hour we get closer to Opening Day, but it will be a while before the Sox start the 2004 season in Camden Yards in April. Right now we are in the midst of the next logical extension of the Hot Stove season inasmuch as things are still mostly about speculation. What will the final roster look like? How hungry will Nomar and Manny and Pedro be? Can the guys who had career years last season—I'm looking at you Bill Mueller and Kevin Millar—pull it off again? Will we stay healthy? Is new manager Terry Francona the guy to keep this group together, to weather the pressure of the Boston fans and media, and to make sure that things on the field are taken care of? And, of course, can we beat the Yankees? It sucks to have to focus so much on a team that we hate so much, but this is the reality of being the perceived lesser in a one-sided rivalry. The fact is that for a record six seasons in a row the top of the AL East has looked the same, with the Yankees in first and the Sox in second. Obviously that eats away at those of us on the Red Sox side, and we want to beat them this time around and beat them solidly.

Curt Schilling had his first serious throwing session yesterday, which is a good way to start off a season in which we hope to reclaim the AL East. He mixed his pitches, he impressed 'Tek (who said Schilling reminded him of Clemens, whom Tek caught at the All Star Game last July), and of course he allowed Sox fans to imagine big things. Here's a guy who stared those Yankees down in the World Series in 2001, who took the Diamondbacks to the Promised Land largely based on the fact that he did not fear and was not impressed by the Yankees and their mystique. He plans to bring that to the Sox this year, and yesterday marks step one of that. The Yankees may have made the last big splash of the off-season, but I maintain that by acquiring Schilling we made the biggest splash, and the one that will have the biggest effect on the division this year.

2

March: In Like a Lion

Monday, March 1, 2004
It's now March. In like a lion? Not where I am. Spring is in the air — it is nearly 70 degrees here in Charlottesville, and naturally sunny skies reign in Florida. Soon spring training games will start up and we'll begin to have some foundation for all of the optimism we've built up over the past few months. Of course spring training has its own rhythm, predictable but no less enjoyable. It is a pretty languid time in Florida and Arizona, unique to major professional sports. Once the season starts up these guys, rich, young, often handsome, are inaccessible to the general public. You see them on television, on ESPN highlights, in magazines and newspapers, or from the remove of the stands, a distance that is far more than the sum of its actual proximity to the players – the field and its green expanses and perfectly manicured topography are a magical, separate world, like Narnia, from the wardrobe that is the stands.

Days play out slowly during spring training. Guys come out, play catch, stretch casually, even interact with fans, often times with the little children they once were and the old men they will someday become, revealing the generational aspect of baseball fandom that gets the poets and essayists swooning. And so if the days play out slowly for players and fans alike, that leaves lots of room for speculation, often about the esoteric. On almost every team, the overwhelming majority of lineup spots are already taken. A young guy or two might impress, and the 23rd, 24th, and 25th spots on the roster might be up for competition. There may be a question of whether or not the manager will go with an extra pitcher or another position player. But on the whole, we know generally what this year's Sox team will look like. Much of what is happening is tinkering. Sure, there are young guys who will claw for a roster spot, but the best of them will go back to the minors and continue to climb the ladder, knowing that getting sent down really is still part of the logical growth process. There also are a few veterans, hanging on to the dream, aware that time is the cruelest opponent and that while early 30s makes one a young man in most professions, a baby in some (such as my world of academia where getting one's PhD before 35 is still a sign of precocity), in professional sports being on the wrong side of 30 begins to put one at a serious disadvantage if he is not a star. It is amusing to think about the idea of "grizzled veterans" in sports – how writers depicted guys like Yaz, Ripken, Fisk, and Nolan Ryan as elderly at the end of their careers, guys who were as close to my age when they retired as I am to a 20-year-old wunderkind.

And so it goes down at the Sox training complex. Most of the spots are filled. But of course there are still questions, and there is the possibility of new acquisitions coming in to camp. The latest is talk that El Duque, Orlando Hernandez, the former Yankee whose tale of his journey from Cuba to the US added to a mystique that briefly made him one of the more formidable pitchers on the Yanks' late-90s staff, might be making a comeback for Boston. Of course the rumor also is that the Yankees will not let that happen. Indeed, among the chattering fans on the Sons of Sam Horn message boards, a website for Sox seamheads, is that Brian Cashman, the Yanks' GM, is keeping an eye on every move Theo Epstein, our 30-year-old General Manager, makes in order to try to counter anything we might do. This is all part of the game within the game, and it gives the lie to any Yankees fan who might assert that there is no real rivalry because of the competitive dissonance between the two teams.

So one of the things we'll be looking for in the next few weeks will be the chess match between the two teams that most experts expect will be fighting it out in the American League East for the next eight months. It started the day the season ended. It will keep going until this one does.

Tuesday, March 2, 2004

Given the rumors and innuendoes, not to mention the fact that baseball was doing very well after last year's playoffs, it was probably inevitable that the issue of steroids would come to a rip-roaring, game-tarnishing, cover-the-whole-thing-with-slime sort of head. I awoke this morning to an ESPN report (I sleep with either television or the stereo on. For some it's a distraction; for me it's soothing.) that Barry Bonds, Gary Sheffield, Jason Giambi and unnamed others had received steroids from the good folks at BALCO, the Bay Area lab that is under serious investigation and with four individuals under indictment for distributing steroids and other performance enhancing drugs.

Now I am not going to kid you. It doesn't exactly break my heart to know that two of the guys caught up in this shitstorm are Yankees. But this is a case where it may well be best for Sox fans to keep our schadenfreude to ourselves. It is hard to believe that, if this thing goes as far as the tentacles look as if they may reach, there won't be any Sox implicated in all of this. While I love Nomar, as long as that insanely ripped image of him from *Sports Illustrated* a couple of years back dances through the transom of our consciousness, it may be best for us all to just keep mum.

This is one issue where the Players Association is 100% in the wrong. I'm about as much of a civil libertarian as it gets. But if these guys give a damn about the game, if they love it even a whisker as much as most of those of us who pay our way into these secular shrines love it, they will go back to Gene Orza of the Players Association and tell him in no uncertain terms: We'll take tests. We'll rewrite that part of the Collective Bargaining Agreement, perhaps with some consideration from the owners, (How about getting rid of non-performance enhancing drugs that have no impact whatsoever on the integrity of the game? I'd trade pot for steroids every day of the week; under the circumstances, so would most fans. Let law enforcement deal with some rookie doing the Chronic during the All Star break.) and make it clear to fans that we are serious about this potential scourge.

And what about records? There is not, in all honesty, much that we can do about that aspect of things. There is no way to place *ex post facto* impositions on players, we can never know who was doing what when, and in any case, there is also no chance that the players' union will even allow that idea on the table. Basically, we have to forget about the damage that has been done. We need instead to deal with the future – we must prevent sins against the game that have not yet happened in exchange for forgiving those that have. It is imperfect. It will not appease those who yearn for blood, who believe in presumptive guilt before proved innocence.

The kid in me does not want to believe the game to be tainted by steroid use and abuse (Say it ain't so, Barry!). But while my love for the game stems from childhood, my understanding of it, and of human nature, makes me fear that the cynics (realists?) are right. And the worst thing is, until we know which guys are cheating, too many will assume that they all are. The good guys will be lumped in with the bad guys. This is unfair. And by continuing this highly legalistic game of obfuscation and excuse-making, the players are only hoisting themselves on their own hypodermic needles. Say it ain't so, indeed.

Wednesday, March 3, 2004

Thus far you would not think that steroid rumors had even hit the Sox camp. Or at least you'd think this was a group immune to the tawdry goings on elsewhere (such as in Tampa, the Yankee Steroid Center, er, training camp site). Sure, Johnny Damon answered a few questions in an interview the other day, but on the whole, the Sox are refreshingly focused on baseball. I like that.

One of the glories of baseball is the rhythm of the season. Everything from here on builds up to Opening Day, a secular holiday that once evoked images of kids skipping school to try to sneak a peek through a hole in an outfield fence. The first few days are all about the thrill of the new season. But then things settle into a pattern. The games all make ESPN highlights. Baseball Tonight provides a safe haven for those of us for whom the obsession does not manifest only seasonally. But for much of the US the game is background noise until midsummer. This year, however, things are already different. Fox, which normally does not even begin broadcasting games until May or so, and which has not shown a midweek game since Mark McGuire hit his 62nd in 1998, is going to show the Sox-Yanks game in Fenway on April 16th, my birthday. On the day I turn 33, the first of sixteen regular season games kicks off in that Lyric Bandbox of a Ballyard, as Updike so memorably put it upon Ted Williams' final game. Suffice it to say, Fox is doing their share to ratchet up the tensions early in the season. The cliché is that baseball is a marathon and not a sprint, but it looks as if the Sox, Yankees, and those with an interest in the season have put the two teams on the line with spikes and blocks and speedsuits. I wonder if anyone is telling the Blue Jays and Orioles that they are not invited. Oh, and the Devil Rays.

In any case, the gang is moving forward toward Opening Day. The Players Association still does not get it when it comes to steroids. And Fox is already going full bore on the hype machine. I think the A-Rod trade is overrated in terms of its value to the Yankees but there is no doubting that it got the attention of the rest of the world. I, for one, cannot wait.

Thursday, March 4, 2004

Today was one of trains, planes and automobiles for me as I made my way from Charlottesville to Washington to Greenville and up to Asheville. I am giving a paper at the South Carolina Historical Association's meeting in Greenville at, of all places, Bob Jones University. I have some interesting things to say about Bob Jones in my paper on civil rights and the Freedom Rides in South Carolina. It should be interesting. In the meantime, I am staying at Matt and Heather's house in Asheville, a place that provides for me many cherished memories.

Matt Dickens is my best friend in the world, my brother, a guy I'd take the proverbial bullet for. We are friends from high school, but in all honesty we were buddies then. In fact we had a bit of an ambivalent relationship up until after we graduated from college and we were stuck in our little hometown feeling as if the world had fallen apart on us. What we call our winter of discontent shaped us both in profound ways, not the least of which being that we established what became a vitally important friendship that has carried us for more than a decade now.

Matt is not a big baseball fan. (I know, I know, there is something kind of eeee-ewww . . .) he is not even a huge sports fan. But he and I have been through an enormous amount together, and even a hard hearted bastard like me can forgive him certain transgressions as a consequence. Plus, I know Matt would be enormously happy for me if the Red Sox were to win the World Series, and that counts for something, right? In any case, as a consequence of my being on the road all day and of Matt not having even basic cable (I indulge my friends as Vito Corleone indulged his children, what can I say?) I have no clue what is going on in baseball or with the Sox. This sort of purging is sometimes good, I suppose. Cleansing, even. (The void is unsettling and bothersome, actually, but I'll rationalize it.)

Saturday, March 6, 2004

Missed my first day of this diary yesterday. Basically, I spent the day with Matt. Went to the Biltmore estate (Matt and Heather received season passes as a gift; I went as Heather) and wandered the grounds (extensive), explored the house (ostentatious), and went to a wine tasting (mediocre, overpriced wine—but the tasting was free). We drank a ton of wine last night and had a nice, big dinner. It was great seeing them. Plus it looks like I might buy their car, a 1995 Volkswagen Passat station wagon. I need a car, they have one, and I can afford it. Everybody gains, and friends can help one another—I can help them get rid of the car and they can help me get one.

I also was offered the Texas job yesterday. They lowballed me on the offer, but it is all negotiable, and I feel as if we can bridge any gaps between us. I'd say the odds are pretty good that I'll be stalking the halls of the University of Texas of the Permian Basin next year. So as I've said, I'd better get ready for satellite television. Maybe I'll go with TiVo too.

Meanwhile, they have reached the next phase of spring training—exhibition games. Yesterday the split-squad Sox had two games against college programs. They beat Boston College and Northeastern handily. Schill made his debut, just threw fastballs for control, gave up two hits but generally got it done. Waker made his debut against BC. He had some minor problems, but he felt good about getting out there. Spring training is a time when it is too easy to read too much into too many things. They key is for guys to hit particular benchmarks, for pitchers to build up to the ability to go 6-7 innings, and for everyone to start to gel and to get timing down.

There are some good signs, however. One huge one is that Pedro seems to have that attitude, that swagger, which makes him nearly indomitable. He put some weight on, claims to feel great, and in what could be a walk year, he has a sense that he needs to prove himself. Pedro on a mission is good for the Red Sox. He's telling anyone who will listen that he is ready for a big year. I know we all think that he is always a pitch away from blowing that shoulder of his out for good, but at a certain point I think we have to trust him. I also would feel really good if I heard rumors that the Sox were sitting down with his agents. Now is not the time for the Sox to make like the Bruins and alienate players by constantly lowballing them in negotiations. In any case, it seems clear that we have loaded up knowing we can compete this year. I don't buy *Boston Globe* columnist Dan Shaughnessy's argument that the Sox have put all their chips in for this season, but this certainly will be the last shot with the lineup as it is currently configured. Some of these guys won't be back. I just hope Pedro won't be one of them.

Today the Sox played their spring training neighbors, the Twins, against whom they will spar all preseason. The Sox lost 6-2 but in spring training it's the sum of parts of the game and not the result that ultimately matters. Yes, they lost, but Byung-Hyun Kim, erstwhile closer who really succumbed to pressure at the tail end of last season, made his debut as a starter, a role he hopes to take over as our #5 guy this season. He looked good, had a couple of really nasty pitches, and provided hope for us having the best rotation one through five in at least the American League and maybe in all of baseball. Kim's situation is one of the many questions we hope to have answered in the next few weeks. Hopefully we'll like the answers we get.

Sunday, March 7, 2004

Yes, it is going to be insane this year. The media. The fans. The players. The owners. The coaches. All are going to fuel this idea of an eight month war, March through October, between the Red Sox and the Yankees. Last night I watched the Duke-Carolina game, and I acknowledge it as perhaps the best rivalry in college sports, certainly in college hoops. But how's this for perspective: Today, on March 7, the Red Sox and Yankees met for an utterly meaningless spring training game. The Yankees won 11-5 and as is typical of these games, every player of consequence was gone before the sixth inning. The Yankees' closer nonpareil, Mariano Rivera, got his inning in the third – not only was he the winning pitcher, this was also the first spring training road trip he has taken since he became a star. Nomar didn't play (some sort of minor Achilles injury, we are told). Jeter and A-Rod were both out by the fourth inning or so. And yet despite this, not only was the game a sellout; not only was it televised in New England and New York and on DirecTV. This utterly superfluous little exhibition game had fans scalping tickets for up to $500 apiece. There was bidding on EBay. People lined up all morning for a small allotment of standing-room-only tickets. I am not going to hear anyone tell me that this is not the biggest rivalry in sports. Not after this foolishness.

Now don't get me wrong. On the whole I LIKE this foolishness. This foolishness is going to make this an epic pennant race (unless, God forbid, these two teams pull a Dan and Dave a la the two great decathletes Dan O'Brien and Dave Johnson in 1992 who were the focus of a great Reebok ad campaign that proved for naught when O'Brien didn't even qualify for the US team). But this foolishness also is largely a creation of a media that increasingly seems to lack perspective that cannot differentiate between the meaningful and the overhyped and that is unwilling to do real journalistic work when there is voyeurism to be had. The Red Sox and Yankees presents an enormity that might even transcend sport, but this was a preseason game, and while this level of hype may pay off down the road, but it simply seemed obtrusive today.

But for full disclosure: Even as I prepared to make a counteroffer tomorrow to UTPB, I received a call today from Salem State College, located in Salem (of Witch Trial fame, of course) in the Boston suburbs. This is a dream location for several reasons, but you know which one came into my mind first? As God is my witness, the first thought I had was that I'd be near the Red Sox. I'd be able to get the *Globe* every morning, would get my coverage from NESN and Fox Sports New England, and Channel 38, would have WEEI on whenever I could stand the get-a-lifers, and I would be there in the middle of the maelstrom. Salem State College isn't Harvard, I'd likely have to teach more than at UTPB, I'd likely get paid less, maybe much less, and indeed from a purely professional vantage point it would not be the greatest decision one could make. Hell,

I'd likely have to break a contract with UTPB. And yet in my heart, I know that it would be totally worth it, and the Red Sox are a much bigger reason for that than I would normally want to admit to anyone. Clearly, I am insane. But if this be madness, count me in. (PS—Today's game means nothing. Zilch. Nada. Anyone who knows anything about baseball knows this. So why do I still secretly wish the Sox had won?)

Monday, March 8, 2004

Here is a somewhat disquieting incident from yesterday's Sox-Yanks showdown in Fort Myers: While the Yanks took batting practice, all of the Sox went in the dugout or on other fields or generally ignored their opponents. Not Nomar. Whether to be petulant or to send a message or out of a sense of goodwill, Nomar went and talked to and hugged A-Rod and Jeter and even Joe Torre. When asked about it later, and whether this was part of some recruiting trip, Nomar was coy. The gist of his responses: Anything can happen, even shocking things, such as the possibility of my being traded this winter. In a Tom Boswell piece in the *Washington Post* this morning about the absurdity of yesterday's overkill, this nugget on Nomar's possible apostasy was by far the most worrisome. Overkill can still feed the larger spectacle, after all. Disgruntled superstars courting the archenemy is another thing entirely.

This is not good. Of course Nomar knows that this is just the sort of thing that will get everyone's goat. And there are those who will complain about loyalty. But loyalty is a two way street. Do I like the idea of Nomar fraternizing with those bastards? No. But how is that worse than publicly hanging him out to dry over the winter? (Nomar learned of the rumors not from Theo or one of the owners, but rather from television) How is it worse than sending him into a contract year without a good faith effort to establish at least parameters for discussion? My hope is that this lights a fire under Lucchino and Henry, and, assuming he has the authority, Theo. My hope is that this seeming apostasy leads not to recriminations but to negotiations. But if this stands alone and if the contract impasse is not settled, I think it will be a harbinger of grim tidings. I don't imagine the locker room will suffer too much. Then again, I would like to think that there are at least some guys who will be rather displeased with Nomar's apparent public courtship of the Good Ship Steinbrenner.

Would he, could he, really go to New York and play second, or perhaps have a lineup shift that gets Jeter out of short? I don't know. But the idea of Nomar and Pedro both hinting that they'll end up just fine and that the Bronx might provide an awfully soft landing is one that should be enough to keep Sox fans up at night all summer. Loyalty runs both ways. I know this may be a romantic notion in a mercenary era, but I'd like to see more of it all the way around.

Tuesday, March 9, 2004

Apparently someone did a statistical analysis, and Theo said it publicly, of this year's Sox team's potential and discerned that they would score 925-950 runs and they would give up 625-650 runs. One might wonder whether the Sox will score more than 925—it seems highly possible, though you have to assume that several guys will not have the career years they did last year. Meanwhile it is even less likely that they will give up that few runs—if all goes well they may have one of the great staffs of the last decade but given that no staff in baseball since the strike season has given up that few runs, this seems an optimistic prediction. In any case, based on some stathead's mathematical formula (The statistician is the inimitable Bill James, who now is on the Sox payroll, and the stat is what is knows as his "Pythagorean theorem" for those of you not in the know), a runs scored to given up ratio like that one is predicted to yield some 107-112 wins. It all seems dubious, but wonderfully dubious.

Today's Sox pitching matchup is not the sort of situation that is going to relieve irrational exuberance about what is to come this year—Pedro is scheduled to make his debut, followed by Schilling. This 1-2 has fueled much of this winter's dreams, dreams that have been remarkably glorious in light of the way last season ended. Granted, last year's Sox team was one of the most likeable ever—lots of gritty guys ("dirt dogs") provided leadership of a tight group of overachievers. No longer the Sox of 25 guys, 25 cabs, the 2004 Sox played through adversity, loved playing with one another, said to hell with talk of curses, and never stopped fighting. The nucleus of that team is back, with the addition of Schilling and Foulke, the closer we needed for far too much of last year.

Although we will have the 1-2 punch of Pedro and Schilling this year, the actual rotation once the season gets going will be Pedro-Waker-Schilling-Lowe-Kim/Arroyo. I like this idea—having Waker in between Pedro and Schilling will provide a serious contrast in almost every series, and especially in those where our 1-2-3 guys go from the first game. But even when they don't, teams will often get Kim or Arroyo, then Pedro, then Waker, or perhaps Waker then Schilling then Lowe. The season won't start out this way—they won't set the rotation until after the early season off days are set—but eventually, this is apparently the route they hope to take. I also feel rather good about there being competition for the 5th spot between two pretty good pitchers. Arroyo was International League Pitcher of the Year in 2003 and Kim has always had good stuff and has preferred to start. This rotation, coupled with strong relief, from guys like Timlin, Embree, Williamson, and whoever doesn't make it as the number 5 starter, to Foulke at the end should put us in the best position entering the season of any Red Sox team I've seen. That, coupled with the return of the gist of the lineup from last year does inspire confidence. If that translates to 950 runs scored and 625 given up, then yes, 110 wins is plausible, and 110 wins would mean good things.

Wednesday, March 10, 2004

It's now truly March Madness. Conference tournaments in NCAA basketball have been underway for a week or so now, but today the major conferences got underway, with the Big East and Conference USA first round games starting this afternoon.

I do not have any built in NCAA loyalties. I am from a region of the country that does not embrace college sports as much as the pros, although I have always been a big college football and basketball fan. I went to a Division III college, and while I am an enormous Williams College fan, that is not enough to get me through March Madness. I went to UNC-Charlotte for my MA, and I am definitely a Charlotte fan. Ohio University, my PhD school, also plays DI basketball, though in the mid-major Mid America Conference, and while I follow them and want them to do well, they do not really hold a place amidst my sports passions. I always rooted for BC growing up—BC has that Boston connection, and they got the most press in the *Globe* and were the only major football program in the area, so I have always supported them in football and basketball. (I do root for UNH in hockey—gotta have some Granite State loyalties, right?). In any case, today Charlotte shellacked Tulane, 78-48 to move into what should be a good matchup with Alabama-Birmingham tomorrow. I'd like to see them get the respect they have earned over the years (there is a reason they call the CUSA tournament the Bobby Lutz Invitational—Lutz, Charlotte's porn-star-moustache-wearing coach always has them ready to play in the tournament, and this year should be no exception; Charlotte has been at least as far as the CUSA semis six of the last seven years. I would like to think that they'll go as a sixth, or better, a fifth seed into the NCAAs. Meanwhile, BC beat Georgetown today rather easily, except they let the Hoyas back into the game. Nonetheless, the Eagles also appear poised to make a big run. Hopefully both of these teams—my adopted Eagles and my alma mater Niners—go far this March.

March Madness is good for Red Sox fans. Sure, we still check out the articles on the Sox first and foremost, and Pedro and Nomar will always matter more to us than Diaper Dandies and Upset Specials and teams on the bubble. But in a sense those of us who are not just Sox fans but also sports fans, which is the overwhelming majority of us, use March as a chance to step back, to defuse the excitement and anticipation of the upcoming season, and to enjoy maybe the best sporting event in America. By the time April rolls around, March Madness has almost provided a respite from what quickly becomes a pressure cooker, especially in years where we are expected to do well. This year certainly fits that category.

Meanwhile, Pedro and Schilling were fine yesterday. Each gave up a run, but both were working on things—Schill is still primarily spotting the fastball, which is getting up around 95, and Pedro was fine for his first appearance in front of another team's hitters this spring. The Sox lost 3-2 to the Reds, but of course that does not matter even a little bit. The key is for these guys to get their innings. They got 5 2/3 between the two of them yesterday, and for Sox fans, it was a nice little bit of March Madness all its own.

Thursday, March 11, 2004

Spring is much like the regular season in very few aspects, but there is one that is germane: It is unwise to get too high or low. Obviously, no fan is going to get into an emotional investment during the exhibition season as they would once they are playing in the big league parks, but there is a tendency to over-scrutinize especially good or bad performances.

A good case of this could be today's performance by Arroyo. As I said the other day, he is supposed to be pushing Kim for the fifth spot. Against the Yankees the other day he had the sort of performance that fuels March dreams of October glory. He shut the Yankees down and made many of us think that we had a new ace in a fifth spot body. Suffice it to say that if he does become a solid guy who helps make us an elite staff, it is going to take time. Today he got shelled. He gave up six hits in two-plus innings. Now you never know—this early guys are often working top spot pitches or are focusing on one pitch. Sometimes they have control issues because they let it fly for the first time in months. Whatever it is, it is clear that there is still time but that we should not begin making plans to send Pedro into free agency because we have the guy to replace him.

Meanwhile after a nice big win yesterday, Charlotte lost to UAB today, and so they are probably looking at a 7-9 seed. BC, however, came from behind to win a game they never led in until the end. That should assure them of a comparable seed as UNCC. I'd love to see one of them make a run in the next few weeks. I'll be in DC for the first weekend and in Boston for the second, so I'll get to go to good places to watch the games. And of course in Boston, I'll get a chance to look at the Sox, a luxury I do not get down here in Charlottesville.

Friday, March 12, 2004

I didn't mention it yesterday, possibly because the steroid question is one that will be in the news constantly and so I will be able to write about it at any given point this season and the purist in me wants to focus on the game on the field when it is possible, but there was a piece in the *Washington Post* sports section that was astounding in its revelation of just how out of touch these players are. The union is sending around a representative to talk to players about where things stand *vis a vis* the steroid issue and the Collective Bargaining Agreement. The players just don't get it. The rep came out of the meeting with the Orioles and he, along with BJ Surhoff, an Oriole who in the past has been a player rep and who has always been active in the union, is by all accounts a bright guy, and ordinarily not inclined to say numbskull things, kept harping on how it would be a dangerous step to reopen the CBA, how the players are united, and on and on. Apparently the Union guy had been to about half of the teams, and the response has been the same.

When are these guys going to realize that this is not an owner-versus-players issue? Yes, there are CBA issues involved, but for all intents and purposes, these are ancillary. This is not about the contract between the players and owners. It is about the compact between the fans and the players, the fans and the teams, the fans and the game. In other words, there is an interested third party that never got to the table and now we are ready to wield our clout, which really could be the fulcrum upon which all of this turns if we start to turn away.

A Senate subcommittee had these guys on the matt the other day. It was perfectly orchestrated. The Senators at the table were a formidable group, with John McCain and Joe Biden in the forefront. (New Hampshire's John Sununu Jr. was there too. I don't count him among the ranks of the formidable.) They had NFL Commissioner Paul Tagliabue and NFLPA head Gene Upshaw marching in lockstep, proud of how the players and owners had come to a resolution long ago to develop the toughest anti-doping program in all of American professional sports. They had an international doping official who said that baseball's system fails every single standard international bodies take for granted to keep performance enhancing drugs out of sport on the global stage. They had Bud Selig, who for once was before Congress and on the side of the angels. And then there was Donald Fehr representing the MLBPA. Fehr has a good relationship with McCain based on their work on the USOC. But McCain and the others really had Fehr on the ropes. McCain made it clear that he does not want to, but he said if he must, he will make Congress passes legislation to deal with this if baseball won't.

One issue no one has raised is that for years and years teams have been holding cities and regions and states hostage. "If you don't build us a state of the art stadium, we'll move to Charlotte..." and so far fans and politicians have felt helpless. Who wants to lose their sports teams? But guess what? Maybe that provides us with leverage now. Boys, you play in a stadium that we paid for. Things are going to change, and we now have the upper hand to deal with it. I am not certain how best to muse that leverage, but I do know that it cannot be insubstantial.

Meanwhile, on the Red Sox watch, apparently the agents for most of our major free agents have been meeting, however tentatively, with the front office brass. The negotiation with the most potential for acrimony (until and unless Pedro gets pissed and begins to feel scorned) is the situation with Nomar and Arm Tellum, his agent. This one has the SonsofSamHorn chatboards buzzing, and while there are some who see Nomar's side, there is a slow and creeping anti-Nomar sentiment beginning to control the tone and tenor of the discussion. Nomar is beginning to come across as bitchy. I think that he has something of a case to feel some resentment, though he has to realize that through no fault of his own, the market has shifted, and this is a phenomenon that has occurred independent of the A-Rod dalliances. In any case, where in his mind he was justified at this point last year to turn down a four-year $60 million offer, things have changed. That offer might not come again, not only from us but from anyone. I think too many people are prematurely forecasting Nomar's decline, and I do think he can have a monster year, but I hope he realizes how the situation is simply different from the heady irrationality of the days when A-Rod and Manny were redefining superstar contracts. That brief era turned out to be like the tech bubble—borne more of irrational exuberance than long-term market reality. I'd hate to see Nomar become a pariah in red Sox Nation, which can be vicious toward its perceived apostates. He is still one of my all time favorites, and I think he has many good, indeed great, years left in him.

On the field, things are progressing. The bats are weirdly silent. For a team that led the majors in just about every offensive category imaginable last year, the hitting has been anemic. This is not especially alarming, as it is early, pitchers are ahead of the hitters, and we have a pretty small sample from which to draw any conclusions. They won't be as potent a lineup from top to bottom as they were last year, but hopefully they will do something that most Sox teams don't always do—score runs well. What I mean by that is that I hope they will score runs in situations where they will matter. I'd rather win 110 games averaging 5 a game than win 90 scoring 6 a game. Too often in the past Sox offensive juggernauts have left the crowds happy in the short run and unhappy when the end result was an entertaining 10-8 loss, or a four game series with two 10-3 wins and two 3-2 losses. In that case the average score may have been 6-3, but there are no credits that teams get to store for future considerations.

BC is up on Pitt 24-21 with just over three minutes to go in the first half of the Big East semis. Have I said that I love March?

Saturday, March 13, 2004

BC lost to Pitt. But they are in the tournament.

Ben Affleck is on my mind. Yes, Ben Affleck of overexposed Bennifer/J-Lo-are–they-or-aren't-they fame. Ben Affleck of the lantern jaw and boxy coiff and piercing eyes and all-around box office verve. Ben is from Boston and is a diehard Boston sports fan. In particular he is a diehard Sox fan. Now normally, this would be of no particular moment—after all, Sox fans are ubiquitous, and so we would expect an overrepresentation of them among the Hollywood set. But Ben is from Boston, and so on the surface he seems like the real deal.

The problem is, he drives most of us who are real Sox fans really fucking nuts. Somehow, someway, the media anointed him the spokeman for all Sox fans. And this off season in particular it seemed as if he was everywhere, and when he wasn't on screen with the J-Lo nuisance, he was blabbering on in a rather unbecoming way for a matinee idol. And so many of us, who already held secret resentment about the fact that he won some sort of gene-cum-looks lottery, were inclined to want to slag him for all of our own shortcomings if not his.

Here is the dirty little secret that I hold: I kind of like Ben Affleck. As I write this he is both hosting SNL and he is on Bravo's repeat showing of *Good Will Hunting*. I also liked him in *Chasing Amy*, and not just for the faux lesbianism. Oh, sure, he has sucked more than stunned in the last few years (unless he was stunning for his suckiness), and the rising of his star seems to be in direct opposition to the quality of what he has done, and so naturally the backlash has been swift, and it has been ugly. And in addition to all of this, he has been put forth as the final arbiter of all things Sox, with his righteous indignation and clichéd emotionalism, when most of us suspect that we all know that we are better fans than him. We know more. We die harder. We feel and breathe and live the history. And even if that is wrong, we still just wish he would shut the fuck up.

By the way, Ben is looking a little bloated on SNL, like a cross between the tubby Baldwin brother and Matthew Perry in one of his heroin binge-and-purge phases. So please, Ben, read your scripts more closely. Date someone with an understated beauty that pisses us all off because of our all consuming jealousy but that does not force us to hear about you in every possible pop culture reference possible. Take more risks even if it causes you not always to be box office draw numero uno (hey, it worked for Charlize in *Monster*. Mmmmmm, Charlize Theron). And please, please, please, if I tell you that we believe that you are a Sox fan, will you follow my advice and just shut the fuck up before you make us look like an even bigger bunch of whiners than the world believes us to be?

Thanks. And I did like you in both *Good Will* and *Chasing Amy*, even if your character really screwed up with Amy. (By the way, the melancholy guy in me gives bonus points to *Good Will Hunting* for two things: 1)the recurrence of Eliot Smith throughout the soundtrack; and 2) Ben's speech about how "If in 20 years you're still living here . . . coming over to watch the Patriots games . . . I'll kill you ... you don't owe it to yourself. You owe it to me . . . you're sitting on a winning lottery ticket . . . I'd give almost anything to have what you've got . . . every day I come by your house and pick you up . . . maybe I'll get up there and you won't be there . . . I don't know much, but I know that." I'll give Ben a lot of leeway for writing and delivering that series of lines.

Sunday, March 14, 2004

Pedro was tonight's ESPN Sunday Conversation, coincident with his stint today on the mound, another successful one for him as he tries to get himself ready to be able to go five or six innings within the next few weeks. One highlight showed him slipping a nasty fastball with lots of movement on it in on the wrists of a hapless Jack Cust of the Orioles. Pedro the interviewee was combative. He said lots of things we had heard before this offseason—indeed, this interview was taped several weeks ago, and ESPN had already run most of the highlights as teasers. His response to the events of Game Three of the ALCS last year was simple—he did not want to hurt Zimmer, but as to Karim Garcia his point was simple: Who the hell is Karim Garcia to challenge me? Seems fair to me. He also sang the praises of the pitching staff, lauding Waker, D-Lowe, and of course Schilling. Hearing that really makes me want the season to start.

Things are progressing well down in Florida. The talks between Nomar's people and the Sox seem to be heating up, which would alleviate a big potential burden for the team. There may be virtue to a motivated Nomar in a contract year, though he is a consummate professional and securing this contract should only make things secure. A happy Nomar is a productive Nomar in my line of thought. Meanwhile it looks like Arroyo will be taking the fifth spot by default, at least for the short term, as Kim is on the shelf for a bit. Hopefully Kim's shoulder is nothing too problematic, but if his taking time to be healthy gives some order to the rotation, that might be a blessing. Wakefield is pitching well, and Foulke made his first appearance of the spring, albeit in the fourth, and was fine. In sum, all's progressing nicely. No major news, so gossip, no malcontents.

The brackets for the NCAA tournament are set. The #1 seeds are Stanford, Duke (despite its loss today in a great ACC final against Maryland), Kentucky, and St. Joe's which slipped in despite its loss. Charlotte got a decent draw—they got jobbed with a 9th seed—this has happened several times now—and they will face Texas Tech, which gives me a good reason to root against Coach Knight, about whom I am pretty ambivalent normally. If they win that game, they get St. Joe's, easily the most vulnerable of the #1 seeds, and the whole east Regional is actually a pretty good one to get. (They are calling the regionals by the city name now, so actually the east Regional is the "East Rutherford Regional" because the other way apparently made too much sense.) BC is the 6 seed in the Midwest (I mean "St. Louis") and they will face Utah. Kentucky is the 1 seed in the Gateway City.

Monday, March 15, 2004

I am really sick of dealing with money and sports. When I was a little kid, during the time that I grew to love the game and to love the Sox and to do so unconditionally, we never thought about salaries. Sure, I remember when Dave Winfield signed what seemed like an impossible contract for millions upon millions in a "lifetime contract." Within a couple of years, Steinbrenner would call Winfield "Mr. May" for his inability to replicate the magic of Reggie Jackson and other past evil Yankee heroes. But on the whole I rarely considered money issues—they did not matter. Sure, those were the waning days of the reserve clause and the early days of free agency, but even then for me it was a matter of losing or getting players. With a child's innocence I did not care that we had lost Freddy Lynn or Carlton Fisk because of baseball economics or as the result of hardball contract negotiations—or in the case of Fisk because of management's inability to know what the deadlines for tendering a contract were—I just cared that we had lost them.

Those were still relatively innocent times. When I'd get the Sox yearbook early in the season, I would pore over every detail, including players' off season occupations. It is almost quaint to note that Yaz worked at a fish cannery in the off season—now granted, he actually owned it as part of an investment strategy, but still—if kids even buy team yearbooks any more (if teams even produce them)—I doubt highly that some little Reds fan will discover that Ken Griffey works in a bakery or Adam Dunn works in construction. Most of the older guys – especially before the 1970s—needed to supplement their income. Yes, they made more, in many cases much more, than the average American worker, but they had short careers too, and most of them knew that once baseball was done they either needed an investment plan or some sort of skill set to fall back on.

There is something noble in that concept. I was reminded of this when I first lived in South Africa and I'd read about the off season endeavors of many of the Springboks, the players for South Africa's national rugby team. At that point they were still making the transition to professional rugby, and so many of the guys did have fallback careers. They played rugby for several hours a day, but they still had to run their farms (lots of Afrikaner farmers at the national level) or their construction company or work in a local garage or keep up appearances at the investment bank. That era too is passing, but it marks a period when sports, while important, were in their place, like they were when we were in high school and only after a full day of school did you go to the locker room and change for practice.

Things have changed. Maybe it is largely because of the off season pissing matches between the Red Sox and Yankees, an arms race that most other teams could not even dream to enter. Or maybe it is because of the fact that the Sox have so many question marks in their future with so many free agents. But at a certain point, the mind boggles. Nomar wants $15 million-plus. The Sox counter of $13 million comes across as an insult. The Pats are dealing with the same thing with all-world corner Ty Law. I wish that tomorrow one of the Sox free agents would say "you know what? I am making a ton of money to play a game that I love. I want to win and I know how special winning here would be. Just be fair. I am not going to talk about respect or insults or anything else. You are offering 4 years $12 million, I have asked for 4 years, $15 million, there has got to be a way to get this done." I know that is not going to happen, but I wish that it were as easy to be a fan as it was back when I was a kid and March was simply an interminable waiting period, a purgatory before I got to see my heroes. Now it is an interminable wait while players bitch, agents play their game through the media, and reporters need to have financial acumen as well as game insight. I want to watch games, plain and simple.

Tuesday, March 16, 2004

This probably won't be the last time I do this before the season starts, but let's take a look at the Sox lineup. Here is how things look now:
C – Varitek
1B – Ortiz/Millar/Daubach (I put Daubach up for sentimental reasons, but obviously he is running more to be a utility guy.)
2B – Reese/Bellhorn
SS – Nomar
3B – Mueller
LF – Manny
CF – Damon/(Burks)

RF – Nixon
DH – Burks/Ortiz/Millar

Of course we have Kaplar looking for a spot as a reserve who gets time. Right now that leaves us with 12 roster spots, plus Mirabelli's backup catcher spot. They are going with fourteen position players, so a lot of guys are working for one place, it seems. Obviously injuries could change this. OK. So far so good.

Possible batting order:
1. Damon (Some folks on the Sons of Sam Horn boards are talking about Nixon here. I don't disagree. But it is not going to happen. Not to start the season, anyway.)
2. Nixon
3. Nomar
4. Manny (obviously the 3-4-5 spots might vary over the course of the season, but if everyone is healthy and happy and productive, this is the ideal in my mind)
5. Ortiz
6. Mueller (This will all shift according to who is DHing, playing first, etc.)
7. Millar
8. Varitek
9. Reese (Depending on his OBP, he may be higher, maybe even a number 2).

Pitching:
1. Pedro
2. Wakefield
3. Schilling
4. Lowe
5. Arroyo/Kim
Relievers:
Williamson, Embree, Timlin, Mendoza (Big wild card—I'm probably being hopeful, both that he'll produce for us and that for once the former Yankee will come back to haunt them) Foulke, and either Arroyo or Kim—that's ten guys. We are going to keep eleven, presumably, and so that leaves one slot. We might want a

complementary lefty to go alongside Embree. Mendoza may not be healthy enough, Kim too, so there is room here for guys to make the staff, but on the whole, this is a pretty good group, certainly the best starting rotation and bullpen I can ever remember the Sox having.

These are the players, by and large, who will get us through the All Star break. Can the offense produce on par with what it did last year? Can Mueller, Ortiz, Nixon, Tek, and Ortiz have the same sorts of seasons they did in 2003? Will Manny and Nomar be as productive as they have been, hopefully more so? And what about the pitching? It seems like the real deal, indeed maybe even better than we might expect (Derek Lowe as the #4 guy—even if that is just a strategic decision to maximize the contrast between Waker and our fireballers—who wouldn't want that?) but of course health and expectations and all sorts of other things can get in the way.

I like this lineup and staff. Most Sox fans do too. We are halfway through March, which means that in less than three weeks we'll have Opening Day. Thankfully we have March Madness to fill the gap more than adequately.

Wednesday, March 17, 2004

St. Patrick's Day—this means only one thing in Red Sox Nation—a spring training game where the Sox wear hideously ugly green jerseys and hats. But the players have to wear them. What I have never quite gotten are the guys you see in Fenway in the middle of July wearing one of those wretched hats that they either got down in Florida, or worse, that they picked up for a five dollar discounted rate at the souvenir shops. Please tell me they got them on sale—no one would pay full price, right? Even in heavily Irish-American Boston?

Of course that means they also had a game today. The Sox won, 5-2, and most important, Schilling went 6 innings, gave up an innocuous run, was sharp, and said after the performance that he was ready to go a full game if the season started today. That is what I want to hear. Nomar also played after a week or so of being on the shelf for a bruise of the Achilles area—he took a ball off the foot, but was in the lineup today. He went 0 for 2 but he had a couple of walks and the main key is that he get some at bats and get his timing down before April rolls around. If he's healthy, Nomar is not a point of concern for most of us. At least on the field. The ongoing contract question is another thing.

Of course now Curt is on tv, articulate as ever, railing on about how the players just simply do not trust the owners. Johnny Damon is asserting that owners actually want steroids in the game because of how it draws fans, and that this is now just a great way to split the players' union. I don't know. The owners are morons, and while they are most concerned about fannies in the seats, I think they all realize that now they need to eradicate steroids. There may be grandstanding on this issue, but that many are finding steroids and the scrutiny this issue brings to the game problematic is not generally an example of that. This sort of player talk is not good for the game, and the players need to know that they are swimming against a strong tide that is not going to calm anytime soon until changes happen.

Meanwhile the government has banned androstenedione, the steroid-like supplement that Mark McGuire was taking in 1998. There are those, including Jeremy Schaap on *Inside the Lines*, who have suggested that McGuire's records carry an asterisk. This is idiocy. For one thing, when he was using andro, it was not illegal! How can you possibly punish a guy for using something not only not illegal, but not on any banned substance lists? Have any of these hyperventilating critics ever heard of *post facto* laws and prohibitions against establishing them? Sure, the Constitution does not directly prevail in major League Baseball, but the constitutional principle—that you don't make up rules and punish people for violating them when those laws did not exist when the behavior in question occurred—still should.

Oh—and Ortiz hit a bomb today, his fifth of the preseason. It may not prove to mean a whole lot, but I still see this as a sign that Ortiz came into his own last year and that his performance was not some sort of outlier. I know there are those who will talk about permanent steroid taint, but there is still something awesome about a guy just crushing a ball. Indeed, it is the inherently special status of the home run that mandates that we restore its purity.

Thursday March 18, 2004

Not a very productive day, I am afraid. Day one of the tournament, so I stayed in and watched the early games (Charlotte fell behind Texas Tech early and never could overcome the deficit) then went to the office. I had to leave at 5 to have dinner with Lon Hamby, my PhD advisor who is in town to give a talk at the Miller Center for Public Policy tomorrow. Lon is a big Cardinals fan. I can live with someone being a big Cardinals fan. There is a hierarchy of baseball towns. Some are just better than others. Atlanta is filled with frontrunners in every sport, and they cannot even sell out playoff games. Ten years of Braves successes have not grown a serious and ardent fan base so much as developed a sense of entitlement. Teams like the Devil Rays and Marlins have not developed a fan identity, perhaps largely because of the itinerant nature of Floridians, who enter the state with their home loyalties, but also because Florida has spring training, in some ways a more special baseball experience than what you'll get in Miami or in St. Pete's bizarre velodrome-looking stadium. But then there are cities that really have a bond with their teams. Obviously I place Boston at the top of this list. But Cubs fans are like this (White Sox fans are not). I'd give Twins fans some credit, even if they play in the worst facility in baseball. And Cardinals fans are truly involved in a love affair with that team. I've been to two games at Busch Stadium, and since they got rid of the turf and did some renovations, it is a pretty good place to see a game. The fans are awash in Cardinals red, they know the game, they are friendly, and they have a long and proud history. They are moving into a new stadium soon – next year, I think – and I imagine the fan loyalty will only continue to be among the best in baseball. I'm glad Lon is a Cards fan. It fits him – he's a native of Missouri (he is of the ilk that pronounces it "Missourah"), salt of the earth middle America type, steady temperament, kind to a fault, and somehow embodying the best of what we think of as Midwestern values. In any case, his being here reminds me of the Cardinals.

Friday, March 19, 2004

If anything can get a Sox fan's heart palpitating and his paranoid, glass is half empty nature kicking into high gear it is injury talk. That talk has been heated among the citizens of Red Sox Nation as there are two really worrisome injuries affecting the team right now. The first is not a surprise, though the degree and extent of it is. Trot Nixon's back continues to flare. He has a bulging (herniated) disc that has caused him to feel pain not mainly in the back, but down in his glutes. The true revelation is that he will be out for six weeks, though when the clock started on that is unclear. Things should not be too bad – we have Gabe Kaplar, we have Ellis Burks, and we can survive until May, though obviously we want him back quicker. There has been idle talk that we might see if we can get Ken Griffey Jr., but I am pretty certain that we won't get ourselves involved in that sweepstakes. Not with Griffey's injury history, not with his salary, and not with Nixon expected to return.

The second injury will be keeping a lot of us awake at night. Nomar, whose Achilles tendon has been bothering him, showed up in camp the last couple of days wearing a soft cast. Achilles injuries are nothing to mess with. And I worry about Nomar's health anyway—good shape as he is in, he seems a bit susceptible to these kinds of things. A soft cast could mean anything—it could be a precautionary measure, it could be a minor injury that needs semi-immobilization, or it could keep him out past Opening Day. This uncertainty is the sort of thing that will cause no end of hand wringing among the diehards.

Last year we got very lucky with injuries for the first year in a long while. The key guys stayed healthy the whole season. We had depth. We had things go our way. That does not always happen. We have to assume that the players will adjust, that Francona can juggle the lineup, and that we are built to withstand these temporary setbacks.

One more off field concern: Schilling has gotten himself into a lot of hot water for comments he made a few days ago indicating distrust of the owners. The owners came back and upbraided him through a league spokesman (Point of Fact: we need a real, independent commissioner) and Schill responded by getting on the Sons of Sam Horn boards, where he was impressive in his ability to convey his opinions articulately in a fan forum, though there were a few self-serving references and he is an ardent union man. Nonetheless, he earns much respect in a lot of our eyes simply for being willing to engage with us seriously.

On the field, the Sox won today. Pedro pitched pretty well—four innings, one earned run, two walks, two hits. He's making progress. Hopefully he'll build his innings slowly and by mid-April he'll be set to go 100 pitches an outing. I'd love 200 innings from him, and having a reliable fifth and even sixth starter should ensure that he'll get optimum rest. They are actually starting to rack up wins fairly regularly, and even if it is only spring training and the results don't count and don't matter, it is good to get a sense that they are gelling and that most of the work is about fine tuning and getting up to speed. That said, I'll feel a lot better when I know that Nomar really is going to be ok.

Saturday, March 20, 2004
Spring training keeps rolling along. The Sox are piling up wins, the pitchers are getting innings under their belts, and on the whole there is not a lot to report. NCAA hoops roll along (Williams lost a heartbreaker today in the DIII Championships: Down 84-82 with almost no time left, they put up a prayer that bounced off the rim—insanely close to a miracle shot). The Sox, meanwhile, seem set to stand pat—it is fans who get in injury crisis mode. Theo and the owners and Francona and the coaches know that as of now we have several guys who have the flexibility that will get us through this. We have a logjam at first and DH, but Millar can play right field, or he can play left with Manny at right. (Nick Cafardo had a nice piece about Manny in the *Globe* today that revealed him as a fully fleshed out person and not as a caricature. It showed how much he seems to genuinely want to win.) Pokey Reese can shift to short and Bellhorn can play second as long as Nomar is out. The sky is not falling. Indeed, the sky is still the limit, no matter how our paranoid Red Sox souls might envision things to be otherwise.

Sunday, March 21, 2004
Many of the daily stories of spring training, indeed in any given day of a long baseball season, seem of little import. That is because most of them are of little import—nagging injuries, small-scale trades, petty bickering, guys miffed about their contracts—these are the things that will fill a beat writer's notes columns every day and yet they may have little bearing on the success or failure of the team as

a whole. Of course sometimes the impact of these little events ends up being a great deal more than one might expect—Jeff Bagwell for Larry Anderson comes to mind. In another sport and another context, the seemingly mundane injury suffered by Bo Jackson to his hip in 1990, or a similar injury to Cam Neely in his prime. Closer to home, Bill Lee's injury in a brawl against the Yankees will always evoke anger. These were stones that produced ripples far beyond what their initial impact would seem to have warranted.

For some reason the following three seemingly disparate stories caught my eye today. All three are probably minor, producing small and inconsequential ripples. But who knows? Maybe one will prove to be crucial. It is just too early to tell, though there will be guys, inevitably full of shit, who will assert later that they knew all along that event x would prove a proximate cause to outcome y.

Probably Meaningless Story Number One: Bronson Arroyo will be the pitcher for the home opener. Initially this would have been BH Kim's slot, and so the plan was to keep the pressure off Kim and have Waker pitch the first game at Fenway. This would have been great. It would have allowed Waker to get some recognition, and undoubtedly the fans in the Fens will go nuts when his name is announced for the first time after all he did for us in the postseason. It would be smart from a stability vantage point—no sense in testing Kim's fragile psyche in his first start of the year after a less-than-savory postseason. Above all it would probably give us the best chance to win the most games early on in a season in which every win will undoubtedly be vital. That said, with Kim out, this makes sense. Arroyo has not had the issues, either in his shoulder or in his head that Kim has shown in the last weeks of the 2003 season or in the first weeks of this preseason. We can thus get an order for the first few weeks anyway, and if we decide to shift Waker to throw between Pedro and Schilling for optimum contrast, there are plenty of off days early in the season to tinker.

Incidentally, it also is reassuring to hear Francona say that he considered throwing Pedro on what would be just under four days rest in that home opener but that he decided against it. Truth be told, that seems a no brainer, and even Grady would not have done it (hell, Grady was cautious with Pedro's pitch count all last year, which is what makes the playoff decision all the more vexing). The only side note to this is that one wonders if Waker isn't beginning to feel a bit taken for granted. I don't believe it—he said all the right things, though one could divine a hint of his desire to get a spotlight start early on if one so chose. Beyond that, it is hard to see how this will be different from every other team's announcement of who their opening day and home opening pitcher will be. It is gratifying for egos, it theoretically gets the pitching rotation set, but in the end, it is long- forgotten by May.

Probably Meaningless Story Number Two: Minor trade consummated today—we gave up Tony Womack for Matt Duff, a St. Louis reliever. Womack might have ended up being one of those Francisco Cabrera feel good postseason stories, but barring that serendipity, it is hard to feel as if this one marks any sort of loss. I'm sure Womack is a fine human being, he probably was a three sport, all state, bang the cheerleaders and charm the moms kind of kid his whole life. He may end up having a respectable career. He'll make more money than me this year even if he ends up playing all season on the Cards' Memphis farm club. But the Red Sox' 2004 World Series hopes simply did not hinge on the performance of a guy who would have been incredibly familiar with the stretch of Route 128 connecting Providence and Boston. Further, something tells me that Matt Duff will not be an enormous storyline for this year's Sox. This will not be Bagwell for Anderson in reverse. And again, I hope I am wrong. I hope we fleeced St. Louis. But my guess is that this will end up being like most of the stories buried in the transactions section of the sports section – of little moment to anyone but the participants and their families.

Probably Meaningless Story Number Three: David Ortiz, arguably last year's Sox MVP and certainly a guy who was the glue from August on, jacked another bomb today. That gives him six for the preseason, which leads the majors. Now this is a meaningless stat except inasmuch as it means that Ortiz is seeing the ball well, he has decent timing, and he is strong (most of these home runs have not been cheap shots). There is little or no guarantee that Ortiz will start the season at this torrid pace. It is highly unlikely that this performance portends a season in which Ortiz will lead the majors in home runs. It would be nice. But preseason numbers are simply not sufficient for predicting anything that will happen once the games count. However, there is a caveat. Ortiz, like several other key guys, is in a contract year. Now many people are asking the obvious question—was Ortiz for real in 2003? If he was, it would be worth signing him to a long term deal before he positions himself to break the bank with us holding the empty sack. If he was not, then it will make sense for us to have signed him just to a one year extension. It is impossible to know now. I sense that he is for real, and that we will wish we had locked him up, and from what the *Globe* said today, Ortiz may well be trying to make a statement from the outset. Again, this is probably a meaningless story, but one worth following, and it is likely the one of these three little spring vignettes that warrants the most attention.

The announcement of the starter for the home opener; a trade of guys likely to spend a good portion of the year in Triple A; and one of the most important performers on the team being on a tear that may well have future contract implications. These are the mundane, banal, meaningless stories of spring that occupy the minds of baseball fans as the season approaches. These are the little stories that make us care, and they are the little stories that make baseball the greatest game, or at least the one that draws the most emotional and intellectual involvement of its fans.

Monday, March 22, 2004

Tonight I participated in one of the great nerd sports fan rites of the age—I took part in a fantasy draft. I have been in a fantasy league or two before, but I almost always am pretty half-assed about it. It is a long season, I often travel in the summer, and while I love baseball, most of that passion is geared toward the Red Sox. I pay attention to the whole game, and of course I love going to other teams' games. In fact one of my goals is to see a game in every major league stadium (I should figure out where I am with that – it becomes tougher with teams moving into new parks, but it is nearing twenty). But good fantasy players log on daily, maneuver their way to good trades, are on top of the waiver wires, and so forth. I usually do not stick with it—but this is a good group of guys, all friends or friends of friends in DC, and as long as I start off well I should be ok.

My team is decent. It is Red Sox heavy, and we'll see what sort of balance I have, but I cannot complain too much. I don't have the lineup memorized yet, but I know I have Ortiz/Millar at first, Javy Lopez behind the plate, Edgar Renteria at short, Manny and Griffey in the outfield, Prior (let's hope he gets healthy), Lowe, Waker, and a handful of other pitchers, including Foulke, and a few bench guys. I bet my friends and fellow players Josh and Don and the rest of the guys can already rattle their lineups off the top of their heads. I cannot tell you my third outfielder, my second baseman, my third baseman or most of my backups, never mind my pitching staff.

In real baseball, the Sox lost 3-2 with the Dodgers' arms pretty well closing down the Sox' hitters. With each passing day the games will more closely resemble the real thing—starting pitchers will go five or six innings, not three or four. Relief pitchers will begin coming in later in games—in the sixth or seventh and not the fourth as has happened for most of the preseason. There are fewer and fewer roster spots available on most any team that has serious postseason aspirations. On the Sox there may be four spots—two regular position spots and two pitching places, and most of these have largely opened up because of injuries, so they are short-term roster places. Of course that is part of the absurdity of the roster at this time of year. Of course the next ten guys on the roster will probably see time in Fenway. Of course making the team at the beginning of April won't matter if you go 0-fer the month or if you get shelled in your first three appearances. In short, we fans may worry about whether or not Terry Schumpert makes the roster in two weeks but even if he doesn't he will likely make the big club at some point and he will be what he will be – a component part of the larger team, a minor player who may get his moment in the sun, who may even be thrust into a starting role if the fates shine on him.

So after dismissing the ultimate significance of these last spots, knowing that no one's dreams end and no one's trajectory is guaranteed in the next two weeks, who are these bubble boys? Assuming that Brian Daubach has a spot pretty well secured, it seems likely that Schumpert, Dave McCarty (who had pipe dreams of being both a pitcher and situational hitter for this team) and Cesar Crespo are the three vying for, probably, two spots. On the mound, we have Frank Brooks, a Rule 5 player from Pittsburgh who will be shipped back to the Three Rivers city if he does not make the big club, and Bobby Jones, a journeyman who has been hot this spring, giving up no runs in 6 1/3 innings, retiring 21 of 23 batters he has faced. Mendoza is dealing with health questions and a big contract that may mean we have to keep him. Kim is guaranteed a spot, but he is hurt and so may well be on the dl for the first two weeks of the season. Jones and Brooks, then, may well have a reprieve for a short while. So this is it, these guys, unlikely to be the determining factors in our hoped-for run to the World Series title, nonetheless are scrutinized this time of year as if they are the final puzzle piece upon which our greatness hinges.

Monday, March 23, 2004

Nick Cafardo had an interesting article in today's *Globe*. Even nine years later, the Player's Union refuses to vote to absolve those guys (some two dozen or so who are still in the majors) who were replacement players in 1995. Now keep in mind the kinds of guys we are talking about—the two affected Red Sox are Brian Daubach and Kevin Millar. Daubach was in A ball and Millar was playing in an Independent League. These guys at the time likely thought they had few options. They were under pressures by an ownership and management group that wielded all the power. A guy in the low minors, however talented, is pretty easy to blackball. Perhaps one can understand the players taking out their pound of flesh but please, Kevin Millar, after all he's done, hasn't earned penance for a mistake he made under pretty serious career duress almost a decade ago? And of course it is not the Sox players who are doing it, though some surely are. Instead it is the whole league.

So here's what I do if I am a former replacement player. It looks less and less likely that you are going to be back in the good graces of the MLBPA any time soon. Let's face it—it's been nine years, and every year Brian Daubach struggles just to make the roster of some team, the Sox or anyone else. He is serviceable, but he certainly has no leverage. In any case, why not tell the union to fuck off, and go against them on steroid testing? Why not discern that the union is the entity blocking some sort of reasonable steroid policy, their obstinacy is forcing all players to carry a cross of guilt, and give the union an option: We are in, or else we are on our own. I know that won't happen. There is a lot of pressure in a locker room, all players do get some benefits under the CBA, and surely lots of guys don't want to take that sort of stance for an array of reasons. Still, if I wanted to clear my name, and after another vote revealed that most of the guys in the league will never let the statute of limitations run out, it would seem like there is little to lose and much to gain for the game.

That's my brainstorm of the day. It would never happen, but someone has to be thinking here.

By the way, today after Donald Fehr met with the Red Sox (Fehr and Orza are making the rounds through training camp – I wonder if Millar and Dauber were not allowed into that meeting and if that is how Cafardo picked up on the story) and afterward he told reporters that the union might be willing to yield to implement more stringent testing. Clearly some guys are beginning to raise hell with the union and I'd love to think that some of that discontent stems from the Sox guys, explaining the timing of this announcement. Something is going to give, probably sooner than we all think.

Monday, March 29, 2004

I just got back from the Promised Land. The Organization of American Historians' (OAH) annual meeting was at the Marriott Copley Place. I was on the program, gave a paper on Friday, and then hung out for most of the rest of the weekend. I spent Thursday night in Worcester at my buddy Rob's—we went out to a sports bar that night, watched all of the hoops games, and won every prize available from a Sam Adams rep. I was the king of Pop-a-Shot, never missing in the competition. It was a good time. The next morning I headed in to Boston on the commuter rail, *Globe* in hand, in pursuit of Dunkin' Donuts. I realized how spectacular and ideal for me it would be to live in Boston and to have that city be part of my routine. But still, one of the biggest lures about Boston would be the Sox.

It is hard to conceptualize why I am such a huge fan of this team. A woman I've been seeing lately asked me why I am such a huge sports fan, and I could not answer very well. How do you explain love or romance? How do you explain just why you like sex? How do you feel what it is like to hit the game winning shot or to win a championship? So many of the good things in my life are in that range of inexplicable things. But then again, saying I love them because I love them is also not sufficient.

A while back, I wrote an essay for a book in which I posited an idea as to why some teams resonate more with certain fan bases and others do not. Of course all teams resonate with some fans. But there are the Red Sox and Cubs and Packers and Redskins and Browns and Canadians. There are lots of teams like that. But there are also a whole lot of Padres, Brewers, Blue Jackets, Hawks, Seahawks, and teams of that ilk out there. Sure, they inspire fan bases somewhere, but people do not write epic poems or essays about the Milwaukee Bucks. And fans from other cities don't know the ins and outs of the long suffering fans of the Arizona Cardinals. I posed a range of reasons for this. One is history—whether long suffering or not, the team in question has to have a past. It can be glorious and victorious, like that of the Celtics or Canadians or, well, that team from the Bronx. Or it can be tortured and heart rending, like that of the Sox or Cubs or Maple Leafs. Or it can fill some extremes in between— the Browns or Philly teams or St. Louis Cardinals. Another factor is geographic ties of fans to their teams. Maybe in fifty years the Rockies and Predators and Jaguars will have a link to their cities that makes the rest of us take them seriously as fans. The Patriots and the rest of the old AFL teams have really only done that in the last decade or more in most cases, and perhaps that only because of football's growing to its greatest popularity during that time.

Obviously the Red Sox are inextricably linked not only with Boston, but with most all of New England in a way that few teams in any sports have ever been. Red Sox Nation, of course, transcends the bounds of New England, but the epicenter is Boston and the Nation emanates from Fenway's cozy environs. And any member of Red Sox Nation could give you a seminar of the past that binds, tortures, mocks, frustrates and makes us what we are. We love them and we do so unconditionally.

But I am irked by an argument that several people have proffered in the last several years. Dan Shaughnessy of the Globe, who lost his fastball soon after Frank Tanana did and who has been milking the insipid "Curse of the Bambino" idea for a decade and a half or so, has been at the forefront of it. In this weekend's *Boston Globe Magazine* Bill Littlefield of NPR gave a similar version. It runs like this: Red Sox fans have suffered for so long that it has become a part of their identity. If and when they win it all, the one thing that has marked them for so long will be gone and the team and its supporters will no longer be special. Now never mind that this utter nonsense ignores the fact that Sox fans also tend to be Pats and Celts and Bruins fans, and the Celts and Pats have won titles in the last twenty years and the Bruins did the spring that I turned one. Forget that other cities with long histories don't lose their identity when teams win—Shaughnessy always mentions Philly, but in so doing he mischaracterizes Philly fans before and after 1980. Further, and most important, so fucking what? We lose this identity, which we don't like, and we get an identity that we all desperately want. I almost feel as if these guys are the types who would tell their best friend not to date the horny supermodel physicist sports fan who really likes them because they will lose their identity as a single guy. Isn't this sort of missing the point, fellas? Maybe this is a just a huge rationalization on their part, but theirs is an idiotic argument.

Look—here's what we want: We want to win the World Series, because we love the Red Sox and have all of our lives, whether we are nine or ninety. For many of us, most of us, the Sox are first among equals. It has been great to watch the Pats win, but nothing like when the Sox win it all. And watching another team jump around the field and spray champagne and weep with joy and kiss the trophy and have the parades, well, it makes us sick, like watching an ex-girlfriend kiss someone else. On national television. With a giant smile on her face. We want to win. We don't want others imposing upon us these images as diehards who dearly fear success. We'll take our chances. We'll run the risk of losing an unwanted identity (and one that entirely misses the essence of being a fan; How do people who clearly do not get sports get to make a living writing about sports?). And we'll get to see that one thing that we've all yearned for over the last eight decades. I know people (ahem) for whom a Sox World Series win, just one, would be one of the greatest moments of their lives, even when placed next to happy families and successful careers and Patriots Super Bowls. And I know Sox fans—within days of the title we would not all be suffering from an identity crisis. We'll be online or in print wondering if we can repeat, complaining (sort of) about how Francona almost blew it in game six by pinch hitting for Ortiz, and starting "Yankees Suck" chants at Patriots games, bars, and anywhere else more than three people with a passport in Red Sox Nation are gathered. That sounds damned good to me. Let me worry about bearing the cross of figuring out who I am after that.

Tuesday, March 30, 2004

It looks as if Derek Lowe won't be signed this preseason. Indeed, with just five days until the opening night game on ESPN against the Orioles, it looks as if most of our potential free agents will be in contract years. This is not necessarily a bad thing. Obviously it is in none of these guys' interest not to be at their very best for the duration of the year, as they are playing for their next contract. Derek Lowe is high strung, but I think he went through the worst of it last year, and I suspect he'll be fine. I feel that way for most of the guys. And many can go into the season feeling as hurt or unappreciated or wounded as they want, but the fact is, we win it all, a lot of that will fade. Further, while we may not sign all of them, we will be in a pretty good position to sign whichever guys are our priority.

So what should be our priority? It seems to me that superstars are the rarest of commodities in this game—in any sport. Derek Lowe is very good, and I would hate to lose him. David Ortiz may have MVP potential, and I would be very loath to lose him. Varitek is the heart and soul of the team and everyone knows as much. So I would guess that we'll sign one of them, possibly (hopefully) more. But Nomar and Pedro are superstars. They are likely Hall of Famers. They are the face of the franchise. Both have had health issues, obviously a serious concern, but if both are healthy throughout the year it seems probable that we have to look to them to carry us in to the future.

For the time being, though, we have to work toward this season, irrespective of contract status. It's almost time to play ball. In fact, it is time to play ball—this morning the Yankees and Devil Rays faced off in the regular season opener in Japan. It was aired live, at 5. I'd love to say I showed the discipline to get up and watch it. I had the alarm set, and I woke up and turned the tv on. I heard bits and pieces of the game. But I did not really wake up to watch a whole lot of it. Hell, ESPN covered the game, but they did not even send their crew to Tokyo—the Baseball Tonight guys covered it from the Bristol studios. So I don't feel that bad—the Sox game is clearly the priority to ESPN. The Yanks and Rays even play once more in the Land of the Rising Sun, but then they actually have exhibition games scheduled! Tell me that's not solely crass commercialism!

Most importantly, the Yankees lost, 8-3. Mussina did not look good and he got pretty well shelled. A-Rod was not a factor, though Giambi played well. So as of today, March 30, 2004, the Yankees are the worst team in baseball. It may be too much to ask for a mini-sweep from Lou Piniella's boys that would put the Yanks in a 0-2 hole. But a guy can dream. Sweet, sweet dreams.

Wednesday, March 31, 2004

I am disappointed to have to write that the Yankees will not go winless in the 2004 season. After yesterday's somewhat desultory loss the Yanks rolled 12-1 in the wee morning hours over in Nippon today. Posada was on fire and Matsui hit a dinger in front of the fans who were there in no small part to see him. So the Empire is 1-1, and tied with the Rays for first. However, if we win on Sunday we are still able to go from pole to pole to win the title.

I say this despite Pedro's performance yesterday. In a span of 84 pitches, Pedro got through three innings. His first inning took most of those pitches. He loaded the bases, gave up a grand slam that was followed by a solo shot. After this performance, which sent most of New England scurrying toward its arsenic supply, Pedro, Francona, and Varitek all said the right things: Despite the end result Pedro was fine, he had good velocity, he was hitting with all of his pitches, he was sharp, and so on and so forth. Now I have to trust these guys. I have to believe in their experience, in their ability to gauge a performance independent of the actual results. I have to think that this is not a big deal. Don't I? Or am I entitled to just a little, itsy bitsy, teensy weensy, yellow polka dot bikini of a scintilla of concern about the fact that our ace, the guy upon whose right shoulder Red Sox Nation's hopes and dreams and prayers hinge, (Curt Schilling's luminous and reassuring presence notwithstanding), has not been sharp, has double the era he had last preseason, and who by the accounts of all semi-objective (writers) and putatively objective (radar guns) sources has been hovering at a less-than-Pedroesque 89-91 miles per hour. Of course Pedro will be fine on Sunday. Right? I mean, there is no reason to worry. Right?

And as long as we are talking about authorities whose expertise I have absolutely no business questioning, why does the Sox medical staff scare the hell out of me? I am sure Mr. Bill Morgan is an elite doctor. At the top of his field. The Sox are in good hands. And yet ... and yet. This Nomar situation is, let's say, worrisome. At first it was minor—nothing to worry about. Then we find that there is a bit of tendonitis—just stay off of it, put on the air cast, give it rest and we'll be set to go. Then suddenly we hear that he may not be ready for Opening Day—now remember, just days before this, we have all been hearing how "if this were a regular season game, he'd be ready to go, but since it is only spring training..." of course Nomar is supposed to be resting his Achilles injury—which is no big deal, mind you—and yet he takes batting practice and infield. Hmmm. And after we find out today that he is going to be on the DL for a while, will almost certainly miss the first week of the season, and might well be out until May. Double Hmmm. Now again, I am not a doctor (well, not the real kind) and so I really should not be asking these sorts of questions, but don't we have a medical staff precisely to keep Nomar from taking batting practice and infield? Isn't it their job to make sure that athletes, with their drive and ambition and unfailing belief in their bodies, do not try to do too much too soon? Further, and this one is a puzzler, why is it that just in the last couple of days that same medical staff—and again, I have no actual training in these sorts of things, so I am basing this on what I would call simple common sense—has decided that maybe, just maybe, our All Star, MVP Candidate, former batting champion, face of the franchise, future Hall of Famer, husband of Mia, and essential piece of the World Series puzzle might need to see a specialist? He's been on the shelf for most all of spring training. He was supposedly getting better but clearly is not, the Achilles is dangerous terrain, and now, four days before the games count, Morgan and company decide that maybe a guy earning millions for his use of his body needs to see, you know, a specialist?

And Nomar's is only the most visible of a skein of injuries that all seem to have followed the same pattern: Injury, followed by mystery, followed by diagnosis, which turns out to be a misdiagnosis, that results in a change of plan—usually two weeks have passed by this point, that Orioles game is right around the corner—followed by a more tentative prognosis, and then, as if this is the first time anyone had ever said these words, with a sense of wonder bordering on the religious—say them sparingly and delicately, as apparently there is some sort of limit to their very utterance us laypeople have not been clued in to—"We are considering sending him to a specialist." If I ever own a pro sports team, I have specialists on staff. If the second left handed long reliever, backup long snapper, towel boy, or, um, All World shortstop so much as farts in a weird way, we're sending him to a gastrointerologist, and if he takes a foul ball of the Achilles tendon, I'm going to go out on a limb and send him to a specialist right away. Again, I'm not a medical doctor, and I am not a sports owner. I'm just a simple sports fan. But I also am not a complete fucking retard. Jesus Christ, rooting for this team is going to kill me.

3

April: Let The Games Begin

Friday, April 2, 2004

Two days. Just two days. The funny thing is that this first game weighs exactly the same as every other game in the standings. But proportion and rationale are not strengths of your average sports fan. By which I mean me. By which I mean Red Sox fans. Part of this, of course, is because there is nothing rational about being a sports fan. There sure as hell is nothing rational about being a Red Sox fan. If on Sunday night, in the game against the Orioles, the Red Sox don't hit, field badly, give up a lot of runs early and give up more late, it will feel like a disaster. This is our fate. This is our heritage.

So let's breathe. Tomorrow does not mean everything. Unless Pedro screws the pooch. Or Foulke gives up six runs in the ninth. Or Manny and Damon collapse and shatter kneebones diving for a ball (ok, wiseguys—it is at least theoretically possible that Manny would dive for a ball).

When you go into the spring on a wave of positivity it is fairly likely that the wave will crash. But why? After all, we were positive going into the spring for reasons that seemed sensible (why am I using the past tense? Fatalism? Damn history. Damn it to hell, or at least to the Bronx.). Our starting staff is outstanding. Our lineup is an offensive juggernaut. We've improved our middle infield defense, which alone should help Derek Lowe. Here's the thing: Like the joke that proved to be the metaphorical foundation for *The Crying Game*, this sort of fear and worry and hand wringing is in our nature. And there is some justification. Just in my lifetime we have a dozen years worth of reasons to worry. We have ESPN reminding us of last year's bitter finish. It's their selling point for tomorrow night's game.

Tomorrow I'll give season predictions. As of this moment I am the only one reading this. Nonetheless, here is a hint—Glory in the Fens. I would not be writing this if I though anything else. Fans don't hope to publish diaries for Wild Card team.

Update Re: The perniciousness of the steroid question: Apparently former White Sox pitcher and sometime rocker Jack McDowell intimated that Mark Prior, because he has had tendon issues that have not healed, might be on the juice. This is such nonsense I do not even know where to start. McDowell never played with Prior. Prior came from college and then the minors, where testing is stringent. I've had tendon injuries. They happen. And they take a long time to recover from. And yet while I think this is insidious foolishness, this is what the MLBPA hath wrought. When no one is substantially tested, everyone is suspect. That said—what the fuck is Jack McDowell doing hinting that other guys might be using steroids? You won a Cy Young. Good for you. Now go back to your horrible, horrible rock band.

Saturday, April 3, 2004

The Sox are in Atlanta in what has become a tradition—play a couple of games in front of a majority of Sox fans at Turner Field before the opener. We split these two games, winning yesterday, getting shut out today, in a situation where quite literally the only concern is staying healthy.

None of the potential free agents signed contracts, and I am not certain what this regime feels about contract negotiations, but my guess is that this is a question that will hover over the team all season, increasing or diminishing in significance in direct correlation with the team's fortunes—if they win, the question will recede into the background, but if things aren't going so well I suspect that the contract situation of the stars will serve as a rallying point for both malcontents and the media.

The roster has pretty well been sorted out. In those final slots we have Brian Daubach, the one-time career minor leaguer who spent several years as a productive Sox first baseman before being released and signing on with the White Sox for last year. He is back and will serve as a left-handed bat off the bench, and perhaps as part of what will be a rotation at first, designated hitter, and possibly an outfield slot if we need him. Cesar Crespo will be our utility guy, a jack of all trades who can play second, short, third, and the outfield. David McCarty is a righthanded hitter who can play first, outfield, and designated hitter, and at least theoretically he can be an emergency (read "lost cause") lefty reliever. He tied for the league lead (with David Ortiz and Hank Blalock) in home runs in the spring, which means nothing other than that he made the decision easier. Finally, Bobby Jones will be the other left handed reliever. He had a solid spring. All of these slots are vulnerable, as we have Nomar, Trot and BH Kim on the shelf for a while, and from here on out, injuries and performance will decide playing time as well as who spends time on the Boston-Pawtucket shuttle.

Daylight Savings tonight. First pitch should come approximately 17.5 hours from now. Go Sox!!!!!

Sunday, April 4, 2004

Tonight's the night. First pitch should happen in approximately twenty minutes. Pedro faces off against Ponson. It is supposed to be some thirty degrees or below with wind chill tonight—not the ideal conditions for a fragile-shouldered ace to make his first appearance of the year. Let's hope he's smart and that the innings are short.

Predictions for the season:

AL East:
1. Red Sox – Hey, I can't go against them, and I think Schilling and Foulke in the end will mean a lot more than A-Rod and Sheffield.
2. Yankees – That pitching staff isn't as solid as it seems.
3. Orioles – I know everybody likes the Blue Jays, but the O's are young and they upgraded pretty substantially over what they had last season, when they were coming together.
4. Blue Jays – Delgado may well be on the trading block by the time July rolls around.
5. Devil Rays – They will be much improved. In the AL Central they might even be good enough to make a run. Respectability in this division will be an accomplishment.

AL Central:
1. Twins – Until someone supplants them, they are this weak division's favorites. Plus I have a soft spot for the Twins now – one positive legacy from my wasted time in Mankato.
2. Royals – I think that they have the talent and I don't think last year was a fluke.
3. White Sox – I am very curious about the relationship between Guillen and Thomas. They did not like one another as teammates. Wait until mid-August when they are ten games out of first.
4. Indians – The Indians are hopeless. But they are young and hopeless.
5. Tigers – They will be better than last year. How could they not be?

AL West:
1. Athletics – The Angels had the best offseason. But the A's still have the best team.
2. Angels – That said, the Angels had a hell of an offseason.
3. Mariners – It still is amazing what they have done in Seattle with the guys they have lost in the last five years. They could well make another run this year.
4. Rangers – I will derive a great deal of pleasure from another steamy suburban Dallas summer of futility.

NL East:
1. Braves – I don't even believe it. But I am not certain I buy the Phillies, and Bobby Cox knows how to reload.
2. Phillies – Still, these guys are going to be much improved, and the Braves will get their biggest challenge yet.
3. Marlins – These guys have two World Series titles. I puke in my mouth every time I think of it.
4. Expos – Major League Baseball is not doing these guys any justice. Baseball in DC!
5. Mets – And no one really even cares.

NL Central:
1. Astros – Better rotation and the Cubs just seem like too chic a choice. But in a shorter series . . .

2. Cubs -- . . . these guys may be tough.
3. Cardinals – Great lineup, but who's going to pitch?
4. Reds – I'd love to see Griffey stay healthy and return to greatness.
5. Pirates – Or maybe the Brewers.
6. Brewers – Or maybe the Pirates.

NL West:
1. Dodgers – Great pitching. Can they hit?
2. Giants – But this is a weak lineup compared to the last few years. Bonds may be lucky to get 350 at bats.
3. Diamondbacks – And it will be worse than this if Big Unit is not healthy.
4. Padres – They will be tough in 2005 or 2006. But not yet. I want to see this new Stadium.
5. Rockies – How can a team playing in that air in that city in that stadium be boring? This year's team will answer that question by example.

AL Playoffs: Divisional Playoffs: Sox over Twins 3-1, Yanks over A's 3-2. ALCS: Sox over Yanks 4-3.

NL Playoffs: Astros over Dodgers 3-0, Cubs over Braves 3-2. NLCS: Cubs over Astros 4-2.

World Series: OK, OK, so I still ultimately am going with the chic choice. Heart rules over head – Sox over Cubbies in 6. Greatest moment ever, Game 6, 9th inning, Fenway Park.

It's game time, or just about. I'll keep periodic updates. The fact is, I do not know how often I'll see the Sox this year. Once I get to Texas, assuming that's where I'll end up, I will try to get a dish, but most of the summer I'll be on the road. ESPN will have the Sox on a lot, especially if we get on an early roll. But I'll have to rely on radio and internet a lot.

Sox lineup:
Damon CF

Mueller 3B
Manny LF
Ortiz DH
Millar 1B
Kaplar RF
Varitek C
Bellhorn 2B
Reese SS

8:07—First pitch to Damon—strike. Damon looks like he is planning to audition for the Charles Manson story. He grounds to Tejada. Mueller too. Getting Tejada was an enormous acquisition for the O's. He and Lopez are a huge part of why I think the Orioles will be better than the Blue Jays this year. Manny is just such an amazing hitter. He gets down in the count and fights and fights and gets a single—and he hustled down the line. Ortiz had a killer spring—how great would a bomb be right now? (That was rhetorical, but it would be very great.) By the way – these stats usually don't mean much, especially once a new season has begun, but Ponson is 1-9 lifetime against the Sox and we've bashed him pretty good. But he just got Ortiz swinging on the high heat. Now it's Pedro's turn. Let's see how that radar gun reads.

OK—One pitch, grounder to Pokey, who shows nice range. I'd love a five pitch inning. Nice movement early on. Ugh—dribbler to third, Mueller comes up with the ball on the run, but the throw is just a bit to the home plate side of the bag and Mora is safe—infield hit. I for one am digging the Lionel Richie hair on Pedro. I hope he grows it out all season into an Oscar Gamble Mickey Mouse ears baseball card look. But first I hope he strikes out Tejada. High fly ball to Manson, er, Damon. Pedro's around 88 or so and his balls are moving—cutters and sinkers it looks like, as opposed to straight cheese. Palmeiro is back with the O's. He hit a little flair. Mora is going for third—Manny throws him out, with Reese covering third. Very nice – assist for Manny. So Pedro gives up a couple of cheap hits but they prove harmless. I don't want him to let it fly, but it would be nice to see a couple of pitches in the 93-94 range when the third inning rolls around and he's warmed up.

Well, I won't do this all game. For one thing, who wants an

inning by inning recap of the entire season? For another, I won't get to do this all year, so no sense only having a game here and a game there.

This is a pretty good Orioles team. There are not a lot of weak spots in this lineup. They have young pitching. Lee Mazzilli, the manager (he was such a pretty boy when he played for the Mets in the 70s and 80s), is an unknown quantity, but you figure he won't screw it up too much. I think the strength of the division is going to cause the Yanks and Red Sox to appear to underachieve at least a bit – with 19 games against each of these teams, we will not both be very likely to hit 100 wins. I still think the Wild Card comes from the east, but as with the past few years, it will be a race that goes to the last week of the season.

Ugh—how, precisely do you get nailed on a strike 'em out, throw 'em out double play to end the inning when Gabe Kaplar is the throw 'em out side of the coin?

Jesus Christ—Javy Lopez' first pitch in an Orioles uniform and he hits a line drive home run that sneaks inside the left field foul pole. Uh oh—Gibbons gets a single to right. Settle down, Pedro. I'm telling you—if you took the DNA of Webster and Lionel Richie, you'd end up with the 2004 version of Pedro. Ooohh—Pedro drilled Segui. I don't think it was intentional—looked like he tried to put juice on it. And now he dumps Larry Bigbie on his ass and follows it up with an inside pitch that is called strike because Bigbie was in position to bunt and could not pull it back. Settle down, big fella. Meanwhile, a chant of "Pedro Sucks" overwhelms the stadium. I won't point out that every time I've been to Camden Yards to see Sox-O's the Sox fans outnumber the O's fans. In any case, Pedro throws the ball away fielding a bunt and a run scores—2-0 Orioles. Second and third, no outs. The *Globe, Herald, Providence Journal, Manchester Union Leader* and so forth will not be kind tomorrow if this keeps going. This is not how you want to start the season. 3-0 now, and still no outs.

Now is not the time to court anxiety. A few years back Pedro got shelled in the Opener against the Blue Jays. He got pounded in the worst showing of his career in the home opener last year. Even in an execrable showing so far, it is only 3-0, and he just struck out Mora, so now he gets to face Tejada with two outs. This would be a key out to get. Keep the damage minimal, get the bats rolling. Well, Tejada got a hold of that ball, but the wind probably kept it down and Damon made a nice little running grab. Still, not an ideal way to start the season. But let's hope Pedro shuts the fuck up about respect for the next few weeks.

Here is the Sox debut for Mark Bellhorn. He got ahold of one — near where Tejada just hit his, but deeper, though not deep enough. Pokey Reese is certainly not here to provide offense, though if we could get some production out of him, which our lineup should promote, maybe he can be a surprise. I really don't want a 1-2-3 inning now. Though I also don't want Pedro coming back after a long half inning. Unfrozen Caveman Damon is up after Pokey got on base with a walk – always good the see the #9 guy get on with a freebie. Oh boy — an interview with Bud Selig. Surprise — he thought the absurd two game Yanks-Tampa series in Japan went well; he thinks "it's better" for the Expos' move "to be done right than to be done fast," which is idiotspeak for God knows what — can't this absurd trope be used forever? It's been long enough now. Then he compounds it by repeating yet another bit of nonsense — about how they take seriously the idea of a team moving into another team's territory. Um, Washington DC is Baltimore's territory? Talk about the tail wagging the dog. By this logic Boston is Worcester's territory. Washington and its suburbs dwarf Baltimore. DC is obviously a more important city with a stronger economic base. Almost all of Northern Virginia is a good hour-and-a-half from Baltimore, and that only is the case if one does not take into account traffic on the Beltway during the exact hours one would head to a night game at Camden Yards, which can make the trip twice that long or more. I lived in Northern Virginia, and trust me — it is not an extension of Baltimore.

Sox are battling. Weird runner's interference call and Damon is out. Mueller gets a hot to drop in. Manny is up — two outs, two on. He smacks one up the middle, off Ponson's ankle (that's gonna smart in these temps — shame) and through for a hit. Men on first and second, one in, Ortiz up. He just hit a ball that must have been flaming when it came back into the atmosphere, and it looked like Mora was dancing around a bit, but he made the play. We got one back. Let's hope Pedro is settled down.

Good enough—de facto 1-2-3 inning after Lopez got on by hitting one through the middle that bounced of Pedro's glove and a play could not be made off of it. Maybe Pedro can go 5-6 anyway—we should score more than three runs, and Ponson has not been unhittable. Tales of redemption are good tales.

We play seven or six games each against the Orioles, Yanks, and Blue Jays in April. I guess our feet are to the fire and we'll see how we do without Nomar and Nixon.

I am already really, really tired of ALCS Game 7 talk.

Bellhorn bangs a double, Kapler to third—he could have gotten home. I hope we can capitalize. Reese is up. He bunts to Ponson who underhands it to first. Damn. I wonder if he did that on his own. Obviously he is not a big run producer, but you still hate to see that play with guys on second and third—he's our guy for the next few weeks at short and for the season at second. Let's at least start the year pretending we expect him to contribute with the bat, huh.

There we go—another easy one for Pedro. 19 pitches the last two innings. Time to let that vaunted offense do its job now that Pedro is doing his.

I never really partook of many of the Opening Day traditions as a kid. I bagged class in college a couple of times, I always watched the games where I could, but I never skipped school or snuck in a transistor radio to the classroom or anything like that. I do remember a few Opening Day games—one time I was sick and got to see the Sox open up the season against the Jays in the mid 80s—Rance Mullinicks, their third baseman, was a Red Sox killer and he drove in 4 or 5 runs that day to beat us. I remember Opening Day, 1986, when Dewey hit a home run against Jack Morris on the first pitch of the season—I did skip school that day, with my friend John Kemp. I spent the night at his house and we stayed home and watched the Sox.

Nonetheless, I always have found Opening Day to be a secular holiday for those of us still smitten by baseball. I know that by most measures football is now our number one sport, but there are only 16 regular season games, and the schedule and format is so tv friendly. For those of us who love baseball, love it to our bones, love it in an irrational sort of way, these April days, though cold and raw and sporadic (there are more off days in April than in any other three months combined, or at least it seems that way) and sometimes sloppy, represent for us all of the clichés of spring. For me spring is a season of renewal and always has been because of baseball. Sure, the snow melting was great, but a late snowstorm was always a possibility—certainly snow after the baseball season had started was hardly enough to get a New England kid to bat an eye. Flowers and trees blooming are fine. Nice even. I'll take late blooming for the crack of the bat on a ball every year. A young man's thoughts turn to love in spring. I suppose. But once you hit adolescence love and sex are a constant—spring was no more or less the horny season than any other, and romance blooms wherever a girl will let you let it, whereas the start of baseball season is a known, schedulable date on the annual calendar.

Pedro just got through another inning. Two guys got on, and the last out was a bit of an adventure. It was to shallow center and the ball clearly was drifting from left to right. Pokey had a bead on it, and he made the catch out past second base, but he and Kaplar almost collided. Kaplar is a solid dude—a serious collision may well have put Reese on the DL. We don't need that.

They just are not hitting today. Or at least they are not hitting enough to drive in runs. Ponson is out, they brought in Lopez, who was beaten out for the fifth starter position and thus should not be able to hold us down for long. He got out the one batter he faced—Damon—but maybe we'll get a chance to try to get to him next inning. It's the middle of the sixth. We'll see if Pedro comes out again—I have yet to see a pitch count, and I doubt they'll let him go much past 90 pitches, so we'll see. One more inning would be great—and he is out there—and just threw his 84th pitch. Johnny Miller just said that Dave Wallace, the pitching coach, projected about 90 pitches, so this will likely be his last inning no matter what. Giddyup – 1-2-3 inning with a strikeout to punctuate it. He's rolling. C'mon guys – score a couple of runs.

Mueller gets his third hit of the night, but then Manny hits into a double play. Ugh. Second inning in a row. Ortiz just hit a bomb, but it was just foul—that wind pushed it just to the right of the foul pole. He walked instead, and Millar is up. Damn—he gets wood on it, but not enough, and the Sox go down again. Pedro can take the loss. He cannot get the win.

Timlin comes in, gets an out quickly, lets three guys on, though one gets thrown out stealing, and then with the shift on against Palmeiro he hits one through the hole at shortstop. Now it's 4-1, which changes things considerably. Dammit. Two more runs on a Lopez double. 6-1—double dammit. Now Embree is on. Ugh—he doesn't look great either, but we are finally out of the inning.

It's amazing how quickly the anticlimax sets in. I've been seriously up for this game for weeks. I knew it was on ESPN. I planned my day, my week around it. And then it goes down like this. But the fact remains that it is early. Pedro started off sloppy and recovered. The bats were not alive, but there is no doubt that they will be. Timlin was sloppy, but this was hardly an ideal appearance for him. It would be nice to rally here in the 8th and 9th innings, even if only to make it closer and get some confidence. With one out Tek walked, Bellhorn got a single, and Francona is pinch hitting Dauber for Reese. The Orioles pitcher, DeJean, is wild, and we are taking advantage, as Daubach just walked too, and the bases are loaded. DeJean is gone. Let's see if we can get to their setup guy, B.J. Ryan, starting with Johnny Damon, who thus far is 0 for 4 with four ground ball outs. And every time he has come up, Johnny Miller has made the same cracks about his hair and what he used to look like and how maybe there is some relationship between Grizzly Damon and his early season 0-fer. I wish Joe Morgan would punch him in the throat. Damon hits into a fielder's choice, but they could not turn two, so Tek scored. Mueller leaves two on base with a meager grounder. Sox have stranded twelve—how very typical. Stranding runners has been the bane of every Red Sox team I have ever followed, including even last year's offensive juggernaut. It's 6-2. Not enough that inning—can't squander those sorts of chances.

Sloppy, sloppy, sloppy. Throwing errors are killing us. Cesar Crespo just made one, leading to another run. 7-2. Williamson is in now. Tonight it does not matter. We get these guys on Tuesday afternoon with Schilling on the mound. It's a long season. It's been a long night. The ninth is coming up, our power guys are set to hit, but a five run deficit in 30 degree conditions seems daunting, especially given our futility tonight. And as expected, we get two quick outs, get two guys on, and do nothing with it. A rather desultory end to a desultory game. Even when we were in it we never were really in it.

So what can we draw from this? Not much. Pokey Reese seems to be the real deal on defense. Pedro may not be where he was, but there is no sense worrying about the roof coming down quite yet. The bats will come around, and we have to assume we'll take advantage of opportunities more consistently in the future. These Orioles are a good team. No sense worrying about it, and we may as well feign that we are not as disappointed as we are. Sigh.

Monday, April 5, 2004

It's a day after the disappointing opener, and the *Globe, Herald, et. al.* predictably walked that line between merely provocative and fully hyperventilating. The big story, beyond the loss, was that apparently Pedro left the stadium last night after he finished. There are rumors that he was in the dugout in street clothes in the eighth, but all reports, with apparent confirmation from Francona and Theo, indicate that he did not stay to watch the end.

This is disappointing for a range of reasons, though of course Dan Shaughnessy was in midseason mode—overreacting, creating a story, or at least exacerbating it. Still, you have to wonder what message he is sending the rest of the guys when Pedro acts like this. He's expressed that he feels disrespected. We get it. But why turn around and disrespect the guys who played out there all night? They didn't give up a home run on the first pitch to Lopez (Pedro did not give up a home run to a righty all last year, I believe) and they certainly did not make the only errors in the game. It is too early to say that this will become poisonous, but the sort of preseason hype we've all contributed to this year could make for a very, very long season if things implode. And this sort of behavior is precisely the sort of thing that could take the sheen off the Cowboy Up diamond. This is why so many people believe Schilling will be our true ace this year. He goes tomorrow. We'll see.

Meanwhile I have not yet figured out if the game will be on Comcast Sports at three tomorrow. Obviously I want to see the game if it is on, but it may be tricky to find out. I'll know if it is on in the DC area by checking the *Post* in the morning, but will it be down here in Charlottesville? And I am pretty certain that I do not have a computer that is able to listen to the games on the internet, though I should buy the MLB.com package anyway, just in case. The first thing I am doing when I get to Texas is getting a satellite dish.

I expect a big win tomorrow—the bats will open up and Schilling's Sox debut will keep the jackals from jumping on the body when it is down. At least for a day. Even in seasons that are supposedly sprinkled with fairy dust and fate's glitter, they clearly don't want to make it easy on us. We're all strapped in for the ride, though. They won't throw us true believers off the bandwagon this early. Most of us are too dumb ever to get off.

Tuesday, April 6, 2004

That's more like it. The sky is no longer falling. The season is not lost. We are not going to end the season 0-162.

Today I played hooky as the Sox and Orioles played an afternoon game at Camden Yards. Schilling was on the mound for us, making his Sox debut and allowing us to breathe again after *l'affaire Pedro (part une?)*. He was what we would have hoped—he scattered six largely harmless hits, struck out seven, walked one, and gave up one run in six innings. I did not catch a pitch count, but I would imagine that he could have gone another inning or two. The relief was fine, and in particular the spring training demise of Keith Foulke may well be overstated, given that he pitched a 1-2-3 ninth for his first save in a Sox uniform. The Sox won 4-1. The bats were sufficient, (interestingly, Manny batted cleanup, rather than third, raising questions as to whether he twisted arms a bit, or if Francona is simply experimenting) but obviously it was not a breakout. Burks drove in Reese for an insurance run in the ninth, otherwise we accumulated all of our runs in the first four innings, including two on a Millar home run.

Tomorrow Lowe goes, and hopefully he'll come out of the gates and state his case for an extension. I think he needs to get off to a good start for his psyche, and a win puts us above .500. Hopefully the bats get rolling tomorrow. It should be televised on Comcast again.

What today's win accomplishes above all is an increased emphasis on the negative. The knights of the keyboards would have had their knives out if Schilling had lost today. Callahan and Shaughnessy both wrote relentlessly negative columns today about Pedro's going A.W.O.L. and Francona's seemingly tepid response. Apparently the skipper's response was something to the effect of: "It's my fault, we never talked about that rule," referring to a rule one would think needed no explication: Don't leave the game before it is over. A win today should help to let this slip into the recesses of our neurotic self consciousness. The writers can focus on Schilling the stopper, the first win, getting on the right track, and all of the rest of the first victory whitewash that will hopefully diminish what would have inevitably festered.

The first win feels good. This is a four-game series against the Orioles. If we can win these next two, we'll be off to the sort of start that we need if we are going to make it through a tough April schedule without Trot and Nomar and even BH Kim. Schilling certainly made the sort of debut we dreamed about on long winter nights. Hopefully today's was the first of a hundred or so of these this regular season.

Wednesday, April 7, 2004

Now this is what we wanted. Derek Lowe has a solid, even a damned good outing, the bats put a hurting on the Orioles' pitchers, we win 10-3, and we take first place early on in this, our season of destiny.

I hate to say that I was right, that I saw the Boston sportswriters for the Pavlovian simpletons that they are, but yesterday's win had the effect I predicted—all of the stories were about Schilling and his meticulous preparation and his professionalism and how he came in and fulfilled expectations—and yet he still isn't satisfied. Now obviously much of the undertone to all of these hosannas was an element of using Schilling as something of a foil for Pedro, still the prodigal son and in the doghouse at least until Saturday, when he can find redemption if he pitches a shutout, strikes out 13, and shows mastery around the plate and in the dugout. You see, we love Pedro's emotions, as long as they are channeled right. The Boston media is ravenous, but predictably so.

Today's game gave a hint as to what these Sox can be. Lowe came in and gave the sort of performance for a third starter that show why all of the promise for this team is so great. He gave up two runs, his sinker was moving, he looked confident, and as important, the guys gave him a lead, minimizing any pressure. Further, this was an away game, and Lowe was horrible last year away from the Friendly Confines, so this too is a good sign. Lowe is like this generation's Bret Saberhagen—every other year he will be outstanding. For Sabes it was odd numbered years that for whatever reason drew out his excellence. For Lowe, the even numbered years are ones to take to the bank. In 2000 he was arguably the best reliever in the American league. In 2001 he fell apart, inheriting the spirit of Calvin Schiraldi and nearly getting himself run out of Boston. In 2002 he went 21-8 and came within a whisker of winning the Cy Young (only Pedro's sublime presence kept him from taking the award). In 2003 he did not fall apart—though that seemed a possibility in August—but while his 17 wins were respectable, his ERA was bloated, and his confidence seemed shaken. But if tonight is any indication, confidence, plus a lack of pressure, combined with the fact that he'll be able to play with some runs most games because the guys should rack up runs against the #3 (or 4 depending on if Francona and Wallace decide to split Pedro and Schilling with Waker) starter of other teams.

The bats were roaring too. Damon broke out of a mini-slump by going 5 for 5, Ortiz hit a bomb, and they scored all ten runs with two outs—7 in the second inning and the rest in the seventh. A range of guys are contributing already, and even the defense is strong—Damon made a catch robbing David Segui of a home run that was the #1 highlight in Sportscenter's Top Ten. Of course Damon will likely keep the serial killer look, which I frankly dig, but which will keep the cracks coming during every highlight and worse, by announcers every game. Don't let anyone try to fool you—sports and baseball are inherently conservative. Guys who would hardly draw a look from fraternity brothers at a Midwestern college campus are looked on as flakes in the Majors—see Wendell, Turk—and someone like Damon, who could be just about any longhair in any town in America, is the source of much bemusement among straightlaced (square?) announcer types like Jim Palmer or Johnny Miller.

But the Sox are in first, and if that makes the whole team adopt the Damon Christos look, so be it. It's less annoying than the rally monkey, and they cannot go back to the Cowboy Up, Rally Karaoke Guy well of last year. Why not go for the barnstorming Christian cult look? It could be a Passion of the Sox sort of thing. Though for the record I still am partial to Pedro's Lionel Richie look. In any case, we're 2-1, the Yanks and Rays are 2-2, The O's are 1-2, and the Jays are 0-3, having been the unfortunate victims of the Tigers revival show that almost certainly will have a short run in Detroit. We finish off the four games with the O's tomorrow. We have Waker on the mound, the bats are rolling, and while it may be premature to say so, going to 3-1 after that Opening Day loss may well mean we never look back at .500, and who knows, maybe we don't look back at all. That would be nice. I would not bet on it happening, but it does give me a warm feeling, like when a "Yankees Suck!" chant breaks out at a Patriots game.

Thursday, April 8, 2004

It's raining in Baltimore. Beyond the Counting Crows reference, that also is the tableaux for the Sox game right now. A game that began at 7:00 is now nearing midnight. It's 2-2, it's in the 13th inning, and the O's are up. There is one out, a man on first, and we are on our sixth pitcher of the night – Bobby Jones has held the O's off for two full innings and this is his third. He just walked Segui, so there is no one out and the O's have Lopez on second, so this is not ideal. Jones has good stuff, but he's a neophyte for the Sox into his third inning in a tight game. And he walked the bases loaded. On a second tight pitch in a row—just off the plate. The home plate ump, Marquez, has been consistent, so this is not outrageous, but the O's have been beneficiaries of this call all night.

A win here would be key. We lost the opener in a flat performance that led to the Pedro fiasco. We won the Schilling outing in a game that was low-scoring and close, but never seriously in question. Last night we won handily. So this is one that would let us all go to bed and sleep soundly. But it does not look great right now.

Jones now has Bigbie at 3-2, and he fouled one off. Damnation. He walks the winning run in. It's raining in Baltimore. Four walks and the Orioles win. So much for waving goodbye to .500.

But this is not wretched. Our relievers came through pretty well. Jones pitched in a situation that he should rarely expect to see this season, and he did not have enough in the end.

Meanwhile Jay Payton just robbed Barry Bonds of what may well have been #660. Obviously that historic home run, tying Willie Mays, Bonds' godfather, is going to happen. Hopefully it will be on so that we all get to see it. Steroid allegations be damned—once Griffey got hurt and Bonds had the seasons he's had the last few years, it became pretty clear that Bonds was the greatest player most of us have seen in our lifetime. My Uncle Nick was the first person who introduced me to Willie Mays, and he always argued that Mays was the greatest player he had ever seen, an opinion I have come to be willing to accept as plausible if not probable, and I have a hard time believing he was much better than Bonds.

My Uncle Nick is hugely responsible for my baseball passion. It's funny, because we rarely talk baseball any more—Nick has four kids, works like a horse, has become an avid golfer who now owns the local golf course that we used to sneak onto and play in my New Hampshire home town, but he still is the one man I look back on as a child (when he was a teenager and twentysomething himself) as being the biggest source of my passion for the game. He taught me the fundamentals—and was probably always disappointed when I did not take to hitting a tire a hundred times a day the way he felt I should to make me a good ballplayer. Nick was an exceptional athlete in high school, and baseball was his love. It is largely because of him, and my acquired passion for the game, that I became a pretty good baseball player when I was a kid and into high school. Unfortunately, my two best sports were baseball and track, and while I made a pretty important All Star team in 16 year old Babe Ruth, track was clearly the sport that was going to allow me truly to excel. The head baseball coach at Newport High, one of my favorite teachers, Larry Carle, made it clear that it would not be feasible for me to play Senior Babe Ruth because he coached that also and he had to go with his high school guys for the sake of the program. I never really blamed him then, though now, having coached high school and college for the last decade, I think that it was a bit nonsensical to say that a kid who wanted to play and was pretty good should not be able to simply because NHS might not benefit in the end. I did well in track, won three state championships and managed to parlay that into a decent college track career, but my love of baseball proved durable, and as much as anything my time with my Uncle Nick, and to a somewhat lesser degree my Uncle John, deserves much of the credit.

I'm honestly not sure if they are responsible for my Red Sox addiction. Surely they are to a good degree, as is my Dad, who would not have allowed any other option even though he was never as big a Sox fan as he was a football guy. I think this is an affliction that is based on geography and my own enthusiasms. I cannot remember ever not being a Sox fan, and I can remember a lot of dumb little kid stuff. I know that by the time Little League began I had been ready to play organized baseball for many years and by then I was a diehard.

And so back to tonight's rainy loss, I can't blame anyone. We could not hit when we needed to, and it is hard to blame the pitching, even poor Bobby Jones, for this loss. It is a long schedule in which even the greatest regular season team in history (the Mariners team that won 116 games three years back) lost 46 times, so there is no rational reason to lose sleep. Yet I probably will think about this one longer than most people think about vexing work or personal issues because, well, that's what we do as Red Sox fans. Languid summers are never quite so languid when your passions are inflamed and every game represents a battle for your heart that can never be won, but that can forestall heartbreak for another day.

Friday, April 9, 2004

Today was the first Sox game of the young season that I was unable to see. It was a 3 o'clock game, I was at the Foundation, and it was not televised anywhere here in Central Virginia. Worse, there is a problem with my computer at work, so it does not get sound. Despite the fact that I subscribed again to MLB.com so that I can get all of the Sox games on the radio, I had to follow along by ESPN's Gamecast, which tries to simulate the games with graphics on the screen, but which can be woefully inadequate, and vexingly slow to boot. Since I could see every game in the postseason and I listened to every regular season game in the fall that was not televised, this was probably the first Sox game I did not either see or listen to since last summer, when I was on the road researching.

I think I am probably just as happy for not having seen what looks to have been a disaster. They fell down early, fought back to make it 4-4, took a lead briefly, but in the end, the relievers, especially Timlin, could not keep us in the game, and we lost 10-5 to a Toronto team that had just gotten over a three game sweep at the hands of the Tigers. This is not good.

Last night's loss was rough and surely did not help—it certainly left our bullpen depleted, especially with Mendoza unable to pitch yesterday and going on the dl today. They called up one of the last cuts, Mark Malaska, a lefty reliever. Furthermore, because of mechanical issues, the Sox flight from BWI did not depart until very late, and they got into Logan at 6:30 and to Fenway at 7:24 on the day of a 3 pm game. Obviously the deck was stacked against them. Despite my optimism of a couple of days ago, and my now seemingly absurd prediction that we'd seen the last of both .500 and the Yankees, at least the bad guys lost today soon, so if we are limping through the first week of the season, so too are our chief allies.

Pedro gets the start tomorrow against Halladay. Both go into this game 0-1 and thus with something to prove. Pedro will be before the home crowd, and hopefully the temps are reasonable, and he'll hit his stride early and will roll. I guess I'll have to drag the laptop to the office and see if I can hook my computer up to get the Sox game. The lengths I go to . . .

Saturday, April 10, 2004

Giddyup. Pedro came out and made some money tonight. Manny and Ortiz hit home runs. Pedro went 7 2/3rds. It was exactly what we needed. Sox won 4-1, and more important, hopefully this performance puts to rest all of the talk about Pedro's arm slot and velocity and importance to the team and all of the rest of the whispers and moans that have characterized Pedro discussion the last few weeks. Pedro outpitched Roy Halladay, the Jays' ace, who gave up a two-run home run to Ortiz, plus a solo shot to Bellhorn. Manny hit a solo dinger off Aquilino Lopez. Foulke had his second save of the season. This was a good, good, win and it put us in position to take the series tomorrow when Schilling gets his chance to sing a refrain of "Anything You Can Do I Can Do Better." Pedro and Schilling will make each other better, just as Johnson and

Schilling had that effect on one another in Arizona. I suspect they will develop a good, friendly, but very real rivalry.

All of this said, what in the hell are the Red Sox doing playing a night game on a Saturday in April? What are they doing playing a night game on a weekend day anyway, unless it is a Sunday night ESPN game? In April in Boston it just gets damned chilly. But on top of that, if weekday games are evening games, if West Coast Games don't start until 10:00 real time, and if playoff games start late, when are kids going to be able to get into the rhythm of the season? As important, when will kids get to go to actual major league games? I love baseball so very much, and I just do not know if MLB and the owners are smart enough to grow a new generation of fans. It seems to me that Saturday afternoons ought to be reserved for baseball games.

Sunday, April 11, 2004

Win every series. That is the mantra my buddy Rob and I long ago established for a successful season. There will be losses. And sometimes you can't win every series. But if you go in and win two out of three most every time, you're on your way to the World Series. After losing on Friday night, the Sox got Pedro's performance last night and there was reason to be optimistic with Schilling making his Fenway debut today.

Schilling did not dominate. But he did his job—he kept us in the game. He gave up four runs in 8 innings. He struck out ten and walked no one. He was down when he left, but the guys rallied, and the game went into extra innings, though with the exception of Bobby Jones, who walked the only two guys he faced after the 13 inning Baltimore game where he walked in the last three in a row, including the game loser, we got good performances from our relief staff, including Mark Malaska, who would end up with the win. And we got that win in the same fashion that we won many games in the second half of last season—David Ortiz jacked one over the Monster with Bellhorn (who is proving to be an on base machine) on first. Walk off winner. The guys formed a semi-circle around the plate to greet Ortiz, their popular clutch hitting teammate. A 4-3 record after a week of play is not ideal, of course, but we are back to having a winning record, and we get a day off that actually is much needed even if it is only the second week of the season. Then Baltimore comes into Boston for a three game set before the first Yankees series of the year, the first game of which will happen on my 33rd birthday. Obviously the O's have shown that they can play us tough, and we need to hope that the Sox don't spend the week with an eye on the Yankees, because the O's are more than capable of putting us on our way to a losing streak.

In order to firm up the pitching staff, we signed the Lieutenant, Frank Castillo, who was last seen in a Sox uniform in 2000-2001, from Pawtucket. We had to designate Daubach for assignment. Hopefully we can get the Belleville Basher through waivers and onto the PawSox (which apparently is something he would be willing to do), because we will surely need him later in the season. Dauber is a quality guy, someone who finally clawed his way to the big leagues after what appeared to be a career destined to be spent knocking around the minors, and he helped the Sox a good deal in his four years before he was sent packing before last year, which he spent with the Pale Hose on Chicago's South Side. I'd as soon see him in a Sox uniform for this run we all hope to make. The problem is that he is part of the usual Sox glut of lumbering first basemen-designated hitters-barely passable outfielders. We have Kevin Millar, Gabe Kaplar, and David McCarty to go along with Ortiz, who obviously is a cut above those guys. When we hit a pitching crunch, that reservoir is a logical place to go to free up a roster spot. Hopefully these guys are aware that in the long run, they will all be able to play a role. Of course, when Nomar and Trot and Kim are ready to come back, we are going to need to free up some space, and several of those guys, along with Cesar Crespo and one or two of the pitchers, need to be prepared to change their Sox, probably fairly often until the rosters open up at the end of the summer. Nonetheless, all of them will have a role to play, just as role players like McCarty and Damian Jackson were vital at times last year. It's a given that superstars have to perform, but so do role players, for a team to achieve the sorts of heights that lead to October glories.

Monday, April 12, 2004

Today is an off day. I hate off days. I suppose this is a trait that one would expect from a somewhat obsessive-compulsive fan, but I really do love the rhythm of a baseball season where nearly every day my team plays. I know they need the day off, of course, especially the game but gimpy bullpen, but I always feel restless on days when they don't play. Worse yet, there is rain forecast for the next few days from here as far north as Maine, so we may well be looking at a few off days.

And it is miserable out. I know April showers bring May flowers, but they are also keeping me cooped up in the house all day—have not yet finalized getting the car I've bought from Matt or securing a Virginia license, which is only slightly easier to do than getting National Security clearance these days. I can hear my grandfather asking me, "What, are you, sugar? You aren't gonna melt." But frankly it is raw and miserable out, and I don't want to risk dissolving.

This is a truly rough April schedule, as we play most all of our games against the heart of the AL East. It should bode well if we can manage to finish the month in first, although the Sox have always had a tendency to play to the level of their competition, so that we can beat the Yankees but somehow the Rangers or Indians will play us tough. We also tend to let the interleague games (get rid of 'em!) throw us for a loop—I am almost positive that we have a losing record against National League teams since interleague play began.

One benefit that we might derive from today but also from an extended break if the weather wreaks havoc up in Fenway is that the guys on the injured list can continue to improve while missing a minimal number of games. I am a bit skeptical about Nomar's injury in particular—this has all the hallmarks of a lingering, and even chronic, injury in an especially sensitive area. Even when he is ready to do full baseball activities, he's going to need some time to recover—he only had eight at bats during spring training, and he was 0 for 8, so his timing will clearly need work. I just hope that when he does come back he does so at full strength. It will also be great to get Trot back, especially to face righthanded pitching and to upgrade an outfield defense that is pretty scary, especially with Damon also missing a few games due to swelling from taking a foul ball off the top of his knee Friday night. Kim's return will allow us to have either him or Arroyo as a swing man/long reliever, which we seem to lack right now, though hopefully Castillo can be a stopgap. Then again, if he were that reliable of an option, wouldn't he have been with us long before now? The fact is that we were lucky last year with injuries. We are somewhat snakebitten now. Hopefully we'll pull through this, some guys will step up and provide us with vital experience that will pay off if we need it down the stretch, and guys will step it up. With our starting rotation, long losing streaks should be rare, stoppers plentiful, though hopefully there will not be a lot of stopping to be done.

In any case, it's a dull, cold, rainy, yucky day, and not one for baseball. At least these three games upcoming against the Orioles will be on television here in Charlottesville, and Friday's game is going to be televised in what I believe will be Fox's earliest ever regular season telecast. That almost makes it worth the wait.

By the way — Barry Bonds hit number 660 today, tying him with Willie Mays. For almost my entire life, the order never changed — Aaron, Ruth, Mays. Now Bonds is among them, and soon he will be pushing 700. I think he'll pass Ruth in May or June of next year, Aaron in late 2006. I hope the steroid talk turns out to be nothing, because right now, Bonds is easily in a conversation involving a very short list of guys: Who is the greatest player of all time? Rarefied air, to be sure.

Tuesday, April 13, 2004

Well, I cannot say that I did not know that today's rain delay was coming. And they announced it early enough in the afternoon to forestall arriving at home ready to watch the game only to find it in delay or postponed late. Still, I hate rain delays and postponements. I hated them when I played sports as a kid. I hate them now when they disrupt the rhythm of the season. Regularly scheduled off days are bad enough, but at least they are the function of the schedulemakers and can be seen as an imposed virtue — yesterday's day off (and I have to admit, today's unplanned respite) will prove good to a bullpen that has been overtaxed in this young season, and provide days for our walking wounded to recover without losing games on the schedule. But rain delays — yuck.

Though at the ballpark I have a few memorable rain delays.

Last summer, for example, my group Fair Game sang at Camden Yards before a planned game with Toronto, only to have inclement conditions wipe the game out soon after our performance (which was riveting, thank you very much). Last summer also I was at a Cubs-Marlins game at Wrigley that took place on a rainy weekend — I got to go to back to back games, both of which were delayed. The first game was beset by a mid-game downfall that was torrential. By the ninth inning, it was summer again. The second day was rainy intermittently, almost never completely stopping, and again by the end it was pretty sunny. I've been in rain delays in Yankee Stadium and Fenway, and probably several other places too, though rarely have I had to deal with postponements.

But a day at the park is a day at the park and carries with it its own virtues. When you are at home, you want the games to be played. You want highlights on Sportscenter, and you want the mini-morality play of how your team performed versus how the bad guys did, who blessed your day with home runs or shutouts or a dramatic play versus who cursed you with errors or 0-fers or the sin of failing to run out a ground ball.

At least tonight the Bruins beat the Canadiens in double overtime to take a 3-1 lead in what has been a thrilling but fortunately thus far ultimately lopsided series. The Canadiens have had a couple of guys take dives in order to try to persuade the refs to call penalties, and fortunately the men in stripes have not fallen for shenanigans and the hockey gods have proved wrathful toward such treachery and deceit. We can wrap it up at home on Thursday, concurrent with the game against the O's in what will be a Boston sports fans spring bonanza.

Wednesday, April 14, 2004

Another rain delay tonight. I came home ready to watch the game, only to see the lowly, wretched, goddawful Wizards on the tv screen. I knew that Comcast could not possibly have a sense of humor that cruel, but it took a while to find out that the game had been officially called.

Apparently we are looking to make these games up during one of the two upcoming Orioles visits to Fenway later in the season. This makes sense for the Sox, who, as I alluded to yesterday, want to have Nomar, Trot, and Kim available to them next time around and for as many games as possible. Nonetheless, while that may be good for us now, racking up doubleheaders later in the season, when there are fewer off days, the summer begins to take its toll, the race is tighter, and inevitably guys are a bit worn may not be wholly in our best interest. At some point you pay the piper, you play the games. Delay can be useful to rest and heal, but not if it happens at the expense of the latter part of the season. It is better at some point to battle through injuries and pitching staff shortages now than to have to confront them closer to the playoffs.

Tomorrow is scheduled to be another home game against the Os. Though it is still a bit on the gray and rainy side, it is drier here than it has been, and Rob thought even that tonight would be clear, so hopefully the weather will turn for the better up North so that we can get one win against the Orioles and be ready for the arrival of the infidel bastards from the Bronx.

Thursday, April 15, 2004

Apparently the Red Sox want to make up for lost time, because they are now in the tenth inning against the Orioles in what unexpectedly turned out to be a truncated one-game series in Fenway, an appetizer before the four game main course that starts tomorrow with the Yankees in town.

Pedro was not Pedro tonight. Or, in a thought most of us do not want to consider, the new Pedro is still coming to grips with not being the dominant force he once was—maybe this, albeit in exaggerated and negative form, *is* Pedro now. Obviously it is premature to throw dirt on the grave, but I doubt we'll ever see the Pedro of 1998-2001, though then again, there may have never been a better, more dominant pitcher than that Pedro. Lowe was supposed to go tonight, but Francona and Wallace decided that they wanted Pedro to go on four days rest, and so he got the start. In five innings he gave up seven runs, never established a rhythm, and certainly did not have the Orioles coming to the plate tentative and worried. He fell down 2-0, the Sox scored five in the second, the O's mounted a little rally, the Sox responded, and when it was 7-4 Pedro's buddy David Segui tomahawked one into the O's bullpen and just like that it was 7-7. Obviously this will start the "what's wrong with Pedro" questions rolling again. It will be overkill, but is there an element of truth to it? The O's coverage on Comcast does not show radar results, but I doubt he got above 91 or even got that high very often. He labored to get through five innings. Since then neither offense has been able to get at the succession of relievers. It is halfway through the 10th and the Sox are coming up—I hope that we can manage to get some runs and leave something in the bullpen for the weekend.

Kaplar singled with one out, and now Bellhorn is up. He's been an on base machine, but isn't really an RBI guy. Nonetheless, we have Crespo coming up, and so we need some production from the bottom third of the order like we got last year. This is where the injuries are hurting us, as missing Trot and Nomar weakens our lineup all the way down the order. Bellhorn walked. Hopefully Crespo can . . . nope—popup to third base foul territory. They are bringing in Groom. He nails Damon with a pitch off the elbow. Damon didn't make much of a move to get out of the way. Mueller is up—long shot to the Monstar, but Mantos makes a grab against the wall, and the rally is done. Ugh. Bases loaded and we leave them stranded. That has the potential to be the big missed opportunity of the night.

Miguel Tejada led off the inning with a home run against Arroyo, Monday's scheduled starter, that bounced right off the top of the Monster—the Monster giveth, the Monster taketh away—that is the epigram of Fenway Park. And just like that, the O's have an 8-7 lead after an inning when the Sox should damn well have found a way to score. Palmeiro beat the shift we always put on him for a single, so the damage could be worse, though a lineout to Damon gets the first out of the inning. You know, it is amazing to me how the Sox have had three off days and yet it still feels as if we are plumbing the depths of our bullpen. Arroyo is the seventh pitcher we've thrown out there tonight. Meanwhile Gibbons bounces one into the right field corner, it got away from Kaplar, and Palmeiro is in to give them a two run cushion. Egads. 9-7. In any case, one of the problems of our pitching staff is that it still bears the marks of the closer by committee – we have a bunch of guys who are built more for one inning than for three. But if the starter goes only five and the game goes extra innings, that leads to a shortage if every one of those guys pitches to only 2-3-4 hitters. In this sense, assuming he can be effective, Kim's return may be as important as that of Nomar and Nixon.

Walk to Tim Raines, Jr. God, I remember his father's rookie season. Sports are a cruel barometer of age, of where one's youth is. For so much of my life, professional athletes were grownup men who seemed not only larger than life, but old. As the years have passed since high school, I've creeped up on them, and suddenly I hear announcers referring to guys my age, especially in a sport like football, or in a position like catcher, as being old, grey beards, risky to sign for their age, and the like. Meanwhile, I am still precocious in my career. But I can feel my body responding much differently than it did even a few years back. I was a college athlete, I competed seriously after college, including playing rugby in South Africa, and yet now if I twist funny in my desk chair I run the risk of pulling something. Of course maybe I'm just in lousy shape.

Sox have let the O's load the bases, there is one out, and Phil Seibel, our eighth pitcher of the night, is making his major league debut, having just been called up from Pawtucket. We got him off of waivers from the Mets in the offseason. Jesus — Bigbie hits a ground ball shot off the glove of Millar. Everyone's safe and Gibbon scores. Bases still loaded and the O's are up 10-7. They scored it an error. That's a tough call. Even tougher is that Seibel walked in the fourth run of the inning. 11-7. And young Mr. Seibel is joining seven other guys in the shower. Maybe Castillo can stanch the bleeding. This is endlessly frustrating. Melvin Mora, bases loaded single, Mantos in to score. Shit fuck damn. 12-7. Hooray! A sarcastic cheer goes up from the rapidly thinning throngs. Casatillo induced a ground ball double play. From 7-7 with our guys on all of the bags to a 12-7 deficit as the pitching staff implodes.

Ortiz – fly out. Manny — K. So we're down to Millar — and ladies and gentlemen, there's your ballgame. No Rally Karaoke Guy tonight. Millar whiffs. The Sox give up five runs in the top of the eleventh and it's done. Nothing to say. Just ugly. Pedro couldn't get it done, the bats scored 7 but none after the fifth, and we use nine pitchers with no real apparent rhyme or reason. And to top it off, the Bruins lost 5-1 in game 5 of their series. We need to forget about this one soon — Yankees are in town tomorrow, and we need to be ready.

Silver lining—National Champion UConn men's basketball coach Jim Calhoun, lifelong Sox fan, told the Yanks to go to hell when they asked him to throw out the opening pitch at one of their games. But apparently he is going to throw out the opening pitch at one of the games this weekend in Fenway. Wake-Vazquez, Schill-Mussina, Lowe-Contreras, Arroyo-Mussina are the pitching matchups in these four games. Let's send a statement.

And God Bless you, Jackie Robinson. God Bless You.

Friday, April 16, 2004

Today the Kid (your friendly diarist, not Ted Williams, the original Kid, aka The Splendid Splinter, aka Teddy Ballgame) turned the palindromic age of 33. Thirty three years of painful losses, near misses, and frustrations. In these 33 years I have probably uttered my ultimate phrase of disgust, "Fucking Red Sox," 33,333 times.

Nonetheless, my birthday present for tonight is a prime time airing of Game one of nineteen Sox-Yankees games this year. We start a four game series against the Evil Empire (I used that damned phrase long before Lucchino did, dammit!) in Fenway. It is starting right now. I'll see the first 2-3 innings here, and then one of my colleagues, Larissa, and I are heading in to town so that I can pretend that I am not pathetic on my birthday, and I can spread the Red Sox love in one of Charlottesville's fine establishments. Barkeep—libations please!

Good first inning. 1-2-3 for Waker, including Jeter and A-Rod. In our half, Damon got on on an error. Mueller came up and blasted one off the façade separating the Yanks' bullpen from the centerfield bleachers. It's 2-0 good guys. I let out a whoop, and my landlord's dogs upstairs got to barking—they won't stop until Eben and Kathy are home. Oh well—all for a good cause. I'll just pretend they are Sox fans arfing at A-Rod. Well, they have a lot to arf about now—Manny just clipped one past the Pesky Pole. It looked like it bounced off the wall and Sheffield thought it to be a foul—Manny would have gotten three bases anyway. 3-0. YeeHaw! Millar just thumped one off of the Monster for a long, loud single. Vazquez is getting pounded. I've said all along that showing potential and talent in Montreal is not the same as dealing with the glare of Boston-New York, even in April. Jeter just made a nice play, diving to his right to stop the ball and throwing from his right knee to clip Millar, nailing the lead runner. I still hate Jeter, the most overrated superstar in some time. He is also the second best shortstop on the left side of the Yankees' infield. Bellhorn walked—he is leading the American League in bases on balls—and Vasquez is getting a little visit from Stottlemeyer. The Yankees' new pitcher seems to have a case of Sphincter-pucker under these bright lights. Derek Jeter, aka Captain Intangibles, just let a ball go through the wickets! Another run in. Hopefully the crowd has started chanting "A-Rod's better!" to foment dissent for the Yanks. The good folks at Sons of Sam Horn have been encouraging this sort of behavior, which I heartily endorse. Actually, SoSH got some good publicity last night on ESPN's Outside the Lines. SoSH is closed to new members, so I cannot even post there! It's annoying, but at least they are trying to maintain quality control. In any case, the Yankees stopped the bleeding and got out of the first. Sox take a 4-0 lead into the second.

Obviously this game has been overhyped. That said, I am glad we got out to this start. It may be overhyped, but certainly every game is going to matter this year, and beating the Yankees always feels good. It goes without saying that no real fan can like both the Yankees and the Red Sox. Certainly one cannot claim to be a Sox fan and feel anything but antipathy and loathing for the Yankees. As I have said, I do not remember becoming a Sox fan—it has always been a part of me, a natural reflex, if not genetic then part of a very early nature-nurture, environmental cycle. Similarly, I do not remember developing a sense of hatred for the Yankees. I just hated them *a priori*. It comes naturally to me, and feels so very good.

Posada just got a run back by taking a nonknuckling knuckler off the wall just to the right of the Monster where it is a home run. I hate Jorge Posada. The damage is contained however, as Wakefield got out of the inning with just that run. We don't look to Waker, one of the least appreciated pitchers in baseball the last few years, for shutouts. We want innings, we want him to provide a contrast from our other guys, especially Schilling and Pedro, and we want him to be a gamer. If he can keep us in the game, give us quality starts, he'll be the best fourth starter in the league.

Interesting Fox quiz geared toward Sox fans—who is your most hated Yankee—Bucky Dent, Aaron Boone, or George Steinbrenner.

Let's scratch Boone. Boone killed us, but he does not warrant mention in the same breath as the other two. Boone was a mercenary wearing that uniform. He hurt us, but he does not embody Yankee-ness in anything but the most circumstantial way. Dent was my initial response. He killed me in 1978. That was probably my formative Red Sox moment—I can remember being a fan before then, and I must have been, as I camped in front of the tube passionate about that game, but that is my first crystalline memory as a Red Sox fan. Scarring as the aftermath of first love. It would be like having your first date with the high school girl you think you are destined to marry end with a kick in the nuts.

Larissa is here. Time to hit a bar, watch the game, and pretend I have a life. . . .

Good times for this 33 year old guy. I may be old, but the Sox gave me a victory I damn well deserved. I was able to see most of the scoring right here at home—after I left the Yanks put up a harmless run, the Sox added one on a Mirabelli ribbie. Waker and then Williamson made it tense, loading the bases in the 8th (after a Manny drop in the outfield, but he hustled after it—leave the guy alone!) but the relief corps, especially Embree (was nasty against Matsui—hmm, could we have used him in game 7 last year when Pedro was laboring?) and Foulke, shut them down. We won. It was a good game. Waker went deep, the relievers did their job, and we took the lead in the series. I got to go out on my 33rd. Larissa and I had a good time. And, as important, my feelings about Red Sox Nation were reaffirmed. We went to Buffalo Wild Wings, a chain that was one of my haunts up in Minnesota and where my buddy worked in Athens, even though I tend to oppose chains in principle, and there were easily 10 Sox fans for every Yankees fan. Yankees fans tend to be visible and loud and opportunistic. But every place I have ever been, all polls about the Yankee fandom (they are bandwagon jumpers—don't kid yourselves) be damned, there have been more Sox fans.

There are three games left in this series. There are more than 150 games left. It is a long season. But don't let anyone tell you that this one was not sweet. It was. Sometimes a taste of sugar is good even if the long-term health benefits are up for debate. By the way, I hate the fucking Yankees.

Saturday, April 17, 2004

It's only April. We still have 17 games against the Yankees, then perhaps a postseason matchup. Next weekend we get them in their place, and their fans will be ready. Still, today Curt Schilling went out and did precisely what we all dreamed about in deepest, darkest winter after he signed with us and rhetorically asked on that first day, "So I guess I hate the Yankees now, huh?" He knows the history of this rivalry. He knows better than to mouth the platitudes of so many other players who insist that all games mean the same, that the rivalry is more for the fans, that they try to win every game. Schilling plays with passion, and he damned well knows that these games are of immense importance for everyone involved. He knows that the fans, especially our fans, are not idiots—if we are this into it, it has to mean something. Indeed, it is fans who determine worth, ultimately, as we are the consumers, the market, the audience.

Schilling was apparently visibly angry in the seventh when Francona went to the mound and took him out with two outs and one guy on base. He wanted the ball in his hands. He wanted to close out the game and to be on the mound when the handshakes were exchanged. But it is Francona's job to manage the staff. He is showing a Sparky Anderson-esque propensity for the hook, but hopefully it will pay off later in the season. Schilling gave up one run and the Yankees never really mounted a threat. The Sox got two in the first on some serious Mussina sloppiness—all of those runs came even though the Sox mustered but one bloop hit, as he walked in one and then hit Bellhorn to walk in the second run. Later Manny hit a home run into the Monster seats, his third of the year. Schilling (1 earned run, 8 Ks, 4 walks, 6 hits in 6 2/3rds innings) and the bullpen cruised, and we won another one where there were few real moments when it looked like things might turn, this time by a score of 5-2.

In other Boston sports news today, the Celts got mauled in Game one of their series against the Pacers, and the Bruins imploded, losing 5-2 to bring about a 7th game in the Fleet, a scenario that most of us hate to see given the tortured history between the Bruins and the Canadiens, our historic tormentors.

Tomorrow D-Lowe takes the mound. This is a big game, but not one where he should be feeling a lot of stress. The Yankees are not hitting well. We are making the most of opportunities and are putting up runs on the scoreboard early. A win would mean we take this series and are set up for a sweep, though Monday's game is the traditional Patriots' Day game, and amidst the earliest start in the majors every year the hoopla surrounding the marathon, we too often get thumped in this little tradition. Nonetheless, this is as good a start as one could have hoped for, and we have a chance to keep it going.

I listened to the game in my office. It was gorgeous out, about 80 degrees with a nice breeze. Summer appears to be peeking out after a too brief, teasing spring. It's perfect baseball weather, perfect Yankee-stomping weather. While it was nippy last night in Fenway, apparently the weather has warmed up in Boston and the conditions were great. Hopefully they'll have to deal with fewer cold days, though there will still be night contests when the mercury will dip, but with May approaching it would be good to be able to rely on cooperative Mother Nature, especially on Pedro's nights. But today was Schilling's. This was the stuff of November dreams of October glory, and is one of the main reasons that the Yankees may well not sleep quite as easily when the race heats up and the fall approaches. They may not be sleeping great now—A-Rod is hitting .171. That will change, but hopefully not this weekend.

Sunday, April 18, 2004

We never expected to sweep the Yankees. We hoped to. Two quick and easy wins gave that hope fuel. But we never really thought we'd sweep. Good thing. Because today we lost, and we lost in a pretty ugly way. Most of that ugliness sprung from the capricious right arm of Derek Lowe. 2 and 2/3rds of an inning. 8 hits, 4 walks and 7 earned runs. Against the Mariners, all of this might be seen as an outlier, a bad performance that we can all pass off as an insignificant performance early in the year. These luxuries will not be afforded a guy whose makeup a lot of Sox cognoscenti have been questioning for years, a guy whose highs have never been given as much faith as his lows have fueled angst, and whose next bad pitch is always more worrisome than his last good pitch has been gratifying. The glimmer of light is that Lowe's performance today might give a respite to the worries over the dark cloud seemingly hovering over

Pedro, whose highs transcend his rare lows by such an enormous margin.

It was an ugly day at Fenway. We started off well, getting a quick 2-0 lead, but by the time Lowe left we were down 7-2 and from there on out we never really challenged. This despite the fact that we clearly were able to get to Contreras, whose ineffectiveness would have been the story of the day had the early lead held. Today our decimated lineup brought about a recurrence of the worried chatter that held sway during the games against the Orioles. Even where we had chances today the weak spots in the lineup seemed glaring. Wins will cover up a multitude of flaws.

I'm not yet willing to worry about Pedro. Similarly, I am sure that D-Lowe will be fine. We are not always going to be on our game. We can not reasonably expect to sweep the Yankees in all of the series in which we'll meet this year. But what is crucial is that tomorrow we face Kevin Brown in a game in which Bronson Arroyo will go out for what on paper is a seeming mismatch. We need a good performance by our unheralded starter, and the only way to think that is feasible will be for the bats to give him some room to work. We cannot expect him to have to go out and shut down the Yankees' lineup. We cannot bask in the ineptitude of A-Rod (0 for 12 thus far in this series and sitting well below the Mendoza Line). We cannot think that getting off to a quick 2 or 3 run lead assures us of anything. Maybe against the blue Jays or Indians or even the A's. Not against the Yankees. We may hate them, but we have to respect them.

Tomorrow is the traditional Patriot's Day game. This uniquely Massachusetts holiday commemorates and celebrates Paul Revere's Ride and the resultant victory in the Revolutionary War. Well, not only are the Yankees coming, they are here, and we need to know that the 2-0 series lead that fueled so much euphoria and gloating is long gone. ESPN will have the game tomorrow. We're back in a dogfight with the Yankees. Tomorrow will be a good test of character and drive. Forget about today and move on and win the only game that really matters—the next one.

Monday, April 19, 2004 (Patriots' Day)

Happy Patriots' Day! And a happy day it may turn out to be. After falling behind by a score of 4-1, we have clawed and scratched and fought and eked our way back.

In the last inning, the eighth, Matsui misplayed a David McCarty fly ball, McCarty was generously given a double, and we managed to get him across the plate on a Gabe "Welcome Back!" Kaplar single. We scored our first run in the second when Kaplar singled, driving in Varitek, who had also hit a single. Our second run came when Ortiz drove in Mueller, who had hit a single. Tek hit a home run to lead off the 6th. Our fourth and tying run came courtesy of A-Rod, who committed his first error of the series. Pokey Reese had gotten on with a single off Brown, who then gave way to Gabe White, who looks like either a porn star or a child molester. Damon singled, sending Pokey to third. Ortiz then came up, checked his swing, but not before tapping a dribbler back to Rodriguez who paused indecisively and then belatedly threw the ball toward Wilson at second, instead sending the ball off into right field, allowing Pokey to score. We went at coming back a run at a time, and Arroyo kept us in the game even after a couple of rough innings.

Foulke is now on to relieve—and he just got Jeter out on a called third strike over the outside part of the plate. Jeter is apoplectic. It was a nice call for Foulke, but not one most guys should think they can take in a close game. Jeter took the chance and it did not pay off. Bernie Williams just hit one to the Wall, and Manny caught it on the run, slightly colliding with the scoreboard almost simultaneously as he gloved the ball. And now A-Rod is at the plate—too perfect. He's 0 for 16 in the series, and now he gets a chance either at redemption or else for us to put an exclamation point on things—he singles to left. So he broke his slump. Congratulations A-Rod! 1 for 17 with a single and no RBI. That's the same number of runs driven in and just one more hit than Nomar had in this series! Of course Nomar did not commit an error to tie the game. In any case, with A-Rod in the of late unaccustomed position of being a baserunner, Giambi is up. He is 3 for 14 all time against Foulke, but 2 of those hits are home runs. It's a 1-2 count. The first finisher of the Boston Marathon (the women started a half hour early for the first time) have crossed the finish line. So have the Red Sox – called strike and Giambi is out. What began as a fairly sloppy start turned out well, we battled back and we managed to take a hard fought series 3-1. Timlin gets the win, Foulke the save. I desperately need to get to work. More tonight after the Bruins' game 7. . . .

Ugh. The Bruins lost 2-0 in what was a fiercely fought defensive game. It was 0-0 going into the third and we seemed to dominate the first half or so of the final period, but then Montreal ran a goal through, and at the end, when we were pressing, they got yet another empty net goal. Season over. This is the second time in three years a heavily favored Bruins team lost to the Canadiens. And this time we had a 3-1 series lead. Not that the Celtics are going to get it done, but many of us just lost out on the dream of a Patriots, Bruins, Sox run in calendar year 2004.

Much to feel good about with the Red Sox, though plenty to worry about also. Pedro goes against the Jays tomorrow. They have been awful, but Pedro has been having a rough go of it as well, so I am hopeful that he can get on track and the bats can start to pick up their production. We cannot let down now that the big series is done, and we have to know that they will be ready to exact some revenge this weekend. They'll deny it, of course, tossing out all of the regular clichés about how early it is and how every series matters, and how the Red Sox are a great team but so are we and blah blah blah. But they know the truth and so do we. They'll be waiting for us. Hopefully we'll go into the Bronx focused — and on a winning streak.

Tuesday, April 20, 2004

I guess we can suppose that the simple answer to Pedro's woes is not simply that he has lost it. Granted, I am at Ken and Michelle's, my dear DC (actually Arlington) friends, so I did not see the game, and I am relying on sketchy reports from Sportscenter and Baseball Tonight. That said, it seems to me that 7 innings, 1 earned run, and 6 hits, if I read the line right, should be cause to praise and not to bury Pedro. We beat the Blue Jays, who admittedly are looking far less formidable than their offseason would have predicted, by a 4-2 score.

This is all good. Pedro pitched well. The bats are still pretty somnolent, but they came through enough to win. They kept up the win streak and the momentum coming after the Yankees' series. This is a series that lent itself to letdown and the guys came through. In all, without having seen the game or any substantial box scores or even highlights, I have to think we are on the right path, even if the Yanks and Orioles won. Let's hope we can score ten runs tomorrow. The offense needs it.

Wednesday, April 21, 2004

The offense did not need ten runs today. All it needed was Wakefield on the mound, two home runs from his private catcher, Doug Mirabelli, and an opponent like the Blue Jays, who have yet to win at home, the longest such streak to start a season since 1995. We pulled off a 4-2 victory, and with Schilling slated to go tomorrow, it is pretty reasonable to think that we can sweep this series and head into the Yankees' game on a winning streak.

There are those who doubt the wisdom or necessity of a knuckleballer having his own catcher, but in all honesty, I don't quite get those criticisms, especially in the case of the Red Sox. Wakefield feels more comfortable with Mirabelli behind the plate — in and of itself that seems pretty important to me. If Wake feels that Mirabelli gives him the best chance to pitch well, how does it hurt? This is especially true since Tek needs to be spelled every so often — this way he knows when he'll be off, and yet he can be ready to pinch hit, especially late in the game if Waker is out. Further, Mirabelli can play. He's not some hack out there just to appease Waker's ego — he had a lot of big hits for us down the stretch and during the postseason last year, and as his performance tonight shows, the guy can win games with his bat as long as we don't go to that well too often, or expect him to be the magic wand for a sputtering offense. So guys like the insufferable Tim McCarver can claim that maintaining a special catcher for knuckleballers is silly. I do not care, Tim Wakefield does not care, Mirabelli and Varitek don't care (I bet Varitek is more than happy not to be chasing that ball all over the place) and as long as Mirabelli contributes to us winning, the rest of the Red Sox fans won't care either. In the end, it is about winning. For this utterly forgettable April game, Mirabelli and Waker were the key players in a victory that, while not especially memorable counts every bit as much in the standings as more publicized, exciting, or sexy games.

Thursday, April 22, 2004

Never assume anything during the regular season. If ever I figured we would win a game and thus sweep a series, it was tonight. Toronto has simply not been very good this season. We had won the first two games of this series and had Toronto on the ropes, with Schilling set to close the series out and lead us into the Bronx Toilet Bowl feeling pretty good. Instead, he appears not to have had an especially good start and we lost 7-3. I do not know any more detail than this—I am in Pittsburgh for my brother's graduation from an MA program at Pitt, sharing a hotel with Dad, and we just got back from dinner, so I have not seen any highlights, or, perhaps, lowlights. While here we plan to catch a Pirates game or two—they are heading into a home series against Ken Griffey, Adam Dunn, and the rest of the Reds, and in my eternal quest to catch games in every stadium (or at least every city—I missed the chance to see a game at the old Three Rivers Stadium, a shame only from a completist's vantage point, as that was one of the old cookie cutter multipurpose stadia that was a blight on baseball for three decades or so) this is a great opportunity.

The Yanks are losing but the O's won, so we are back into second place in the East. They are en route to New York now, and D-Lowe takes the mound tomorrow after his rough Sunday outing. Hopefully he, like Pedro, will find his groove again and we can continue this early season run against them. Just as Schilling's early season dominance provided no guarantees of success tonight, Lowe's struggles on Sunday do not of necessity mean that his sinker won't befuddle the Yankees tomorrow. This is what makes baseball so wonderful, frustrating, vexing, and above all, unpredictable. This is why, as they say, they play the games.

Friday, April 23, 2004

Hey—who just won, 11-2? I'll tell you. The Sox just did. And they did so 11-2. By which I mean we kicked their asses. We hit four home runs, including a three-run shot by Bill Mueller and by Millar and Bellhorn (back to back) and Manny. D-Lowe carried a shutout into the seventh inning. Mike Timlin and newcomer Lenny DiNardo took over took over the last three innings to close out the game. Meanwhile the Yankees' fans, God bless their tiny brains and withered souls, booed A-Rod and Contreras. The Yankees, with their $185 million payroll are now 8-9.

No sense making too much of this, of course, but the Yankees are suffering something that usually afflicts the Red Sox, and as a consequence, their fans: Frustration at expectation. That lineup, that offense, was supposed to be a juggernaut. And realistically it probably will be. (To put things in comparative perspective, the Red Sox 6-9 hitters have hit better, driven in more runs, hit more home runs, and scored more than the Yanks' 1-4 slots in the five games head to head this season) But the Yanks are struggling right now, and those fans are not a patient lot. It is early, of course, but just as I want to put the Orioles away, to erase any fantasies of them being able to compete for the duration of the season, I would love to see the Yankees fall several games below .500. They radically changed their pitching staff and they brought in several free agents over the course of the offseason—say this about them, after losing the World Series the Yankees don't stand pat—and at least early on, it seems not to be working. Surely when we get down to the wire the Yankees will be the team to beat, but it is nice to see them scuffling, and it is especially nice to see us as the team largely responsible for it. Right now, a tenth of the way into the season, we are better than they are.

Saturday, April 24, 2004

This is almost too enjoyable—we beat the Yankees again today, this time in 12 innings, 3-2. In six games this year, we have beaten them five times. We have beaten them in blowouts, we have beaten them in nailbiters, we have beaten them when we came from behind and we have pulled out to quick leads and never had to look back. We have beaten them with Schilling and we have beaten them with Arroyo. With that one exception last Sunday, the one constant has been victory.

Today's was as peculiar as any. We left 19 men in scoring position without driving in one, something that has not been done since 1974 or 1977 depending on whether one believes Baseball Tonight or Sportscenter. Leaving men on base has always been our big Achilles heel, but somehow we managed to get it done today, largely because of our stellar relief pitching and a sacrifice fly by

Bellhorn in the 12th (apparently they are talking about official at bats, because Manny was on third, so obviously Bellhorn drove him in). Arroyo kept us in it again with an outstanding start. Further, while A-Rod has started to hit, Jeter is in something like a 0 for 40 slump right now. Apropos of nothing save my own schadenfreude, Roger Clemens is hitting higher (3 for 9, .333) than any Yankee starter.

Obviously this will not last forever. The Yankees are too talented not to right this ship. Steinbrenner will not allow them to fade, and he will not sit idly by as the Red Sox run away from them. Further, at some point our bloopers will not fall in, our knucklers will not befuddle them, passed balls will find their way into catcher's mitts. Their hits will fall, their fly balls will soar over the fence, their pitches will break sharper. This will be a race until the end, and given history and the weight on our shoulders, we would be best off not to be smug about all of this.

Sunday, April 25, 2004

Sweep! With a version of Pedro that looked remarkably akin to his vintage incarnation keeping the Yankees' bats silent, the Sox completed a three game sweep in the Bronx. It was not televised, but I got to follow the score through a rain delay at PNC Park, the Pirates' beautiful home stadium on the Allegheny River.

On Friday Dad and I had walked a long route down the river and then around the two stadia, Heinz Field and PNC. PNC does a great job of evoking the Pirates' history, and while the stadium is obviously part of the trend of retro parks, it does not do so self-consciously, and it does not try to be too cute. It is a good old fashioned, fan friendly baseball stadium. And today, at least, the home team put on a good show. The rain delay was three hours, and in fact Marcus, my newly minted MA brother, will get to use the tickets for another game because the delay was so long, but they did get in a game. The Pirates won 6-0 in a game in which their starting pitcher, Oliver Perez, threw a complete game shutout, keeping the Reds to just a handful of harmless hits. The Pirates hit a couple of home runs, and once the game got going, it was a nice, sunny day. Marcus, who as a result of some sort of bizarre atavism is not a huge sports fan, nonetheless enjoyed himself. We walked much of the stadium, had perfectly acceptable bleacher seats that were nice enough that we did not feel compelled to move elsewhere, and we had ballpark food, a beer, and just a nice time. I can now add Pittsburgh and PNC to the cities and ballparks where I have seen a game.

7 innings pitched, 4 hits, a walk, and 7 strikeouts. This may not be the Pedro of 2000, but it sure stands as a line that once and for all should erase those worries that Pedro cannot get it done any more. As so often has happened in the past five years, the guys did not give them a lot of runs, but two (on a Manny home run that he absolutely crushed) proved to be enough, and some credit should go to Vazquez, who finally showed up. So in a series where we did not exactly score a ton, we can pull out the brooms. We have taken 6 of 7 against the Yankees. We are in first place. Around the corner we will get Nomar and Trot back to bolster the offense which, for all of the pride in how we have played, has not exactly been a juggernaut. And we will get Kim back, who should be the final piece of the puzzle for a pitching staff that has really come around – the bullpen is on a serious hot streak: in consecutive days Foulke, Timlin, and today Williamson racked up saves.

Tomorrow we get another off day, this one well earned. I travel back to DC early in the morning (up at 4 – 4 1/2 hours from now—for a 6:00 flight) and will probably try to get right back to Charlottesville tomorrow, unless someone is around and wants to do something— unlikely since it is Monday and Ken and Michelle are out of town, plus I have to be back in Fairfax on Thursday, and thus back to DC on Wednesday night. April is winding down, the Bruins and Celtics (Indiana finished off an ugly sweep of us this afternoon) done, and the NFL draft over, it is definitely time for baseball, baseball, and more baseball. We swept the Yankees, we are in first, and we are not even at full strength. Hopefully this bodes well and is a starting point rather than an early peak.

Monday, April 26, 2004

Today was an off day as Mondays so often are. No real news from Red Sox camp. A day off is a day to heal, to rest, especially for the pitching corps and the injured guys.

There were only two American League games scheduled for

today, the Jays beat the Twins 6-1 and the Orioles-Mariners game was postponed due to the rain deluging much of the east coast.

The Sox are in a nice position now. They face off against the Devil Rays starting tomorrow before starting a series in Texas against the Rangers. Both of these teams are much improved, not to be overlooked, but certainly they are also not teams about which we should lose sleep.

Thursday, April 29, 2004

After Monday's off day and Tuesday's unexpected respite due to the rains in New England, the Sox picked up where they left off in their sweep of the Yankees. Any worries about letdown have flown out the window after another big sweep, albeit against a less inspiring foe. Nonetheless, six straight wins and nine of ten, not to mention a streak of 32 scoreless innings that lasted from the weekend through the second game of today's makeup doubleheader, including three straight shutouts.

In the first game of the series yesterday, Curt Schilling had his best outing as a Sox pitcher, going 7-and-a-third and keeping the Tampa Bay hitters befuddled as the Sox won 6-0. Today they played a day-night doubleheader (when is the last time there was a regular back-to-back doubleheader in the major leagues? Why doesn't a small revenue team like Milwaukee or Pittsburgh give fans a chance to see two games consecutively?) and the Sox swept. The first game was perhaps most rewarding. Byung-Hun Kim is back, and while I tried to temper my expectations in the early phases of his comeback, his line tonight validates bringing him back earlier than expected – he went five innings (giving Waker, who sacrificed his turn this week much the way Lowe did last week, a chance to get in work in-game rather than on the side) and gave up only one hit. The Sox won in yet another shutout, 4-0. Ortiz was the man, going three for three with a two-run home run and two doubles. In the nightcap, Lowe went 7 innings, gave up but one earned run, striking out three and walking one. Tek kept up his recent roll, hitting a three run bomb in a 7-3 win.

The pitching has been the key. Obviously Kim's return opens up so many options for us, allowing us to have Arroyo as the swing guy, our long reliever who can also spot start if something goes awry with the starters. Lowe had another outstanding outing, indicating that his fiasco from a while back really was the result of him having had too much rest, which can be problematic for a sinkerballer and especially for him. Schilling was incredible and will be our stabilizing force for the season, even if Pedro is still the ace. And in the biggest twist from last April, our bullpen is the best in baseball. They have now gone 32 1/3 innings (and counting) without giving up a run.

It is really difficult to temper my enthusiasm for this team right now. Even if the Yanks swept the A's the last few days, as our lineup gels and guys start returning from the DL (Kim's performance tonight, Nixon's minor league Florida appearances, and even Nomar's light fielding drills all are indicative that maybe we will get back to full strength soon) it is easy to see the Sox building on what has been a fantastic April. Tomorrow they start a series in Texas, which will mark our first trip out west this season. We'll finish April and start May deep in the heart of Texas.

Friday, April 30, 2004

April showers are supposed to bring May flowers. The Red Sox hope so, and so do their fans. The east coast rain that has so characterized the early season snuck out to Arlington, Texas and caused yet another rain delay in this young season, a delay that we will make up tomorrow in another doubleheader. Arroyo was going to go tonight, revealing how important he can be in this swing role, but we'll have to see what we do tomorrow. I would suspect that we'll still throw him out there in order to maintain the rotation, and we'll follow him with Pedro in the nightcap and Waker in the getaway game on Sunday, though we might switch and have Pedro do the earlier game.

April is now done, and we head into May. This is a big month for us. The Sox have a schedule that could allow them to feast on many of the mediocre teams in the league—teams that will not be horrible, perhaps, but that will not be very good, or certainly that won't be a factor when September rolls around. It is time to do something the Sox have been notoriously bad at these last few years—putting a foot on the throats of our lesser. We tend to play to the level of our opposition. I want to play the role of bully this year—I want to kick the shit out of teams that are smaller and weaker than we are. But unlike a bully, I also want us to stand up to the tough guys, which we have done by kicking sand in the faces of a Yankees team that, early impressions aside, certainly are not 98 pound weaklings.

It's hard not to be optimistic right now. Our bullpen is the best in baseball. Our starting rotation may well be the best as well. Our depleted lineup nonetheless has been able to produce enough, to provide enough run support, to win. Indeed, we have the best record in baseball. We've similarly started off well the last few years—we are 15-6, and in every year since 1999 after 20 games we have been 14-6, so it isn't as if this is unprecedented. What is unprecedented is that we seem built to maintain this sort of pace. The superstitious guy in me doesn't want to say as much, but I am not especially superstitious, so I'll tempt fate—this is a team that has 110 wins and historical greatness written all over it. We'll have to see, of course, if that can pan out, if we can remain on the nearly 116 win pace that we are on currently. So much—injuries, slumps, running into hot teams, dissension, complacency,—can happen in a long season, but there is an equal element of Morgan Magic and pre-collapse 1978 dominance in the air, with a little lingering Cowboy Up tempered by perhaps a little less naivete. I doubt highly that this is a team that would celebrate a Wild Card berth as they did last year. They have a sense of mission. Where last year Kevin Millar was the posterboy for the Sox, with his Cowboy Up, dirt dog, Rally Karaoke Guy overachieving public face of the franchise, this year's team is Curt Schilling and Jason Varitek, Dirt Dogs no doubt, but a little less goofy, a little more driven, a little less likely to be content with anything short of the ultimate goal, and a little more talented. And in both cases, we are fueled by the joie de vivre of David Ortiz and the hitting savant that is Manny.

All of this comes with the passage of just a month, the shortest of the season, but certainly Red Sox fans can and should feel good about things. There may well be time for negativity down the road. But today this is a cynicism free zone.

April

AL East Standings after April 2004:

Team	W	L	%	GB
Sox	15	6	.714	—
Orioles	12	9	.571	3
Empire	12	11	.521	4
Tampa	7	14	.333	8
Toronto	7	15	.318	8.5

4

May: Keeping it Rolling?

Saturday, May 1, 2004
Jesus Christ. I wake up this morning and Pedro is bitching about his contract. The Sox have not met his needs. He is done entertaining negotiations until the season is over. This is the big story on the SoSH Boards. As well it should be. We get off to a great start, and our supposed star goes off on a rampage about his contract. It's all about disrespect I guess. Oh, who am I kidding—after a 15-6 start to lead the league, I don't know what the fuck it's about.

And so tonight we have a doubleheader against the Rangers because of last night's rainout, and what happens? Arroyo holds up his end of the bargain, but the offense cannot produce, and when we give our best shot, Millar thinks he has hit a bomb, and instead he is still standing flatfooted at home when his shot hits the wall. He gets thrown out at second. He cost us at least two runs. Had that happened to Manny it would have been all over the papers tomorrow. But Millar has somehow made himself immune. I wish I knew how that happened, because Millar could not hit a camel in the ass with a bass fiddle, and yet if Manny, who usually has a slugging % well above .500, whose worst attribute is better than Rally Karaoke Guy's best, screws up, it is front page news in every Boston area paper. The *Manchester Union Leader* never quite notices that Millar sucks, but if Manny neglects to run out a ground ball, well, there is angry white hell to pay.

Meanwhile, Pedro picked the worst time possible to have a shitty game. In today's paper we got reports of his discontent. Pedro, who is earning $17.5 million this year, is feeling disrespected because we have not yet offered him a multiyear deal. And so, as if to prove his point, Pedro goes out tonight and . . . gets his ass handed to him. Apparently this is some sort of cunning stratagem. Or maybe Pedro is feeling unappreciated. Whatever it is, when you are a professional athlete, and you grandstand one day, you'd damned well better justify it the next. Or as Chris Rock has said, no one is above an ass kicking. Pedro ran his mouth. He whined. Then he got hammered. We're not Los Angeles fans. This could get ugly. And Pedro brought it upon himself.

Believe it or not, after all of the greatness of April, the hope is that tomorrow we can just salvage one game of this three-game series against the Texas Rangers. Jesus, the Red Sox know how to squander goodwill.

Sunday, May 2, 2004

Was it really just a week ago that we were basking in the glory of a sweep over the Yankees? Was it really just three days ago that I was writing projections of well over 100 wins and how we should be happy and cynicism free?

Hopefully today is the season's low point. We lost 4-1 as the Rangers completed a sweep that would have seemed highly improbable just 48 hours ago. Waker gave his best, pitching into the 8th, giving up two earned runs, never more than one in an inning. It was not his best performance, but he certainly pitched well enough to win.

But the bats are still silent. And it is getting a little tiresome to blame the absence of Nomar and Trot. First, their return may well not be a panacea—Nomar has not gotten a hit, preseason or otherwise, since last fall. Second, this lineup as currently configured should be hitting a lot better than it is. They may not be at full strength, and obviously any lineup that has David McCarty, Cesar Crespo, and Pokey Reese getting regular at-bats is scuffling, but with Manny, Varitek, Ortiz, Mueller, and Damon healthy, there is no excuse for putting up only 2-3 runs per game. It's maddening. They are not waiting for their pitches, they are not capitalizing on mistakes, they are not going deep into counts, and they are not moving guys along on the basepaths. And as always, they are leaving men on base in alarming numbers.

As Texas showed, teams are not just going to bow before the majesty that is the Boston Red Sox. Meanwhile the Yankees have swept consecutive series, have won six in a row, and are within spitting distance of us in the East. Tomorrow we get the Indians. Hopefully that will be good for what ails us. Texas is overachieving. Cleveland truly stinks. We need to go out and pound them with the bats and shut them down with the arms. In this four game series, anything less than 3-1 is truly unacceptable.

Monday, May 3, 2004

Pathetic. Teams slump—we know this, it is hardly cause for alarm. But after getting swept by Texas one would think this team would have gone in with a bit more urgency to face a Cleveland team that is not mediocre—it is downright bad. Schilling certainly did his part, keeping the Cleveland bats pretty well silent with the exception of one 2-run home run. But this isn't the National League. He can't bat and help his own cause. He needs at least some help. And yet tonight we go out and lose 2-1. Pathetic.

It is hard to discern what is truly alarming and what is just part of the ebb and flow of a long baseball season. The pitching on the whole has been solid, at times great, from the starters to the bullpen. The defense has been fine—there have been lapses, but nothing that we can point to that would be the cause of a losing streak. Reese so far has shown some spectacular ability with the leather though there have been some routine plays that he has made harder than need be, and I am not certain that his defense, even when stellar, thus far is enough to justify his bat, which has been wretchedly limp. And that is the problem—as former Celtics coach Rick Pitino might say, the offense stinks and it sucks and it stinks. And everyone seems to think that when Nomar and Trot walk through that door, it will be the magic elixir. I'm not convinced. It seems pretty clear that we are setting these guys up as saviors. Nomar will already be pressing. He knows well what his presence means to the team, but also to his bottom line—missing more than a month, he needs serious production to have any leverage in the free agent market. Trot won't have the same level of pressure as Nomar, but the expectation is that he will bolster an anemic bottom of the order. And by their productivity, it will supposedly give the guys around them better pitches to hit. A rising tide lifts all boats, you see. Of course all of the men left on base cannot be attributed to

Gabe Kaplar and Pokey Reese, can they?

We shall hit, of course. And over the long course of a season, if given a choice between what it looks like this pitching staff can do and the prodigious offense of last year (which still left tons of men on base and shut down for stretches of the season at bizarre times) I'll take this staff. But we need to strike a balance. It is no more satisfying (and is much more frustrating) to lose 2-1 than it is to lose 9-8. And at least when you are down 9-8 there is reason to believe that the bats can produce another run. The way things have been going, when we've been down in the late going, I've hoped we could produce, but I've come to expect that we probably would not.

We should take three of four against them. But losing today was not the best way to start a series against a bad team. And it was an especially bad situation to squander with Schilling on the mound. This losing streak will end and hopefully we'll purge this little bout of miasma. To make matters worse, it was on tv, but I had a date so I only saw the last inning—and she's probably freaked out, as I dragged her into a bar I saw the television as we walked by and she got to see me react to a wretched loss. They can even screw up my love life.

Tuesday, May 4, 2004

At least we are finding innovative ways to lose. This team of destiny, this pitching rich band of men, this one-time offensive force, has now lost five in a row, two to the hapless, no-name Cleveland Indians. Here in Charlottesville I could not watch the game, and I had a dinner to go to that prevented me from listening to it on the internet. This may have been for the best, as my computer at the VFH is the property of UVA and the Commonwealth of Virginia, so putting a fist, bottle or forehead through the screen would cost me more than I can afford now. But the frustration is palpable. I got to the office late, checked out ESPN's Gamecast, and we were down 7-1. By the time I took the bike ride home and settled down for NYPD Blue, the Sox had lost 7-6.

What is there that is left to say or write? Without seeing the numbers, it is clear that D-Lowe did not come through. Bill Mueller made two errors that cost us the game, and that somewhat take

Lowe off the hook, but obviously we are not getting it done on D or on the mound. It is equally obvious that rallying from 6 runs down and coming up short, while Pyrrhic in nature, really does not matter. This team is in a serious funk. Not hitting when it matters is still not hitting. Stat padding looks good on the AL Leader lists, but there are always Red Sox on those lists. I'd accept our absence among the individual leaders for a World Series win.

Meanwhile the Yanks won in a come-from-behind win, as did the Orioles. It was always going to be a race. We were never going to run away with this. But I had every reason to think that we were going to keep April's run rolling in some way shape or form. It's too early to invoke the Who and claim that I won't be fooled again, and despite what must be going on in the world of the Boston talkfest of WEEI radio, I am not quite ready to despair. But like just about everyone in New England and in all of Red Sox Nation, I am really, really frustrated. The regular sportswriters throughout New England have to fill deadlines with set amounts of words. Fortunately, I don't. This is getting old. We've lost every game so far this May. Now we have to hope that we can split this series with the Indians. Talk about diminished expectations.

Wednesday, May 5, 2004

We can breathe again. We can step away from the Tobin Bridge, take our heads out of the oven, put the shotgun away, screw the top back onto the bottle of pills, and climb in off of the ledge. The Red Sox won again, the dry spell is over, and we can return to some semblance of normalcy—for Sox fans this means your usual neurotic, borderline psychotic throwing stuff at the television mania, as opposed to, you know, excess and lack of perspective.

The offense was roaring again. David Ortiz was the key—he hit two dingers and drove in four runs. When he plays the role of The Man, the team seems a lot more confident and loose. Bill Mueller also had a three-run home run, and the bullpen staff got a good bit of headway into another shutout streak. Kim did not have a great start, though as with Lowe yesterday he was victimized by several errors—three in one inning alone (were it not for the woes of the offense and the Pedro follies, the defense's problems of late would be cause for alarm) but Arroyo bailed him out, and Williamson and

Foulke kept the Indians from mounting a comeback. Kim will need to build up his innings, but today gave a pretty good indication as to how valuable Arroyo can still be for us as the swing man—he actually got the win tonight.

This was the worst May start in quite some time, but this win was good for us, if only to put a stop to any prolonged losing streak that could fester into a self-fulfilling crisis. We're tied with the Yankees again (well, we're up half a game, and the Yanks and A's are tied in the top of the 9th inning) and we have one more game against the Indians—we can actually pull out a tie in the four game series with a win tomorrow. The schedule is still soft, and if we can just get consistent production from the lineup, we should be able to mount another win streak. It's incredible what one solid win can do.

This was the first major crisis of the 2004 Red Sox season. One can rest assured that it will not be the last.

Tuesday, May 11, 2004

A great deal can happen in a week of baseball. I've been gone for the past six days, in DC and Birmingham. The latter was for a conference, the Alabama Historical Association, which was quite the travel travail, but the conference itself went well, I was able to get a great response to my paper, and I like Birmingham and always enjoy being in the South, however briefly. (Yes, Virginia is southern, but Charlottesville is a different South from that of Birmingham).

In any case, the Red Sox had a good but not great week while I was gone, going 4-2 against the Royals and Indians. It culminated today with Pedro having a second straight strong outing (7 innings, 4 hits, 11 K's, 2 earned runs) in a no-decision that the Sox won 5-3, with Embree getting the win. Pedro obviously is rounding into form, though for the second straight appearance he gave up two runs in the first before pulling it together. Last Thursday he did the same thing, but he settled down, throwing 7 innings, giving up the two runs on four hits, walking three while punching out eight. Manny hit a home run and Pokey Reese hit a double to put us ahead. On Thursday, as tonight, Pedro outdueled the Indians' ace, C.C. Sebathia, who is fast becoming something of a hard-luck story for the relief-poor Indians. Pedro coming around is a good thing for the Red Sox.

The next night, in the first game against the Royals, the Sox kept it going. They were down 6-2 in the eighth when they mounted a comeback. In the ninth Bellhorn, hitting in the second spot, hit a game tying two-run home run. The go-ahead run came on a Varitek double that drove in Manny, who scored standing up on a close play that would likely have resulted in an out had he slid. Waker went eight, giving up all six runs, but only four were earned, and he continues to be quietly reliable. Timlin got the win. In the second game against Kansas City, the Sox won in a blowout, 9-1. The improbable hero was Pokey Reese who hit the first inside-the-park home run in the majors this year and the first one for the Sox in years. He added a more conventional blast later in the rout. Schilling held down the fort and pitched his first complete game for the Sox, scattering five hits and no walks while striking out eight. Adding to all of this good news was a report that Nomar is excited about the progress he is making in his rehab. He took swings in the cage for the first time and says that there is daily improvement.

The next two days were not so good. Lowe took another loss in a rough outing against the Royals, with the Sox going down 8-4, giving the Royals a win rather than the Sox a sweep. Last night Kim took the loss after spotting the Indians a bunch of runs, and the Tribe took the first game of a four game series, 10-6. Kim's first outing gave most of us hope that he would step up and shine, pushing Arroyo to the bullpen and thus strengthening the staff immeasurably. Indeed I thought that Kim's return might be more important than both Nomar's and Trot's. I may have been premature. The Sox sent Kim down to Pawtucket today. Maybe this will give him a chance to get some innings under his belt—we brought him up earlier than expected and obviously he was not ready. Hopefully Arroyo will continue his roll, and my thought is that he may well keep that fifth spot, at least until Kim proves that he is worthy of supplanting Bronson in the rotation. I don't trust Kim's psyche, and he may not be equipped to start on this team.

We are still in first place. Pedro is coming around, Schilling is rolling, Waker continues to be an unsung hero, and even when we lose our fifth starter we replace him with a guy who arguable deserves the slot more and who has been a revelation for us. The bats are no longer quite so anemic, the schedule is friendly, the temps are heating up, and we seem to be gearing up for the long haul. We have another five days until our next day off. Hopefully we can finish off the Indians by winning tomorrow, setting us off on another roll.

Wednesday, May 12, 2004

Apparently this Red Sox team that hopes to beat the Yankees on their way to a World Series title is not quite capable of beating the Cleveland Indians. We played our last game against them today, Waker got off to a rough start, we fell behind, and we never were able to catch up. Due to the exigencies of the unbalanced schedule, we are done with the Indians for the season, and so our season record against them ends at a confounding 3-4 without us winning a series against them.

In the first inning we had our best shot. Manny drove in a run with a double, then a couple of batter later on a single to left third-base coach Dale Sveum waved him in when he had no business doing so. This killed an inning that showed some promise and we never really recovered. In the end, Waker was ineffective, the defense was sketchy, shoddy baserunning coupled with bad coaching decisions, and of course intermittent hitting, doomed us tonight. In all, it was a very frustrating performance by what thus far is a frustrating team.

Thursday, May 13, 2004

Huh. This wasn't supposed to happen. After nearly a month in first place we were not supposed to go on a losing skein. After last month's series against the Yankees, when we finished off a sweep and took 6 of 7 over two weekends, they were supposed to be in our back mirror. After the Sox loss against the Blue Jays two weeks ago when Schilling gave up the lead in the 8th on a grand slam home run, we were not supposed to get shelled with Schilling on the mound, set for revenge, against those same Blue Jays. We weren't supposed to misplay popups. And certainly Schilling was not supposed to get shelled throughout the five innings of his start.

In the end, we lost 12-6. We started to mount a rally, coming within a couple of runs after falling behind 6-2. Schill's control was off, he could not spot his pitches, and so when he came in with his fastball, the Toronto guys sat on it and it was bombs away. We got off to a bad, bad start in this four game series. The Red Sox are scuffling. Schilling did not play the role of stopper. The bats are not getting the job done. The fielding is abominable. Our baserunning, historically not a Sox forte, continues to run us out of innings.

The Yankees won today, pounding the Angels in a game in which the Yanks pitchers did not exactly inspire confidence. With our loss, that vaulted them into first place by half a game. What is most alarming about that is that while New York is playing the A's and Angels and winning, we are playing the Indians and Blue Jays and losing. Their schedule will get easier. Ours will get harder. May was a month in which I honestly felt we needed to take a pretty big lead, beating up on the chaff while the Yankees struggled with the wheat. So far, this has not happened.

I remember well being a Red Sox fan in the years after those great teams of the 1970s fell apart and we were left with a mediocre agglomeration of decent hit, no pitch, ho-hum 84-78 teams. Those teams had very low expectations imposed upon them and they met those expectations. In the half decade or so before Roger came onto the scene, when Yaz was playing out the string, when Rice and Dewey were the holdovers from the 1975-1979 era, when individual accomplishments and 25 cabs for 25 guys reigned, the Sox were dull. As a ten year old, I always thought they could compete, but the reality was, they were not good enough. Over the course of the last few years things have changed. The expectations are high. The team is, or at least should be, pretty good. And yet this team, with its high-priced stars and glamour and grand expectations, is 20-15, is in second place, is pitching poorly, hitting worse, and is so frustrating as to not be entertaining.

We face off against Toronto in Sky Dome tomorrow. Hopefully we'll come out swinging and will even up this series. Hopefully we'll catch fire. But I have to say, after today's game, the euphoria of the offseason, the feelings of invincibility that accompanied the Schilling deal, seems a long, long way away. This will pass, inevitably. But right now it seems like we're running in sand.

May 14-31, 2004

I've been out of commission for more than two weeks, and we'll have to see if this is a salvageable endeavor. It was not my fault. Out of nowhere my laptop crashed. Stupidly I had not saved in almost a month, and so the last date I had saved was in mid-April. It would not even have made sense to keep this going. Then, as mysteriously as it crashed, I got my computer back, and was able to transfer what I did have to disk. I'll see if I can catch up and give reflections on the past couple of weeks.

During this time the Sox played quite well, actually. The offense began to work its way out of its malaise even without Trot and Nomar in the lineup. We have gotten solid contributions from role players, though also inconsistent ones—we never know when guys like Pokey or Daubach or McCarty will come through, and most of the time they don't, but they are allowing us to keep our heads above water. Kevin Youkilis, the "Greek God of Walks" of Moneyball fame, has had an auspicious beginning to his Sox career, Bellhorn continues to lead the way with his walks even as his batting average has begun to creep above the Mendoza line, and guys like Damon seem to get it done, if barely. Of course it does not hurt that Manny has been a monster, near the league lead in every significant category. And Ortiz has continued to contribute as well. The Sox went after the low hanging fruit to sign him to a long-term contract for the next few years—it is looking like a brilliant investment.

Pedro continued to come around, Schilling was a rock, though for a range of reasons he did not get the wins that he deserved. Waker continued to be the inscrutable knuckleballer—not outstanding, sometimes dangerously off, but in the end solid because he is wily and gutsy and smart and dedicated. Arroyo has shown signs of why he is a 5th guy, though he still has promise, and we need him to be big with Kim on the shelf indefinitely for either health or head problems, depending upon to whom one talks. Lowe has been a nightmare, his ERA creeping ever closer to 7, his head clearly fragile, his pitches not showing the bite that almost won him a Cy Young two years ago. He has always been something of a head case, but more important, since I deride most of the pop psychology that characterizes sports fans and media these days, is the fact that his stuff seems to be failing him at a time when clearly he is not dealing with it all that well. It is hard to know if there are mechanical issues, physical ones, or something else.

If the starters were supposed to be the strength of our team and have not been quite as good as advertised, the relief corps has been better. Foulke has been the relief ace we lacked the last couple of years, closing out every game that has come his way (until blowing his first on Sunday the 30th, and even then we came back to win on a McCarty walkoff) and allowing Francona to begin to set roles for everybody, though his handling of the pitchers has undoubtedly been the source of biggest concern in the first two months of the season. But we have gotten great performances from everybody, at least all of the key cogs. Scotty Williamson is on the DL, but we have so much depth right now that guys have stepped up and if our starters can just go 6 we know we have a great shot at shortening the game and giving us distinct advantages in the later innings.

Defense continued to vex during this time period, and for a while there it seemed as if we were making two errors a night, many of which proved costly, as errors are inclined to do. This will continue to be problematic, but we can hope that Nomar and Trot will shore up the defense (although we probably lose with Pokey out, we also get stability rather than musical chairs at short) as much as the offense, where they have been sorely missed.

In all this has been a good stretch. We began the month 9 games over .500 and playing at an unbelievable clip. Then we slumped. But by month's end we were 11 games above .500 and playing, if not inspired or great, at least well enough to contend, to allow us to enter June with a realistic shot at taking the division. The Yanks have awoken from their early somnolence, and as usual, the teams in the west are not about to roll over, but hopefully we have the personnel to get to where we need to be. June is a vital month for us, as we often seem to swoon when the summer rolls around and school lets out. This may be a crucial month. Then again, in a pennant race, they all are.

May

AL East Standings, May 31, 2004:

	W	L	GB
MFY	30	19	—
Sox	31	20	½
Orioles	24	23	5
Jays	22	29	9
Rays	18	31	12

5

June: The Race is On

Tuesday, June 1, 2004

Tomorrow I leave Charlottesville for a few weeks in Ferrum, Virginia, two to three hours southeast of here where I'll be participating in a National Endowment for the Humanities seminar at Ferrum College.

I am up late because tonight we begin our first west coast swing of the season. We started out in Anaheim, which appears to have its 2002 form back. It did not go well. We got off to a 4-1 lead and then promptly let it all go to hell. We could not pitch (Arroyo scuffled after he was spotted the lead—the Bronson of Yankee killer fame is slowly fading from memory—and the bullpen did not have it). We could not hit (runners left on base killed us again, including another bases loaded gem with Millar keeping his form of late). We could not field (two key errors, including a wretched throwing error by Daubach, who is bringing little to the table in the field or at the bat). We could not run (Manny picked off first.) We could not manage (Tito needed to take Arroyo out earlier than he did). At the end we made a run, Dauber hit a window dressing two-run home run, and it proved not to be enough. We lose 7-6.

This is only a two-game series, and tomorrow (actually, later today) Pedro goes out hoping to salvage a split. It will be a long day here as I still have work to do (I am keeping my office here in Charlottesville for the month) and the game won't come on until late (it's on ESPN—we'll see later in the week if my MLB radio works). Hopefully we get back on a winning path. We'll see. Yanks are up by a game now. Nothing to fret, but we cannot keep playing like this.

Wednesday, June 2, 2004

Criminy. Even the transition to Ferrum, Virginia (a good three hours from Charlottesville, where I am doing this NEH seminar on Appalachian studies) does not seem to have helped the Sox. Of course only a fan could understand such an absurd statement, but it is true. The little things we do in life effect the team. Sit in one position while they rally, and you'll relive that position, no mater how uncomfortable, unwieldy, or inappropriate, for a week's worth of games. Order pizza in the 7th inning and they come back? Thank God you like pizza. Go take a leak and watch the other team come back? You'll let your bladder distend next time rather than piss again. It's the nature of the beast—no one can disprove the effect your acts have on the game, and proof of causality be damned, even those of us who in our regular lives demand strong evidence and good arguments for just about anything turn into something not much better than ouija board and tarot card devotees.

Tonight Pedro got the start. He did not fare especially well. There were moments of brilliance, but those were peppered with innings when his ineffective fastball did not provide the sort of contrast that makes his offspeed stuff traditionally nasty. It has been a back and forth game, and right now it is more back than forth—Vlad Guerrero just hit his second bomb of the game, and we are now down 8-7. One reassuring fact, which also prevailed last night—on the audio it is clear that Sox fans are dominating the hapless Anaheim fans. "Let's Go Red Sox!" chants have provided the soundtrack for a night when we have desperately needed whatever help we can get. It's the seventh inning now, and soon it will get a lot tougher, as it will be Francisco Rodriguez time, and that kid has been close to indomitable the last month or so. We need a rally. We need to hold them and hope that we can push a few across. Otherwise we look at a two-game sweep and the fact that we have lost five of seven (not that four of six is exactly good).

Fortunately I am still unpacking and can watch this while I get my room into tip top shape. It's a dorm, which feels weird, yet comfortable—I've done dorms a lot, between my own time back in college, and in summer teaching gigs and the like. In a sense it is like a form of regression, but since I have (relatively) little stuff, I can appreciate the compactness of it all. Nonetheless, it will get old soon. The campus is beautiful. We're in western Virginia, south of Roanoke, on a sprawling little campus with lots of space and verdant green. I'll need to buy computer speakers (I've bought at least five speaker sets for computers, but I left the ones I just got in Charlottesville, and I won't be able to get them until at least this weekend, if I go up then.) to hear the games, but it is a pretty good little set up.

Jesus. How's this for faith in the team right now? It is the seventh inning, we are down by two, and we brought in Foulke, our freaking closer. And he is looking wild. Things are just not good right now. The 8th and 9th will be interesting. We need to find a way to get to Rodriguez. This is not a World Championship team right now. And Vladdy came up and got his ninth RBI of the night, setting an Angels team record and matching any asskicking I've seen by one player. Fuckity. 10-7. The AL single game RBI record is 11, by the way, owned by Tony Lazzeri of the Yanks, 1936. The MLB record is 12 by the inestimable Mark Whiten.

So we get to the ninth. It's still ugly. And the Angels, whose manager actually apparently pays attention to his bullpen, is going with Francisco Rodriguez, portentously nicknamed K-Rod, rather than imminently hittable Troy Percival. I safely can say I hate life right now.

Leading off with a walk is good. Youks striking out is bad. Ortiz absolutely driving one to right is good. Guerrero catching it is bad. And we're down to one out. Yeah, this bodes well, even with Manny up. 0-1. Great breaking ball for 0-2. Froze Manny. Way outside, 1-2. Cheese. Manny swung through it. Damn, Rodriguez is good. Damn, the Red Sox are bad right now. It's 1:06. I have to be up and smart in a handful of hours. God, these guys are going to kill me.

Thurday, June 3, 2004

Today is an off day as the guys head east, tail between their legs, for a series in Kansas City. As the Sox traveled, the Yankees finished off a sweep against the Orioles, a team that manages to play well against us even as they are schedule padding for the Yankees. That puts the Yankees up by 2 1/2 games, a margin we cannot afford to have open much beyond.

Reports are that Nomar is very close to returning. He may be back as soon as Tuesday when they start a homestand against those traditional rivals, the San Diego Padres. He wants to get a few more games in with Pawtucket, to work up to 7 or so innings. Hopefully he'll provide a spark not only on the field, but also with ripple effects throughout the lineup and the clubhouse. That will be the first truly good news in some time. The last few days have hopefully been just one of those spells that hit during a 162-game schedule. Nonetheless, we cannot afford too many of these, not with the Yankees surging and the West seemingly determined to compete for two playoff slots. That Wild Card has never been something we could take for granted (think 2002) and we do not want a dogfight against both the Yankees and the West's second best.

Kansas City has never been good to us, but hopefully tomorrow we get back on a roll. We almost have to improve in every facet of the game, because in all of them we have looked like a second division team.

Friday, June 4, 2004

Another loss. What more is there to say? In the last 33 games we have been a game below .500, 16-17. We lost to Kansas City and the Royals 5-2. ESPN made a big deal about how the Royals had not yet thrown a shutout this season, and we scored two runs, but in the end it was a giant blueball. We lost. We had one inning where we posed a serious threat. What more to say? We are not a very good team now, and as a Sox fan, I have to say, we are playing in a more disappointing way than any team I can remember. After all, this year we were supposed to win it all. Now we are 3 1/2 games down on the MFY (Hint: Last word is "Yankees," first word refers to a maternal figure.)

Saturday, June 5, 2004

OK, breathe a sigh of relief. We won tonight. Schilling came through with a reasonably big performance, a stopper's performance. He held the Royals to three runs, six hits, and a walk in seven innings while the bats woke up and hit when they had to. Ortiz, Bellhorn, and Youkilis (who is earning his reputation as an on-base machine, as has Bellhorn—maybe there is something to this Moneyball stuff) each hit a three-run home run, and we beat the Royals 8-4 in Kansas

City. Ortiz continues to be the king of the extra base hits, as he was last summer, to the point where even when he struggles he is a threat. With the offensive explosion, there was no way that Schilling was going to be denied and hopefully he helped to settle down a staff that has gone from being ranked first in ERA to one that is in the middle of the league rankings. Francona (and, one presumes, Wallace) chose to flip-flop Schilling and the struggling Lowe in the rotation, and it bore fruit. Hopefully Lowe follows Schilling's lead, or at least can appropriate enough of his mindset, tomorrow in a getaway game that they really need as they head into the house of mirrors that has been interleague play for Red Sox teams past.

Sunday, June 6, 2004

Derek Lowe has clearly decided not to make it easy for himself, or for the rest of us. But after one shaky inning in which he gave up two earned (in the fifth he gave up a third run that was the result of his throwing error) he pitched well enough to help him get the win, although the Sox scored all five of their runs only after the fifth, which would prove to be his last inning in the game. Johnny Damon is probably playing as well as he has yet as a member of the Sox, and today he had three doubles, putting him on base and driving in runs. Mike Timlin came in and threw three innings of hitless ball, after which Foulke came in, closed the door, got the save, and sealed a win that was more important than it probably ought to have been.

Now we begin interleague play. We have not been very successful when we have played our National League brethren. Even in years when we have been good, which has been for most of the duration of this interleague experiment, teams that had no business beating us pounded us like nails (the Marlins in their post-1997 incarnation come to mind) and teams that should have beaten us (the Braves) fulfilled their expectations. On Tuesday the Padres come into town. We'll have a day off, and we should have Nomar in tow, barring some sort of catastrophe. Given how we have played lately, there are no guarantees. But one has to think that we will come out and will play well, even if Nomar scuffles while feeling his way back into the Major League routine. We took two of three against Kansas City. Hopefully that bit of momentum, coupled with a serviceable if not outstanding start by Lowe, will kickstart us into the middle phase of the season.

Monday, June 7, 2004

Mondays are often off days in Major League Baseball. The Collective Bargaining Agreement mandates a certain number of days off per month. The Sox will be off almost every Monday from now until mid-July.

We are about to embark on the somewhat daunting 12 game run against National League teams in the Little Shop of Horrors that is known as interleague play, at least as far as the Sox are concerned. This week we face San Diego and the Dodgers at home. Next week we head out west to face Colorado and San Francisco. Obviously the Dodgers and Giants are the daunting teams of the four, the Padres and Rockies less so. But with this year's Sox team, and our history against the Senior Circuit, we can take nothing for granted. I am excited to see us hit in Coors Field, and to see our guys take on Barry Bonds. We are an obvious historic matchup against the Dodgers, who have been much improved this year and who are the exact type of team that will give us difficulties. The Pads are basically anonymous, which of course means that they may make us look like fools.

Nomar should be back tomorrow. He has gotten a few games in with the Paw-Sox, and while he has not hit especially well (last I saw he had gone 0 for his last 9) one can only assume that he is working on timing at the plate and comfort in the field. He will give the Sox a boost, and we just need to cover him while he gets back into the routine. We need to get on a roll. The Yanks still have us by a couple of games, and we need not only to keep them in sight, but to get back in the driver's seat. A run through the National league and into the All Star Break would be great now. So there is only one thing to say: NOMAHHHHHH!!!!!

Tuesday, June 9, 2004

PEDRO!!!! PEDRO!!!! PEDRO!!!! For one night it was 1999 all over again. Tonight marked the first interleague game of the 2004 season. Sox against the Padres, making their first-ever trip to Fenway. Pedro against old Sox nemesis David Wells.

About this matchup Pedro proclaimed that everyone must be sick of these two (himself and Wells) facing off, that they were old goats who were going to be tossing doo-doo across the plate. I have no idea what that means, but it proved to be true. Wells was virtually unhittable, and the Sox managed to squeeze across but one run, when Damon hit yet another double (after shaving his beard in the last week or so in May he appears to be growing it back) and drove in Kaplar.

But vintage Pedro makes something out of being spotted one run. And so he went 8 innings, gave up two hits and a walk, struck out 8, was often over 90, his curve was nasty, and he threw more than 110 pitches. Foulke came out and closed the door. The goats were tossing the doo doo but the old goat from the Dominican apparently threw it better. Messier? Nastier? Whatever the appropriate term, he did it.

Despite expectations, Nomar did not come back. He is taking one more game in Pawtucket after which point he will have another examination on the delicate, precious Achilles tendon. If all goes well, he'll finally make his way to Fenway. If Pedro really is back, the pieces will come together. Nomar, Trot (had a start in Double A yesterday), and Scott Williamson are on their way back. We got off to a good start in interleague play. We beat the Padres in an epic midseason pitching matchup. Life's good.

I mentioned Pedro circa 1999. Pedro is the best I have ever seen. I am relatively young, coming to baseball in the decade of my birth, the 1970s. I've seen the Ryans and Seavers and Palmers and Carltons. I saw guys like J.R. Richards and Dwight Gooden and Fernando Valenzuela who had brief but brilliant peaks. I've seen great pitchers come up huge, such as Hershiser in 1988 and Morris in 1991. I was convinced that Clemens was the best I had ever seen and still argue for his all time greatness, even if he turns my stomach for his sundry apostasies. But Pedro Jaime Martinez from 1997, when he won his first Cy Young for Montreal, until his last healthy go round in 2002, is the best, most dominant, most charismatic, most awe-inspiring moundsman I have ever seen. I never got to see Gibson. And probably more apropos, I never got to see Koufax, with whom the career parallels are frightening. He has struggled through injuries nagging and major. He has gotten off to a slow start this year. But tonight reminds all of us who love this team and who are hoping for greatness this year not only of the Pedro who has sparked so many dreams of October Glory, but he reminds us of the kind of Sox team that wins and that does so with panache and glory and dominance and style. Pedro healthy and dominant is transcendent, an artist. He plied that artistry tonight, and all of Red Sox Nation can go to sleep dreaming of Game Sevens to come.

Wednesday, June 9, 2004

It is a stormy night up in Boston. The Sox went down 4-0 through 6, the result of some really shoddy defense—three of the runs were unearned. Then they had a rain delay of over two hours. I had hustled back from Charlottesville in order to catch most of the game. Within just a while of when I got back and got the tv on, they pulled the tarp on the field at Fenway. It's been a miserable spring up in those parts. I'm glad to have been here in the Southland.

Before that break at least one good thing happened—Nomar made his debut. He played reasonably well—made good contact both at bats and got a single in his first appearance of the year. He turned a double play and he made another nice play, though it was muffed at first base. Which brings up the big complaint of the night—we've had far more injury issues than any team deserves, but that does not completely explain some of Tito's personnel decisions. I can understand him wanting to get guys in, wanting to find combinations that work, but it seems that we never have a set lineup. Every day it is something different. Today was one of the most quizzical—they sent down Daubach when they activated Nomar. They kept Andy Dominique. That may make sense if they want to have a third catcher, but then they start him at first base tonight. This is not a kid ready to play first at the major league level—he did not even play much down in Pawtucket. One thinks Buddy Bailey, the PawSox manager, and Tito should have had a conversation. Then Dominique goes out and not only makes a couple of really bad plays, including one or two that led to runs, he also did nothing at the plate. Meanwhile McCarty is there and could have played better at first and probably made a better showing at the plate too. We have guys who can play first. This is a decision I simply don't understand.

Arroyo got the start, and he pitched well. The errors killed him. Waker came in to relieve him. They were down 4-0. It's now 7-0 with DiNardo on the hill. I think we can write this one off, although we can always hope for a rally. This is not what we all hoped for when Nomar came back, but I guess it just reaffirms that simply adding Nomar into the mix will not on its own produce a more consistent team.

Damon leads off the 8th with a solo shot about 30 feet or so left of the Pesky Pole. Maybe the rain delay hurt San Diego's relievers. Bellhorn gets a hit. Yes, maybe Jay Witasick is just the medicine for the few remaining fans at Fenway. Of course then Ortiz, Manny, and pinch-hitting David McCarty go down 1-2-3 and it is the 9th inning. We can just erase this one from the memory banks.

Final Score: 8-1. Yuck. Consider it erased. Schilling goes tomorrow, 7:05 at the Fens, and we win this series, hopefully with a much needed offensive explosion.

Thursday, June 10, 2004

A baseball season can be broken up into almost infinite chunks. Look at it one way, and a team has lost 17 of its last 30 games. Look at it in another way, and they have won 7 of their last 10. I thought of this tonight when musing about the Red Sox. Since April 30 they have not been very good. In the two weeks before last weekend they had been wretched. And yet with a huge, fun, rollicking win tonight, they have won four of their last five.

Nomar went 1 or 4, but that one hit was a two-run double that sounded awfully close to a gland slam, and he drove in two runs. Plus Pedro did a little goofy dance when Nomar smacked the double—that's a clubhouse thing, and it is good. Manny had three RBI and one came on a two-run dinger. Schilling threw seven innings, gave up two runs, walked two, and struck out seven. He played the role of stopper, getting us the win and catapulting us to a series against the Dodgers. We won 9-3, based primarily on the middle of the lineup getting a clear boost from Nomar's presence and a little bonus from Pokey Reese, who went 3 for 4 with an RBI on his birthday. It is too early to proclaim that Nomar is fully back. I am going to expect that he will struggle in the next month—he'll slump a bit, and thus he'll press. But in the long run, this is the time to get him back. He obviously still has everything that it takes to be a great hitter.

The Yankees maintain a 3.5 game lead right now, but for a while it really looked as if we might be getting ready to hemorrhage. We are holding steady in the early phases of interleague play. The Padres are not the Yankees, but the important thing is that no matter who the opponent, we won the series. Pedro dominated his start, Schilling basically did his, and we got Nomar back. So we've played just over .500 ball if you measure it from April. But we won tonight. And the great thing about baseball is that you can always envision that you'll win tomorrow.

Tuesday, June 15, 2004

I've been out of commission for a few days. I had a wedding in New Hampshire this weekend followed by two unexpected days in Harrisburg, Pennsylvania as I waited for my car to be repaired. Two extra days and more than a thousand dollars later, I am back in Ferrum. I cannot tie the Harrisburg debacle in to baseball, try though I might.

The wedding was great—it was my cousin Nicole's. Nicole is the eldest of my cousins, the oldest daughter of my uncle John and Aunt Antoinette down in Massapequa, on Long Island. John, my Dad's brother (Dad is the oldest, John next of the four boys), is a huge baseball fan, and his two sons, Joey and Michael, were both very good high school players; Joey starred at Columbia. John taught them well—even as New Yorkers, they are big Sox fans, especially Michael. It was also great to be able to see the games with the local coverage—Jerry Remy is a cult hero, and understandably so—a Massachusetts native who played for the Sox and who is a respected analyst for NESN.

The Sox have had a good run of it since last I wrote. They took two of three against the Dodgers, including two pitching duels (one with Lowe prevailing—obviously huge in the scheme of things—and one with Pedro) sandwiched around a game in which Waker and the rest of the staff got pounded 14-5. After a day off, the Sox lost to Colorado, a team that had lost eight straight prior to tonight.

The weekend has to be seen as a positive. Taking two of three from a pretty good Dodgers team after two of three against the surprising Padres gets us off on the right foot. Lowe's appearance was a great sign that maybe we can have the rotation we dreamed about in spring training. He did not get the decision—Foulke actually blew the save in the ninth, and Ortiz had to drive in his second RBI of the game to give us the win in the bottom of the inning, giving Foulke the win. But it all goes directly to Lowe's credit. He's had a rough year. But he got the decision in his previous start and then went out and pitched seven innings, scattered five hits, struck out four and walked four (control still not perfect, but improving) and looking like the D-Lowe of old. His fragile psyche is legendary, and probably overstated, but on the whole this was a good win for him and for us.

Saturday was a washout. Waker was off, we fell way behind, and we never were seriously in the game. The less said about it, the better. We came back Sunday and got the getaway win. Pedro was on again—he was not quite as flawless as he was in his last appearance, but he kept the Dodgers off balance, and though the relievers almost let the Dodgers back in, they closed the door on a 4-1 victory. Pedro went seven, allowing one earned run, seven hits, two walks, and five strikeouts. Pokey Reese was probably the star of the game. In the seventh he made an amazing play in which he leapt high in the air and snagged a line drive that would have signaled trouble for Pedro. Pokey is fast becoming a Fenway favorite for his magic with the leather. He also had a two-run double that provided the difference. He is making the Bellhorn-Reese decision a very difficult one, but so far Tito is juggling lineups, getting both players in, often with Bellhorn at third or dh. If Pokey hits some, it will give us some enviable luxuries.

If the weekend was good, tonight's game marks an inauspicious start to the away component of this interleague swing. We got off to a quick lead but could not hold on. Arroyo has not won in five starts, and while his outing was respectable, he gave up four runs in a 6-3 loss and he has not won in five outings. The bats are struggling a bit. We had a good beginning to interleague. We cannot get off on the wrong foot this time around. We are better than the Rockies. We need to win these next two before facing Bonds and company in San Francisco.

Wednesday, June 16, 2004

What can you say? If we are not good enough to beat the freaking Rockies, with Schilling on the mound and Trot back in the lineup, something is wrong. No one wants to overreact to one game, but this was one that should have been chalked up in the win column, especially after we lost last night. So we come out, let the Rockies stay in the game, while Schilling is clearly dealing with an ankle that is not 100%, and the Yankees continue to win. We are now five-and-a-half games behind them. It is only June. But it is June.

Meanwhile, the Rockies have won six times in twenty six games, and two of these wins have come at our expense. Schilling has traditionally struggled in Colorado, but this is absurd, especially with this lineup. Trot hit a dinger, but that welcome home did not much matter. We almost came back from down several runs in the 9th, but we should never have been down by that much. Were I to bet, I'd say that Schill will be on the DL soon. Too bad we did not find out before this start.

Thursday, June 17, 2004

Redemption comes in many forms, some large and some small. In the grand scheme of a long season, today's redemption will probably go down as a small one, but it felt pretty big.

There is no ideal Platonic form when it comes to a baseball game. But if there were this one came pretty close. D-Lowe came up big, going seven innings in heavy rains, giving up four hits and four walks, no runs, and three strikeouts. Perhaps most important, in Colorado's thin air, 17 of the balls in play off of Lowe were ground balls, meaning that his sinker was at its peak form. Of twenty one outs, twenty came either on grounders or strikeouts, with the last being a fly out. If Lowe is pitching like that, and this is his second consecutive stellar outing in a row, he has pitched 14 innings of shutout ball, so we have reason to believe that he will, we suddenly have what is arguably the best pitching staff in baseball. In Lowe's 100th career start he was the central player in only the 25th shutout in the history of Coors Field. Scott Williamson came in and pitched the eighth—his return has been less heralded than Trot's and Nomar's, but in returning he also gives us our preferred relief rotation. DiNardo pitched the ninth.

And a pitching staff that gets eleven runs has a lot of room for error. For most of interleague play the offense has scuffled. Not today. Ortiz had a career high five ribbies, one on a shot of a home run in the 7th with one on. Reese continued to solidify himself as a fan favorite by driving in two, Bellhorn also had two RBI, and McCarty and Varitek each pushed one across. Nomar went three for five with a triple, and Trot went 2 for 3, though apparently he was limping quite a bit, revealing that we need to be careful with him and his balky quad.

So it was a good day in Denver. It was an afternoon game, so they were able to get away for their trip to San Francisco, which should be a good matchup. The pitching was sterling, the Derek Lowe reclamation project continues apace, and the offense revealed flashes of last year's wallbangers with a lineup that no longer resembles a spring training split squad game (Cesar Crespo sightings should be mercifully infrequent). Losing a series to the Rockies is unacceptable, but we salvaged a win, and it looks like my prediction about Schilling was wrong, that he will be ok. At least until the next start. Somehow it seems appropriate that after such a good win there would still be some anxiety.

Sunday, June 20, 2004

The NEH seminar has moved base to Caretta, West Virginia, which is about as isolated as a place can be. We will be working on service projects during our time here in one of the poorest little nooks in the country. This is not good for me now, as I am in a bit of a downward spiral that, shockingly, is not Red Sox related. At my friend Steve's wedding this weekend I met a girl. A beautiful, smart, sexy, funny, interesting girl. It sounds inane, but after just one night I know that this is a girl that I could marry. Except that she lives in Montreal. And she has a freaking boyfriend. I feel like a jackass, but this has sent me into a pretty serious depression, probably tied to the sorts of emotions that single women are supposed to feel at weddings — lack of self esteem, envy, self loathing, and paralyzed be ennui covers it pretty well. I have not been so smitten since the early days of Katherine. I'll probably never see her again. It was great to see all of my Ohio friends, although it was a bit of a sticky situation, because I also invited an ex-girlfriend from those days, and she was my date, and then I blew her off at the wedding reception as a result of my newfound crush. I am a cunning one.

And on top of all of this, I do not know the outcome of the rubber game between the Giants and Sox. It was tied 0-0 in the fifth last I heard, so Arroyo obviously was doing his job. They won on Friday after falling behind 7-2. I discovered this because one of the guys in the wedding party is a huge Giants fan, and he was taunting me. The Sox won 14-9 largely because of several home runs and some especially bad outfield defense. Yesterday we lost, with Pedro on the mound, after coming from behind again only to see Embree give up a two run home run to give the Giants the win.

So silly as it sounds, I fell half in love this weekend, which led to a serious crisis of confidence, and now I am in Caretta hoping to help people improve their own lives when I cannot even do the same for myself. I remember reading a review of a Pete Townsend song in the early 1990s (I was working as a bartended at a dude ranch in Michigan—and yes, I realize how absurd that sentence is) that quoted a lyric I always remember. I've never been a big fan of The Who or of Townsend's solo work, but this line sticks: "Every so often you meet a soul and you fall in love and there's not a thing you can do about it." That about sums it up. Hopefully the Sox won today.

UPDATE: 4-0 Giants. They won on a Jason Schmidt one-hitter. The Sox apparently let a popup drop between a few guys allowing the Giants to break the scoreless tie. Arroyo was wild, walking five and hitting a batter, but he kept them in the game until the 7th. Obviously we still do not have the hang of this interleague thing. We cannot keep losing games when the Yankees are as hot as they are. We went .500 this go round. Tomorrow is an off day, followed by a series against the Twins, and then back to the National league with a series against the Phillies.

Monday, June 21, 2004
They were off today, which is just as well. Caretta is insanely isolated, and I hate getting bits and pieces of the games. I do not even have access to a decent newspaper around here, never mind the fact that my internet access is minimal when it exists at all, and

so I can forget about listening to the games on MLB radio. I'll be happy to get back to civilization. As for the other thing: I'm still smitten. Not much will change that anytime soon.

The Sox need to start playing better. This is becoming a mantra. When they pitch well they do not hit. When they hit well, the pitching falls apart. It is still relatively early, though the All Star Break is coming up in just a couple of weeks, and that is the traditional point at which the standings start to matter. The Yankees have been slowly stretching that lead, and we have not responded. Off days generally are bummers, but with me being stuck here in McDowell County and the Sox scuffling toward mediocrity, maybe today's respite is the best thing for them. Hopefully we'll win this series against the Twins in spectacular fashion.

Tuesday, June 22, 2004

And so a win in spectacular fashion we got. I feel a bit as if I am living in the 19th century frontier and I am awaiting the delivery of a message from the Pony Express telling me if the Red Sox won or not and, space permitting, what scant details a telegram will allow. Nonetheless, we won after the off day giving us much needed momentum and hopefully giving us something from which to work from now until the All Star Break.

On Sunday, Tito rested three starters, making many in the media (and had I known, me as well—have I pointed out that being this out of touch is killing me?) wonder what he was thinking with an off day to come on Monday. But last night the guys apparently looked rested and ready to work. Schilling gave us another 7 innings of solid pitching, and his record is now up to 9-4. When the game was still vaguely in question, Nomar finally hit his first home run of the season, and he did so with a little panache, crushing a grand slam to seal the win at Fenway. Ortiz and Manny also had bombs, and they hit several doubles as well.

The Sox are now 4.5 games behind the Yankees, yet they have the third best record in all of baseball, second best in the American League. The West and Central teams may hang around all season, or one or two may separate, but with all of the uncertainty and mediocrity and frustration, the Sox still look ready to make a run. They are in position to play well, even if they have not done so yet. The Twins are a good opponent in this sense—they are looking to make the playoffs, but we should be beating them, and so how we play against them should give a good indication as to where we stand. A revived D-Lowe goes to the mound tonight and a win would put us in a position to sweep, to enter what ought to be a good dogfight with the Phillies, a team we may well get the chance to see down the road if all goes well. For now, going well would be Lowe continuing to stake a case for his standing as maybe the best #3 in the league, to be the guy who got lots of votes for the Cy Young two years ago. If he keeps coming around, the second half of the year should be fun indeed. And maybe Nomar will get rolling again too. After my nightmarish Minnesota experience, I love the idea of beating the Twins soundly.

Wednesday, June 23, 2004

Unfortunately, I will not discover until sometime tomorrow whether or not we did in fact beat the Twins soundly. Apparently the Pony Express got held up overnight. The internet is down here at Big Creek People In Action's clubhouse o' Fun. So I'll have to wait to know the results of Derek Lowe's start (they should be in the 7th or 8th inning by now). Maybe he had another seven innings of sterling sinkerball goodness, drawing grounders, making hitters get bad wood on the ball, and generally keeping them off balance and letting the infielders do the work. Maybe the bats keep rolling. I honestly cannot think of the last time in the United States that my access to scores was so consistently sketchy. Hell, even in Africa most of the time, or in Ireland, I was able to get scores soon after the games were done. Only at times in Namibia, Botswana, Zimbabwe, and at times in Israel have I been I this consistently out of the loop. I'll have to update tomorrow. But I'm feeling oddly confident—which is a good thing, because Rob and I have noticed that almost every time I leave the country for extended periods of time, the Sox struggle. Apparently the same does not hold for being isolated within the United States.

Saturday, June 26, 2004

God, these Red Sox are a challenge to support. It is a bit like watching a schizophrenic argue with himself. From a voyeuristic vantage point, it is undoubtedly entertaining. Let's face it—traffic slows at accidents largely because we want to see the carnage. But if you care, deeply and profoundly care, about the schizophrenic, what beauty you get from whatever lucidity he comes up with pales when placed next to how difficult and painful and awful it is to watch the struggle of internal incoherence that is fundamentally harmful to him. So it goes with the 2004 Red Sox.

I simply could not write these past few days. We lost a series to the Twins, the last in 10 innings. I asserted earlier that a team such as the Twins, one that has playoff goals but that we should still beat, would be a good gauge of what kind of team we are. Obviously we are not a very good one. The bats are failing us. Nomar is not where he needs to be, and his hyperaggressive approach, one that has served him well for several years, is counterproductive. He stubbornly insists upon swinging at the first pitch in a way that must be reminiscent for old timers of how Ted Williams refused to go to the opposite field when teams implemented the Williams Shift. The starting pitching has been fine. In a time when the mean earned run average is above four, and with our offense, we should win 90% of all games that our pitching staff allows only four runs to cross the plate. We are not doing that.

Further, when we score 9-10-11-12 runs in one game, and then lose 9-2 the next, it really obviates the importance of what suddenly seems like a superfluous offensive explosion. This is what has happened in the first two games of this Phillies series. Last night we mashed. Manny had 5 RBI, we pounded the Phillies from the outset, and we won 12-2. Good feelings all around. Then today we go out and lose 9-2. Good teams, and certainly great teams, do not do these sorts of things.

I am writing this from Breaks Interstate Park, a gorgeous setting on the Virginia-Kentucky Border. We left Caretta earlier today and headed out to this, our last stop in the NEH seminar and my last before I take the long trip to Texas. The Pony Express phase of the summer is done. The hotel rooms in Breaks, a gorgeous setting deep in the mountains, have ESPN. Unfortunately, what I get to see today is another ugly performance. .500 ball is not going to get it done. This team continues to disgust because it continues to underachieve. There really is not much reason to recount these games every day until they play the sort of baseball that this team is capable of. We can break this ugly streak of losing series with a win tomorrow. Then we get the Yankees. This is a far different team from the one that pounded the New Yorkers back in April. Maybe we need to face them to overcome this schizophrenia. But we don't get to play them every day.

Sunday, June 27, 2004

Breathe a sigh of relief. Hold off on the hyperventilation. Step off of the side of the bridge. The Sox have won a series. Against the Phillies—a good National League team. They scored another dozen runs, with Ortiz, Bellhorn, and Manny driving in three each. Schilling kept the Phillies to three runs over six, and he became the fourth pitcher this year to reach ten wins, the first to have seven at home. I still would prefer that he not start off by falling behind 3-0 on two home runs. But by the 6th, when he was gassed, he reached back and got it done.

And of course I am feeling good again. Which might make me the fool. Nonetheless, we won, we took a series in interleague against a potential World Series opponent (note how easily that term reemerges), and we came back and scored a ton of runs. If this team hits, and if it hits consistently, we will not be beaten. It is tough to trust them right now on that front.

By the way—as I write this I am watching the treacly handjob of an introduction to the Yankees-Mets game tonight. I want to puke. God, when it comes to baseball, I hate New York. Oh—and as Joe Morgan and Joe Miller talk about this Yankees lineup as the best they have seen in 25 years, I have to wonder if the remember last year's Red Sox. It is hard as a Boston fan to be taken seriously if you bitch about a pro-New York media—it is not like we are not a popular story, but the stroking the media gives the Yankees is vomit-inducing. I hope we pound them this week.

Wednesday, June 30, 2004

I'm in Memphis on my way to Odessa. The Sox got hammered last night. I watched them tonight, with Brendan, one of my best friends from high school, and his wife Andrea, with whom I went to Williams, though we did not know one another then, at a local burger joint. They lost. They lost in egregious fashion. Ortiz made two ugly errors, one that forced ESPN to evoke Bill Buckner. I am growing to hate ESPN and their utter lack of imagination, their inclination to go for the obvious, their pandering to the lowest common denominator of fans. Maybe we'll pull out the win tomorrow and salvage something from this. I am not especially hopeful. This is not a good time to be a Sox fan.

AL East Standings:

	W	L	%	GB
Yankees	49	26	.653	—
Sox	42	34	.553	7.5
Tampa	38	37	.507	11
Toronto	34	44	.436	16.5
Baltimore	32	42	.432	16.5

6

July: The Dog Days Come Early

Friday, July 2, 2004
I'm in Texas, my new home state. But that's not important right now.

Another day another ugly loss. We are playing the Braves, who suck this year, and yet we are apparently the tonic they need. We lost in extra innings and I could see it coming because it had all the trademarks of a 2004 Sox game. They got a lead but kept blowing opportunities. The starter, today Arroyo, who has been on a recent run of hard luck, did his job, limiting the Braves to 2 runs through seven. But we stranded guys on base. We let them stay in it. We got ahead in extra innings only to give the run back. I could go into details. But what's the point? My good friend Rob, who lives in Worcester and with whom I exchange several emails a day, has decided to take some time from the Red Sox. I wish I could do so. I've had to miss so many games this year and I hate to miss ones that are on tv. But right now it is ugly. The manager is making dumb decisions, the guys are not meshing, the defense is sub-sucky (we have given up something like 60 unearned runs in 75 games), the vaunted bats only hit in games that are out of hand, and the relief corps does not have that intimidation factor they had the last part of last year and the first part of this one. Even the starters are not getting it done consistently enough. I feel as if I could cut and paste the same post for the last week and it would hold. There is always tomorrow. I am not certain how many more of these tomorrows I am ready to face.

Saturday, July 3, 2004

Schilling is the stopper of this team. Amidst the maelstrom, as the sound and fury rages around him, he comes in and salves our wounds, which have been oozing something awful. After last night's awful loss, (which followed the previous night's awful loss, which followed . . . oh, never mind) we needed something to staunch the flow of blood, and we got it today. Schilling went the whole way, throwing a complete game, striking out 10, and giving up but one run in a 6-1 Sox victory. Nomar went 3 for 4 with a home run to give us a 1-0 lead that lasted for much of the game, which may help to halt some of the vocal sentiment beginning to well up against him—my guess is he's going to get the hell out of here as soon as this year is done, no matter what we do and no matter what he is saying. But the big blast was a Mirabelli grand slam that opened the game up wide and pretty much assured Schilling's eleventh victory of the season.

So what does it all mean, if anything? Not much. This is a team that has some serious problems. They leave way too many guys on base. They give up an unconscionable number of unearned runs, mostly because of our porous defense. Francona's affable style is undermined by an inscrutable strategic approach. And then we have had a rotating cast, largely because of injury, that is no one's fault but that nonetheless has hurt this team in the field and, I would posit, in the clubhouse, though that sort of speculation is best left to people who know better. Scott Williamson is back on the disabled list, and we keep trying to find the pieces that fit. Hopefully we'll get it straightened out. I maintain that in the postseason we can be a better team than the Yankees. Just as April's poundings of them don't mean a lot now, so too can we envision these last games not meaning much. Meanwhile tomorrow we can win this series. We cannot win it all back at once, but hopefully we can make steps to get back on track. ESPN clichés aside, it is far too early to rule anything out this year.

Jesus Christ. One win and I'm waxing optimistic, despite all that has transpired this past week. I really do deserve whatever happens to me.

Sunday, July 4, 2004

Yes, whatever happens to me, I deserve it. The Sox were swept by the Yankees, got off to a wretched start with a punch to the gut loss against the Braves, have not looked truly good in weeks, and I let one win derail my realism. It did not help that we got off to a 4-1 lead today and everything looked good.

Then the Derek Lowe Face reemerged. The Derek Lowe Face is one of the creations of Bill Simmons (aka ESPN's The Sport's Guy, previously Boston Sports Guy). He actually has a pantheon of faces—the Troy Aikman Face captures that utterly out of it look that Aikman got when he was being besieged by defenders, especially when he was going through his multiple concussion phase. The Derek Lowe Face is one that haunts Sox fans. We have all seen it. Lowe gives up some hits, then a few runs, and where some guys, the best ones, buck up, Lowe gets this bewildered, hurt, somewhat crestfallen look of someone in the process of inevitable defeat. It is not much of a sight to behold. I hate psychological explanations most of the time, but boy, the Derek Lowe face does seem to give away a fragile psyche beneath.

Four-and-a-third innings, 8 hits, 8 runs, all earned, with his era ballooning to 6.02. Newly acquired and promoted Jimmy Anderson came in and gave up the final two runs of the ugly nine-run fifth, but by then the damage was done and we were on our way to our fifth loss in six games and eighth in eleven. We are 28-31 since April and are 18-23 on the road.

We are off tomorrow, and on Tuesday the A's come into town. Oakland has moved well ahead of us in the Wild Card race, and we have Waker on the mound facing Zito. I imagine the reception they get from the Fenway Faithful will be resounding in its clarity of our displeasure. And if I were Terry Francona, I would not start making plans for leaf peeping in New England on off days this fall. The knives are out, and whether or not we as a sports society are too quick to fire coaches and managers, the fact remains, Tito's head is on the chopping block. I await the inevitable and damning vote of confidence from Epstein.

I'm off to catch my first Midland Rockhounds game. They are a Double A affiliate of the A's in the Texas League, which has some old, historic teams and some of the best nicknames and mascots in organized baseball. It's the 4th of July, so there will be a Fireworks display and I plan on partaking of several hot dogs or whatever local specialties might be on offer. I bet the Midland Rockhounds won't break my heart. I also doubt they'll strand eight guys on base and make three errors on a nightly basis. Happy Birthday, America!

Tuesday, July 6, 2004

Victory, sweet victory. But knowing the Sox, this 11-0 throttling of the A's (if you're going to pound someone, may as well make it be a Wild Card rival, and for the record, of course I am rooting for Texas to take the West so that I may be able to see a Sox-Rangers playoff matchup) will be ephemeral. Tomorrow they could come out and score 2 runs and make the guy they are facing look like Sandy Koufax redux. But these days, given that we've lost 5 of 6 series, I'd say any game-one win has to count as a good one. Tomorrow night's game is on ESPN, so I'll get to see if they can build up a little momentum before they take the All Star Break.

It was a good win. Waker was on the mound, and he was masterful. He went seven, gave up but three hits, striking out six and walking only one. His ERA has dropped below four, and all in all, he is making a case yet again for why maybe we should not overlook him the way we often seem to do. We always seem to preface conversations about Waker with caveats about his knuckler—"you never know with that pitch," or "depends on if he's on or off," and yet as the years have accumulated, you do know, and more often than not he is on. "Underrated" is one of those words that we use all too easily, and yet has it ever applied more than it does with Tim Wakefield?

This club was built on two things. The first is obviously starting pitching, which on the whole we have gotten even if it has been inconsistent, and even if Lowe is still a huge question mark. (Now with Lowe you really never do know whether he'll be on or off, and his sinker is far more vexing than Waker's knuckler.) The second thing upon which this club is based has been the lineup. They have underachieved, even if the cumulative stats do not indicate as much. But tonight went well—A lot of guys saw time in the blowout, which began with three runs in the second (on a three-run Mueller home run, his sixth, and his 23rd, 24th, and 25th RBI), four in the fourth when the Sox loaded the bases and just bled the A's, and four more in the fifth when they did the same. Damon went 5 fore 6, setting the table all night. Bellhorn had two hits, two RBI, and two runs scored, Nomar went 2 for 5 with 2 RBI (though he also left five on base), Manny went 0 for 3 but walked twice and drove in two runs, Dead Man Walking Kevin Millar managed to go 3 for 4 with 2 RBI, Mirabelli gave a slumping 'Tek a rest and went 2 for 5 and scored twice, and Mueller went 2 for 3 with the home run and three driven in and he scored three times as well. Alas this laundry list stands out all the more for its relative rarity this year.

It's pretty clear that we Sox fans are a resilient lot. And while we bitch and moan and complain and swear (and swear, and swear) the fact is, we do still have faith, and we hope they have faith too, because we still believe that this is the year. Why, I do not know, but we do.

By the way, I attended two Rock Hounds games on consecutive nights and they won both times. I don't want to imply any causality, but they started the second half of the season (when records are wiped clean after the first half winners garnered playoff spots and the second half is up for grabs) 2-8 and now are up to 4-8. So draw from that what you will.

Wednesday, July 7, 2004

What was the line from *The Shawshank Redemption?* "Hope is a good thing, maybe the best of things"? Well the Sox are giving us hope. They pounded the A's again today, plating another 11 runs, this time in another walkover, 11-3. It's hard to believe it, but could could the catalyst really be the successful return of Bill Mueller to the lineup? He's back from the DL (and Cesar "Bling Bling" Crespo mercifully accepted his being sent to Pawtucket, where he belonged all along—a world where Cesar Crespo is a contributing player on a team that dreams of the World Series is a world in which the living would envy the dead) and is hitting ninth, a spot in which he is comfortable and which automatically makes our lineup look a lot more like last year's. There were several games earlier in the year, especially when Nomar and Trot were also out, that our back half of the order was laughably inadequate.

Pedro had another good start tonight, winning his fifth straight in a laugher that took any pressure off of him, and thus hopefully that right shoulder of his. Pedro rarely gets run support, so this has been a good omen. If we hit and he can have a cushion, we will really do some damage in the second half of the season. He went seven innings, gave up five hits, had only one rough inning, the third, in which he gave up three runs but because of an error only one was earned, his only earned run of the night. He walked one, struck out seven, had good control (70 of 102 pitches were strikes) and, notably, in the 7th inning he was throwing in the low 90s. This is all very good. He's getting that Pedro swagger, he drilled Bernie Williams last week and was unrepentant, he's hugging guys in the dugout, and he is giving us the ace that we know and love.

Meanwhile the bats are flourishing. Nomar is on fire (that snapping sound you hear is the breaking of ankles all over some rather shameful provinces of Red Sox Nation from jumping off, on, off, and now back on the Nomar bandwagon). Damon followed up his five-hit day yesterday with two more hits and three RBI. Nomar hit a home run for his 500th career extra base hit, Bellhorn popped one out, and Manny prevented an 0-fer the first two games of this onslaught for him and Ortiz by hitting an absolute blast that banged off of the coke bottles in left and somewhere into the parking garage across Landsdowne Street. We've scored 22 runs on 32 hits in two games, shelling Mark Redman tonight after humiliating Zito last night. Tomorrow we go for a sweep. And we get to take on the Rangers over the weekend, meaning I should get to see all of those games leading into the All Star break.

Yes, hope is a good thing. There is no sense getting ahead of ourselves, but we are playing the sort of baseball we anticipated when this all came together in the cold New England winter. The Yankees have lost five of six, getting swept by the Mets and following that up with two of three against Detroit, and we get to face off against them again after the Break. There may be nothing like a two-game offensive explosion to get that short-term memory to fail us. Let's pull out the brooms in Fenway tomorrow. For now that would be the best of things.

Thursday, July 8, 2004

OK, which Sox team is going to show up in the last two innings? At one point we were up 7-1 in this game. In the last four innings we have given them seven runs. Schill had an ok performance, but he was reaching a pretty high pitch count (The A's were playing Moneyball) and was gone after five-and-a-third in which he gave up three earned runs. The bullpen then came out and imploded. Timlin gave up three. Foulke gave up one, though he also let in some of Timlin's runners, and the A's tied it in the top of the 8th.

We just got up, Damon got an infield hit, but Mueller flied out on a hit and run and Damon was doubled off easily. Ortiz, who has had a hell of a game (3 for 5 with an RBI on a blast) popped out high but harmlessly. And the A's are up in the top of the ninth. Manny has also had a good game—he is leading off the ninth, and it would be nice for him to add to a night in which he has already gone 2 for 3 with a home run and three RBI.

On a positive note, after last night's game, someone went into the clubhouse to tell Manny he had been chosen to be in the Home Run Derby to be held at the All Star festivities on Monday. Manny immediately asked about Ortiz, and upon being told that his friend was not invited, Manny gave up his spot for Ortiz. Apparently the powers that be acceded to Manny's request, and Ortizzle, who also made his first All Star team (it would have been a travesty had he not) will get some spotlight at the Home Run Derby, which has become one of the most popular events of any sport's all star game. The fact is, Ortiz might be more naturally suited for this sort of contest than Manny. Maybe he can come out of nowhere and do what Garrett Anderson did last year. This also points out something that I have suspected for a while—the team takes most of its cues from the Latin Troika influence of Pedro and especially Manny and the affable and popular Ortiz. It is worth noting that we have seen no appearances of surly, brooding Manny this year and instead have seen a boyish, joyful, happy, ebullient Manny. And is it a coincidence that he is having a monster year? (Granted, Manny almost always has monster years. He really is a freak of nature at the plate. And he is becoming a serviceable left fielder, much as Jim Rice did).

In any case, Manny is at the bat. I'd love to see them end this now, escape with a win that was more difficult than it ought to have been, and get ready for Texas. My buddy Rob and I just exchanged an email as the tide began to turn in this game, and he observed that a loss tonight, especially in this way, would pretty much erase the good vibes of the last two nights, making appearances like those seem like the anachronisms. I agree. It seems to me that a win is a win. If we pull this one out, it won't matter that we almost pissed it away, and in fact it might even be one of those that goes down as a test of team character that they can say proudly that they passed. But there are different kinds of losses. This one would be a bad one.

Ugh—Manny got a reprieve when Hatteberg muffed a foul ball. Then he took it deep into the count, and ultimately he struck out, looking pretty bad in the process. Nomar is up, and he just ripped a line drive, but it was foul (naturally it was on the first pitch). A slider away for a called strike makes it an 0-2 count. Ugh—another strikeout. Now Trot Nixon is up. Trot hits a somewhat controversial triple! Apparently a case could be made that a fan touched it, but the umps either did not see it or chose not to call it. Now it could all rest on the bat of David McCarty, who has had a couple of late-inning hits to impact games. But he grounds to Hatteberg, who takes it on a tough hop and wins a footrace to first. It's going into the tenth. Forgive me for feeling a bit tense—of late extra innings have not exactly been beneficent to the Sox. They are 3-5 this year in extra frames, and some of those losses have been wretched, gut wrenching, painful, nightmare-inducing, therapy-requiring affairs.

Lefty Curtis Leskanic is pitching. A quick 1-2-3 inning is in order. We acquired him from Kansas City recently. He was 0-3 with them, is 0-1 with us so far. But he's induced a couple of outs, including one on a K. Still, I cannot say that my ideal conception of an extra inning game against one of our key rivals has the ball in Curtis Leskanic's hand, but that's what we got, and he just got Eric Byrnes to fly out to Pokey for the third out.

Now the bottom of the order has to get it done. The good thing is that they have their rookie, Justin Lehr, out to face us, and we pummeled him last week. I hope this is not too evil, but let's destroy this poor young guy's psyche. Let's go 'Tek! OK, 'Tek struck out.

Let's go Pokey! Wait, Pokey, who's been ineffective of late (0 for 4 tonight, 1 for his last 20) gives way to pinch hitter and on-base machine Mark Bellhorn. Let's go Horny! OK, ground out to first. Eeeeesh. Let's go Damon! Single to left! Winning run on base, with Bill Mueller, Your 2003 American league Batting Champion, at the plate. Let's Go Mueller! (Annoyed yet?) YES! YES! YES! Mueller delivers! Damon was taking home on Sveum's urging, and he scores on a Mueller double to left center! It wasn't easy. It wasn't pretty. But it was a win. 8-7. And it is a sweep! As I said, it doesn't matter how you win. Just that you do.

Friday, July 9, 2004

The beat goes on, with Captain Caveman (my favorite nickname of the generally imagination-challenged comments dopey announcers have made about the hirsute centerfielder), Johnny Damon, leading the way on offense while Bronson Arroyo, he of the hardest luck in baseball this season, pitched a masterful eight innings of shutout ball against the Rangers.

I was able to watch the game from what I suspect will become my favorite sportsbar in Odessa, Zucci's. It's a good, dark bar with several screens and even NTN trivia. Since we were playing the Rangers I was in the minority, though most people were not all that interested in the game. Philistines. In any case, I am hoping for a sweep for the obvious reasons, but also because I made a bet with one of the guys last night, who insisted that the Red Sox are incapable of sweeping this Rangers team.

We won 7-0. The bats are still hot, with Damon continuing his 14-game hitting streak. He is now hitting .319, and has gone an electrifying 19 for 32 in the last six games. He's scored in every game but one in the last 14 and he has five home runs in his last ten games, including two last night. The appreciative fans cheered until he gave a curtain call after the second of the two solo shots, waving his cap and revealing his shaggy joyousness to all.

Even Kevin Millar is contributing. He played a legitimately solid first base yesterday and he continues to improve at the plate. He also stole a base, the fifth of his career.

But if there was one truly auspicious sign, perhaps it was that Arroyo finally got a win, something he had not done since May 21.

He kept Texas hitters off balance all night with an array of pitches, all of which were hitting their spots. He only gave up three hits, two in the first inning, and he was hitting in the low 90s with his fastball. If Arroyo can pitch like this against the best hitting team in baseball, we really might be set at starter, especially if Lowe can somehow pitch his way out of this slump. He goes tonight against a team that will be looking for redemption.

It is also rumor time in baseball, as the end of July and the trading deadline approaches and teams need to decide if they can win or not. Two of the most interesting rumors involve the Sox pursuing Randy Johnson and Roger Clemens. Neither is going to happen, in my estimation. No way Drayton McLain, the Astros owner, trades Roger. And I think we won't get anywhere with Johnson, who may or may not even be on the market. The Yankees are said to be interested too. (Somehow Steinbrenner managed to say he would love to get Johnson for hi staff and did not get nailed for tampering, yet our owners get chided when they refer to the Yankees as the "Evil Empire." It would be nice if Selig would get his hands out of Steinbrenner's pants long enough to realize the rampant hypocrisy of how he deals with them and how he deals with everybody else). In any case, I would love to see Johnson in a Sox uniform, but I do not know what we could give for him, and while it would be nice, I'm not convinced it is necessary. And I am not sure Johnson would waive his no-trade clause to pitch in Boston—apparently the big ugly bastard has declared that he'd prefer living in New York over Boston.

In any case, there are two games before the All Star break (Schilling has pulled out of the game to save wear on his ankles and to get time with his family, a decision for which I am thankful) and it would be really nice to continue this roll for the next two games. We need Lowe to come through tonight – hopefully whatever Arroyo has is contagious—and Waker to do so tomorrow. The bats should take care of themselves.

Saturday, July 10, 2004

That rat-a-tat-tat sound you hear resonating throughout New England and Red Sox Nation is balls bouncing on, off, and over the Green Monster. We just won our fifth in a row over the meat of the American League West. Today it was a 14-6 victory. D-Lowe stumbled again, giving up six (all unearned after a Bellhorn error on a play that would have ended the inning) in the second inning, but the bats just kept swinging and connecting and scattering the ball all over Fenway, and Lowe only gave up one hit after the second and he pitched into the eighth. Dealing with adversity has been his difficulty this year, and he did a good job of it today. We got a season high 21 hits tonight, most by the usual suspects. Manny hit two home runs (with five RBI total) and Bellhorn, Nomar, and 'Tek added one each. Damon continued his torrid pace by going 3 for 6, hitting in his 15th straight. This was his seventh straight multi-hit game. This is the Damon we all dreamed about seeing when we first acquired him. Bellhorn, Nomar, and Manny each had four hits—it was a career high for Bellhorn. The top four slots in the order went 15 for 21 with four home runs and 10 RBI. Nomar hit his first home run playing a position other than shortstop, as he was the DH today. He has gone 18 for his last 35 and has hit three home runs in his last eight games. A hot Nomar might be the best news of all given that his mood has seemed surly of late. Any way you look at it, these guys are on fire, and despite the confidence of the old guy in the bar, they are poised for a sweep. They smacked possible All Star game starter Kenny Rogers around, and he left in the second. Lowe stumbled but we were able to pick him up and he got the win. In all, it was just another great game for the Sox. And as a little bonus, when Rogers came out, the Rangers replaced him with old friend John "Way Back" Wasdin, who gave up a double to Nomar that drove in a run and then Manny's two run blast.

The Yankees are unfortunately rolling right now too, so we are still six games behind them. But if we are playing like this, we will be formidable. They'll stumble at some point. I've no doubt that the AL East race is not over and that we'll close this gap. We almost should not want the All Star break right now, in case three days off cools down the bats, but at the same time, we may as well get guys rest where we can as the hottest part of the year is upon us, and they need to be fresh for the stretch run. Damon has historically been a guy who has great half seasons, but he never can seem to maintain it. Maybe this year he'll be able to keep his pre-All Star game performance going after the midseason classic is done. Pedro was given permission to head home to see his family, but unlike in the past, it is not a source of controversy. Manny is playing unreal baseball. Ortiz gets to have his first All Star and Home Run Derby appearance. Nomar can use this time to get healthy, ditto Schilling and Pokey, whose thumb has clearly been bothering him more than he has let on. The break gives Tito a chance to reset the rotation to set us up for the second half.

Everything is going well right now. Tomorrow is a big game because we can keep this streak going, continue to send a message to the rest of the league and maybe gain a game on the Yankees if Tampa can manage finally to eke out a win against New York. As bad as I felt a week ago, I feel that good now. Have I pointed out what a bizarre, weird, nonsensical thing it is to be a Red Sox fan? It's self induced of course, but no less chaotic as a consequence.

Sunday, July 11, 2004

I am going to sound like a fool, but it never crossed my mind that the Sox would not win today. With the way that they had been hitting, with the way guys had been coming through, I really thought that a victory was inevitable. Instead they lost 6-5 in a game when they fell behind and battled back, and managed to tie it at 5-5 (on another big Damon hit, a solo home run in the eighth) but then Foulke gave up one run and we could not quite scratch back. Damon got on in the ninth, then stole second and when the ball got away on the throw (Damon may have inadvertently but fortuitously kicked it away) he took third. But we could not advance him, and the game ended with Bellhorn looking at strike three. A game should never, ever, ever end on a called third strike. Ever.

Still, there is much to feel good about right now. After the worst stretch of the season, we rebounded, won five of six against the Rangers and the A's, one of whom is likely to win the west, the other to be a candidate for the Wild Card slot. We are hitting the hell out of the ball. Waker was not especially sharp today, but on the whole the starting pitching has either been good or they have at least battled to keep us in games. They have the look of a team that is ready to do some damage. In all, if we could not pull off the sweep, this was actually not so bad a game. We were down 3-0 and then 5-2, came back to tie it, and an over-rested Foulke just was not sharp today. On the whole all is going ok given how we shot ourselves in the feet for most of the two months preceding this past week. Hopefully this is the real incarnation of the 2004 Red Sox and not what we have seen too often. If the guys are hitting, we are as dangerous as anyone. If not, it will be a long second half.

Monday, July 12, 2004

The All Star Break marks the traditional halfway point of the Major League Baseball season. True, teams hit the 81 game mark, the literal halfway point, a week or so ago. The Red Sox, for example, have played 86 games. But baseball is a metaphorical game, in which traditions play a role. That we have not played precisely 50% of our games should not matter. The All Star Break provides a league-wide opportunity to take pause and to assess where we have been and where we are going. Without ado, (well, ok, there will be a little ado) I am going to engage in one of those cheap, lazy sportswriter's parlor games and present to you my grades for the first half of the season.

First, the AL East Standings at the break:

	W	L	%	GB	H	A
Yanks	55	31	.640	—	33-12	22-19
SOX	48	38	.558	7	30-15	18-23
Rays	42	45	.483	13.5	23-18	19-27
Jays	39	49	.443	17	23-23	16-26
O's	37	48	.435	17.5	20-26	17-22

Clearly, we have much ground to make up. The Wild Card race, though we do not want to think about it yet, looks like this:

	W	L	GB
Sox	48-38		0
A's	47-39		1
Angels	47-40		1.5
Twins	47-40		1.5

Obviously, nothing is guaranteed, but certainly we still can look forward to the postseason, and hopefully we can rally enough to win the division, despite the formidable but not insurmountable deficit. Now the grades:

Hitting: For much of the year the hitting statistics have made the guys look better than they have been, truth be told. It seems as if there have been an awful lot of games that we have lost 5-3 and left a dozen guys stranded on base for every 9-3 win we have had. For so much of this season they have seemed incapable of hitting in the clutch. Obviously for much of that time we missed Nomar, Trot, and Mueller, forcing us to send out the notorious split squad teams. But even as constituted with the injuries and with guys who should have been getting at bats in Pawtucket and Columbus, not Fenway and the Bronx, we should have been doing more. Manny has had one of the great first halves in Red Sox history, and Ortiz is not far behind. In the last couple of weeks Damon has been unstoppable. Nomar took a while, as many of us suspected he would, to recover from his spring training Achilles injury, but he is on fire as well. On the whole, then, it seems that there have been three distinct phases for the batting order, that month in April when we seemed capable of outhitting anybody. The nine-week period after April when we looked pathetic. And the last week or so. The pessimist in me knows that a week does not a trend make. The optimist thinks that this is more like the team we will see in the second half. The professor in me knows that even periodic greatness cannot allow one to overlook sustained mediocrity. So in the final analysis, for the first half they get decent, not great, grades.
First-half Grade: B

Starting Pitching: The expectations were obviously huge on this front with the acquisition of Schilling and the presence of Pedro. The belief was that Schilling strengthened our staff because suddenly Lowe could face #3 starters, Waker #4s, and the tandem of Arroyo/Kim could split between the #5 slot and the bullpen. It has not quite worked out that way. While Schilling has been as good as advertised, making the All Star rotation and likely the starting slot had he not begged out to give nine days of rest to his balky ankle,

and while Pedro overcame a rough April to rebound and look at times like the Pedro of old, there have been a few glitches. Lowe has been woefully inconsistent, and at times just plain woeful. He had a tirade last week against the media, and the speculation about his psyche, while unfair, is probably inevitable in a media culture such as Boston's. The hope is that he'll come around and give us the form we've seen in the past. I still give him all sorts of leeway after last postseason, but in the end, he still has to get it done on the mound. Waker has been typically reliable, even if his won-lost record does not indicate as much. Arroyo has had some of the most rotten luck in recent memory and Kim has been injured and otherwise out of commission and has not contributed. Maybe we'll get him in the second half, though the Sox would be wise not to bet on it. This has not been what folks may have hoped, but it has certainly been a strength of the team. The inconsistency at the bottom of the rotation, no matter the reason, costs the group an A.
First-half Grade: B+

Relief Pitching: These guys started off slow, then became the best in the game, and in the last few weeks have backslided. We've had some injuries that have kept us from being able to have our ideal knockout combination, and Foulke, who was lights out for most of the year has had some rough outings of late, including yesterday's, where he was, by his own admission, pretty bad. But on the whole, keeping in mind that relievers often come in as the result of someone's failure and thus in vulnerable situations, this has been a strength. They have lost very few games for this team and most often have kept us in games so that we could win them. When they are healthy they should be even more of a pillar, supporting the already solid rotation and shortening games.
First-half grade: A-

Defense: The Sox in the field have put the "Ugh!" in ugly. They are arguably the worst defensive team in the league, and have given up something like 70 unearned runs. That is an awful lot of runs. And they translate out to a distressing number of losses. Interestingly, there have been at least one or two revelations in the field, most notably in the form of Pokey Reese, whose glove has made him

a beloved folk hero, and of all people Manny Ramirez, who has played not only passable, but good and sometimes outstanding defense. Even Kevin Millar has been a standout of late. But a few bright spots cannot cover up for a multitude of sins, and if this component of the game does not improve, we could be watching while other teams play in October.
First-half Grade: D-

Running: This is another weakness. The American league simply does not call for a team to be the Go-Go White Sox of 1959. But we only have one guy who can be called a serious and smart baserunner, and that is Johnny Damon. On the other hand we have a lot of really dumb baserunners. And we have generally smart players who nonetheless have done dumb things. Again, perhaps surprisingly, Manny has not been one of the biggest culprits. If they cannot be fast, at least they can be smart. So far, this has not always been the case.
First-half Grade: C-

The Bench/Team Depth: Most of us hate to admit it, and it gave us lots of fodder for screaming at the tv or radio, but while our depth was a joke, it also saved us for much of this year. The Pokey-Bellhorn combo that was supposed to struggle for playing time this year suddenly became our double play combination for most of the first half, and on the whole acquitted themselves very well. When things were going well it seemed like someone different came through every night—David McCarty or Gabe Kaplar or Kevin Youkilis or Brian Daubach or Andy Dominique or, God love him, Cesar Crespo. The problem was, with all of the injuries that we have, good to passable bench guys, guys who provide depth and insurance, were pressed into starting detail. Oftentimes several of them at once. That is not good. But that we have them all is. We weathered an injury bug this year that we avoided last season. Some of these role players are going to have a lot to be proud of if and when we do make a run in the postseason, because without them we would not be where we are.
First-half Grade: A-

Managing and Coaching: The rule of thumb in Red Sox nation is that everyone thinks they could do better. Every farmer in Framingham and teacher in Tewksbury and nurse in Newport and bartender in Bennington knows what to do in situations where our coaches and managers, who have devoted their lives to playing and coaching and knowing the game, have allegedly screwed up. Of course screwing up is, for one thing, a post facto assessment. A decision that fails is always noticed. One that succeeds rarely is. And that soccer coach in Saugus who gets to second guess after a loss is never in a situation to make the decisions that matter, time after time. He is not in a situation to be questioned after innumerable bad judgment calls—and if you think they don't make those bad judgment calls, go look on the message boards or listen to talk radio and listen to the irredeemably dumb things that people say but for which they are not held responsible. I think it is a bit early to judge the Tito era. Yes, I agree with my critical brethren that Tito does some things that invoke head scratching—his pinch running choices and his use of the bullpen in particular raise questions. I too wonder if he is too soft, too much of a player's coach, too much of a pushover. I think he sounds a bit too much like former Pats Coach Pete Carroll after losses. But for now I am willing to give him the benefit of the doubt. Players tend to win and lose games. If this changes, we can go with the hook. For now, managing is not the problem in Boston.
First-half Grade: B-

Health: OK, I am not certain how you grade something like this. If I am judging the witch doctors who seem to make up the medical staff, it seems that they deserve an F and perhaps need a refresher course with the Simpsons' Dr. Nick. If my grade is simply a way to mark the general health of the team, it cannot be much better. Nomar, Trot, Mueller, Williamson, and Kim among those expected to be major players for this team spent significant time on the disabled list. Mendoza, Burks, and others have seen little or no time this year. Manny's hamstrings, Schilling's ankle, and Pedro's fragile shoulder all have fallen under scrutiny. Last year this sort of thing did not happen. So I am not certain who I am grading here, but due perhaps to circumstances beyond their control we have to wish for better in the second half.
First-half Grade: D

Intangibles: This is supposed to be where we assess things like clubhouse chemistry, where we include the quality of guys who cowboy up, of how happy or controversy- ridden or dysfunctional the clubhouse seems. On the one hand we have D-Lowe's blowups and Schilling's alleged clashes with Scotty Williamson and then yesterday Manny, and Nomar's undertones of disgruntlement. Then again we have Varitek's leadership and Manny's seeming contentment and the overarching influence of Papi Ortiz. When we lose, the former stuff matters most. When we win, it is the latter. At the end of the day, winning will make for a happy and productive clubhouse. They have weathered a lot of storms. They seem to support one another and they seem optimistic.
First-half Grade: B

So on the whole the Sox are doing ok. They are not the juggernaut we all hoped to see. But they are firmly in contention to go to the playoffs, which means they are in a position to do what we all yearn for them to do: Win the World Series. That is a pretty good placement, and hopefully it will get better.

Wednesday, July 14, 2004

All Star Games, the Midsummer Classic, rarely live up to their billing. Last year's was an exciting affair, with Hank Blalock providing the dramatic home run off of Eric Gagne (He of the splendid and just ended record consecutive games without blowing a save streak) that also gave the American league the home field for the World Series. But as a general rule, these games are all pomp and no circumstance, with the rhythms of the game constantly disrupted, especially in recent years, so that managers could play Little League coach for a day and make sure everybody got in.

The only solace one usually has is that your guys might get in and do something special, which is relatively rare. I can remember very few great Sox moments in All Star games. Roger in 1986 was great. Obviously my elders will recall Ted Williams' performances, especially his epic 1941 blast at Briggs Stadium that won the game 7-5 for the American League and his 1946 performance in the 12-0 laugher at Fenway. In both years he won the game's MVP.

It is hard to believe, but there was once a time when the All Star game mattered. Of late there has been the prattle that "it counts," but even if it counts (and people are pretty undecided as to whether it is dopey to have an exhibition game have any actual implications or whether it is really, really dopey) it does not matter. Most guys today would never think of a career highlight coming from an All Star game, and yet in another era, the guys cared, beating the other league was important, and someone who proved to be a star among stars would place that performance up there with their all-time memories. Today the guys seem to love the atmosphere (at least those who don't decide to skip the event entirely) and it is great to see a guy like Adam Dunn videotaping every moment for posterity, or at least his grandkids. But it is not the same. One can easier imagine Pete Rose being named chair of a Major League Baseball ethics panel than one can envision a collision at the plate in one of these affairs, as happened when Charlie Hustle trucked Ray Fosse back in 1971, a collision after which Fosse was never the same. The guys make too much, with free agency and interleague play the lines between the leagues are fungible, and, perhaps rightly, no one wants to cost their own team as the result of going at it too hard in a game that doesn't really count, World Series implications notwithstanding.

Last night's game was pretty typical of these matchups. The American League jumped on hometown hero, and really the focal point of the day, Roger Clemens (not a lot of broken hearts in Red Sox Nation over this one, I'm afraid, and doubtlessly not many more in New York or Toronto) and before the first inning was over, the score was 6-0. As a Sox fan I always root for the American league, so of course I was happy. But more importantly, Manny hit a laser shot that landed in the third row of seats in left field for a two-run dinger. Later in the game, Ortiz blasted one of his moon shots off of old friend Carl Pavano. Ortiz also walked twice and scored another run, so he would have been in line for the game's MVP trophy if Alfonso Soriano (he of the indeterminate age) had not hit a three-run homer in that decisive first inning. The final score was 9-4. The AL won, and the two Sox players contributed to the victory.

As important to the whole weekend, Ortiz added a level of joy to the proceedings that shows why he might be the glue in the clubhouse for this team. He was clearly enraptured to be there, and even after only hitting three home runs in his Home Run Derby appearance, he was supportive of everyone lese, including the eventual winner, Miguel Tejada (he and Lance Berkman of the Astros put on an eye-popping show), for whom he pretty much seemed to serve as coach, trainer, and mascot. It was fun to watch such unfettered joy and to see a reminder that for many of these millionaire athletes, it is still a game that they love to play and from which they derive joy.

Today is the last day of the break. Then on to Anaheim and a three game set with potential Wild Card (and Randy Johnson) sweepstakes competition (if the prognosticators are to be believed. I still do not believe them.) the Angels. We have played sub-.500 ball on the road this year, and that is an area that needs marked improvement soon. Hopefully everybody is rested but still possessing that edge that took us back from the brink last week. The All Star Break is done. Things are serious from here on out. (As opposed to the frivolity I've surely conveyed for the last five months.)

Thursday, July 15, 2004

It's the second half of the season. Red Sox fans could not be more excited. There is a buzz in the air. And a good number of us won't have any damned idea what the hell happens in these games until the next morning. The Red Sox tonight start a span of games in which they play 18 of 24 on the road, with the home games being a series against the Yankees and one against the Orioles in which we have a doubleheader. Given our road woes in 2004, this is where the rubber meets the road. This is where we find out just what sort of team we have. If they come back from the next month or so within shouting distance of the Yankees and still have a solid grasp on the Wild Card, this team is for real. If not, well, how 'bout them Patriots?

I suspect that we will be fine. Now maybe I am whistling through the graveyard right now, but this is a different team from the one of even two weeks ago. Admittedly, inexplicable and at times downright surreal things happen to Red Sox teams with the weight of expectations on their shoulders. But the reality is that this is a formidable lineup that just now is beginning to gel.

The Dog Days Come Early

The pitching is still potentially the class of the league. They are playing hungry. The AAAA lineups and batting orders should be behind us. Big Papi and Manny and Nomar should haunt the rest of the league's moundsmen while Pedro and Schilling and Waker bewitch and bedevil the rest of the league's lineups. D-Lowe will be a reclamation project and Arroyo will get the breaks he did not get up to now. Or at least both of those guys will benefit from consistent run support.

And this all will start tonight, at 10:05 Eastern Standard Time (or what this provincial easterner likes to call "real time"), 7:05 on the west coast, and here in flyover country, were it to come on at all it would be at 9:05. Ending well after midnight, these games will be unsolved mysteries to a goodly proportion of Red Sox Nation, who will thank their various Gods for morning Sportscenter repeats and high speed internet access. In New England, I used to wake up and before I'd brush my teeth, or go to the bathroom, I'd turn on the radio to hear a score. Of course in the wilds of New Hampshire, we did not have cable, and this was largely before ESPN made it a world worth inhabiting, and even the editions of the *Boston Globe* that made it to the Granite State were early editions and thus did not have game results. I honestly am not certain how I survived such a savage, barbarous world.

In any case, the last time we faced them, Anaheim started us on a swoon. Vlad Guerrero had himself a 6 RBI night as the Angels rolled. Things are different now. I expect Manny and Ortiz to keep up their All Star run and D-Lowe to induce the Angels' hitters into harmless ground balls. I expect that there will be some late nights here as I await the word from Baseball Tonight. My suspicion is that this week of west coast games will drive me into the arms of DirecTV as soon as I rent a place (I'm staying at one of my new colleague's house).

One last thing—in his latest column on ESPN.com, Tim Kurkjian did one of those gimmicky but delightful "Ten Questions for the second half" columns that are just about ubiquitous in sportswriting (note that I did one with the midseason grades a couple of days back). I should say it was delightful until I saw that one of his questions was "Will Vlad Guerrero win the Triple Crown." I was almost apoplectic (Note to self: getting apoplectic about sports columns is a sign that you have a problem. Response to self: Bite me.). So I wrote Kurkjian an email that will be deleted by some pimply intern forthwith. So I thought I'd share it with you. (I share because I love.):

> Tim—
>
> Am I missing something? In your question, "Will Vlad Guerrero win the Triple Crown?", and in almost every first half MVP ranking that I have seen, I cannot help but wonder if everyone is not being intentionally obtuse. Anyone who would ask about Vlad Guerrero winning the Triple Crown would have to willfully ignore Manny Ramirez, who only leads Guerrero by 6 home runs, is tied with him for RBI (wanna bet which guy gets more chances to drive guys in during the second half of the season?) and is behind him by a negligible .001 in batting. Now one could argue, theoretically, that if Player A had a history of being mediocre and Player B had a history of being outstanding, then Player A would revert to the mean. The problem is, this isn't theory, and with a bat in their hands, Vlad Guerrero, great though he is, is no Manny Ramirez. Manny may be the best pure hitter in the game, and with Ortiz and the rest of the Sox hitting like they are, it is pretty hard to avoid Manny in the order. He's going to see pitches. On the MVP front, I am equally as befuddled. Pudge is having a great year, but for a team that is going nowhere, and I'll place bets as to whether or not a catcher maintains a .370 average. But ok, I can see being enamored of him. But I've seen guys place Michael Young and Vlad Guerrero and a whole host of other guys ahead of Manny, who at times has carried the Sox when Nomar, Trot, and Mueller were out. This is long, you get dozens of letters a day, and I know the tone of this is probably snarky enough to have earned instant delete button, but still, help me, before I think I am the one-eyed man in the land of the blind.

At least we know and appreciate Manny's sublime gifts. Like all sublime gifts, they come at a cost. But I'll pay that price.

Friday, July 16, 2004

Ugh. Last night Derek Lowe wobbled through four innings, letting lots of guys on base but giving up no runs. Discerning fans foresaw disaster if the offense did not manage to muster at least a few runs early on. And in the 5th, with D-Lowe's pitch count already at about 100, those predictions came true as the wheels fell off. Guys got on, this time Lowe could not muster up the magic or the luck or the karma, and the Angels started scoring in bunches. And when Lowe left the game, the relief staff caught whatever had infected the big sinkerballer, and before long it was 8-1 and over. UGH!

And of course this morning the recriminations came, mostly involving why Tito gave Pedro the whole weekend off when he was slated to pitch Sunday's game, the tough 7-6 loss, and barring that, why Pedro was not starting last night. To an extent this is understandable—with the way Lowe has been scuffling, and with the fact that Pedro has shown a little bit of 2001 in the last two month, it would seem to make sense to maximize Pedro's value while minimizing Lowe right now. But in the end, if they come back and win the next three games, this should pass, especially if judicious use of Pedro means we have his right arm all the way through to game seven in late October. What more is there to say? You can't unring the bell, you can't get the toothpaste back in the tube, and you can't undo a loss. Let's just hope that they shook the All Star Break grogginess out last night and they show up ready to play in Anaheim for the remainder of the weekend.

Saturday, July 17, 2004

Any night when the normally affable David Ortiz utterly and completely loses it in a confrontation with the umpires is going to stick in the craw.

In the seventh inning Big Papi was called out on a pitch that was at best borderline – letter high and on the inside portion of the plate—and he started jawing with the home plate ump Matt Hollowell. It soon escalated to the point where Hollowell gave Ortiz the heave ho, and the big fella just lost it. He went absolutely berserk. Terry Francona had to use every bit of his might (Francona is a former major leaguer and not a small man) to keep Ortiz from making contact with Hollowell, who typical of umpires, kept the argument going rather than diffuse it. One of these days a mouthy ump who thinks the show is about him is going to get torn asunder by one of these guys. The men in blue sometimes forget that these are professional athletes, and not Little Leaguers, whom they oftentimes provoke, antagonize and instigate into fights.

In any case, it took Francona and hitting coach Ron Jackson to pull Ortiz from the fray. Then once he got to the dugout Ortiz launched two bats in the general direction of the umps. I think he was just trying to toss them on the field and be a general pain in the ass (may as well give the fans their money's worth) but not knowing his own strength, Ortiz almost kneecapped two of the umpires with the bats. Yes, yes, yes, inappropriate and unacceptable and horrifying. But amusing. Definitely amusing. Unfortunately it will prove to be a rather expensive amusement, as one has to think that when Bud Selig and his minions see the tape, they won't be happy, and they'll express as much in the form of a hefty fine and a lengthy suspension. Since Selig wears Yankees underoos beneath his suit, one can be pretty certain that he will encourage the discipline czar, Bob Watson, (Let Him Play! Let Him Play!—Bob Watson-inspired Bad News Bears reference there, folks. Gratis. I'm clearly the hardest working Red Sox diarist in the biz. And shame on you if you do not get the reference.) to pile on. Some are saying this could be as much as a ten game suspension-worthy offense. That strikes me as absurd, and I would think he'll get 5-6, reduced by a game on appeal.

Oh yeah. About 41,000 fans went to the David Ortiz fireworks last night, and a baseball game broke out. With Pedro turning in another solid outing (6 innings, 110+ pitches, 2 earned runs, 8 strikeouts) and the Sox won one they had to have, 4-2. Nomar and Gabe Kaplar were the sparks at the plate. Kaplar (If I hear his name 70 years from now, I am certain it will still evoke the Welcome Back Kotter theme song by, I believe, John Sebastian), also had a couple of spectacular plays in left field, where he was substituting for Manny, whose left hamstring is still tight. Manny did plunk a single into left-center field when he took Ortiz's place in the batting order in the ninth inning. Perhaps most reassuring, and maybe a bit of vindication for both Pedro and Francona, who has taken a lot of heat for Pedro's early departure to the Dominican last week, Pedro's velocity was the best it has been all year. He said after the game that he felt as good as he has all year, and he could have gotten it up to 95 had he needed to. He now has 10 wins. This is all good news.

For reasons unknown, except perhaps that the Angels want to do their part to kill baseball by making it difficult for young kids to watch and go to games, tonight's is another 7:05 start, 10:05 in the east. When I am king of the world (and I will be, mark my words [note to editor of *Bleeding Red* book on tape: insert sinister laughter here]) there will be no such thing as a nighttime start on a Saturday or Sunday.

I hope Ortiz gets on a bit of a roll and can contribute with the bat, because my guess is that he is soon to take a long vacation courtesy of Major League Baseball. Let him play! Let him play!

Monday, July 19, 2004

In the sort of rationalization that is the only way to get through inconsistent and at times mediocre play, I will assert that we should be able to feel pretty good about splitting a four game series with the Angels, who are a good team and potential Wild Card or American League West contender. What is disquieting is how we earned that split. By now it is pretty well established that Pedro and Curt (or Curt and Pedro) are a formidable 1-2 punch. The Sox are 27-11 when those two take the mound, and they have lost once combined since mid-May. The problem is that we are 23-29 when others start, and they've lost twice as many since Thursday than those two have lost in about two months. We continue to scuffle along at below .500 ball on the road. We go into Seattle tonight for a two game set. Hopefully we assert our will and dominance against one of the weaker teams in the American League.

That said, Schill really was dominant yesterday. He went eight innings, giving up a run on three hits in eight innings when, with the exception of a Bengie Molina home run in the third, it did not seem as if they could touch him. Timlin struggled a bit in the ninth, but he closed it out. Ortiz decided to give himself some RBI in case he loses time as a result of his tantrum the other day, driving in four runs and missing the cycle by a double—interesting that he'd miss that one given that he leads the American league in two sackers.

There also was almost a beanbrawl. In the sixth, after Ortizzle went Quadrangular, John Lackey hit Nomar in the left forearm. Immediately home plate ump Kevin Kelley warned both teams. Nonetheless, in the eighth, Schilling drilled Molina, his only walk of the night, and yet he did not get tossed. Mike Scoscia argued (rightly) and ended up getting tossed for his efforts. Schilling got away with one, but he also stood up after Nomar had taken the pitch in the arm, so even if he had gotten himself thrown out of the game, it was the right thing to do. That will go a long way in the locker room. And Schilling knew it.

On Saturday night the Sox came out with another half assed performance. Waker got shelled, literally, as he took a line drive off the shoulder (X-rays have come back negative. He's day to day. As Charlie Steiner always says, aren't we all?). But I don't want to write about that loss. And you know what? I don't have to. This is my book. But hopefully salvaging the four game split will give us a little push as we head up to Seattle. We have a lot of games coming up, including a doubleheader on Thursday against the Orioles and then the next installment of Sox-Yanks this weekend. There is a lot of baseball yet to be played, but we should have a good idea of where we stand after this week.

Tuesday, July 20, 2004

Last night's was the worst Sox loss of the season. It was worse than the 13-inning epic at New York. It was worse than any of the blown leads, or no-hit good-pitch games, or anything else. Bronson Arroyo threw perhaps the best game by a Sox pitcher this year—he went seven innings, struck out a dozen, including an eye-popping eleven in a row, and gave up three hits and one run. He was awesome after giving up a run early, and he gave us every opportunity to win that game. For most of the game the offense could not get a run across the plate even as the pride of U-Mass, Ron Villone, was letting guys on base at an epic rate. And the defense, though only on the hook for two errors, made a series of gaffes, blunders and, as the Brits might say, cockups, which made things tense.

And yet for all of that, in the eighth inning Varitek hit a bomb to right-center that gave us a 4-1 win and surely a win for Arroyo. As Lee Corso often says on College Gameday, "Not so fast, my friend." In the bottom of the eighth a Mueller throwing error cost the Sox a run after Timlin came in to relieve. But no worries—Foulke was coming in to close it out.

The problem is, of late Foulke has not closed out a whole hell of a lot of anything. Instead, Foulke has been giving up runs at an alarming rate from the one position in the rotation, closer, where runs are most deadly. Further, last night's nonsense—ineffectual hitting, wretched defense, dumb baserunning, lack of intensity, and dumb bad luck—made it one of those games where fans had an impending sense of doom, a sense that was affirmed when Foulke gave up two solo shots, to catcher Miguel Olivo and to wily old Edgar Martinez, in the ninth. And just like that it was 4-4, Arroyo was not about to win, and what was an uneasy feeling across Red Sox nation was suddenly a collective knowledge that things were going to go very, very wrong.

This is not just idle speculation or artistic license either. Making this ever more nerve-wracking was the fact that I was at home (well, my colleague's home—I'm still a man without an address) and my only way to follow the game was through MLB.com's Gameday (Gameday is just a simulated version of the game in which you can follow the action sort-of live, but it can be frustrating and slow and it is simply not the ideal way to follow the game, especially when it is all going to hell. I cannot get the MLB radio to tune in at Jaime's house) and the Sons of Sam Horn game logs, which usually provide as good a minute-by-minute sense of the pulse of Red Sox Nation as any other. The crowds at SoSH all had that feeling that things were just not right. Folks were pretty mad about the way the Sox were playing. I was exhausted, we had it and lost it after Tek's home run, and it just was a mood with bad tidings attendant.

Foulke somehow managed to get through the 10th, but when we entered the 11th we still had not scored and Curtis Leskanic was on the mound. Before long he loaded the bases. Bret Boone came up. It's too easy to make the parallels between the Boone brothers. But in any case, with the bases loaded, he jacked one out, Game over. What was once a 4-1 Arroyo masterpiece ended up as an 8-4 loss in the most wrenching of fashions. Meanwhile all of us who go the distance for the Sox had stayed up very late for a west coast game that went extras. It was excruciating. Worst loss of the year. My mood this morning was foul, and that lasted throughout the day.

I'd love to tell you that as I write this I am feeling much better, as the Sox broke this afternoon's game open with an 8 run fourth. It is now 8-3, and Lowe had a solid appearance, giving up two runs. Manny and Ortiz have hit bombs with most of the guys contributing. But last night the Yankees lost, the Angels lost, the A's lost. We could have made up ground, gotten within 6 of the Yanks, and shaken off this road funk we've been on. Instead we are forced to be happy with another split against another West Coast team. And of course it is 8-4 now with the Mariners making a bit of a run.

This Sox team is just not that good right now. They are playing bad baseball. I suspect that will change because I am a fan and I thus have no choice. And maybe this is really the year and this is just the test of faith. If so, they are doing a pretty good job of sending boils and plagues of locusts our way. Hopefully we win this one.

UPDATE: My God. It is heading into the ninth inning, and as if we have been cursed to suffer the death of a thousand cuts, it is suddenly 9-7. This really is excruciating. The SoSH game threat is also full of angst. The thing is, that is indicative of how this team has been since April. When things are going well, these sorts of games are exciting because you think somehow they'll find a way to win – that is what started happening by this time last year. Instead this season, when the other team starts chipping away, you get that sinking feeling in the pit of the stomach, like the second after your girlfriend says, "We need to talk."

Perhaps the most daunting thing is that even with a win, we are absolutely wasting the bullpen arms. We are down to almost nothing in the pen right now—Foulke, who uncomfortably is suddenly in a position to get the save, Jimmy Anderson who, well, don't ask. And Ramiro Mendoza, whose presence on the roster right now can only be explained by the fact that he was out of options and we are not quite yet ready to give him away. It's the bottom of the ninth, we cling to a two run lead, and Foulke is in, hopefully to throw water on the fire. Ichiro leads off with a single and then steals second. Varitek has taken over behind the plate, possibly because they had been stealing on 'Belli all day. Meanwhile randy Winn walks on a check swing. Now Bret Boone is up. It need not be pointed out that he represents the winning run. OK. Breathe.

Strikeout. Now Edgar Martinez is up. Exorcise that demon for us too, Foulke, and for yourself. Another K. Now their wunderkind is up, Bucky Jacobsen, who has become a phenomenon in his couple of weeks up in the league. He has a big hitting streak on the line. This is going to kill me. Strike three! Game over. I am going to go and take nitroglycerine pills now.

Wednesday, July 21, 2004

This is getting pathetic. Pedro comes out and gives up 8 runs in 6 innings. The offense is just horrid. The defense would not be acceptable in most high school programs. And I know I rail against armchair psychology, but there is absolutely no heat coming from this team. We are getting shelled by an Orioles team that is 1-8 against the Yankees. I have nothing more to say now except that I am really, really depressed, but also really, really mad.

Friday, July 23, 3004

The Red Sox are not getting any less frustrating. They managed to salvage the second game of the doubleheader yesterday on a masterful and gutsy performance by Waker, who went seven and pitched shutout ball, as they won 4-0. Nonetheless, losing a series to the Orioles, and especially with a horrid loss Wednesday night and an equally bad one in the afternoon game yesterday, is not good. The following is what I wrote my friend Rob last night. It sums up a lot of what Sox fans are feeling right now:

> Roberto —
> Got home, drank some beers, came to the revelation that I needed a break from the Sox, drank more, realized the break from the Sox was untenable, paid attention via the web and SoSH game thread, and am not certain if I am happy about the win or not. Bottom line: We are Red Sox fans. We live day to day. But what has happened of late is intolerable. What tonight's win means is exactly this: We managed to take one game from the dregs of a division we once thought we might win. Even if we sweep the Yanks? We'll be behind by 6 games. Yippee-fucking-doo-da. This team sucks. And you know how I am about managers—but you know

what? Tito is simply not up to it. It is almost always a lame excuse to fire the manager. Not now. Fire him, trade Lowe for prospects, trade Millar for a [bag of balls—trust me when I say that what was in the e-mail was far too lewd for publication], entertain the idea of Nomar for prospects, not to get Johnson, but to say you know what? You guys decide. You guys decide if half-assed play and desultory acceptance of .500 ball is what you want. Ortiz (who will be missing five games now, possibly four on protest) is not enough. Manny, great as he is, is not enough when he is also going to be the cutoff king. The fact is that we keep throwing out lineups that make no sense. No fucking sense whatsoever. And we couple it with atrocious use of the bullpen, some of the worst defense and running (ie: fundamentals, after Tito in spring training said: We'll play the game the right way) in all of baseball, and certainly in recent baseball history of any team that thought they had a shot at a World Series title. We won tonight. Which I am afraid will just perpetuate what we've seen the last few weeks. Hell, what we've seen since April. And you know what? I wrote this to you just venting, but I cannot bother to think any more about this club right not, so this is also my Red Sox Diary entry for today. Faithful readers just go to the box scores for details. Sox won the nightcap 4-0. Whoopee.

We are 9 games aback the Yankees, who come into town tonight. Schilling is on the mound. We must win. Simple as that. We must win, or the race for the East is effectively over.

Saturday, July 24, 2004

So I guess the A.L. East race is effectively over. Curt comes in, gives up seven runs including five in one inning, and that makes it nearly impossible for us to come back. The nattering nabobs on SoSH cast a lot of blame on Millar's defense, but from what I can tell, some of that blame is misplaced inasmuch as at least twice he may not have had any play at all to make. Plus, he hit three home runs on a night when the offense otherwise was leaving loads on base and in scoring position. Manny has looked execrable of late. We did tie it up in the 7th, only to have Foulke blow yet another game.

Today Sox-Yanks are the national game on Fox, kicking off at 2:19 CST, or in about seven minutes. I am at school now, trying to get something done. I am a glutton for punishment, so I am going to go watch the game. But boy, is it tough to muster up a lot of enthusiasm over what would normally be the highlight of the week. As Rob wrote me this morning, this team just does not have it. Even if they make the Wild Card, they do not have it. Unfortunately, the reality is that he's right. Things can change and there is still a lot of baseball to be played, but this is definitely not a team that deserves a Wild Card berth. Forget about the division now. At a certain point these guys should just be playing for a modicum of respect.

Saturday, July 24, 2004 (Redux)

YEEEEEEEEESSSSSSSS!!!!!!! Billy Mueller hits a bottom of the ninth walk-off home run after easily the most contentious regular season game between teams that matter in years. Tek smacks A-Rod then lifts his whiny ass off the ground. Tanyon Sturtz (Oh, sorry, "Worcester's Own Tanyon Sturtz [or WOTS]) makes the colossal mistake of grabbing Gabe Kaplar (no doubt about it, the baddest, best built mofo in all of MLB) and he leaves the game with a "bruised pinky" even though in reality he had blood running from his face. (And somehow, some way, Kaplar gets ejected but Sturtze does not.) It went back and forth—at one point the Sox were down 9-4, and with Rivera coming in it was 10-8. This was a visceral game. As one SoSHer wrote; "This whole season feels like the playoffs last year."

If it has been impossible emotionally to recap too many games over the last few weeks because of the anguish involved, it might be just as impossible emotionally to recap this victory, which is one that every Sox fan feels in the guts. Was it as well played as the 13-inning game in the toilet in the Bronx in early July? For purists, maybe not. But if you are a Sox fan, and if you were watching and hoping even when we were down 9-4, and if even after all that has gone on you never fully lost faith, and if you let out a scream and lacerated your hand against the lights on the fan above your head (ahem) when jumping out of your seat as Mueller hit the bomb to beat Mariano Rivera (aka "Fruitbat"—maybe the best, most descriptive insulting nickname ever) then this was the greatest regular season game imaginable. Can we win the east? I don't know. But we did maybe the next best thing last night—we went toe to toe with them, we showed them we have balls, and we showed them equally as much that we have heart.

Tomorrow's confrontation is the Sunday Night ESPN game. We'll get to see 'Tek jack A-Rod in the face at least 20 times, which is fine with me. If this is what it takes to stop those simplistic ESPN jackasses from going back to that same Aaron Boone footage then I am perfectly content. D-Lowe needs to come through big time. But for now, it is just time to bask in the glow of what was clearly the best win of this season. The season just began in earnest.

Monday, July 26, 2004

And the world is suddenly a good and virtuous place again, where children laugh and women smile at me and beer flows like water and pork products are in abundance. For all of the sturm and drang, the Sox wrapped up the series against the Empire last night with a satisfying 9-6 win that nonetheless still had its moments of exasperation—most notably in the 1st inning, when we fell behind 2-0 because of our horrid defense; the 7th, when Lowe came out of the game after 6 and 2/3 innings and Timlin gave up a grand slam to Matsui to make it uncomfortably close; and the 8th, when for a while it looked as if we might piss away the lead. Fortunately we held on. The offense was prolific, especially in the first couple of innings, when they broke it open after back-to-back home runs by Johnny Damon (Kevin Youkilis predicted that one with almost eerie precision, as he was mic'ed up on ESPN and he could be heard calling for a three-run yakker off the Pesky Pole, which is precisely where Damon knocked it) and Mark Bellhorn. Kevin Millar continued his Lazarus act by hitting another home run. He went 10 for 13 in this series and he has hit six home runs in the last five games.

The fact is, for all of the inspiration that Saturday's win provided, a loss last night would have undone most all of that. Instead they went out with a mission and got it done. Foulke came out with one out in the 8th and stopped the bleeding on a bizarre play in which a Jeter line drive ricocheted off his leg and back to Mirabelli, who threw to first but nailed Cap'n Intangibles in the back. Miraculously the umpires went against their nature and ruled against the Yankees, deciding, rightly, that Jeter had been running inside the line the whole way and that he thus was guilty of interference. Rather than a single that drove in a run, then, Jeter was out. Foulke made quick work of the remaining batters and the Sox finished off the mini-home stand.

Tonight's game and this whole upcoming series against the Orioles is crucial. It will be telling to see how well we recover from what was an emotionally draining series for all involved. The Orioles are 6-3 against us this year, and clearly we need to be able to beat teams like this if we plan either to start pulling away with the Wild Card or to make a run at the Yankees, against whom we face off 6 more times in games that could be of vital importance for the postseason picture. Pedro gets the start, which should bode well even if he got shelled last time out and even if the Orioles have proven to get the better of him all season. Pride coupled with momentum (Oh, I believe in momentum) should mean that we go in on a roll tonight. I want an easy win for once. I want us to go in, treat their starter like a batting practice pitcher, and let Pedro roll. It seems as if even our wins this year have been nail-biters. For once I want to go in and just assert our dominance as the clearly better team. Tonight provides a chance to do that, to build up some steam, and to get on a Morgan Magic-type of run. The rest of the season started on Saturday. We have faith.

Wednesday, July 28, 2004

I think one key to this year's Red Sox from here on out is simply not to get days off, or at least not to get days off if we have started hitting. We piled up runs throughout that Yankees series, and then on Monday night we pounded the Orioles in a rainy night at soaked Camden Yards. We won that one 12-5, and those last couple of Orioles runs came only because Pedro got a little tired after sitting for twenty minutes while we scored runs and the rain intensified. At one point he slipped and tweaked his hip—he never should have been out there, so if he had gotten seriously hurt, we'd probably have a new manager – Francona is just terrible at handling pitchers. He is maybe as bad as Grady, possibly worse.

In any case, after a game that started off poorly yesterday, the rain proved too heavy and the umps called the game, which was fine since Waker did not have it and we were down 4-2 when they called it in the third. The makeup date has not yet been scheduled. We play Baltimore in Camden yards to end the year, so the assumption is that we will make this one up only if it will make a difference in the postseason jockeying.

Tonight the offense came to a complete halt. It is the top of the 9th and we are down 4-0 and have not mounted a serious challenge. Dave Borkowski and then B.J. Ryan have pretty much shut us down—though Ortiz just hit a home run off of Ryan, who up to that point had been death to lefties. And then Manny strikes out to end the game, and we leave Baltimore with a split of a truncated series. Schilling pitched well until the end, when he gave up a couple of extra runs. He gave up four through seven innings, he did not walk anyone, but he also only struck up two, and as important, he gave up two home runs, which were more than enough to provide the margin of defeat for the Sox.

From here on out we have to adhere to the simple philosophy that I have espoused before—just win every series. If we win two out of every three games we will be in great position come August. And if we can win the first game of every series, it will take much of the pressure off of us. There is plenty of time to go, and we do not need to watch the scoreboard every day (though we fans will, let there be no doubt about that). We get an off day tomorrow (off days after we suck are probably ok) and then we fly to The Cities (as Minnesotans solipsistically call Minneapolis-St. Paul) to take on the Twins in the Metrodome. Hopefully we come out firing on Friday and can get the first game of that series. I have a special urge to beat the Twins these days after my miserable stretch in the Land of 10,000 Lakes from August 2002 to December 2003.

Saturday, July 31, 2004

Today marks the Major League Baseball trade deadline, or at least the deadline where teams can make trades without squeezing guys through the waiver wire, a complicated and difficult situation that means it is almost impossible for truly substantial deals to happen. Thus far across baseball there have been a few big trades, but none

The Dog Days Come Early   161

have involved Randy Johnson, and closer to my heart, none have involved the Red Sox. There are still rumors that we are negotiating with the Cubs, with Nomar and possibly Matt Clement at the center, but I would not want Clement straight up, and if our goal is to get better for this year, prospects, unless they are out of this world, simply will not do. The other main rumors seem to involve Derek Lowe, and I suppose tonight's scheduled starter is still on the block, but I am not certain what sort of matchup there is that is still possible and that makes sense. I might be a blind optimist, but if we don't find a fit with which we are comfortable, I see no need to trade him just to make a trade. I think he will continue to show improvement, and can be a suitable #4/5 for the playoffs, or a swing man, who can start or relieve, much as we envisioned that Arroyo or Kim would do earlier, before Kim crapped out and Arroyo became one of our top 3 pitchers.

Arroyo had another wonderful start last night. On the road this year he has the second lowest ERA in the league. His home splits are not so good, but hopefully he will settle down at Fenway by the time September rolls around. In any case, we were on the road in Minnesota last night, which was good news for us and bad news for Twins hitters. Over 7 1/3 innings he gave up two runs, eight hits, and struck out eight while not walking anyone. His overall numbers are not that impressive, as he is 4-7, though his 4.08 ERA now is lower that Pedro's. In any case, right now he is on fire, he obviously recovered from last week's fiasco against the Yankees (A-Fraud and 'Tek were given 4 games each, Sturtze, Kaplar, and Nixon were given three games – I disagree profoundly with Nixon's and especially Kaplar's suspension – and they were all fined, as were Schill, Ortiz, and Lofton – one can quibble with some of these, but none of it is really surprising.)

We won 8-2 last night, which would indicate that we were running on all cylinders, but in fact we lefty loads of guys on base and as much as the final score makes it look like a really great win, we should have scored several more runs. Nonetheless, in what must be some of his last games before he has to serve the suspension for the Angels game a while back that he is appealing, Ortiz went 3 for 5 with 2 RBI, bringing him to 93 on the season. Kaplar also had a great game at the plate, getting three hits and driving in three key runs. He also shined in the field—in the seventh he made a throw from deep in right field that nailed Justin Morneau, the super-prospect who is making the Twins willing to trade Doug Mientkiewicz (who drove in both of the Twins' runs in going 3 for 3), possibly to Boston. That gundown reminded some observers of Dewey Evans, Jesse Barfield, Dave Parker, or Roberto Clemente. If Kaplar can get it done in the field as well as at the plate, and if he can provide the spark this year that Millar seemed to offer a year ago, I am not so certain that it is a vital to get someone to replace him in right as some are suggesting.

There is a potential downer, beyond the fact that some likeable guys might be traded. Not only do the rumors about Nomar persist, but after an off day, and after a week when another games was shortened and postponed because of rain, he sat last night and is probably going to sit tonight. Some speculate that this is because of the trade rumors—he is about to be dealt, thus in good faith they do not want to play him. Others—and this is the official line—simply say they are being cautious, that they have several games in a row on turf, and that since Nomar is experiencing tightness in his Achilles, it is best to play it on the safe side. But the other speculation is that the injury is worse than we all had been led to believe, and that this is being done less out of caution than of necessity. Obviously we won't know until we have some sort of confirmation, but losing Nomar to injury rather than trade for the last half of the year would be the worst-case scenario.

They play the Twins again tonight. As I said, our scheduled starter is D-Lowe. But it is 12:30 Central Standard Time, The trade deadline falls in two and a half hours. There may well be a need to update a bit later, as a lot can happen in that time. I just hope that if Theo does execute a trade it is for smart baseball reasons for this year. I do not think anything else—fear of losing our free agents, trading just to trade, shaking things up, saving money, or getting prospects—would justify making a move. I guess we'll know in 2:28:42.

A.L. East Standings after July:

	W	L	%	GB
New York	65	38	.631	—
SOX	56	46	.549	8.5
Tampa Bay	49	54	.476	16
Baltimore	46	56	.451	
Toronto	45	58	.437	20

7

August: Gut Check Time

Tuesday, August 3, 2004

OK, several days have now passed, and the Sox have started off this series against an improved Tampa Devil Rays squad by winning two straight, so I am finally ready to talk about recent events. On the field, in all honesty, there is not a whole lot to say. After taking the first game against the Orioles we went right back into our little cocoon, losing two, both of which we should have won, and both of which were the result of blown relief outings and some generally bad play, coupled with the sort of untimely offensive slumps that make most of us realize that for all of the talk and all of the inflated stats, this is simply not a great offensive team.

The last couple of days have revealed some strengths against a Tampa team that is young, fast, athletic, and talented. They are not ready to compete seriously yet, but they might be a threat to contend next year if they keep this rate of growth. In any case, last night Waker was masterful, keeping the Rays off balance and parlaying an early lead into a 6-3 victory. Tonight, Schilling was equally sharp, throwing a complete game, giving up only two runs, with the second coming when we were up 5-2, and generally assuring that we had a shot to win when by the sixth the O had put up the five runs that would provide the final 5-2 score. These are good wins that we need.

But of course this is not the big news in Red Sox Nation, or, as so often happens when something big happens at the Fens, nationally. As the trade deadline ticked to its inexorable conclusion, it appeared that the Sox were going to stand pat. Nomar and Lowe would remain Red Sox, and, in the words of former NFL Houston Oilers and New Orleans Saints coach Bum Phillips, we'd dance with what brung us.

But then within a few minutes after the deadline, 4:00 eastern, 3:00 here in the Central time zone, the rumors started flying—Nomar had been traded. Floating out on the web were all sorts of scenarios, almost all involving the Cubs and another team or two. For a while it looked like we might get Matt Clement, Orlando Cabrera, and possibly someone else in exchange for Nomar and Lowe. This was something most of us could live with, as many of us thought that Clement would be a significant upgrade as a 3rd-4th-5th starter.

Then it all changed. It came over ESPNews that Nomar had been traded. And for 15 or 20 excruciating minutes, there were no details. We were left to wonder—did we get Clement? Did we part with Lowe? Just what had we done? The reality was less than enthralling. We had traded Nomar, one of our top prospects, Matt Murton (our 2002 first round draft choice) and cash to the Cubs. We got Doug Mientkiewicz from the Twins and Orlando Cabrera from Montreal, who each got various parts from the other teams involved in the trade. This was, to say the least, not what we were looking for. The rumor had been that Mantkiewietz was potential waiver wire material, that we could have gotten him for very little a few days later. Nomar alone for those guys was insane. Theo had clearly gotten jobbed, fleeced, robbed, outclassed. He'd stared experienced general managers eyeball to eyeball, and he had not only blinked, but when he reached for the Visine, he instead handed away a top prospect and cash. Injury? Hi, I'm Insult.

Lots of folks started the spin machine whirring. Theo himself explained that as constituted, the Sox could not win with that defense. Perhaps. The D has been wretched, and Nomar's injury hurt his range tremendously. And our D at first has been terrible save for when McCarty has been in the game. But Cabrera and Minky (not surprisingly, most people who write about the Sox, whether in the press or in places like Sons of Sam Horn, have been desperate for a nickname. Minky is obvious shorthand, though I am somewhat fond of "Eyechart,' since that is roughly what "Mientkiewicz" looks like) have been wretched at the plate this year. Truly horrible, though both have had better seasons in the past, and there is hope that being in the Sox lineup will return them to such form. It looks as if Minky will be a platoon player with Dave McCarty. Cabrera is a serious defensive upgrade, but unless he returns to form is a liability at the plate. The trade, on paper, does not look great.

But as is always the case, there was more to it than all of this. On a player-versus-player basis, clearly the Red Sox got robbed, it would seem. But there are some other facts. Nomar is hurt, and will have to miss games. He was clearly not happy and simply was not planning on signing with Boston over the winter no matter what. Our defense has been terrible. And there were rumors that Nomar had not so subtly hinted that he would rather tank the rest of the season than play for a World Series title. This latter question has been much disputed over the last day or so, and it seems that whatever Nomar felt on the way out, he never would have mailed it in.

So what happened? Nomar was one of the most popular players ever to wear a Sox uniform. Ted Williams thought Nomar was another DiMaggio. He was surely the greatest shortstop in Sox history, and in the greatest era of shortstops the game has ever known, he was most always one of the top two, definitely top three. He is one of my favorites of all time. He played hard, he played well, he worked his tail off, and he just seemed like the sort of guy destined to be a lifer, a Williams or Yaz, someone who always belonged in a Sox uniform, who would retire in it, enter the Hall of Fame in it, and embody the franchise for his generation.

So what instead turned him into the Carlton Fisk, Mo Vaughn, Roger Clemens, or, I think maybe most appropriately, Freddy Lynn of our era? It is easy to lament what has happened, easier still to lament what has not. Like Fisk, there was the free agency issue. Like Mo there was a suddenness to how things changed. Like Roger, there were almost immediate recriminations (not to mention now there are also fears that he'll go back to that Hall of Fame trajectory, and we'll have to watch him win MVPs for a decade). But above all, he reminds me of Lynn: Preternaturally great, graceful, strong, unimaginably talented, attractive and charismatic, and Californian to boot. But like Lynn, whose potential Hall of Fame career was cut short due to fragility, and who left under a cloud, Nomar seems mostly a victim to his body's betrayal of his gifts. First he had the wrist injury in 2001 and now the Achilles. Nomar has never returned to his 2000 status, and many Sox fans had reconciled themselves to the fact that he never would again, a curious stance in an era when medical science can do things that Fred Lynn could never have even fathomed, but one that nonetheless was pervasive among Sox fans. Never mind that for most of 2003 he was an MVP candidate—by the playoffs he had slumped for so long some even took to calling him a weak link. Never mind that even with all of the time that he had missed this year his numbers at the plate seemed poised to catch up with Jeter's full season numbers.

Never mind all of that, because on top of it all was the "Unhappy Nomar" trope. And it is true that Nomar seemed less joyous than any of us had ever seen him. More sensitive than most, surely at least in part because he was so much more committed than most, the A-Rod issue cut him to the rawest nerve during the off-season. True, he had allegedly turned down a monster contract (4 years for $60 million the rumors went—Nomar and Arm Tellem, his agent, had seemingly not adjusted to the market realities in baseball post A-Rod's and Manny's deals) and the Sox had gone from that alleged first offer to a lowball 4 for $48 million in one season. But true too, the Sox mismanaged and bungled the A-Rod talks from the outset, though Tom Hicks' insistence on running his mouth is what caused the leaks to get out in the first place. And then, just as the possibility for redemption came, just as spring training was underway and performance on the field might have proven to salve his wounds, he got injured. Again. Perhaps not as serious as the wrist tendon fraying that caused the first serious downturn, the heel injury was nonetheless nothing with which to take risks, and so he had to shut it down again. Soon rumors started that he was dallying with his return, maybe engaging in a slowdown to show the Sox something, to send a message.

And when Nomar returned, the perception had become reality: Nomar was unhappy. He would never re-sign with the Sox again. He had to go. That cannot be good for his market value. Then again, it would have been nice if Theo or the ownership group (with whom Nomar's relationship was by all accounts either hostile or nonexistent, maybe hostilely nonexistent) had worked to allay that unhappiness. That brought us to last week. That and the crappy defense and the underachieving and the dubiousness of winning even the Wild Card and the generally disappointing tone this season had taken on.

Gut Check Time

And so before we knew it, Nomar was gone. Traded to the Cubs for guys whose very names would have been mocked and scoffed had a similar offer been made a year, a month, even a week ago. But this is what it came to. Lots of recriminations are flying around. Nomar is making calls to the media to salvage a reputation that clearly matters to him. The owners are sending out negative vibes, likely to try to ease the pain of losing a guy who seemed to represent this franchise better than anyone had in many a year, maybe since the heyday of Yaz, or the Gold Dust Twins, Rice and Yaz.

In any case, he is gone. Nomar is a Cub. The Sox try to get back on the right track. I am a 33 year old man, and yet even days later I cannot but help to be saddened. Yet the Red Sox are the Red Sox still. I think of it more romantically then to say that I merely root for laundry, but I root for an institution. Nomar was a vital part of that, and I hope I will always be a fan of his. But sad as it is, it is time to move on. I wish him well, and another tiny little part of my youth is now gone. But if we can get on a roll, and can start to make some ground, the World Series is not yet out of reach. It is just a shame that Nomar won't be part of it when it happens.

Thursday, August 5, 2004

Hard not to draw the conclusion that this Sox team that we are seeing on the field, and not our conceptions of what they might be able to be, represent the reality. Despite the personnel changes, the fundamental ingredients are the same as they have been all year and are not worth going over again. What is most bothersome is how dumb we play. Physical errors are one thing. They happen. Those balls are moving fast, it is not easy to be a major league fielder, and I can live with that. But when you play 162 games a year you have to understand intuitively the job of the cutoff man, or the rudiments of baserunning. And the coaches have no excuse for the sorts of dumb, mental errors they are making—they do not play the game—their contribution is overwhelmingly mental. If they consistently screw that end up, their *raison d'etre* becomes difficult to justify.

Last night's game is a perfect example of all of these little maladies. Each loss seems more horrific than the one before it, though at least this time we managed to win the series, something we have not done on the road since early June. But taking two of three is less fun when you are in a position to sweep and you take a 4-1 lead into the seventh inning. This is precisely what we did.

Arroyo was masterful again last night, at least for six innings. But then he started to struggle a little in the seventh, letting the first two batters on base, at which point Francona should have lifted him, if not before. Instead he let Bronson pitch to Julio Lugo, who hit a grounder to Youkilis that should have resulted in a double play. The ball took a funny hop, Youks misplayed it (funny hop or no, he ought to have made the play) and the bases were loaded. Francona still did not react, even with no outs and the bases loaded. The other day he took Pedro out when he was absolutely dealing, and last night Arroyo struggled and Tito left him in. It is uncanny the way he manages to misjudge when to lift a starter almost every time. In any case, Toby Hall, Tampa's catcher who was on a 0 for 18 streak prior to that at bat, came to the plate and worked to a 1-2 count. Arroyo shook Tek off a couple of times, and threw a sinker that Hall blasted for a grand slam. And just like that it was 5-4, Tampa.

Even then the game was not over. The meat of our order went 1-2-3 in the 8th, but one thing about this team is that the contributions come from all over the lineup. In the ninth Millar singled and was promptly pinch run for, with newcomer Dave Roberts, one of the fastest guys in Major League Baseball, taking first. He advanced to second on a wild pitch. Then Mientkiewicz came to the plate, and he drove a single to center field. Despite the fact that Baldelli scooped the ball up before Roberts had even gotten to third base, Dale Sveum, who almost makes us yearn for the days of Wendell Kim, waved him home. Baldelli made a perfect throw, and Roberts, fleet afoot though he is, never had a chance. Letting Roberts try for home when you are only down one and could have had guys on first and third was colossally stupid. It would be one thing if we had not been beating this team. But we had easily taken the first two games, and it is not as if the Devil Rays relief corps strikes fear in the hearts of men. If we cannot get a guy across from third with no one out, we do not deserve to win. Mientkiewicz had advanced to second on the throw. Mueller grounded out, but advanced Minky to third, and Kaplar took one for the team, advancing to first after being hit by a pitch. Even after the Sveum screw-up, there was a shot to get the tying run across, but Damon popped out to first, capping an 0 for 5 night at the plate, and the Sox lost 5-4.

And now rather than an off day during which to get some rest and enjoy the fruits of a sweep they have to stew over a game they had won, gave up, and should have taken back. What more to say than "UGH?" Tomorrow we head into Detroit, another team we should be thinking that we can sweep. But the sure thing is never sure with this team.

Monday, August 9, 2004

The Red Sox return to the Friendly Confines today after an eleven game road trip that in many ways embodied the 2004 Red Sox—disappointing and frustrating, but with just enough promise to keep us from losing faith. After another frustrating loss on Friday night, in which Lowe gave up only four runs but the offense could only muster three, the Sox came back and won the next two to take the series. Saturday night Pedro played the familiar role of stopper, giving up only two runs en route to a 7-4 Sox victory. Yesterday was one of the more peculiar games you'll ever see—Waker gave up six home runs, the Sox gave up seven in all, and yet they managed to win 11-9 largely as a result of Youks hitting two home runs and Ortiz throwing in a 3 run bomb for good measure. Obviously he gave up mostly solo shots, but Waker's struggles of late are a little disconcerting.

Today we start a four-game series against Tampa, a team that we have owned. We are 7-2 against them this season, and hopefully that, coupled with the fact that we are back in Fenway, will allow us to build a much-needed win streak. Schilling gets the start tonight in a game that will be televised on ESPN 2, so hopefully they play the sort of game we need from them to start building some momentum through this month.

One of the amazing facts about this team is that for all of their struggles and as painful as they have been to watch on a daily basis, they are tied for the lead in the Wild Card race with Anaheim and Texas. Of the remaining contenders (including those leading their divisions) we have easily the kindest schedule, with fewer games against teams with records above .500 than anyone else and with more home than road games, which is especially good for us given how well we play in the Fens and how poorly we play when living out of suitcases. Those teams out west will continue to beat up on one another so that no one runs away and no one falls too far behind. I am still rooting for Texas to win their division so that I can see some games up in Arlington, but above all, it is time for the Red Sox to go on a run over the next ten days or so, when we get to play at home against teams we really should be beating soundly, including these four against Lou Piniella's rejuvenated Devil Rays, three against the ChiSox, and three against Toronto. 8-2 would be really nice. We are ten behind the Yankees, and I still have not entirely given up hope on that front. Which just proves that I am insane.

Tuesday, August 10, 2004

In a lot of ways, I was forged as a fan between 1978 and 1986, between the two horrific losses that most created the modern Red Sox fan. In 1978, the infamous Bucky F!@#ing Dent game was my first real painful fan experience. I watched it on the living room floor at my grandparents/dad's farm, where I spent a good percentage of my formative years. The details of that game are well known, I have covered them elsewhere, and suffice it to say, that game was the sort of introduction destined to foster a life of heartbreak. If our relationships with our mothers largely dictate how we men interact with women for most of our lives, then our connections with our sports teams as a boy have a similar effect on our relationships with those teams until we die.

If the 1978 game marks one bookend of those formative years, the 1986 World Series forms the other. Again, no detail needed, as lazy journalists and networks have used the stock footage of the Buckner play so many times that their telling of the tale has prevailed, despite the fact that in this little narrative Bob Stanley and Rich Gedman never appear, and they never bother to make clear that game 6 was not the last game of that series.

But the years in between are just as important for someone my age. For in the eight intervening years, the Red Sox were the worst of all things—they were mediocre, especially after that great team of the 1970s fell apart so that by 1981 or 1982 a team that had shown so much promise to emerge as a consistent powerhouse instead became a non-factor. These were the first years when I attended games at Fenway, which, at an hour and a half to two hours from my small hometown of Newport, New Hampshire, was the equivalent to going to Mars. These were the years when hopes would start off so high and soon would be dashed. These were the years when I grew to hate, to loathe, to despise Yankees fans. From 1978 to 1986, two years that brought us unbelievable highs and crushing lows, was forged a new generation of Red Sox fans. Those were somewhat dreary years, and in a sense the last decade or so has marked a transition. The Red Sox historically are almost always good, rarely are they horrible, a few years in the 20s and 30s, 60s, and 1992-1993 notwithstanding. But in the last decade, we have been consistently very good, and in some years outstanding.

But I have come to realize in the last few weeks that maybe this team is a lot more like those teams of the early 80s than I thought. Sure, there is more talent on paper. But these guys are equally as frustrating. In a listing of the truly frustrating seasons in this team's recent history there are a few trends. One is that after years in which we defy expectations and/or go a long way, we tend to build up expectations only to see them dashed—1968, 1976, 1979, 1987— these were all seasons we entered expecting great things only to see it all go awry. 2004 looks a bit like these years. But recently these sorts of seasons have seemed to happen more and more often, 2002 being a prime but not lone example. I am certainly not giving up hope, and I do not buy into these trends as determinant or even predictive. But they are at least worth noting even if I have no idea what they mean.

I say all of this in the context of last night's loss, yet another one not worth rehashing. Schilling got crushed, giving up three homers. The bats never got going. It was effectively over by the 4th inning. And all of this against a team we should be pounding soundly at a time of the season that will make or break us. There are three more games in this series. It would be really, really nice if we could play the sort of baseball that will let us win them. I was a lot more resilient in 1984 than I am two decades hence.

Thursday, August 12, 2004

It was like 1999 all over again in Fenway today, and for the last three days it has been nothing at all like the early 1980s. The Sox recovered from the first-game Schilling drubbing to take the last three games of this four-game series, and somewhat quietly they have won 7 of 10 and look really, really good. If the last two nights were enjoyable—especially last night's 14-5 pounding of the Rays, today's matinee in Fenway was ambrosia.

Pedro was vintage. He pitched a complete game shutout, his first since he beat the Rays in that famous game that started off early on with the brawl, in which Pedro punched out 17 and gave up one hit. He was not that dominant today, but he did strike out ten, giving up six hits and walking no one. His pitch count was low all day, giving him a shot at the complete game—always good in and of itself, but especially so because we have six games more before our next off day. It was just a pleasure to watch (it was the ESPN Day Game) and hopefully it is a sign of good things for the next month or so. This is about as good as I have felt about the Sox since that series against the Yankees last month. Now we get the White Sox and the Blue Jays, two more teams we can beat. The ChiSox have been somewhat tough, but Toronto has been awful. We just need to keep it rolling.

I think it's safe to say that with Nomar out of the fold, it would be a good time to start hinting to Pedro that we're ready to make him happy with the contract. There is no reason to think that his shoulder is going to disintegrate, he has helped carry us this year, I think he wants to be in Boston, and at this point, an aura of goodwill on all sides might get a deal done. Pedro's looking a bit like his vintage incarnation. The defense is certainly improved. The bats are hot. We are winning at the time of year when winning is most important, and I expect this to continue.

Friday, August 13, 2004

Yes, it may be Friday the 13th, but nothing can dampen my enthusiasm about the Red Sox right now. And it is contagious. The glass-is-half-empty crowd at Sons of Sam Horn is as contented as they have been all season. Dan Shaughnessy, whose columns in the *Globe* have been increasingly sour as the years have passed, was a downright Pollyannaish optimist in his column today. He pointed out that Game 7 of the 2004 World series is scheduled for October 31st, and since the American League won the All Star Game and thus home field advantage, not only could that game happen at the Fens, but he also pointed out that the traditional victory parade would be scheduled for Tuesday, November 2nd—Election Day. When Dan Shaughnessy is speculating about Sox victory parades, it is safe to say that Red Sox Nation is infused with a positive aura that is seldom seen in these parts.

Pedro's stellar performance yesterday plays a huge role in all of this, of course. If Pedro is even remotely close to the indomitable force we've known for his Red Sox career, it means that our postseason rotation will be menacing. A menacing postseason rotation tends to yield fruit.

It seems as if everything is going well. Yesterday on consecutive plays dale Sveum challenged Rhode Island's own Rocco Baldelli by running on him, despite the lesson one would have thought he should have learned last week. Both times, Baldelli made the picture perfect throw, nailing Millar and Varitek (not exactly Raines and Henderson on the base paths) to end the fifth inning. When he held up a baserunner at third in the sixth inning, the crowd gave him an explosive sarcastic ovation, to which Sveum tipped his cap. Had we lost yesterday, Sveum may well have had a difficult time getting out of Fenway alive. But in a win and during a streak in which we have taken three straight, five of six, and seven of ten, Boston fans will give him a little more of a leash.

In any case, October 31 is a Sunday. I have class on Monday morning, but if we get to a game seven in Fenway, I'll be there, even if it means I am among the madding crowds pressed against one another at Jillian's or the Cask and Flagon. Hope floats throughout Red Sox Nation right now. The Chicago White Sox are in town, though Boston is apparently pretty besotted with rain. Hopefully we'll all be feeling just as good on Sunday night. It's amazing how quickly our mood can change. We're a resilient lot, I guess.

Saturday, August 14, 2004

It's never ok to be happy after a loss, and certainly at this time of year, with the mess that we've made for ourselves, all losses have ramifications, but we need to keep in mind also that sometimes a loss is just a loss. Surely this year has been pockmarked with a lot more gut wrenching, kick in the groin losses than any season in recent memory. Certainly we've squandered lots of opportunities in games we should have won. Absolutely this team should have ten more wins than it does. No question, there have been a good half-dozen games after which we moaned that this was unquestionably the worst of the year.

Last night's loss was not one of those. Granted, Tim Wakefield's erratic performances of late continued last night, as he got hit around pretty good. And we did give up an early lead. And we did come up just short in a comeback that would have been defining. But it was just a loss, and we've been losing the first game only to come back and win series a lot lately. Had Ortiz been able to get another foot from his warning track shot to right field in the seventh inning, things would have turned out differently. Rather than a three run shot that would have made it 7-6, he had to settle for a sacrifice fly that made it 6-5. This sort of thing happens. Millar hit a two-run bomb that brought us to within one run in the ninth to continue his rejuvenation. It was not to be, however, and we lost 8-7. There is no sense making it out to be more than it was—a loss in a long season to a team that itself has postseason aspirations. They left too many guys on base. Wakefield did not come through. But this isn't a loss that will require folks to consider jumping off the Tobin Bridge.

Tonight we get Schilling on the mound. There are whispers that his ankle is acting up again and that this is limiting his effectiveness. Obviously we hope this is not the case, and as importantly, we hope that he is doing whatever we need him to do so that he can perform at the highest level not just now, but also when it matters in September and October. If this means missing a start, I think he needs to consider it—but only he and (maybe, given their track record) the Sox doctors know.

One bit of bad news that is beyond spin is the fact that Scott Williamson apparently has a tear in the elbow or forearm that has been so troublesome for him all season. I think people underestimate the effect that not having him has had on this team most all year. Our bullpen has been thinner, it has had to be overworked, and in places where S-Willy would have been in there, instead we have had guys like Curtis Leskanic step in, who either are not up for the task or who are not suited to that particular role. The ripple effect has affected the other guys in the bullpen, especially Timlin,

Embree, and Foulke, who showed how lights out they could be in the postseason and earlier in the year when we did have a full complement in the bullpen. Hopefully we can find a way to work around this, though it is disquieting that one of Francona's biggest weaknesses is his management of the pen. It has been nice that Timlin and Embree got something of a break over the past week, though at the same time they seemed a bit rusty last night, so there needs to be some effort to strike a balance. One can hope that the re-emergence of Ramiro Mendoza—despite the fact that he was not quite able to squeak out of a tough situation last night—will prove to be the perfect salve. He's been there before with the Evil Ones. This would be a good time for that magic to make its return, but to be used for good.

In any case, if he is healthy, Schilling should be able to play the role of stopper tonight. Surely Pedro's big outing on Thursday was not lost on the hypercompetitive Schilling. And his last outing must be eating away at his considerable pride, so perhaps the talk about the ankle is much ado about nothing, and he'll come out and shut the Pale Hose down, propelling us to the win, and another streak.

Monday, August 16, 2003

Doug Mientkiewicz, who caused the jaws of more than a few Sox fans today to drop when he jogged out to the field to play second base rather than his customary first, had a good game in the Sox 8-4 win over the Jays today and so was just interviewed by Jerry Trupiano on WEEI. Minky agrees with me—if you win every series, you will be in good shape come the accounting for the postseason. The Sox could not pull off this weekend's series against the White Sox, taking only the middle game (on the strength of two home runs by Ortiz and one by Manny to give the Sox a 4-3 win) and losing the rubber match 5-4 on a dreary, rain-soaked day in Fenway. They are 5-3 on the road trip after tonight's win, and they are a half game ahead in the Wild Card race, though that is mostly because Texas has not finished their game against the smoking hot Indians, who are close behind in the rear-view mirror, and the Angels do not play tonight.

The weekend showed some of the Sox strengths and weaknesses, but they battled in each game, and as I said after Friday's loss, falling in that series is not as bad as others we have seen. We lost Youkilis indefinitely to an injury yesterday, which precipitated the unorthodox lineup that put Mientkiewicz at the second sack, where he made a couple of sterling plays, including a 4-3 double-play in the early going. Tonight's win had D-Lowe dealing well for most of the night. He went 7 innings, gave up 4 runs, 3 earned. It almost got ugly when the Blue Jays closed it to 5-4 in the 7th, but we stopped the bleeding and added a few insurance runs. And one of those runners who scored was Delgado. Earlier in the game Delgado had taken a cheap shot at our Gold Glove first baseman-turned-second baseman by forearm shivering Mientkiewicz as he broke up a double play. When Delgado led off the 7th, Lowe, who sometimes has not shown a stomach for such things, drilled Delgado in the ass. It almost came back to haunt him, but he had to do it. Lucky for Delgado he did not pull that crap with Pedro on the mound, or he'd have taken it closer to his earhole than his other one.

It would be nice to sweep the Blue Jays. They are not very good. We are. Even with a couple of losses the last few days, this just feels like a better team. I suspect that this feeling comes about because they are better. Usually, over the course of a long season, better teams rise to the top. It's rarely a fluke to win out in a 162 game season. Of course now it comes down to some four dozen games. The old truism about baseball is that the season is a marathon, not a sprint. But from here on out, a better metaphor might be that it is like a 400 race, a long, sometimes grueling sprint, but a sprint nonetheless.

Wednesday, August 18, 2004

Sweep! We took the Blue Jays down in three, although it was not as easy as it could or should have been. Yesterday we had to win with a walk off double that drove in Damon to make it 5-4 and tonight, much like Monday, we had it in hand except toward the end we let in runs that never should have scored. Foulke struggled a bit tonight, and so while we were up 6-2 we ended up winning 6-4. Still, this is a good way to go into an off day. We just went 7-3 on this home stand and we are setting the pace in the Wild Card chase. The Twins have broken their streak of futility against the Yankees and have taken a couple in a row, so though it is unlikely that we can catch the Yanks, we are at least going in the right direction in the division. Will the Yankees have an epic collapse? Not likely. But it is a nice idea.

Yesterday's game was a good one. Pedro started off a little rough, and it looked like he might get banged around, but in a sign of how much he has become a pitcher, and not just a fire thrower, he was able to use savvy and smarts to settle down and get through seven innings and give the bats a chance to eke out the runs we needed. The fact that Cabrera had the game winning RBI is a great sign, as the incomparable Fenway heat was beginning to descend from fans and media, and so he chose the right time to start hitting. There was an incident after Ortiz was hit with a pitch. Former Yankee Ted Lilly came up and in and hit him on the wrist, and Ortiz lost control a little bit, but things were restrained before anything major happened, and if Ortiz reacted badly, Lilly was much worse. There was surely an element of rollover from the previous night, when Lowe hit Delgado in retaliation for the incident on the base path. The fighting spirit is nice to see, actually, though they need to be smart about it.

Cabrera continued his hot streak tonight. And Kevin Millar, who was the target of much of the ire of Red Sox Nation as recently as last month, is on an absolutely torrid pace. Wakefield had a nice outing after a couple of shaky ones, giving up two runs on five hits in a lightning fast game, and while the end was dubious—Foulke struggled in a game in which he may not have belonged, and Sveum managed to get Mueller thrown out at the plate by what by all accounts was a good thirty feet were the lowlights of the last couple of innings—nonetheless we waltzed out of there with a victory, and since the trade deadline we are playing well above .600 ball, which obviously is what we want. The guys are hitting, and the starting pitching has been pretty spectacular for a week or so, during which time every starter has made it through more than six innings. These are all good signs.

Once again it is August and we are beginning to spend a good deal of our time scoreboard watching. Now obviously the ideal is to do what we need to do in order to make the performances of other teams irrelevant, but since those teams are not about to roll over, the reality is that we likely won't get much of a rest when the season comes to a conclusion even if we do end up taking the Wild Card. But this team is not one that is going to die, and they have played through a whole range of adversity. Even now, they are playing even more shorthanded than they have been, as Youkilis and McCarty are out with injuries. Tonight Earl Snyder made his Sox debut at third. He did not have a great outing, though he did get a hit – indeed, it is possible that Sveum sent Mueller in that ill-advised attempt (it was a single to shallow left and the left fielder had the ball in hand before Mueller rounded third) in order to get Snyder his first Sox RBI. That is sweet, but ill-advised, especially under the circumstances.

We're off tomorrow, which seems to happen far too often when we get on a hot streak. Schilling goes to the mound on Friday in the New Comiskey, so hopefully we can get off to a good start in the Windy City and exact a little revenge for this last lost series in Fenway over the weekend. The Sox are 15 games above .500 for the first time this season, for at least the moment the Sox lead the Wild Card chase, and could maintain it depending on what goes on with the A's and Rangers. This is a fun time of year. It is much better when they start playing the way they should have all year.

Friday, August 20, 2004

Today one of my best friends, Josh, came into town to pay me a visit here in the heart of Texas' Permian Basin. Pep (his last name is Pepin) is also a diehard Sox fan and a fellow New Hampshire boy. I suspect that there will be beer involved. The Sox are the national Fox game tomorrow as well, so we'll get to watch them.

Strange though it may seem, if we win tonight we will have the exact same record that we had at the same stage of the season last year. For all of the romance attached to the 2003 team, the fact is that for much of the year they were almost as perplexing as this year's bunch. The expectations may not have been quite as high, but we still figured them to contend, and teams that can contend are always thinking World Series. But the reality is that the bullpen often killed them last year, a season in which they gave up many, many late inning rallies and some excruciatingly painful walk off home runs. In August and September, though, they started to pull it together. It is true that all games count the same in the standings, but playing well now is far better than playing well in April and May when teams effectively position themselves for the heart of the season. We need to gain a little more ground by winning this series in Chicago. Schilling takes the mound tonight, and the rumors are afoot that he will be taking a shot for his bum ankle, which, if it helps is fine with me. In any case, let's hope for some Pep Mojo for the boys in Chicago—coincidentally enough, Josh is flying down from Chicago, where he spends his workweek—he lives in Boston, Greatest City On Earth.

Sunday, August 22, 2004

The weekend was all that we expected and more, as Josh and I had a crazy fun time. We did not treat our bodies especially well, and I desperately need tonight's sleep, but it was worth it.

Not surprisingly, one of the focal points for the weekend was yesterday's Sox game, which was the national Fox telecast. We went to Vette's, a local sports bar and had a bonanza of sports, with not only the game, but also the golf tournament, the Little League World Series and the Olympics. The Sox won again, and while Arroyo did not have his best outing he got it done because for once the Sox put runs on the board for him. Tonight they go for a sweep in another nationally televised game, this time on ESPN. They have begun to be the team we expected from the start—and I still maintain that the Yankees simply are not that good. If we can finish off the sweep tonight we will go into Toronto on our best roll of the year.

Classes start tomorrow here at UTPB. The start of a fall term traditionally means that the pennant races start to heat up in a big way. The Red Sox are starting to peak at just the right time just as they did last year. Hopefully we can keep it going, because this is the best I have felt about the Sox this year.

Monday, August 23, 2004

First day of classes here at UTPB, and my students undoubtedly will benefit from how well the Sox are playing. It's sad but true—the Sox affect my mood, and my mood in so many obvious ways affects my students. Of course it goes without saying that Yankees' hats are strictly verboten in my class, which usually garners a whole lot more support than it engenders hostility. In any case, I'm only draconian where I must be, but Yankees' hats are a must quash situation.

Today the mood was good. The Sox won last night, completing a second consecutive sweep and revealing how the bounces are suddenly going our way. In the 8th Manny slipped and allowed a ball to go past him and tumble around the base of the wall before Johnny Jesus was able to get to it and toss it toward the infield with his noodle arm. Nonetheless the ChiSox base runner assumed Manny would catch it, so he went back to first and thus could not score. They got guys as far as second and third with no outs, and yet Midland, Texas' own Mike Timlin got us out of it unscathed. This is a game we would have lost a month ago. We fell behind 5-4 late, and the next inning Manny went deep giving us the 6-5 lead that would prove to be the final score.

Last night we flew from Chicago to Toronto, where the Jays will surely be intent on getting a little revenge for our sweep of them last week. We, meanwhile, have Schilling and Pedro going to the mound, as well as Waker, so we are pretty happy with our odds, all things considered. Apparently the clubhouse attitude is great. Meanwhile, though he has been hitting, it sounds as though Nomar might be hurting again, as the word from Chicago is that he is going in for an MRI after having missed two games. Minky is playing brilliantly in the field and he is swinging the bat well too, and Cabrera is becoming more reliable. We are on a roll this month, and Toronto is a good team against which to keep that trend going. If we do, I'll be happy, which will make my students happy. And selfless guy that I am, it's all about keeping the students happy.

Tuesday, August 24, 2004

Unfortunately, the Red Sox do not understand the whole chain of happiness. Last night they were shut out, 3-0, by Ted Lilly and the Blue Jays. This is not cause for too much alarm. The Jays played just about the perfect game for them—Lilly gave one of the great pitching performances in franchise history, they got to Pedro with two quick runs right away, and yet even with this nearly flawless game, they only won by three runs.

Furthermore, if this team is able to bounce back with Waker on the mound tonight, it will hearken back to the last few months of

2003 when different guys consistently stood up even after some of our big guns have failed. This would be a great time for Waker to start regaining his form and for the guys to put scads of runs on the board against Batista, who has not given us much difficulty in the past.

The reality is that it would be a huge disappointment not to win this series against the Blue Jays, but I would suspect that we will come through tonight. What is amazing is that as hot as we have been, we are still in serious danger of losing a lot of ground if we go on even a short losing streak.

There are traditionalists out there who loathe the Wild Card. I just do not get it. They prattle on about the integrity of the regular season, pretending to stand as the gatekeepers for the game, and yet it seems clear that these critics are willfully or otherwise unaware of two realities in the last few decades—one of these is that there are a lot more teams now, and that the older models no longer worked. One team running away with a division is not fun for the majority of fans. This system gives so many more fans a reason to care about their teams. Despite what the nincompoops say, then, the Wild Card makes the regular season more meaningful for more teams. How that is a bad thing, I do not know. The second reality is that with a Wild Card, teams are rewarded for good seasons and not punished simply for geography. There were many years in the old AL East-AL West setup in which the two teams with the best records hands down were in the east. How, exactly, does that reward the integrity of the regular season? So let's assess: the Wild Card makes the regular season matter for more teams and more fans; it instills excitement where there otherwise would be far less; it rewards the best teams. How is this hugely problematic?

So even as I hope that the Sox can close the gap on the Yankees, I have no problem saying that we would otherwise want to win the Wild Card. Of course we would. Those are the rules as they exist, and if we win it all within those rules, there is absolutely no reasonable way to invalidate the accomplishment. In the end, the most important thing is playing them on the field eventually. When the postseason rolls around, we are going to have to beat two of the four teams, and the other team will have already been defeated by a team we'll have to overcome, so I am a big fan of this setup—more teams get to compete to see which really is the best. We believe that it can be the Red Sox.

Wednesday, August 25, 2004

Within any season there are dozens, hundreds of little plots and subplots to occupy the most fervid fan's waking hours. The Red Sox seem to have more of these petit dramas in any given year than most teams.

This is probably true more because of the scrutiny on and coverage of the team than it is on the actual reality of the existence of these dramas. All teams, after all, deal with injuries and suspensions, and prima donnas and the trade deadline and playoff pushes and criticisms of the manager. But in Boston these things are magnified by the ubiquitous nature of the media, for which the Red Sox are without peer. *The Boston Globe,* historically one of the most respected newspapers in the United States and a very important one for its coverage of politics (though it is nowhere near what it once was – a relatively recent transformation that may well be tied to its being owned by *The New York Times* – of course there is a New York connection to blame) probably has the local baseball team on the front page more often than any newspaper in a major league city of any in the country.

And of course because the hopes of all of New England, save for that peculiar little pimple west of I-91 and South of I-84, rest similarly on the boys who ply their trade in Fenway, not only do the Boston and larger Massachusetts papers converge on Yawkey Way, so do those in Rhode Island and New Hampshire and Maine and Vermont and the respectable parts of Connecticut. Everyone wants a scoop, or at least an angle. This is great for the fans most of the time, as this competition leads to a lot of information. And information is plasma to the sports obsessive.

I was thinking about this because of Jason Varitek. The biggest of the many big subplots interweaving through this season is his scuffle with A-Rod in Fenway a few weeks back. That will most likely be seen as the defining moment of this team when everything plays out. I have the image prominently displayed in my office. Well, long after most folks have consigned this to the "yesterday's news" bin, Sox fans get to be reminded of that weekend because

Gut Check Time   185

Tek decided, wisely in my estimation, to serve out the suspension. He figured that these four games are ones the team can win without him, and it is better to miss a series against Toronto and a game against Detroit than to be absent when we hit the big boys again in the next couple of weeks. Tek has been rolling lately—he has raised his season average above .300, his OPS is climbing, and he is back to being the heart and soul of the team.

Fortunately, Doug Mirabelli, blasted a three-run home run that might still be soaring across Canada had it not encountered a wall 420+ feet from home plate. Mirabelli has served most of the season predominantly as Waker's special catcher and as needed to spell Varitek. And he always seems to get at least one big hit when he does play. These are the little things that help a team get to the playoffs. Even the most durable catchers need a spell, and to have someone in whom the pitchers have faith and who is a force at the plate and in the clubhouse, well, that can make a huge difference. And Mirabelli's stint as the man right now is even more vital, because he is really the last line of defense—we chose not to go with a backup, and so if something happens to Mirabelli, we will go with Minky as our backup and Millar is our emergency guy. I think Minky is great, do not get me wrong, but gold glove or no gold glove, it was quite enough of a heart-tester to see him get a start at second last week.

Another story that has lingered through the season, longer than the A-Rod situation, which on the whole was good for us, maybe decisive, has been Tito's handling of the bullpen. True, Dave Wallace, the pitching coach, deserves equal scrutiny, but at the end of the day the manager is often the final arbiter, and even if he is not, he is responsible for the pitching coach. Tito's biggest two problems have been the timing of his use of the bullpen – almost always he's pulled a guy 2-3 pitches too late. It would be humorous were this not so serious. The other problem he has had is in use of his big guns, Embree, Timlin, and Foulke. Of course this is a bit more difficult to pin down, especially given that we lost Williamson, and that has been huge. Tito has tended to overwork some guys (those three) and seems to be underutilizing others, namely Mendoza, who appears to have regained some of his old form, which could do wonders for the bullpen if he can consistently produce. Last night Timlin was lights out when he came on in the 7th, which is another key. If he keeps pitching well, if Tito can develop a consistent use pattern, the pen will return to being a strength of this team, which could be a decisive development.

Tonight the Sox are rolling. This was exactly the outing they needed. Schill has scuffled against the Jays all season, with a record of 0-2 and 6.00+ ERA. We needed the bats to come in and just pound, and this is precisely what they have done, with the big boppers hitting home runs – Manny hit his 34th and Ortiz his 32nd and 33rd. Cabrera continued his hot streak, adding his own home run to continue to bring Red Sox Nation around on this trade. With the lead Schilling has been predictably solid, and barring the sort of catastrophe the very thought of which makes my stomach turn we should have this one in the bag. And the Sox just stretched the lead to 9-1 on, yes, Mirabelli's RBI single, so I cannot envision catastrophe right now. The Jays' radio announcers are talking in terms of Wally Pipp with regard to Varitek, which is obviously not something Tek has to worry about—at least until contract negotiations this winter—but which indicates just how hot 'Belli has been of late. And now it's 10-1—Schill is out after a solid outing—6 1/3, 8Ks, 0 walks, and 1 run. Another series win.

Next we are off to a four-game set against the Tigers, a team we should be able to mash over the next few days. All of the little stories give the season flavor. But the only way the stories will lead to a happy ending is if we keep winning. Right now, cue sunset, because things look good on the storyboard.

Friday, August 27, 2004

For all of the sturm and drang, the 2004 Red Sox are two games ahead of the pace set by their much more lovable (at least knowing what we do now about the season) 2003 forebears. That is a remarkable fact, and one trumpeted pretty clearly in the *Globe* today. Dan Shaughnessy wrote a fairly gushing piece, yet another example of the kinder, gentler Curly Headed Boyfriend revealing himself from his hardened soul.

Of course a streak of nine wins in ten games will tend to have that effect. Last night the Sox won again, defeating the Tigers 4-1, highlighted by Bronson Arroyo fulfilling the Tigers' deathwish in a 7 1/3 inning, 8 strikeout, one-run performance. Timlin once again came in and did his job, putting out a minor fire in which Detroit had Higginson on second with one out. He struck out I-Rod and then induced a Dmitri Young lineout, closing the last, best chance the Tigers may have had. Foulke came in and shut the side down in order in the 9th. Outside of Arroyo and the pitching, it was a pretty lackluster win, but one we would have managed to turn into an adventure a month ago.

Tonight Varitek returns from his A-Rod-smacking-induced suspension, spelling a hot Doug Mirabelli who may well have earned himself at least a couple of appearances more than he might have gotten, and a DH slot or two should Ortiz enter the field or simply need a rest. Lowe hits the mound, and hopefully will continue to show the fortitude that seems to have returned to him these last few appearances.

The Red Sox have 36 games left on the schedule and are 5 1/2 aback the Yankees in the East. They lead the Wild Card by a scant 1/2 of a game. I am more worried about the latter than the former. And if the Blue Jays are reading, last night you were up 4-0 on them and still lost. A little help here!

Saturday, August 28, 2004

I am setting myself up for an enormous, crashing fall by being as stoked about the Sox as I have been since the April evisceration of the Yankees. Last night they continued their hot streak (10 of 11 and counting) by beating the Tigers 5-3. Derek Lowe went eight innings, a season high, and gave up three runs on the way to the victory. He has now only lost once in his last six appearances, and many, including *The Globe's* Bob Hohler, are speculating that Nomar's trade helped him more than anyone by improving the infield defense and thus helping the sinkerballer's cause. Obviously it is impossible to prove whether or not this is so. I believed that Lowe would right things in the second half of the season anyway, but if he is more confident in the defense, and that helps explain his recent performances, there will be no complaints from this corner.

It is hard to overstate how important it is for the starters to eat lots of innings in their appearances. This is not because our relief corps is unreliable. On the contrary—they are becoming a linchpin for this team again, but for any relief staff to do their job, they cannot suffer from overuse. This happened to the guys for much of that dreary middle part of the season, and we paid a steep price for it. It was all the worse because of injuries. But if the starters can go 6-7-8 innings every time out, we will have flexibility in the bullpen.

One scary moment occurred in last night's game, which I only was able to follow after the fact (new faculty had dinner at the president's swanky house, and then we went out for drinks). Manny fouled a ball off of his left knee, causing him to leave the game and making him day-to-day. The x-rays were negative, and our crack medical staff has diagnosed him with a contusion. It could be worse, which of course is easy for me to say, as I did not take a foul ball off of my knee less than 24 hours ago.

Pedro goes tonight. In his last outing he was bested when Ted Lilly threw the game of his life. Pedro had a decent outing, but my guess is that he will want to come out throwing smoke tonight. Overthrowing is actually a particular bane to this incarnation of Pedro, but if he does not overdo it, and if the guys give him a lead, we could be in pretty good shape to accrue yet another sweep, this time in a four game series.

As is the case with every team at this time of year, injuries could be the determinant factor in our late-season success. Right now things are not ideal on that front, as they have not been all year. Besides Manny's knee, Bill Mueller did not play yesterday because of soreness in his ankle and foot; Minky continues to sit because of the shoulder injury he sustained the other night; and Foulke's back stiffened up on him and he was unavailable last night. This last development has caused the accursed words "closer by committee" to cross some lips, with the committee consisting of Embree, Timlin, and Leskanic, though one hopes that Mendoza's name will start being uttered in more and more crucial situations with the way he has been throwing. Bill James, of course, has made the case that the closer is overrated and that you should bring the best guy in for a situation irrespective of whether or not it is the ninth or a save situation. And this may well be true, at least in the abstract. But the Red Sox do not play in the abstract. So I'll gladly welcome Foulke back in a traditional closer's role any time he is ready.

Pedro's on the mound. College football kicks off tonight. The Pats are on national television (yes, it is only an exhibition game, but still . . .), I am having folks over to Casa de Catsam this evening. The Red Sox simply must win for perfection to reign, at least temporarily.

Sunday, August 29, 2004

Six in a row, twelve of thirteen, fifteen of eighteen, eighteen of the last twenty-two. Sometimes numbers can be eloquent in their simple explication of complex reality. I am not certain that I am thrilled about tomorrow's off day, but I do know that as well as we have been playing, it is all prelude to the next couple of weeks. The Wild Card is a dogfight right now, as the Angels, A's and Rangers are playing nearly as well as we are. We get a shot at all of those teams in our next three series, and this is when it is essential to gain ground. We can effectively eliminate each of them as a serious contender if we win each of these series. Right now we have a game-and-a-half lead on Anaheim.

Last night I hosted a soiree at my place that went rather well. Josh was at Fenway last night, having bought standing-room-only seats from a scalper before the game. He kept calling my cell with updates from the game. Pedro did well, going seven (apparently the Sox have had their starters make it through at least 5 innings for an astounding 40+ games.) and giving up just one run. One indication of how they are playing is that they are eking out runs even when they are not hitting especially well. My phone rang constantly as the Sox pulled away, which was a source of amusement and mystery to my guests, who inexplicably are not Sox fans.

Today's game marked yet another outstanding appearance by a starter. Waker went eight innings, he gave up just three hits and one run. He struck out seven, and as an indication of how on he was with the knuckler, of 99 pitches, an astounding 72 caught the plate for strikes. This is the rotation we dreamed of, with Arroyo instead of Kim, and it is really bearing fruit now. Kim might be close to a return, along with Nixon, whose quad is almost fully healed. And Manny played today. Since the rosters are on the cusp of expanding to forty, all of these additions will be able to help us in the stretch run. I cannot imagine anyone wanting to face us in a five- or seven-game series.

Great as the pitching is, everyone seems to be playing his part.

Astoundingly, the Sox had seven steals in this series. Bellhorn hit a bomb, Mirabelli has been playing well, Kaplar has been great, the relievers have been money, and of course Manny and Ortiz have continued to pile up MVP numbers. I hope the off day does not harm our momentum, and that we can keep playing this kind of baseball in this most important stretch of the season.

Monday, August 30, 2004

It is time for me to make an admission that has been scaring the devil out of me for two months or more. As my faithful readers, and even a few faithless ones, might have divined, I do not much go in for the Curse of the Bambino hooey. Red Sox fans may well be sinners in the hands of an angry, vengeful, and even arbitrary God, but it is a God that allows us to our own devices.

That said, there is one curse in which I not only believe, but for which I am wholly responsible. It is a powerful curse, and one I am not certain I am able to counteract. Fortunately for Dan Shaughnessy, whose grandkids will be going to college on the spoils of *Curse of the Bambino*, my curse has neither the pithy title nor the broad appeal of his (and it is not really even his theory, but he has stolen judiciously, and for that we should admire him.) The Curse of Derek Going Abroad (which I am hereby naming Yank Abroad Not Knowing Sox' Status Unusually Capricious as a Konsequence—acronyms are fun!) is one that has ample evidence to bolster its existence.

Basically, the curse runs along these lines: Every time I leave the country for an extended time during baseball season, the Red Sox swoon. On occasions this is a season-long phenomenon, such as in 1997 when I lived for the duration of the year in South Africa and the Sox had a decidedly mediocre season. At other times, it manifests in short losing skeins that seem to overlap almost directly with my absences, such as for two or three months in 1999 when I was back in South Africa, or in 2000 when I left for the summer in Ireland and Northern Ireland. Both times the Red Sox had summers that were pretty woeful, and while the Sox occasionally come back from such nightmares, it still is a bit more than I like to be responsible for delivering. Last year when I left for Israel for ten days, the curse did not manifest as strongly, but it was not until I was back in the States that they began to recover from a pretty lackluster mid-season.

Gut Check Time

This brings us to my impending trip to England for some ten days. I have two conferences, one this weekend at the University of Kent in Canturbury, the other at the University of London the following weekend. In the interregnum I will do some traveling, a bit of research, and as much catching up with some friends as possible. But I am scared. I am very scared. You see, in a season that has been fraught with some pretty remarkable nadirs, I am tempting not merely fate, but I am tempting a curse the mojo of which has proven to be almost insurmountable. And I do not mean to be solipsistic about this. But it really is all about me.

The Sox play 11 games during my absence, depending on how one sees the game on the 12th, which starts at 4:00, when I will probably have landed in Dallas but will not have arrived in Midland/Odessa. So call it ten games. (It figures, of course, that my hubris is rewarded with eleven days in a row of games with nary an off day in sight during the entire length of my trip. And this is not an easy stretch—while I am gone they finish the Anaheim series, they play three against Texas, three against Oakland, and after all of that they have a four game series with Seattle. Yes, the Mariners stink, but their stench still comes after nine huge games that may make or break the season.

So what to do? The dumbest thing would be to just whistle through the graveyard, to pretend that the curse is not REAL and thus not worth acknowledging. (Remember that I do not believe in curses. But I'd be a fool to deny this—I mean, it is ME, I am IT). And so instead what I hope to do is to blog through the graveyard. To stay up late or get up early, to know in as close to real time what is happening in Fenway and out west, and to hope that fate knows that I am on the case, and that still, I believe.

I acknowledge that I am treading on some dangerous ground here, and that my chutzpah might be swiftly and resoundingly punished, and for those of you who are Sox fans out there, just know that this is going to hurt me a lot more than it does you (really). But I am brave. And you should be too. For if this truly is the year, the guys are just going to have to break on through to the other side of this vexing hex. Like other alleged curses, this is one we simply have to overcome. And we shall overcome.

Tuesday, August 31, 2004

Today was a good day. It was a great day. Were it not for Mike Myers (no, not the one of Austin Powers fame, and despite how it looked, not the one of Halloween fame, either) giving up a ninth-inning grand slam to make a laugher a 10-7 game, it might have been a historically great day. Oh hell, given that Foulke came in to close it out, and that the Yankees lost by what might be an American league record in a shutout shellacking at the hands of the Indians, 22-0, and that we closed the gap to 3.5 (at one point they were up by 10.5; at the beginning of the month the lead was 8.5 games), and that we are up on the Angels by 2.5, and that the Rangers are losing, it was a pretty historically great day.

Despite the late inning ugliness, we had this game from the outset. In the first two innings, Manny hit two home runs and we were up 5-0. From that point on, it was a matter of adding a few runs (a 4-run 7th proved to be huge, with Dave Roberts' three-run home run proving to be the difference maker) and holding off an Angels team that, whatever our bullpen's shortcomings today, deserves credit for being tenacious. They do not say die (though Scoscia did pull some of the starters, which I bet he regretted in the 9th when Foulke came on to earn a much unexpected save). Almost getting lost in those last inning fireworks was Schilling's sterling outing. He went 7 and 2/3rds innings, scattered nine hits that produced three earned runs, and while he only struck out four, he walked none. That earned him his 17th win, tying Mark Mulder for the league lead. So while the end taints the whole a little, it is easy to say now that we won a big game in a big way, and the series advantage is in our hands. That feels nice.

And what of the big doings in the Bronx? This is a tough balance. On the one hand, I want to gloat, to enjoy the fruits of schadenfreude, to dance on their graves. On the other hand, this should not be about the Yankees.

Oh hell—I am ecstatic about this. This morning's *New York Post* had a picture of Alfred E. Neuman in a Yanks' hat asking "What, Us Worry" as some of those guys claimed that they were not at all concerned by what is appearing more and more like 1978 in reverse. That they came out tonight, 4.5 up, playing a swooning Indians team while we had to start a run against the meat of the American

League, and they not only lose, they not only get shelled, but in the Toilet Bowl in the Bronx they get beaten by a margin that forced statisticians and historians to the record books (Rennie Stennet had seven hits in a 22-0 Pirates mauling of the Cubs in the 1970s; otherwise, apparently, one would have to go back to the 1880s). But beware, Sox fans—we can be happy, even elated, but tonight has nothing to do with tomorrow, the Yankees have too much pride to let even the ugliest loss mean much for tomorrow, and if they win and we lose, they'll get this game back. The ugliness is nice to see, and one cannot help but wonder if the Yanks are not imploding just a little. I am all for such an implosion, and will relish tonight's results for the next 20 or so hours, but tomorrow's games are no less important than tonight's even if the YANKEES LOST 22-0 AT HOME TONIGHT.

But back to the Sox. It is now seven in a row, 13 of 14 (and remember, the loss was the Ted Lilly game in which Pedro gave up but three runs) and we finish August with a 21-7 record. On August 15th we were down by 10.5 on the Yankees. We enter September down by 3.5. What seemed a matter of speculation and wishful thinking and hopeless optimism now seems very real. We can win this division. The Yankees know it. Most important, so do the Red Sox. Yeah, this was a damned good day.

A.L. East Standings After August:

	W	L	%	GB
MFY	81	50	.618	—
SOX	77	53	.592	3.5
O's	59	71	.454	21.5
Tampa	59	72	.450	22
Jays	54	78	.409	27.5

8

September: The Stretch Drive

Thursday, September 2, 2004
I am in a bit of a frenzy to get everything I need to done before I head out of here for my London trip. But not wanting to tempt fate, and knowing that this is a key ten-day stretch in the season, it would be irresponsible for me not to write before heading off to the Midland airport for my trip to Merry Olde England.

Another day, another win. I do not want to sound flip about this, as if I am merely taking it all for granted, but it is a refreshing change from most of this season when I wake up expecting the Red Sox to win that day and end up disappointed when they do not. Last night's game was a bit of a circus, with both starting pitchers getting pounded early and the teams swapping runs. The Sox prevailed 12-7, simply showing more firepower and almost as much aggressiveness as the go-go Angels. After Bronson flamed out in the third, we got solid relief pitching from Mike Myers (of Tuesday's meltdown—Tito's thought process probably is that we need him, and thus his confidence, down the road) and Terry Adams, two guys pretty far down the depth chart, but whom we may well rely on to provide some innings down the stretch. Everybody did their part—indeed every player on both teams had at least one hit. Millar appears to be getting hot again. He hit an absolute bomb that provided some insurance runs in the sixth. Bellhorn, Cabrera, Damon all contributed in important ways.

As of this morning we sit in a pretty good position, 3.5 ahead of the Angels in the Wild Card race, still 3.5 behind the Yankees for the American League East. As I expected, the Yankees shook off the 22-0 shellacking, proving it to be at least something of an outlier, even if a beautiful satisfying one. A sure sign that this is the year will come if they can overcome my absence. I'll be watching as closely as one can from a country where cricket is more important than baseball, and football more important than, um, football. It is going to kill me to miss these games. But I have confidence that the Yankees will be feeling our breath on their necks and the Angels and Rangers and A's will be in the rear view mirror, not closer than they appear.

Sunday, September 5, 2004

Greetings from England, where a five-hour time gap (and six from my expatriate base in Texas) and sketchy access to news about the Sox has not deterred this intrepid diarist. Despite a loss last night, the first in nearly a fortnight, the Red Sox are sitting pretty despite my prolonged absence from the country. The Curse of Derek Leaving the Country may just be a thing of the past.

In my absence the Sox have gone 2-1 and have closed the gap on the Yankees by yet another game, dropping it down to a mere sliver, 2.5 games. Even as Steinbrenner idiotically compared the 22-0 loss to the Indians to the carnage of 9-11 (where do these people get their educations these days?) the Sox keep chipping away. Suddenly we are within a series sweep of the lead in the American League East. And we still have several games to go before our next showdown. First we need to win today to take this series against the Rangers. Then we need to face off against the white hot A's, who in addition to being on a roll of their own are also a team we may well face again in the playoffs, so this is a pretty big series coming up.

I am in a land where 'football' is king, and rugby and cricket are at least in the royal family. Baseball? Not so much. But hopefully I can keep abreast of the Sox and they can continue to overcome the Curse I bring. Keep it going, boys. I'm behind you all the way.

Monday, September 6, 2004

It is nice to wake up to a Sox victory. If I am going to miss these games, at least knowing that they are continuing this glorious run is of considerable solace. Despite almost giving it away in the 9th inning after Schill went 8 and 1/3 with double-digit strikeouts and left with a 6-1 lead, we managed to stave off a furious rally by the Rangers to win the game and thus the series. The Yankees defeated the Orioles 4-3, so their tenuous lead in the East remains at 2.5 games. With the Sox traveling to Oakland to take on the Athletics, things certainly do not get any easier for the good guys, but they have continued this roll against the meat of the American League. No reason to think we will not be able to keep it going against the A's.

Not shockingly, I get a good amount of grief here about American sports. The Brits just simply do not get baseball (as if cricket is simple to grasp; I like cricket, but let us not pretend that it is not a rather Byzantne game) and of course they constantly echo the refrain of those folks from rugby-playing nations who deride football for its padding. I try to explain how football is simply a more explosive game, that the lack of constant action that they also tend to mock means that it is simply faster. They do not buy it. If I like cricket, I love rugby, having played for Rhodes University in 1997, but the games are different, and one can appreciate both. In any case, I try to spread the gospel about the Boston Red Sox here in England, but it is a tough sell. Crumbling empires can be so set in their ways.

Tuesday, September 7, 2004

They just keep winning. Each series that has come has seemed tougher than the one before it, and yet the Red Sox have shown that if they are playing well, nothing else matters, they can beat anyone. While the Yankees are raising a squawk about games against Tampa being postponed due to the hurricanes that have struck Florida, asking for forfeits (very gutsy, George, though the way things have gone of late one can see why you might not think your best approach will be to win on the field) the Sox went into Oakland, the toughest place to play this year, and beat the A's 8-3 last night in a game that was far closer than the final score indicates.

Arroyo recovered from the pummeling he received at the hands of the Angels last week, giving up a couple early but keeping us in the game. Manny and Ortiz helped to break it open at the plate, and we held them off for a great and important win. Waker has been struggling of late, but hopefully he'll take the ball tonight and put us in position for another game win, another series win, and maybe another series sweep.

It is difficult to have to follow this from afar, relying on intermittent internet access and emails from Rob. But it has become a nice ritual. Five times now I have gone to find a computer not knowing how the Sox did just a few hours before. Four times I discovered that they won. It is a routine that is tough for me, because I want to be there to hear or see games. But they are winning, and in less than a week I'll be back for the homestretch. The Yankees should probably look for alternative ways of getting wins, because we are not going away.

Wednesday, September 8, 2004

We have now taken on the meat of the American League West and the heart of the toughest part of our schedule, and we have won every series. Last night's 7-1 pummeling of the A's, with Derek Lowe at the helm on the mound (I believe yesterday I averred that Waker would be pitching—clearly being out of the country has been bad for my attention to detail—mae culpa) and the bats continuing to fire on all cylinders. Tonight we go for the sweep with Pedro on the mound against their ace, so this should be a pretty epic game. Sadly, it is on ESPN2 but obviously I will not be seeing it. Though being on the west coast, the game will end not long before I wake up tomorrow.

In theory the schedule eases up for a while until we face the Yankees, next week, but in reality, the games count the same. Losses still hurt in our quest to overtake the Yankees and to continue to lead the Wild Card with ease. Wins still keep us in the hunt. It is no good to slice through these solid teams and then to crumble against the Seattles of the world. Hopefully we keep it up again tonight with Pedro atop the mound.

Thursday, September 9, 2004

So in the most important stretch of games all season, the Sox sweep the Angels, take 2 of 3 from the Rangers, and sweep the A's in rather humiliating fashion (8-3 last night, Pedro pitched a two hitter, they rolled in the first three innings, pretty much putting the game out of reach, even if they did yet again give up runs in the 9th that made it look closer than it was—a slightly worrisome trend). The Yanks could not get their doubleheader in last night, so we gain a half game on them and maintain our lead in the Wild Card, a lead decreasing in significance as it widens and as we close in on the gasping Yankees.

It is becoming alarmingly clear what an obsessive I am. The first thought in my head when I awoke this morning wasn't about my train ride to London today, or my pending conference paper, or my last morning in Cornwall. It wasn't about the blazing need to brush my teeth or the itching desire to take a shower (or simply to scratch myself) or the pressure on my bladder. It was not about eating. It was not even about sex. No, the first thing on my mind was "How did the Sox do?" Every day this past week or so, I have been able to wake up happy. Still, for a grown man this should be an alarming fetish. Instead, it is one that I embrace.

I'll be back in the States in four days, at which point I will be able to follow pitch-by-pitch, news story-by-news story, rumor-by-rumor, speculation-by-speculation. The gratuitous overkill will be especially fabulous after this respite. The trip has thus far been truly wonderful, but I am missing the Red Sox.

Friday, September 10, 2004

Naive and foolish as it seems, when the Sox have been on this roll, I have begun never to even conceive that they might lose. And certainly the idea of them losing to a team like the Mariners, or them losing games (a whopping 1.5 as the Yanks swept the Rays in that long postponed doubleheader and we lost) seemed almost unfathomable.

And yet lose they did, and in fashion reminiscent of the old Sox of July. Waker gave up seven runs, and yet only two were earned, with the Sox committing two deadly errors and the bats falling asleep. Obviously there was a bit of letdown against a lesser team after the roll we went on against the teams we had to beat. Problem is, we have to beat everybody. No sense reeling off 8 of 9 against the big boys only to lose 7-1 to the minnows.

Perhaps if my curse is done, and even more powerful one has set in: The SI cover jinx. I do not necessarily believe in such things, but I do not necessarily not believe, either, if that makes sense. Last week Tom Brady was on the cover of the SI football preview (which will be awaiting my return). This week the Sox made the cover, which I cannot wait to see. Nonetheless, it should have hit mailboxes yesterday. Then they lost last night. Hang on lads, and defeat that jinx as you so nobly defeated mine.

I'm in London now, visiting my cousin, a Long Island born—and bred—Sox fan (my Uncle John did yeoman's work on that front) and getting ready for a conference on "South Africa Ten Years On" from the end of apartheid, at which I am giving a paper. I'll be back in the country in two days, and cannot wait to see the Sox again. And now the Pats as well—they beat Indy 27-24 last night to extend their win streak to 16 games. But first and foremost, the Sox now need to get it done.

Saturday, September 11, 2004

Like most Americans, even (maybe especially) those of us who are abroad, it is hard not to be thinking about the horrific events of three years ago. It hit particularly close for me since at the time I was living in Washington. One of my first thoughts on a day riddled with disjointed pondering was of Williams, my alma mater, and how very many of my classmates and other fellow alums work in the world of finance in New York, and how many work in government in Washington, and one of the little reliefs of that day was knowing that for all of those numbers, we lost relatively few.

There is no way to make a graceful segue here, so I will not even try, save to say that I simply wanted to acknowledge that on this particular day, baseball is not the priority.

That said, one of the things sports can do is to bring joy and happiness and release in people's lives. From several thousand miles away, the Red Sox are certainly doing that. Last night Schill took on his increasingly unfamiliar role of stopper (by definition a stopper stops losing streaks, something we have had a blissful paucity of in the last month or so) by pretty well shutting down the Mariners, though with the way the guys swung the bat last night, they put him in a position where he could have stunk up the joint and they still would have won. 13-2, the Sox came back from their loss and earned the win. With the Yankees' 14-8 loss at the hands of the frisky Orioles, the Sox are back to being 2.5 back.

Manny took control last night, though Johnny Damon drove in three runs and Ortiz blasted a home run. Manny, however, had two bombs (marking the twelfth time this year he and Ortiz have jacked in the same game) including his 17th career grand slam, which ties him with two former Sox, Jimmy Foxx and Teddy Ballgame, for fifth on the all-time list. He passed Babe Ruth and, I think, Hank Aaron with the shot last night, and he passed another Sox legend, Dewey Evans, on the career home run list. In all, ManRam had a hell of a night.

Now the hope is that they keep it up. We earned our stripes against the mettle of the American league. Now we finish off against teams with sub-.500 records, save for the six games against the Yankees. We are still behind, but in a lot of ways, we can control our own fate. That's all one should ask for in September of the baseball season.

Monday, September 13, 2004

I am back from England, and wouldn't you know it, the Sox have an off day. Which in all honesty, is probably good—I am exhausted, had to teach three classes today, including this last one that ends at 10:00 at night, and I am as drained emotionally as I am physically. It is almost nice not to have to worry about how they are doing on top of readjusting to life back on the vast, dry, hot expanses of West Texas. I got back yesterday, was awake for more than 24 hours straight with the whole range of the long travel experience, and was able to watch some football.

But I cannot completely avoid the great race in the AL East. The Yankees are playing the Royals, who crashed hard this season after last year's unexpected successes. Nonetheless, Tony Pena's boys are doing well, as they are beating the Yanks soundly, 12-3, late in that game, so as we travel east, we get to make up a half a game that we lost yesterday in a 2-0 defeat in which we never threatened. Lowe pitched well again, which is good, but it was not enough. Ortiz sat, apparently resting the still-acing shoulder he hurt when Sveum waved him in a couple of weeks back despite the fact that Ortiz cannot run and the leftfielder had picked the ball up before Ortiz even rounded third. It was a cunning display of misjudgment and now we are paying a price for it.

Tomorrow we start a three-game set against the Devil Rays, and we cannot overlook them as we get ready for the big Yankees series this weekend. The Yanks are playing the Royals, and while the Kansas Citians are helping the Sox cause tonight, we have to expect that any loss will lose us a game in the standings from here on out. This weekend is huge, but at this stage of the season, every game is magnified.

Tuesday, September 14, 2004

Before tonight the Red Sox were a shocking, indeed, almost unfathomable, 0-6 against rookie pitchers. After tonight's ugly performance, the likes of which we have not seen in well more than a month, make that 0-7, with the Sox making tonight's Rays' starter Scott Kazmir, who came into the game with a record of 1-1 and an ERA of 4.50, look like Sid Finch. It is the 8th inning right now, and of course you never want to rule anything out, but if the form holds, we are on the way to our 3rd loss in 5 games, which pretty well erases much of what we gained in the previous couple of series. These games all count the same whether they are against the Angels or Devil rays. Too bad the guys started off this series looking like they do not know this.

Pedro got the start tonight, and he struggled early on. His control was a problem, but he gave up just two runs in his somewhat labored six-inning outing. From that point on, the Sox bullpen was ineffective, they got a few bad bounces, the Rays were aggressive enough to avoid some double plays, and before we knew it the floodgates had opened.

Here in the 8th the Sox are showing signs of life. Nixon just hit a pinch hit home run where the bullpen splits with one on, and it is now 5-2, but a Damon fly-out means there are two outs and Bellhorn, who has struck out three times tonight, is our hope to salvage the inning and get us to the big boppers, who have not bopped very big in the last couple of games. Moot point—Bellhorn strikes out. Looking. Again.

We made a run in the ninth. After getting a couple of runs, we eked out two walks (one on a hit-by-pitch in which Varitek pretty much leaned in to the ball) and Cabrera, the tying run, came to the plate. He hit a line drive to right center field, but it is not enough. Game over. Two-game losing streak. Ugh.

So what was it? Were they looking ahead to the Yankees? Was a prolonged hangover and letdown from the nine games against the big guns from the west inevitable? Is this just part of the regular ebb and flow of a season? Is it a sign of fundamental weaknesses? All of the above? None of the above?

It does not help that the Yankees are winning, meaning we could be four back after tonight. Each game we lose looms larger as the remaining schedule gets skinny. But perspective might be in order: When we first started to get things straight, we lost several first games and still came back to win series. We need Waker to come up big and Schill to continue his roll. We need to hit. If we take two of three, we'll be fine. Still, every loss now hurts just a little bit more than normal.

Wednesday, September 15, 2004

While I am sure the phrase was around a lot longer than my recollections, the first time I ever heard the term "winning ugly" used was to describe the 1983-1984 Chicago White Sox. That was the team that changed uniforms again, that time into something remotely resembling the beautifully hideous rainbow unis of the Houston Astros. It featured a hirsute pitcher, La Marr Hoyt, who was their ace. Carlton Fisk was their stalwart at catcher (a thought that still makes Red Sox fans wretch nearly a quarter century after Haywood Sullivan let him escape to Chicago because we tendered him a contract offer too late). Harold Baines, Greg Luzinski, and Ron Kittle were their offensive backbone. It was a team that won, taking the west in 1983 before losing to the Baltimore Orioles who went on to win the World Series against the Phillies, but they won ugly — lots of error-riddled 9-7 games and the like.

I bring this up because tonight the Red Sox won, but they won ugly. Waker was decidedly not on, but every time the Rays pulled ahead or pulled even, as they seemed to do every time they stepped up to the plate in the first six innings, the Sox came back to tie or go ahead. It went this way until we pulled ahead 8-6 in the 6th, and that is how the game ended. Each team piled up the hits against a succession of pitchers who simply did not get the job done. For the Sox Timlin and Foulke were the exceptions, each pitching a perfect inning, Foulke's for the save, but before that, nothing was automatic. On a day when the Yankees won early to go up by 4.5

games, putting us in jeopardy of falling behind by five, we simply fought and scuffled and worked, and at the end, our bats were a bit better, or our pitchers were not quite as bad. We were paced by home runs by Bellhorn and Millar, Bellhorn's putting us ahead 2-1 in the first and Millar's pulling us ahead 6-4 in the fifth. It was Millar's 100th career home run. In the 6th Manny drove in the go-ahead run with a sac fly. We added a run in the 7th when Trot hit a ball that snuck between Julio Lugo's wickets, driving in Dave Roberts. It is nice to have Trot back, even if that RBI was sheer luck.

Do we worry about Wakefield? He gave up four runs on six hits through five innings and is winless in his last three starts. Still, we all know what Waker can do for us, and at some point in the next six weeks we will need him at a big moment. I am confident that he will come through, even if he is scuffling now.

Tomorrow Schill takes the mound in another must-win game. We need to keep pace or gain a game as we head into this series in New York. Both Friday's and Sunday's games will be on ESPN, and I have to assume that Fox will carry the Saturday game, so I will not have to take any drastic measures to see all three of them. But first things first—at this time of year we need to think in 24-hour increments. It was ugly, but we won. That's all that matters. Now we need to take this rubber match tomorrow and head off to New York ready to do battle.

Friday, September 17, 2004

I've been giddy and worthless all day. Hearing that there might be a rainout in Yankee Stadium has me both disconsolate and apoplectic. There is no way this game can be postponed, canceled, or otherwise delayed, lest my head explode. This series is enormous, with huge implications for the Sox.

Last night things went on as I had hoped they would. The Red Sox pounded the Rays from the outset, Schilling rolled for 7 2/3 mostly unscathed, and they won in a laugher, 11-4. It was the ideal sort of game—we won the series, we saved the arms in the bullpen, the bats are swinging well, and they even gained half a game on the Yanks, who did not play last night.

Normally I reserve my Red Sox writing for this diary, but on my weblog, "Rebunk," I decided to write about the upcoming series, and while some of this will be old hat for followers of this diary, I figured I'd save a bit of labor and reprint it here:

> This weekend the Red Sox are at what threatens to be a rainy Yankee Stadium (aka "The Toilet Bowl in the Bronx") for a three-game series that will help settle the American League East race. But it means so, so much more than that.
>
> Currently the Yankees have a 3.5 game cushion and the Sox are comfortably ahead in the Wild Card race, so whatever happens, both of these teams should easily make the playoffs. Nonetheless, I have been giddy all day, nay, all week, about these three games (all of which will be on national television, which is manna from heaven for this Texas cowpoke).
>
> On August 15th, the Yankees held a 10.5 game lead on the Sox. Now they can feel our breath on their necks as we close in on them. The logical parallel is with 1978, the year the Sox collapsed (though the apex of their 1978 lead came in July) and the Yanks came back. In the last week of that season the Yankees opened up a lead from which the Sox recovered to force a tie (People always forget that part) and a one-game playoff, the results of which have been lost to history, never to be recovered.
>
> Suddenly the glove may be on the other hand. The Red Sox have been playing first-rate baseball. The Yankees have shown that their aging dynasty is more age, less dynasty. They are ever dangerous, of course, and no one in Red Sox Nation takes them lightly, but they are vulnerable.
>
> In September of that fateful summer of 1978 the Yankees played a four-game series in Fenway in which the pinstripers pounded the Sox by an aggregate score of 42-9. It has forever been known as the "Boston Massacre," and even as a professional historian, whenever I hear that name, I do not think of the event that helped to precipitate the Revolution by showing the lengths to which the ruthless

Redcoats would go to suppress colonial intransigence, but rather it conjures up events that cause night sweats in any respectable Boston fan.

So this weekend (and next weekend, when the two teams will meet in Fenway, aka "God's Favorite Place") is huge. The AL East is at stake, home field in the American League playoffs is at stake, but beyond that, intrinsically, the games themselves each simply mean something, everything. My apologies to fans in other sports or of other great and storied rivalries, but this is the best, most heated, most intense rivalry in sports. It is Athens v. Sparta, USA v. USSR, Rocky v. Apollo, all rolled into one. It is the only event that matters on the calendar this weekend. It is what September baseball is all about -- rivalry and joy and tension and release and glory and imagination and hope. Always hope.

Go Sox!!!!!

Saturday, September 18, 2004

I think they gave me an ulcer last night. In the last two years the Red Sox-Yankees rivalry might be the only seemingly over-hyped sporting matchup that nonetheless actually manages to surpass the buildup. And it does so every time, no matter who wins, no matter which team you support.

Last night's game was no exception. In a game punctuated by two rain delays, one of more than an hour, the Red Sox triumphed in a ninth inning comeback against Mariano Rivera, also known in Red Sox Nation as "Fruitbat." (Do a Google image search of both names and see if it is not one of the greatest cruel nicknames of all time). It was a 3-2 game characterized by fireworks appropriate for a game with three times as many runs.

Bronson Arroyo weathered both rain delays and dodged a few bullets, one in which Manny made a spectacular, Espy-Award-type catch to rob Miguel Cairo of a home run. Cairo was so certain that it was gone that he finished his trot by crossing home plate and trying to get some love when he looked around in disbelief after finding out what Manny had done. Oh, and if one wants to measure the superiority of Sox fans v. Cubs fans in terms of baseball smarts, note that the Sox fans lining the left field wall did not interfere and indeed pulled away from many to allow him to make a catch that will be burned on my brain forever, to be pulled out and savored in offseasons to come. Note also that when the Sox made big plays or got big hits and audible roar came from the crowd: Embedded Sox fans in the Toilet Bowl. You won't hear Yankees fans in Fenway next weekend, I'll assure you of that. In any case, Tito too dodged some bullets when he left Arroyo in for one inning too long, though Bronson, who is growing up before our very eyes, was able to pitch a 1-2-3 6th. He had given up a solo home run to Olerud to lead of the fifth, which for most of the rest of the game looked as if it was going to hold up as the winning run.

The Sox got to El Duque early, with Manny Ramirez absolutely tagging him for what appeared to be a home run, only to have it overruled by the umpires, who had a wretched game overall even if they got that call right. Especially horrible was home plate umpire Tim Wendelstadt, who was calling pitches six inches off the plate for strikes. Maybe part of his thinking was that he wanted to get a game threatened by rain past the fifth, but his horrible plate umpiring continued even after the game would have gone into the books. In any case, the Sox squandered a bases-loaded opportunity in the first, but Johnny Damon hit an upper deck blast on a not-so-fast Hernandez fastball in the third that held up as the lead for two innings and a couple of hours due to the delays.

In the ninth the Sox were magical, even if that is when my ulcers probably fully appeared. Facing the bottom of our lineup (Nixon, Varitek—who had a horrible night in his first trip to the Bronx after l'affaire A-Rod—Millar, and Cabrera) Fruitbat was uncharacteristically wild. He walked Nixon, for whom Tito wisely pinch ran Dave Roberts, who kept Rivera off balance, especially after Roberts stole second when Varitek struck out. He then drilled Millar with a pitch, causing Wendelstadt to warn both benches. Arroyo had hit a batter earlier, also clearly unintentionally, but this was absurdly premature—no one in either dugout believed hitting Millar could possibly have been an intentional, and these guys have to be able to play, which includes pitching inside. In any case, Cabrera dropped a single into right field that allowed the speedy

Roberts to tie the game up. One batter later Damon continued his heroics by singling in Gabe Kaplar, Tito's choice to pinch run for Millar. This goes to show just how solid the Sox depth is, which could be huge as the postseason approaches and progresses.

Keith Foulke did his job, shutting the yanks down 1-2-3 in the bottom of the ninth to preserve the win and earn the save. Today's game is just about to start, so I need to go home and bunker down. D-Lowe against Lieber. I suspect a lot of firepower today. I also expect either a win or another few holes in my stomach lining. Nonetheless, it is a glorious form of stress. I cannot wait to see what these two teams come up with today.

Sunday, September 19, 2004

Yesterday's game did not happen. Oh, there are delusional ne'er do wells who will claim that they saw a game, and that it ended in a 14-4 romping and that Derek Lowe lasted just 1+ innings and gave up an absurd amount of runs (6? 7? Remember—it did not happen, so fake numbers are unimportant.) Those same jokers will tell tales about how the Sox defense absolutely fell apart. But remember— there was no Sox-Yanks' game yesterday. So today's game is not an absolutely critical rubber match that will keep alive the Sox' best bet at catching the Yankees. It is not a huge game for Pedro. It is not another ulcer-inducing showdown in the Bronx. Because whatever you hear, yesterday's game did not happen. Thank You.

Monday, September 20, 2004

There reaches a point when even the most studious denial becomes obvious to the denier himself. Denying the 14-4 trouncing was an effective defense mechanism when it seemed like a blip on the screen, and when the presupposition was that we would bounce back, win the series, and give the Orioles the business. But the reality was rather different—we got pounded yesterday 11-1 in Pedro's start and then today we had a third straight horrible outing by a starting pitcher when Waker lost 9-6 to the Orioles, who have had our number all season. And to add insult to incompetence, the Yankees lost tonight, so we blew one of our few remaining shots to catch up and take the AL East, an eventuality that simply seems more and more remote with each passing defeat.

There is time of course. After our roll through August and the first half of the month, it was probable that we would come back to earth. Still, my mood is foul right now, and it can be largely attributed to the play of the Red Sox. When they are good they are very, very good. But when they are bad they are nearly unwatchable. I am more than ready for the good Red Sox to return.

Wednesday, September 22, 2004

It is that time of year when the phrase "Magic Number" appears on lips across this great land of ours. It is a phrase that is thrown around a lot, but most people do not really understand it. I'll admit that every year I have to re-learn how to calculate it. There are actually a couple of ways, but here is one of the easier: Take the number of games remaining and add one; subtract the number of games ahead in the loss column your team is from the opponent against which you are trying to figure your magic number.

So, the Angels have 11 games remaining. Add one, which makes 12. We are six games ahead in the loss column. Subtract that from the games remaining +1. Our magic number is thus 6. Basically, we would have to collapse not to have some combination of 6 wins and Angels' losses in the next two weeks. The Yankees have a magic number of 9 right now.

The main reason that I can write about the Magic Number at all is that the Sox (barely) were able to stop their own blood flow last night, pulling off a nail biter of a 3-2 win. The Sox led 1-0 going into the 9th when Foulke came in for what should have been the save on a Schilling masterpiece. Schill went eight, struck out 14, including the last three batters he faced in the 8th, and of 114 pitches he threw an astounding 90 for strikes. Foulke had converted 16 straight save opportunities, and so it seemed logical to bring him in. Instead of things going according to plan, however, as Tejada singled and Javy Lopez hit a bomb over the Green Monster to make it 2-1, deflating all of Red Sox Nation and costing Schilling a much-deserved win. Fortunately, in the bottom of the 9th, Mark Bellhorn managed to drive in Youkilis and Mueller (who had four hits, including a double that pushed Youks, who had walked, to third) with a single on a 2-1 count to win the game. It must have been a nail biter in Fenway, but it was a needed win, even if the bats still are largely silent.

Hopefully they can manage to take these next two games, starting with Arroyo's outing tonight, and get on another win streak heading into the series this weekend against the Yankees. Maybe the three days before last night's games were the worst, last bad streak we'll see in 2004.

Thursday, September 23, 2004

Twelve innings. Another ill-timed home run off Foulke in the ninth to tie the game. Another bases loaded, no runs lack of capitalization by the Red Sox. Another hero stepping on to the main stage to help us pull off an epic win—this time Cabrera with a blast over the Monster on the 400th pitch of the game, but also an unheralded group of relievers parading one after the other after the 9th to hold down the fort and give us a chance to win. This is the sort of litany of the improbable and the unexpected that characterizes the 2004 Red Sox.

Last night's was another chaotic and vertiginous game at the Fens, but we emerged on top 7-6 after squandering another lead The whole game was a see-saw battle in which the last at-bat was perhaps the most important thing we had in our favor. Foulke is going through a spell like he did in June, but he righted himself then, and I suspect he'll right himself now. Arroyo was not as sharp as he was on Friday night, but he kept us in it. Because of defensive changes and pinch hitting and seemingly profligate bullpen usage (but ultimately effective—Tito seems more confident in his handling of the relief corps, though I suppose by "seems more confident" I might simply mean "now it is working") just about everybody on the roster who could play seemed to get in last night. In some ways this will serve as an audition for the postseason roster. But it also shows the depth that we should bring to bear when October rolls around.

Perhaps best of all, the Yankees lost again, and so we are within 3.5 again. Last night's game thus is something of a microcosm of the last two weeks, when we ended our big winning stretch and started to scuffle: No matter how much we seem to put ourselves out of any game, or the AL East race, we always do something to get ourselves right back in the mix. The fact that the Yankees cannot put us away is part of the problem for them. But to our credit, we also refuse to be put away. We scratch and we claw and we fight and even when others have given up, the guys in that clubhouse battle to the last out. I know I sound like a cliché-addled manager after a big win, but it is more than a little bit true. Like last year's team, these guys have faith in one another, and they never think they are out of a game. That bodes well for the postseason.

The Yankees won today, so we need to do the same to keep pace. Indeed, they clinched a playoff spot, so once again, we will have to go through them in order to get that prize we have eyed from afar for so very long. But that is as it should be. Tonight Derek Lowe gets his chance to redeem himself after Saturday, when he pissed down his leg against the Yankees. The current rumor going around the web and other seedy spawning grounds for rumors (which I am not above repeating) is that on Friday night, Lowe and a number of the guys were so certain that Saturday's game would be delayed or canceled due to rain that they went out on a Dionysian spree in New York. That is dumb on so many levels I can hardly contain myself. But it also provides a nice way to rationalize Saturday's game (which, as faithful readers might recall, did not happen).

Friday, September 24, 2004

Derek Lowe went five innings, gave up five runs, four earned, and exited after 5 down 5-3, though the Sox scored two in the fifth to tie it up and take him off the hook. From that point on, the game was the bullpen's, which given the overtaxing from the night before, was probably way too much to ask. The O's went up 7-5 and scored two runs in the ninth off of Byung-Hyun Kim, making his first appearance since he went insane, I mean, got hurt, months ago. We got back two in the 9th, but it simply was not enough, and the Orioles continued their spell against us. They lead the season series 9-6 against us. We close the season with four more against them. Ugh.

So now we are 4.5 games back, meaning that realistically, with ten to play, we need to sweep the Yankees, take care of our own business, and still get some help from their remaining opponents. Home field will be a huge factor this year—playing Minnesota, which seems likely, is a lot more daunting when they get last raps (old Little League/playground term for last at-bats) in the

Metrodome than when we get to rely on Fenway Magic. Tonight the Yankees roll into town in a game that will be on ESPN. Pedro gets to try his hand against Mussina again, and we also get Schill on Sunday, so if Waker can take care of business (and he did a side session yesterday with Charlie Hough, who spun knucklers well into his mid-40s, so hopefully he'll get back to form) maybe we can pull this off.

A couple of happy-happys, as they say on PTI: The Sox did a classy thing and activated Ellis Burks, who since April has been on the shelf and gone through two knee surgeries. He is retiring at the end of the year, capping a wonderful career in what must be a disappointing way. Nonetheless, the guys really seem to want to include him and get him a ring, and he got a single last night in a pinch-hit performance. If he can get a couple of hits that help lead the way, the tale will be all the better. I still remember Burks when he and Mike Greenwell were something of a Rice-Lynn, Gold Dust Twins Lite. Burks had the bearing of a young Reggie Smith or Lynn, with a grace that belied his power. He left the Sox to sign as a free agent in Chicago with the White Sox, and as so often happens with Sox players, there was a hint of acrimony to the divorce. Nonetheless, he went on to shine despite knees that would have frightened Joe Namath or Mickey Mantle.

Meanwhile, Manny and Ortiz are beginning to compile numbers that make their partnership this year worthy of historical notice. Two nights ago Ortiz hit his 40th home run, making the two the second pair of Sox teammates to hit 40 each, joining Yaz and Rico Petrocelli, who accomplished the feat in 1969. If the guys on ESPN were accurate, they are also the first pair of American Leaguers to combine for 40-120 since Ruth and Gehrig did it three times in the 20s and 30s, and they are the only pair of teammates to have hit 40 homers and 40 doubles each in a season as well. On top of all of that, Ortiz's home run the other night was his 86th extra base hit, tying him with Big Jim Ed Rice in 1978 and Teddy Ballgame in 1939. Obviously, the Manny-Ortiz pairing will be crucial to our postseason hopes.

Tonight the epic rivalry continues, this time in the Fens. I'll be glued to my tv screen, fully believing that they'll get it done. Pedro will deal. The Wonder Twins will both go deep. We'll get to Mussina early and often. We'll shave a game off of their lead.

Sunday, September 26, 2004

Barring some sort of Yankees collapse and the Sox running the table, we are likely not going to win the American League East. Our only realistic hope would have been to sweep this series and then hope that they lost and we didn't on a couple of occasions in the next week or so. After a galling loss on Friday night, the reality became clear: We will win the Wild Card, we will play either Minnesota or the winner of the West on the road (Go Rangers!) and we will not see home-field advantage until the World Series if all goes as it should.

Friday night Pedro again took it on the chin against the Yankees, and while it is too soon to panic, and while Pedro's own self-criticism has been harsher than anything in the media or among the fans, it seems fair to say that Pedro has not been at his best against them one team we need him to be at his best to face. Tito kept him in too long Friday night, and the Yankees battled back for a 6-4 win in a game that we had taken the lead in with a Manny bomb, and when it all was over, we were 5.5 back.

Yesterday's game salved the wounds a little. Waker has been another problem point for us, but he kept us in the game. We were up 5-3 but they came back to tie it 5-5, and that sinking feeling slowly began to set in. But then we started rolling, and before long, in the 8th, we got a few hits, even Varitek, whose slump of late has been alarming, got into the action, and we ended up with a 12-5 victory.

Even if we cannot expect to pull out the East, a win today wins the series. It is worth noting that by winning yesterday we assured ourselves of taking the season matchup against the Yankees. Today we get to face Kevin Brown, who will heavily pad the glove on his injured hand, which he broke while throwing a temper tantrum a few weeks back. The fact is, with a win today we'll still sit back and say "if x happens and if y happens we might be able to steal the division," which is to say that even when the average Sox fan has given up hope, he or she has not really given up hope.

Happy Birthday, Mom.

Monday, September 27, 2004

Even if we end up taking second in the AL East for the seventh season in a row (adding to what was already a rather bittersweet major league record) we can relish in one fact: We beat the Yankees eleven times this year, which we have not done since that joyous season of 1975, and of course we took the season series from them 11 games to 8. We took a game off of their lead, bringing the margin down to 3.5. And of its own right, yesterday's was a pretty nice win, 11-4 with Schilling continuing to pitch masterfully as he gears up for the postseason, in which he will be our number one guy. Obviously the bats were roaring, and the Yankees have much to fear when it comes to choosing a number four pitcher. Yesterday Kevin Brown lasted 2/3 of an inning as we ping-ponged his ineffective pitches all over the little bandbox. Schilling, meanwhile, gave up two runs but only one hit and we were never in jeopardy. He is our ace right now, which is why we pursued him to begin with last offseason.

This last fact is not insignificant. On Friday night after his loss to the Yankees Pedro gave a rather bizarre and melancholy accounting to the media in which he said, among other things, that this year the Yankees have been "his daddy." I am not the first to point out that his unfortunate choice of words will be fodder for tee shirts that have likely already been printed in the Bronx. Nonetheless, I think it is easy to make a mountain out of this particular anthill. Pedro is emotional and he tends to wear his heart on his voice box. He was frustrated and bothered by his inability to finish off the Yankees when Tito brought him back for the 8th in Gradyesque fashion and then left him in for too long to give the Yanks the lead. In any case, I like to think that we still have a pretty good 1-2 combo for the postseason.

And it should be but a formality for us to win the Wild Card. Our Magic Number is now two, so we could conceivably clinch a tie tonight with a win and an Anaheim loss to Texas, an eventuality for which I am rooting in any case, what with my interests being firmly in the success of the Rangers.

Two other salient points from yesterday: Things continued to be chippy, with near-beanballs flying and even a half-hearted bench-clearing in which no punches were thrown. That will percolate for the next couple of weeks, I should think. And finally, Ellis Burks did not play but he got a nice ovation when prompted to step out of the dugout in his last regular appearance in Fenway. Sox fans are generally a classy lot, to be sure (though I would not encourage you to show up to Fenway with your little kid in a Yankees hat; there is a limit to that class).

Let's pound Tampa. Make it easy. Let some borderline guys prove their worth for the postseason roster. Get the pitching rotation and bullpens set. Win. It's almost playoff time.

Tuesday, September 28, 2004

Let's hear it for your 2004 Boston Red Sox, playoffs—bound again. It is stunning to think about, but the Sox are going to the postseason for the second consecutive season for only the third time in their history. 1915-1916, 1998-1999, and 2003-2004. That is shocking. One of the arguments I have always made about the tragedy of the Sox is that unlike, say, the Cubs, the Sox have almost always been good. Since the 1920s they have not had an entire decade when they were dreadful. Yet only thrice have they gone to the postseason back to back. What is heartening is that two of those have come in the last six seasons. Obviously that is attributable to the Wild Card, but also to our consistency.

Last night the Sox got it done in a game marred by some beanball silliness in which we were the key beneficiaries. Arroyo, who I just do not believe is a headhunter but who nonetheless leads the American League in hit batters nailed two guys in the fourth. The next inning the nearly unhittable (for us this year anyway) Scott Kazmir retaliated by hitting Manny in the legs, then managed to drill Millar on the next pitch leading to the benches clearing (Millar started toward the mound, which I am convinced was a ploy simply to escalate and thus assure that Kazmir was tossed) though no punches. Once Kazmir was out and Jorge Sosa was in for the Rays we scored quickly, with Damon continuing the heroics that are inspiring a little bit of talk involving him and MVP votes by hitting a three run home run. Manny blasted an epic bomb in the next at bat after his plunking, and Varitek and McCarty added solo shots as the Sox rolled 7-3 to give Bronson his 10th win. He did well, going six-and-a-third and giving up only two runs.

When all was said and done, the guys went to the locker room and engaged in a celebration involving a bit of champagne and a lot of spilled Bud Light. Some have criticized them for this as they did after their much more ebullient celebration after they clinched the Wild Card berth at home last year. I don't get that criticism. They had a tough season and achieved one of their major goals with a week to go in the season. They clearly like one another, and they wanted to show it. They all said the right things—when asked about who would be the number one starter in the postseason Pedro said that all he cares about is getting a ring. And Millar complained that they were wasting good alcohol by spraying and spewing it across the locker room. They were enjoying themselves. Their celebration last year did not hurt them in the postseason. If we've reached a point where a team cannot celebrate after locking up a postseason berth, I think we are missing the point about the joy of sports, for us, but also for the athletes. We cannot complain that they do it all for the money and are mercenaries and do not care and then at the same time chastise them when they show a little bit of joy and life. In other words: Screw the critics.

Tonight is proving to be a vexing game. We started off well, getting a 1-0 lead. But in less than three innings Lowe blew it, looking awful and likely pitching his way off the postseason roster in the process. By the time he left it was 5-1. In the fourth the Sox managed to tie it up. Terry Adams gave the lead right back to them in the bottom of that inning. In the fifth we scored two and took a 7-6 lead. Adams promptly gave that lead back with two in the bottom of the inning. Five innings, five lead changes. And now in the 6th Cabrera got on with a bloop hit, and many just drove him in with a double that Baldelli briefly lost, allowing Cabrera to scamper across the plate. It is now tied 8-8. Millar just got hit by a pitch, and he is the second Sox hitter to take a ball off the body, but there is no tension and have been no warnings. The Sox have the bases loaded. And Mirabelli hits into a 6-4-3 double play. It's 8-8 midway through the sixth. I am going to listen while I do some work and report back . . .

Now THIS is the Red Sox team that I want to see heading into the playoffs. No, not the one that engaged in a see-saw battle with a frisky but overmatched Tampa team for seven innings, but rather the one that kept it going until the eleventh before Kevin Millar hit a two-run home run to give us the 10-8 win and get us within 2.5 of the rained-out Yankees, who suddenly are in an interesting position. They obviously lost half a game by virtue of us winning and them losing. And now they have to play a doubleheader tomorrow, which, given their pitching staff and bullpen, is not good for them. And even if they get a win, we could gain ground if Minnesota earns the split. And if we win and the Twins take both games, well, then things become very, very interesting for everyone involved.

Thursday, September 30, 2004

There were a number of possible scenarios for yesterday's games. The best was for us to win and for the Twins to sweep the Yankees. The worst was for us to lose and for the Yankees to execute a sweep. Anything in the middle would have been of varying utility.

The worst-case scenario happened. So in the age-old tradition of being a sports fan, let me spin this into a little bit of sweet lemon rationalization: If we were going to lose, a day like today was good for us. For reasons that this diary has chronicled ceaselessly, we came up a bit short, and a 4-game Magic Number, which the Yankees had going into yesterday, is a razor-thin margin. At least with three games cut from that magic number we now can get ready for the playoffs knowing that we will have to get it done on the road. We can rest guys judiciously. We can position ourselves. Better for that to have happened yesterday than for us to have left it all on the field over the weekend only to come up short and to have left ourselves in a less-than-ideal position for Tuesday when it all matters most.

Two main issues right now: The first is that, without recounting yesterday's loss, which was not pleasant, Pedro's performance is suddenly a source of concern in a way that it has not been since April. He has lost four starts in a row. He has lost two in a row to the Rays. He lost that one to the Yankees last weekend. He has not looked good. There is no intimidation factor. Maybe he is fatigued, and if that is the main cause, he should get rest between now and next week. We cannot win the World Series without Pedro being a factor. The debate over who our #1 starter is has long been decided. But he is a vital piece of the puzzle, and we cannot afford to have him spin out of control now.

The second issue is how we prepare for the playoffs. I think we need to continue playing most of our main guys on most days. Every year at least one team that has secured its place in the postseason shuts it down. Then when the playoffs kick in they expect to get back to where they were when they were at their peak. That does not happen, and even a little slippage against a playoff team can be fatal. Rest a few guys a day. Get the pitching staff in line. Do not let the relievers get stagnant, do not let them get tired. Do that and we'll be in good shape. I have faith. And even weakened, I want to beat the damned Orioles.

AL East Standings:

	W	L	%	GB
Yankees	100	59	.629	—
SOX	95	63	.601	4.5
Orioles	77	81	.487	22.5
Rays	68	90	.430	31.5
Jays	65	93	.411	34.5

9

October: This Is The Year! (Is This The Year?)

Friday, October 1, 2004
There are four games left in the regular season of the 2004 Major League Baseball season. While there are still plenty of playoff slots to be determined, and this may be one of the best closing weekends in baseball history, the Sox just need to keep themselves fresh and get into a playoff mentality. They have 95 wins now, so they might want to add to that for aesthetic purposes, but the fact is, no matter what happens from here on out, on Sunday or Monday they will get on a plane and fly to Minnesota, Oakland, or Anaheim.

Tito does have some decisions to make. Who will be our number four starter? What will the playoff roster look like? But on the whole, he knows that most of what is to come will happen between those white lines. Obviously a manager can have an impact on the game, and Francona's impact has been for ill as often as for good in the past six months, but hopefully he knows his club better than he ever has and understands that, for example, keeping Pedro in after seven is inadvisable unless he is absolutely dealing, his pitch count is low, and the lead is large. And even then, why do it? He knows he needs to have a fast hook for D-Lowe, and that he has to be judicious and smart with use of the bullpen. He knows not to over-manage. He knows these things. Or he should.

But there are five days until then. Tomorrow is a doubleheader, the result of a rain postponement earlier in the season, and thus is potentially dangerous. In that second game in particular I hope he just sends out waves of guys on the bottom tier of the 40 man roster and at the back of the pitching staff, Bud Selig be damned. Selig, of course, will argue that for the integrity of the game teams with secure playoff berths must make honest efforts this weekend. Not to be graceless, but screw that. Whatever integrity is lost in resting guys in the second game of a largely meaningless doubleheader is more than gained when teams are at what they believe will be their best for the playoffs when not only the packed stadia but the tens of millions watching on tv actually give a damn. No Sox fan will care if they see a game that resembles something played in Fort Myers in March, and as for Orioles fans? Well, that's the price of playing sub-.500 baseball all year (except, of course, against us. Bastards).

Saturday, October 2, 2004

The Sox are tuning up for the postseason, even if they still do not yet know who they will be playing. In a bizarre twist, the Twins, who need to sweep the Indians to have the chance to face us at home, were tied 5-5 in the eleventh when their game was suspended so that the folks in the Dome could change over for the Minnesota-Penn State football game tonight. The game was suspended sometime around 2:30 so that they could prepare for the game. That's right—a playoff-determining baseball game that was in the 11th inning was called in order to plan for a football game that would start 4-5 hours later. In my mind this automatically disqualifies Minnesota as a good baseball town. In a choice between starting the football game late, or interrupting a game tied in extra innings, the good folks in Minneapolis decided to call the game, delaying the Twins' ability to determine if they would have home field advantage in the playoffs. Let's just put it this way: This confirms something I discovered from hard-earned experience: Minnesota sucks.

Meanwhile, the Sox have determined their pitching rotation for the postseason. With a solid outing in which he only gave up 2 runs in 6 innings, Waker earned the fourth slot for the playoffs (presumably—he and Arroyo could go in either order, 3rd or 4th). The Sox were down 2-1 when he left, but in the top of the seventh they tacked two on the board en route to an 8-3 win. The rotation thus should look like this: On Tuesday Schill will take the mound. Wednesday will be Pedro's shot. After a day off on Thursday, Arroyo will get his shot at home, and then if necessary, Waker will take the mound for game 4 on Saturday. Lowe will be something of a swing man from the bullpen, and while it is highly unlikely that the sinkerballer will get a start, his role may prove crucial, just as he and Waker did last year when they made multiple appearances from the pen even when they went in as starters. This should be a bit more stable. We are apparently going with ten pitchers for the division series, with Williamson the odd man out and the rejuvenated Ramiro Mendoza to take that slot, which, if last year was any indication, will probably matter.

The Sox also won today in the first game of a virtually meaningless doubleheader against the O's. Arroyo pitched three innings of shutout ball, and the Sox scored six in the second, allowing Bronson to leave with a 7-0 lead. Despite leaving Manny, Ortiz, and Millar on the bench, the Sox held on for a 7-5 win, assuring them at least a split in this series, which in turn means that they have won 13 of 14 series since August 16. They are also an impressive 43-17 since August 1st.

Now who will we play? If the Twins finish off the sweep tomorrow, and the A's win at least one game in the epic matchup out west, we'll play them in the Metrodome starting Tuesday. The Angels just guaranteed themselves the AL West, knocking the A's out of the playoffs and ending Oakland's attempt to gain entry to the postseason for a fifth consecutive year. The A's can thus only serve as spoilers if the Twins cannot beat the Indians tomorrow in the finish of today's game and in tomorrow's scheduled affair. In any case, one has to assume that we're ready to face whichever team emerges with the best record of the three teams. I am pretty comfortable with our chances. For now, Schilling, who has been better on 5 or more days of rest (he'll have had 8 by Tuesday) than on 4, which is an omen with which I can live, needs to shut down the bats he faces on Tuesday. If we get that first game, we will be in damned good shape.

Sunday, October 3, 2004

When asked today about not starting in the postseason, Derek Lowe, who went just two tune-up innings today, giving up one run, said that he would like to start, of course, but that he would gladly serve in any capacity. Then he said something interesting. "They're not called the Derek Red Sox. This isn't about me." That may be so, D-Lowe, but I like the ring of that, the "Derek Red Sox." Sometimes given my emotional investment, it sure seems that way.

So we're playing the Anaheim Angels. We avoided playing Minnesota when the Indians beat them in that second game (the "Collegefootballismoreimportantthanthe-TwinsinMinnesota" game ended with Minnesota winning 6-5) and the Angels completed a sweep of the A's. The Yankees get to face Johan Santana in the first game. But now we have to wonder if this won't be one of those "be careful of what you wish for" situations. The Angels are not exactly pushovers, and by being tested near the end of their season, they may be as playoff-tuned as any team in the league right now. They have guys who have given us trouble (Eckstein, Guerrero, eg.) and they have a lights-out relief corps that shortens their games, with K-Rod nearly unhittable at times in that setup man role that he conquered in 2002. We'll see on Tuesday, but I think we should be able to handle the Angels, even if we have to start off in Anaheim.

Today Tito clearly had one goal: Get through the game and avoid injury. The highlight clearly was David McCarty pitching two innings of shutout ball and striking out Palmeiro. Swilly got the lost, but the run he gave up in the fifth was unearned, and there is no word as to his postseason status, though I think he is still on the wrong side of the bubble, especially if we are going with 10 guys. We lost 3-2, and I do not imagine that anyone in the Sox clubhouse even remembers today's game. The Sox did bash their 373rd double of the year, tying the Major League record, but right now it's all about Tuesday. First pitch should happen in Anaheim at 4:09 EST, 3:09 here in Texas, where I'll be glued to the television. Nothing beats playoff baseball when the Sox are involved. This is what we've waited for. It begins now.

Monday, October 4, 2004

The first pitch in Anaheim should go off in almost exactly seventeen hours. It may well be seventeen long hours for the Red Sox fan. Today actually flew by faster than it might otherwise have, though for at least one reason I'd have preferred not to have been diversionary: In yet another day with torrential rainstorms here in West Texas, I got caught in a flash flood, my car died out in two feet of water, and while two guys pushed me to safety, we'll have to see if the Passat will survive. Twice I've tried to start it today and both times it did not look good. Since more of the wet stuff is scheduled for the next two days, it may be awhile before I am on the road again, which is rather enervating. (I'd say emasculating, but I am a good progressive guy who came of age in the 1990s and I know that my manliness is not tied up in my ability to drive an automobile. It is obviously tied up in my commitment to sports).

But back to the game. Last year the Division series began disastrously, with two ugly Sox losses in which the bats seems to have gotten lost en route to Oakland, and the pitchers seemed to forget that the object was to keep guys from crossing home plate. Then we came back and won the next three, which helped to make last October one of the tensest months in my life. It would be very nice if we could get to the Angels sub-par (for a playoff team, anyway) starters in the first few innings and make them bring their big guns from the bullpen a little earlier than they would hope and pitch more innings than they would want. Playing from behind is always tough, and it is especially so in the playoffs when runs tend to be at a premium. Hopefully the days off will not hurt our guys, though it has seemed as if every break in the schedule has had a deleterious effect on the batters.

In any case, all systems are geared toward being in front of the tube at 3:09 tomorrow afternoon. Having a car that runs will be nice, but at least for tomorrow it will not hinder my ability to watch every pitch of every inning of every game. Buckle up. It's going to be fun.

Wednesday, October 6, 2004

9-3. In game one of the 2004 playoffs, the Red Sox beat the Angels 9-3. Those are the facts, the ones that matter. Schilling gave us 6 and 2/3 innings in which he gave up 3 runs. This was not really vintage Curt, save for the fact that he was staked to an early lead and he got it done. He is now 6-1 with a 1.74 earned run average in the postseason in his career, and this is why we got him.

One win down, ten to go, and we have Pedro on the mound tonight. It would be easy to get cocky, to talk about impending titles, to think about how our pitching staff will line up against the MFY's (or, more likely right now, the Twins, who beat the Yanks last night 2-0 behind Johan Santana). But reality comes easily to

Sox fans, so I'll be the momentary fly in the ointment: When the Angels won the World Series in 2002 they lost every single game one in the postseason. The Yankees have lost something like eight of their last thirteen playoff openers. Last year we were down the first two games to the A's before we rallied to take the last there and seemingly seal our team of destiny status.

But the fact is, one game is just that: One game. One wonderful incredible game in which we did the things that the Angels were supposed to be best at—a little small ball, such as Minky's drop dead perfect bunt for a single down the third base line that scored an eighth inning insurance run; some stellar fielding, and not just from the usual suspects, but from, of all people, Kevin Millar who made a couple of great plays, including a breathtaking diving stop to rob a hit. But they also brought out the whuppin' sticks, with Manny and Millar smacking taters to put us in the driver's seat for not only the game but also the series.

Don't get me wrong. I was absolutely elated with their performance yesterday, if only because it allowed me to breathe freely for the first time all day. And it was made all the better by the Yankees' loss, though in all honesty I do not much care what goes on in that series. A huge part of me knows that the perfect scenario would be to beat them in the ALCS, but seeing them lose is always a pleasure, and in any case, if it requires us beating the Twins to go the distance, then so be it. If the Yankees cannot get by Minnesota, it will not lessen the experience for me one bit, and for reasons personal, beating the Twins would be great as well.

But as I said, such speculations are for the future. For now, we have a huge game tonight. Pedro needs to show flashes of the Pedro of old, or at least of the Pedro of August. If he is on tonight, we have the 1-2 punch that we have dreamed about since November. I have faith that he will do it. I have faith that when I go to bed tonight we'll be up two games to none. I have faith that Pedro will shut them down and the bats will knock them out. Schill did his job last night (and to make it all the more sweet, he even went on Sons of Sam Horn and started the game thread yesterday, and since he led us to the win, he followed tradition and started it again today) and now it is Pedro's turn. It would be fantastic for him to prove to us that we do not have the best 1-2 punch in the league, but that rather we have the best 1-1a punch in the league.

One win down. Ten to go. This is the year.

Thursday, October 7, 2004

Red Sox fans carry two things with them at almost all times: An almost inexplicable sense of hope, and an impending sense of dread. To know a Red Sox fan is to know someone deeply internally conflicted. There is no doubting our love for our team, a love that I would argue surpasses that of any other fans for theirs. I'll argue it because it is impossible to prove. But that dread, which of course stems from doubt, is borne of hard-lived experience.

Right now the hope prevails, it is the dominant trait, it is pushing dread into the recesses of our consciousness. The Sox have taken a 2-0 lead in this series against the Angels and we did it in ways that cannot help but draw a smile from even the most hardened soul in Red Sox Nation. They took two games in Anaheim. They won both by (seemingly—as I'll soon explain, last night's game was a whole lot closer than it seemed) handy final scores. Pedro, who went into the series with all sorts of creeping doubts as a result of a September that will go down as the worst month in his hallowed career, was sterling last night. And we get the next two games in the sacred ground of Fenway, where we can imagine the stuffed-past-capacity crowd (there were thousands of Sox fans in Anaheim the last two nights, a trend that will not be reciprocated in the Fens, one can rest assured) providing Bronson Arroyo with the push that he needs to get him over the anxiety he is sure to be feeling in his first playoff start. The team that led the majors in runs and several other batting categories will pepper the Monster with rocket shots, knocking a few over it in the process. The relievers will come in and close the door. The Sox will celebrate a Division Championship, a small but critical step en route to the final goal.

That's the optimist speaking.

But deep in every Red Sox fan's heart we fear the opposite. We fear some sort of epic collapse. We fear having to go to Game Five, even if we know we'll have Schill on the mound. We fear that something will happen again to break our hearts.

The optimist, the hope, however, prevails. Things won't go awry. Not this year. No chance. Not against the Angels, not in Fenway, not with this bunch of self described baseball idiots. This is our year.

And what of the other division series? What is a good Sox fan to think? What is the loyalist, brimming with hope, pushing away the dread, who is prepared to pull out a "Yankees Sucks" chant at any moment—at a Patriots Super Bowl parade, say, or a friend's wedding where there are Yankees fans who have slipped through the cracks—to think about the Yankees-Twins series that is now tied at one game apiece after the Yankees slipped by the Twins in 12 innings last night only after Rivera blew a save? For whom do we root? Obviously we cannot root for the Yankees per se. At the same time, while there will be nothing to diminish our conquest if it goes through Minnesota and the Dome, don't we all know in our hearts that there would be nothing sweeter than vanquishing the Yankees? That there would be nothing that could surpass drilling those arrogant bastards and their troglodyte fans in the Toilet Bowl in the Bronx? That capturing the American League pennant by defeating New York is the way the fairytale has been written? (Yes, yes, and yes).

And so what do we do? Well, the last two times we went to the ALCS we faced the Yankees. We took our division series to the full five games, both times coming from a 0-2 deficit to win in dramatic, epic, heart-palpitating fashion. The Yankees had a much easier road. They could rest, work their pitching staffs, and come in with the ideal lineup and rotation to face us while we went with whoever was freshest. It would be nice if we could take care of this early, if we could win in a sweep, or at most in four, setting Schill up to pitch the opener of the ALCS. So what we want is for those two teams to pound the hell out of one another. We want extra innings. We want games where the teams combine for 400 pitches, four relievers each. We want a war. Good for the fans, good for the networks, good for the Red Sox—this would best serve the common good.

Just a few words on last night's game: Pedro showed a lot of heart. He also consistently showed a 94-95 and even once or twice a 96 mile-an-hour fastball. He gave up three runs, but two of those should have never happened, as in the bottom of the second a lazy can of corn fell in between Manny and Cabrera, neither of whom had any idea what the other had in mind. The Angels squeaked across two runs that may never have happened. Our lineup also squandered not one, but two bases loaded situations, in the first and second, that could have opened things up. But when we most needed it, Pedro gave us seven innings including a seventh in which he battled and won the tenacious but slightly overmatched Angels, especially that pain in the ass David Eckstein who fouled off ball after ball before Pedro got him to fly our harmlessly to left. Pedro's last pitch was a 94 mph heater to end the inning on a K, and to bring his outing to a conclusion. In the top of the inning Manny had driven in the go ahead run with a sacrifice fly (the Red Sox have done a far better job of manufacturing runs than the Haloes even though that was one of their stocks in trade coming in to this series), so Pedro left with the lead, and when he hit the dugout there were hugs all the way around. Those guys know how much that appearance meant for Pedro, but as importantly, for the team (and its faithful throngs). The Sox opened it up in the top of the ninth, getting to that vaunted Angels bullpen and showing that we are not afraid when another team's supposed shut down arms come in the game. Our much less ballyhooed pen, meanwhile, mowed the Angels down, with Timlin continuing his postseason excellence, Mike Myers (whom I did not want to see, to be honest) and Foulke (who secured the last four outs) taking care of business.

In the internal battle, then, hope is kicking the crap out of dread. We feel good. Red Sox Nation is smiling. This is the year.

Friday, October 8, 2004

Being a serious, diehard sports fan brings with it certain, shall we say, bizarre behaviors. We fans are a superstitious lot, perhaps because it gives us a sense of control, however false, over games that mean so much to us. If we fail in our superstitions and they lose, we feel responsible. If we do something and they win. We'll continue that for as long as it takes. I've known guys who would not shower or shave or change underwear if they felt that it was contributing to winning mojo.

When the Patriots made their run in 2001-2002, my friend Rob and I were difference makers. He was in Massachusetts, I was in DC, and we started eating chili dogs every weekend. Rob had begun the tradition when he and his father started doing so midseason, when the Pats were pretty mediocre but were about to go on an epic winning run. The next week, I felt the chili dog magic and I picked up the routine. We never missed a week. That Pats did not lose. There were some close calls—I remember sitting at the Hard Times Café in Arlington, where I had rushed to get my friend Josh and me dogs for the AFC Championship game against Pittsburgh. Josh had been roped in to chili dog magic, and we just knew that we needed to get those dogs scoffed before the game. I arrived at his place, dogs in tow, with about two minutes to spare. We wolfed them down, and Bledsoe came in after Brady was shaken up and led us to the victory. The chili dogs played a role. We just know it. It is not rational, but then again neither is being an obsessed sports fan.

This year's late-season and playoff run is no different. My own peculiarities thus far are still in flux. I own a dozen or more Sox hats, and since they have been winning, I've been wearing my red hat with the traditional two red stockings logo. I wore it to my classes today, warning the students that they probably ought to get used to it. If the Sox continue this run, the red hat may well be the cosmic reason. If they lose, it will be time to change hats. It is a delicate game, and so far not too obsessive. All bets are off if the Sox make an epic comeback when I happen to be eating tripe, or standing on one leg, or sitting Indian style.

But once again, Rob (oops, he wanted me to refer to him as "Big Poppa," or "Thunderstick") is carrying a particular form of mojo that has proved powerful if, frankly, disturbing. (Warning: Adult Material Follows. The delicate or prudish or young may want to avert your eyes). It started a few weeks ago. Do not ask me how—I have not asked and do not want to know. In any case, if the Red Sox fall behind and need a comeback—so this is clearly close-game, playoff or pennant-in the-balance stuff—Rob engages in, um, onanism. Self love. Or as we prefer to call it, "running to the car." And I swear, it has worked. Look, I have not tried to be gratuitous here, but it is true. We are sports fans. This is what we do. Or in this case, this is what, er, Big Poppa does.

Meanwhile, Curt Schilling continues to start the SoSH Game Threads and he has asked a simple question every time, and one that may become a bit of a rallying cry: Why not us? This year's team just FEELS different from past teams. As I was telling Rob earlier, we do not feel like underdogs this year. We do not feel like a team of destiny. We just feel like the best team. So, indeed, why not us?

Saturday, October 9, 2004

Wow. Wow! That was a hell of a game for the Red Sox. They took a 6-1 lead, squandered it when Vladdy Guerrero bashed a grand slam off of previously imperturbable playoff pitcher Mike Timlin, and then in dramatic fashion won it when Big Papi David Ortiz hit a home run into the Boston skyline and into history in the 10th inning to give us a dramatic 8-6 extra innings win in Fenway.

I think it is safe to say that I went a little batty throughout the whole game, which I watched at Vette's sports bar in Odessa. I nearly got thrown out of the bar after Vladdy's MVP-affirming Grand Slam when I let out an explosive F-Bomb in the bar. One of the customers took umbrage, he's a regular, and a bit of an ass, and he went to the owner. I offered to leave, reminding them that my rather sizeable bill would remain open if I did, and they asked me to settle down a bit. They were ready to throw me out after Ortiz's home run when I went nuts, which strikes me as the dumbest attitude ever. This is a sports bar. They claimed that they don't advertise that way, which is bizarre, since the sign out front says rather clearly "Sports Grill and Pub."

No matter. This was one of the all-time great Sox wins to cap our second postseason series sweep ever (in 1975 the Sox swept the defending World Champion Oakland A's to get to the Series). D-Lowe came in to relieve Foulke, who struggled but did not give up any runs. He ended up getting the win, something that I would suspect is gratifying for him but also for those of us who remember the cajones he showed in the postseason last year. Damon was simply an on-base machine and Millar and Manny did what we've come to expect from them in big games. Arroyo was outstanding. And the whole lineup just scratched and clawed, making great plays in the field (Cabrera), getting timely hits (Trot) and never giving up (Ortiz!!!!).

Schill had "Why Not Us?" T-shirts made up and some of the guys were wearing them in the locker room where champagne and beer doused victory cigars. Fenway was alive, with "D-Lowe" chants and general merriment. The Sox are rolling. We do not care which team we play, Twins or Yankees (The Yanks took a 2-1 lead in their series last night by bashing the Twins 8-4 but even with that lead their bullpen is so ravaged they actually had to bring in Rivera for the save – a very good omen).

I do not know how I will survive the next three days, but we're returning to the ALCS, and I am exuberant, if a bit hungover from celebrating in the appropriate excess. Hope continues to push dread into the recesses of our consciousness, one Ortiz bomb at a time. If it takes me getting thrown out of every bar in West Texas, I'll make those sacrifices.

ALCS: Sox v. The Evil Empire

Sunday, October 10, 2004

Bring 'em on. The Yankees won yesterday, erasing a 5-1 deficit against the Twins to bring about the series that everyone wants to see. It was well nigh impossible to root for the Yankees during the series, but now that it is done, I am glad the Yankees won. This is the way it is supposed to be. I do not mean that in any fatalistic sense, and I do not believe in Destiny, the dirty harlot who courts Curses, but I mean it simply in the sense that getting to the World Series by beating the Yankees is just right. It is what we want, it is what Yankees fans would demand, and the ratings this next ten days will bear out that sports fans across the country cannot wait to see what the next installment of this rivalry offers.

In his column this morning, Dan Shaughnessy raised the old issue of "be careful what you wish for . . ." but that is of no moment to most of us. As I said the other day, we fans, and from all I can tell, the guys in the clubhouse, sincerely believe that our guys are the better team. We want this matchup because we want to beat them. There is nothing more to it than that. We want Curt Schilling toeing the mound, even with a balky ankle, in Game 1. We want Pedro to prove that no one in the Bronx is his daddy. We want young Bronson Arroyo out there to engrave his name in Sox lore. We want Manny and Ortiz and Millar and Tek blasting balls deep into the night off of the Yankees' staff, and we want Damon and Bellhorn and Mueller on base constantly. We want to be able to barrage them with depth and with the best defense of any Sox team in history. We cannot wait for the gritty Trot Nixon to make some magic. We cannot wait for D-Lowe's continuing redemption, for Waker's flutterballs, for the adroit leatherwork of Cabrera and Minky and maybe even Pokey Reese. We want to beat them with our talent, wear them out with our depth, crush them with our intensity. This is the series that we have looked forward to since harsh winter days during the Hot Stove League. You need to be able to beat everyone, but even given that, it would be disingenuous to deny that the Yankees were always first among equals, and that beating them en route to the World Series is the only imaginable scenario.

It looks like there will be a bit of a dark cloud hovering over the series, however. The details are sketchy as of my writing, but apparently there was a major tragedy at Mariano Rivera's Panama home. It has to do with his electric fence surrounding his pool and a couple of family members who went swimming and apparently both ended up being electrocuted. It is heartening to see the Sox fans at Sons of Sam Horn, from whom I have been following the story, showing true compassion. I hate Mariano Rivera between the lines, mostly because he is simply a warrior on the mound, and he has bested us often. But obviously this is a human tragedy beyond the realm of sport. I promise that Sox fans will give him an ovation during pregame introductions in Fenway before Game Three on Friday. Not that he will ever see it, but from this tiny corner of sports fandom, my condolences go out to him and his family. I still want desperately to beat him and his teammates, but I hope he can overcome this awful turn of events.

Monday, October 11, 2004

I am a historian. This is why I think I am pretty well qualified to proclaim that history is largely irrelevant when it comes to this Red Sox-Yankees showdown. Everyone invokes ghosts and curses and especially the past, as if the past always dictates what comes next. If being a historian gives me any particular insight here, however, it is that history is most misused when people try to use it to predict the future, either short- or long-term. That is not to say that history does not tell us anything of course—trends matter, the past and present and future are inextricably bound, and I do think historians can have important things to say about the present using our perspective and insight and acumen. But it is to say that most people who talk about the Red Sox and their oft-tortured past misuse history as something that is somehow inevitable or predetermined, that history is a force independent of the variables that weigh upon it. This is, of course, nonsense.

I raise this today because, not surprisingly, in the quest to fill column inches for the insatiable Red Sox Nation, the hackneyed questions about the past came up today in the *Globe* and elsewhere. It happens every time the Sox make it this far. Ryan or Shaughnessy, or, today's culprit, Bob Hohler, goes in and surveys the players who almost universally respond the same way: "History has nothing to do with if we win or lose. We were not here in (1986, 1978, etc.)." And so forth. Usually the reporter then paints the Sox players out as cliché-spewing jocks. But the reality is that the question, the conceit, is the cliché. And when asked a clichéd, indeed stupid, question, athletes are inevitably going to respond with less-than-unique responses. The only serious alternative answer would be something along the lines of "Yes, Bob, we are burdened with a historic yoke here and we are likely to lose, probably in self-immolating fashion." And what athlete would ever say something so foolish and self-defeating?

Again—history is not predetermined and there is no such thing as historical inevitability except in the narrowest sense—at a point things become inevitable only because they happen, but at some point most all historical events are avoidable, or more significantly, could play out in vastly different ways. To pretend otherwise is not to think historically, but rather in ways best categorized as historicist. Historicism believes that events are preordained. Historicism believes that history involves the inevitable. Historicism believes in the Curse of the Bambino. Historicism believes that 1918 determines 2004. Historicism is intellectually sloppy. Historicism is dumb.

Tuesday, October 12, 2004

I honestly do not even know what to write. Sox fans have been waiting for this series for a year, but really forever. We believe this is the year. We believe this is the time. We believe. Most of us have been worthless all day, checking Sons of Sam Horn and a dozen other Sox-obsessed websites every twenty minutes, emailing friends, poring over the *Globe* online, or ESPN.com, and snooping in on the New York media. This is simply going to be an epic series, and we have Curt Schilling going to the mound tonight to lead us.

Obviously this is all about winning. Most observers are talking and writing about how this is destined to be a classic. How it will go seven games and will add to the lore of this great series. And if we win in seven, it will indeed be historic. But lots of us would be just as happy to win in a sweep, or in five. Readers of this diary have encountered my buddy Rob on a somewhat regular basis. This is how he phrases the internal thought process we are all experiencing in the inimitable way only Rob can bring to the table:

> It's the kind of game that you say you want your players to win and win with class, but really, you hoping for a 20-0 win in which after you get the lead, your pitcher beans A-Rod, Jeter and Sheffield, gives the finger to the entire Yankee Stadium crowd as he walks off, collects the hardware and then has sex with the wife of every Yankee fan that was in the crowd.

As Kent Brockman once said: "Strong, disturbing words." But words with a degree of truth to them.

Hate is a pretty strong word. But as an institution, I hate the Yankees. I loathe them. I want to beat them. I want the Sox to pound them relentlessly. This is the year. This is the time. This is the series. 7:00 CST cannot come quickly enough.

Wednesday, October 13, 2004

You know what? This might be typical Sox fan rationalization, but that was about as productive a loss as you could imagine—interesting, because it could have been the worst imaginable loss. Had we lost 8 or 10 to 0 with Mussina twirling a no-hitter or perfect game, I'd say that might be so crushing that we might go down in 5. But this loss? Jesus—that Yankee Stadium crowd just died. It was 8-0. Then in the space of an inning it was 8-7. Our guys never relented. Timlin choked, but not as bad as Tito did in keeping him in when Myers was available to pitch to a lefty, which would have had Timlin out of the game and someone else in who may not have given up a two-run double. That's a different game if Nixon does not have to go up there in the ninth hacking at the first pitch to try to get us one run closer with one swing.

Yes, in pro sports there are no good losses, no moral victories, but as great as Sox fans are, anyone who was not counting this as a loss when we fell down by so much, hoping for a Pedro rebound, wondering what our psyche would be like is either lying or is eight years old and thus full of irrational thoughts. The game nearly killed me. I was an emotional wreck. For 6+ innings I was disconsolate. But the key is that we did what this team has done all year—we never gave up hope, we never faded, we never stopped fighting. There are no good losses, but this one could have been a lot worse, and I expect what we did in the 7th and 8th inning to carry over to today. (But don't you wish Ortiz was just a little faster, or that he had gotten one more pound per square inch of force on that ball?).

The thing is, Mussina took a perfecto into the 7th, our leadoff hitter struck out four times, our manager forgot what game they were playing, and even when things did go well, Ortiz's ball manages to stay in the park. Schilling was awful, likely because of the ankle injury. The bullpen was inconsistent when not simply mismanaged. And yet with all of that, we almost came back and won. Surely we'll improve in many areas tonight. Surely they know how big this is -- game one is never a must win, and no one thought Schill would not find a way to pull it out. Now the guys know what the situation is, and it is as close to a must win as things get. This series will go deep, it will go back to New York, and we all knew that would be the case.

Now, in maybe the ultimate sports cliché, we just have to take one game at a time. The most important game is the next one. If we win with Pedro on the mound, we have earned a split in Yankee Stadium and this becomes a five game series with us having home field advantage. If I'd been offered that scenario on Sunday, I'd have taken it, as would any sane Sox fan, and even most of us insane ones.

I think some of the edge might be off for me now. Yesterday was tough—I was pretty much worthless once I finished running errands. Now, though, I can deal. I still want 7:00 to roll around, of course, but with somewhat less of the desperation of yesterday.

Then again, for the last hour or so, all I have done is deal with baseball. So maybe I am just kidding myself. Yes. I am kidding myself. I won't function right for the next three weeks. I am a Red Sox fan. That is the reality.

We win today. Pedro may think the Yankees are his Daddy. But there comes a time in a boy's life when he needs to whup Daddy in one-on-one, to show that the boy is a man. Tonight Daddy gets that whuppin'.

Thursday, October 14, 2004

What is there to say? I've recovered from the worst of last night's loss, though the bottle I threw across my living room at the last out of the game that bounced off the wall and shattered into a million tiny shards on my kitchen floor still sits in a pile in the corner.

The reality is that we face a 2-0 deficit in this series that we all so anticipated. Our ace starter who was supposed to be the biggest difference maker is suffering through a worse injury than we expected, a tear of the sheath that covers the tendons on his right ankle, the leg from which he pushes off to give him drive on his pitches. He may well be done. He certainly will not be at full strength. Our hitters are not getting the job done, too often swinging at the first pitch and popping up harmlessly to shallow right field. Both games saw us mount a comeback, but in each case we fell short in the ninth inning, with Rivera slamming the door. This is not the team that pounded the Angels, even if Pedro did come out and, despite a couple of rough innings, do enough so that he should have garnered the win (though that home run ball he served up to Olerud was really deflating on a night when we made Lieber look like Bob Gibson).

But I do not despair. Oh, I fume, rage, scream, and throw bottles like a madman. But I do not despair. I have not given up hope. My utter certainty may be on the ropes, but I think we can win this series by getting the job done in Fenway. The key is to get out to a good start, to get some runs on the scoreboard, and to take pressure off of our pitchers. We need to win tomorrow, then let the weekend take care of itself (though it looks like the weather in Boston might be so bad that they will not get the game in, which would cause me no end of anxiety, even if it might be for the best for us). I see Schilling coming through with a Willis Reed (or perhaps Pedro against the Indians in Game Five of the 1999 Division Series) moment in game six or game seven. I see us taking one blowout, one nail-biter, and one comeback in Fenway. I see us going back to the Toilet in the Bronx with a chance. Right now, that's all we want—a chance. I still believe.

Friday, October 15, 2004

And now, as if we have not suffered enough, there is a strong possibility that this game will be rained out. It has been pretty raw, dark, and miserable in Boston all day, and the latest reports indicate that there may be no way to get a game played.

So is this a good break or a bad one? As ever, it depends. The fact is the Sox hitters have been notoriously bad this year when given extended rests. They cannot be much worse than they have been, of course, but I would like to see them get up and smack a few balls off the Monster. On the other hand, this can only be good for the rotation, especially as Pedro will get to start Game 5 in Fenway and it gives Schill another day for the Medical Miracle 'neath the Monster to take place. They have him all tricked out in a new brace-shoe combination and apparently he threw from the mound today. No sense hoping for anything at this point, but that cannot be a horrible situation.

But whether it is good or bad from a baseball vantage point (and my guess is that it is a wash), it is decidedly not good for me. I run the risk of going mad. I want them to get out there and start this drive toward redemption. I want them to get the Fenway hit parade off and running. I want a victory under the drizzly Friday Night Lights. I want the young gun Bronson Arroyo to get out there and snuff out those dastardly Yankee bats like so many flickering candles. Selfishly, I want them to play.

Saturday, October 16, 2004

Last night I had the pizza on its way, the beer in the fridge, a friend on the way, and the good Sox mojo going when MLB finally called the game just before the scheduled opening pitch. I have not yet checked the Boston weather, but I have to assume that they are going to try to get this game in no matter what. I can feel myself getting really, really nervous. I cannot imagine what it was like in the 1975 World Series, when they had several days of rain delays. Then again, I'd guess that the intensity level in Red Sox Nation is a lot higher almost thirty years later.

Still, with the rainout we got another day to see if the Schilling Miracle can take place (the new brace did allow him to throw off the mound for twenty or so minutes yesterday, a nice sign) and even if he cannot start, maybe we can get a bullpen appearance from him. We also get to have Pedro a day earlier and in Fenway Park, which does benefit us substantially.

Tonight's the night we get the first of the eight wins we need.

Sunday, October 17, 2004

There really is not much to say the morning after a 19-8 massacre in a game that for all intents and purposes was a must win. Because faith is blind, I spent most of the afternoon wondering if we could not be the team to make history, to win a series after being down 3-0. These are the longest of odds and we are playing a team that knows how to keep its foot on the neck of its opponents once those opponents are down. Emily Dickinson once wrote that "Hope is the thing with feathers." Hope, Ms. Dickinson, is the thing wearing the Red Sox hat today. And we still have hope. But it is fading.

Here are my first impressions of the game, written in an email to myself last night:

> Immediate, if drunken, responses: I did not bring this upon myself. None of us did, really. You commit yourself to a team for reasons you never really understand, mostly related to geography, history, and perhaps a hint of daddy-did-it genetics. You wish and you hope and you love. And it sure enough is unconditional -- it is not as if you expect Derek Lowe to send you a card or Johnny Damon to call you on your birthday. All you ask is that they return it. That they return it with effort. That they return it with grit. That they fucking return it somehow.
>
> I am a 33 year-old man. I have a PhD, a good job, a great girlfriend, and frankly a life worth living. And yet

. . . and yet. This team, this team I have yearned for and dreamed about and gushed over, this bunch of guys mostly younger then I, well, they can put me in this state. . . . And in this state, I am the bad guy—I have lost faith. Never mind that I did not give up 19 runs. Never mind that I was well aware that a loss tonight meant we were done. Never mind that . . . oh, never mind. Some years just hurt more than others. (Oh—and fuck Tim McCarver for railing on Manny in the second inning for trying to take third when, by the way, he was safe—the ump fucked up, not Manny, you sanctimonious, out-of-touch ass.) My affliction is one that is unconditional. Tomorrow I'll rationalize why they can win four in a row, despite the fact that no team has ever done so in baseball. Tomorrow I'll deal with the calls on my cell phone. Tomorrow I'll start dealing with, well, tomorrow.

So tomorrow is now today, and we have Derek Lowe going to the mound, most likely against an El Duque who will have no reason to feel any pressure. A win will give us one more game. Right now that is all we can play for—the chance to play one more time.

Monday, October 18, 2004
At this point you've either given yourself over to belief or you have not. At this point you are either fer us or yer agin' us. At this point you are hardened, cynical and jaded or you are willing to hang on to hope.

No one could honestly blame the hard hearted. I gave up hope briefly myself on Saturday night, as yesterday's diary entry attests, but it did not last long. It was a test of faith, I was Job, and while I doubted, I never left the fold. I never strayed from the flock. But those of you who think you know better, well, you may simply be the wise ones. Or perhaps you are inuring yourself to the pain you fear. Or maybe you just hate puppies and children and goodness and America.

All I know is that last night's game was reason enough to keep our dreams of October glory alive. How can I even try to capture it in words? It was the sort of Sox-Yankees battle that everyone envisioned from the outset, with the Yanks taking a 2-0 lead, with us fighting back to go up 3-2, and with unlikely (but seemingly foreordained) hero Derek Lowe giving us a chance through five and a third. He gave up a triple in the sixth to Hideki Matsui who has just been unconscious, and Mike Timlin came in but could not hold the lead, and suddenly it was 4-3. Innings began slipping away as the Sox could not mount a rally. Then, against Rivera in the 9th, we drew blood. We got to the supposedly indomitable closer. We squeezed the tying run across when Millar walked to lead off the inning, Dave Roberts pinch ran for him, making it clear that he intended to steal second, and doing so. Billy Mueller then singled to drive in the speedy, intrepid Roberts and tie the score. I like Bill Mueller up against Rivera in a tight game. We had the chance to win that inning but Rivera shut the door, and one had to wonder how many more chances we'd have.

The key to the game was the stellar, inspiring work by the relief corps. While Timlin faltered and Mike Myers was unable to get out Matsui, the lone batter he faced, in the 11th, the rest of the guys came up big. None more than Foulke, who gave 2 2/3rds innings in which he silenced the Yankee bats, Embree, who evoked images of his performances in the 2003 postseason, and Curtis Leskanic, my favorite whipping boy of late, who kept the Yanks at bay long enough to set up the heroics of the 12th and to earn the win.

If David Ortiz was not already a Boston legend, climbing slowly and inexorably up the pantheon, he certainly is solidifying his claim now. In the wee hours of Monday morning, in the 12th inning, against former Sox righthander Paul Quantrill, Manny led off with a single to right field to become the potential winning run. Ortiz came up, the only Red Sox player who has done substantial damage against Yankee pitching this season. He had hit the two-run single to put us ahead 3-2 back in the fifth, but had looked horrible in his two appearances against Rivera. But against Quantrill, Ortiz got a 2-1 fastball over the inside portion of the plate, and he was able to drive it. It was a no doubter that blazed a path into the Yankee bullpen. 6-4. Bedlam overtook Fenway. Once again, his rapturous teammates mobbed Big Papi.

Now, of course, comes the question of what does this all mean? The teams meet again this afternoon, 5:00 Fenway time, for game five. Pedro will face off against Mussina, against whom we will have to do a whole lot better than we did last week when he stymied us with a perfect performance through 6 innings. Pedro needs to come ready to keep the Yankees off the scoreboard. We cannot afford to tax the bullpen. Even if we win, odds are long. Let's face it—we are looking for a Rasputin-like performance from Schilling in one of the remaining few games, followed by a motley starter-by-committee approach in which we will throw Waker and Arroyo and Lowe and Mendoza and whoever else at the Yankees hoping to keep them at bay while we get to their similarly patchwork quilt of weary and wounded wings.

My buddy Tom called me last night and asked why Major League Baseball has not cracked down on Tim McCarver wearing his Yankees' hat and "I ♥ Derek Jeter" t-shirt in a the booth. I did not have an answer. Tom thinks the former catcher's naked Yankee support is all part of McCarver's long-term goal to be Jeter's personal fluffer (giving new meaning, I guess, to "naked Yankee support"). But much to McCarver's chagrin, no doubt, the Red Sox did what they have done all year—fought and rallied and believed and clawed until someone, or in the case of last night, many someones, could contribute and just get the job done.

There was much joy in Red Sox Nation due to the heroics not only of Ortiz, but of an entire group that has never given up, and that still believes. If they do, then we should too. Today, we have Pedro on the mound. We still are in a deep hole of our own digging. But we get one more game. At 4:00 today I will be in front of the television. I've cancelled my night seminar knowing that this game will not be done in three hours. No longer does it matter that no team has ever come back from a 3-0 deficit. Now the math has for all intents and purposes changed. Now it is a 3-1 series. The odds may not be much better, but better they are, and 3-2 is even more surmountable. In a sense, there is no pressure on us now. They just need to go out, give Pedro some run support, and keep the magic coming.

We believe.

Tuesday, October 19, 2004

I think that the tightness in my chest and the tingling in my left arm have just about subsided. I think I am breathing normally now. I think I can get down solid food. I think my vocal cords are beginning to stop bleeding. I think my knuckles are no longer pure white. I think that must mean that the next game is to start in just a few hours.

My God, is this not the most incredible imaginable postseason? Let's put last night's game in perspective: As a story, on a national level, it dwarfed a game played almost simultaneously (even though that one started 3+ hours later) in which the Astros and Cards went through eight innings with a grand total of one hit. In which the teams were tied 0-0 in one of the greatest pitching duels in the history of baseball. And that game was a distant second on all of the highlight shows and on almost all lips this morning. I live in Texas. No one has said a thing to me about the Astros' game last night, a 3-0 win courtesy of a Jeff Kent walk off blast. Everyone is talking about the Red Sox.

And when you talk about the Red Sox these days, you talk about Big Papi, David Ortiz. David Ortiz!!! Again? Are you kidding me? This is Yaz in '67, Rice in '78, Tiant in '75 type-stuff. For the first time in the history of the postseason the same guy gets a hit to win in walkoff fashion. And these two happened in extra innings. And of course there were other heroes—Roberts did it again on the basepaths; Waker (who got the win) was a God, as were all of the relievers (more on them momentarily); the list goes on. Just when we thought it would be impossible to top Sunday night's game, last night they go 14 innings, things were even tighter, and the stress level was even higher. Our bullpen was somehow more lights out than the night before, pitching 8 innings of shutout ball, with Timlin, Foulke, Arroyo, Myers, Embree, and Wakefield coming on in succession to relieve Pedro who tired after 6 and gave up a 2-1 lead in the 6th, allowing the Yankees to take a 4-2 advantage that for a while seemed like it might hold.

But in the end, their bullpen was almost as tough, save, of course, for our runs in the 8th, 9th (another blown save for Rivera—looks like we have found Rivera's kryptonite and it is us). There were moments that made fans scream at the television set. We taxed our capacity for superstition (Rob got the Thunderstick up twice last night, yeoman's work). We certainly taxed our constitutions. Last night's was the longest game in terms of time in postseason history, surpassing the night before. And of course the previous night had been the longest 9-inning game in postseason history. We are getting our money's worth, even if national productivity is waning discernibly.

And I am going to say it: If you listen closely, you can hear the anxiety in New York. Oh, they would never admit it. Being a bunch of frontrunners, bandwagon jumpers, and NAMBLA supporters, the fans of the Yankees will insist that they are not worried, that they know the Red Sox never beat them, and that they have 39 pennants that reassure them that they have nothing to worry about. And I am going to call their bluff: Bullshit. Not once in the last ten years, even in losing World Series, have the Yanks looked this vulnerable, this beaten, this mystified. They tossed their best at us, they got to their vaunted bullpen with leads, they had the meat of their order up several times with a chance to take the lead. And every single time the Sox either stifled them or else had a response.

Don't get me wrong. This series still is in their favor. The Yankees have the home field now, they only have to win one, and we may well have spent ourselves in catching up. But, boy, it does not feel like the weight of things runs their way, does it? The Yankees certainly are not invincible. And let's keep something in mind—the 19-8 humiliation warps our perspective on this series. In every other game, including those first two in the Toilet Bowl, either team had a shot in the end. In games one and two, the Sox came up in the top of the ninth and had the tying or go ahead run on base or up to the plate. Either team could have won. The last two nights were extra inning epics.

Of course one of the themes of last night's game is second guessing. Did Tito let Pedro stay in too long (YES—Jesus, do we never learn anything when it comes to our Dominican Dandy?) I was dumbfounded by the situational use of Myers to face only Matsui when we are clearly taxed out in the pen (though it did work. Then again, just because something works does not make it a good idea. If someone successfully drives home drunk the success not make the act a smart one). I still think Mirabelli ought to have come on when Waker did, and Varitek's fielding of the mighty knuckler almost cost us dearly. It is not as if Mirabelli cannot catch other guys, and he has been remarkably productive at the plate in the at-bats he has had. People will question Damon's steal attempt, though it took a perfect throw to nail him—if they did—and had he not run, people would have raised questions about that too. Obviously Ortiz's steal attempt, perhaps humorous in other circumstances, was ill considered. However, keep this little hidden tidbit in mind—he was safe. Just as Manny's much-maligned attempt to take extra bases the other night fell victim to crappy umpiring. And as long as we are taking about our blunders, what about the huge one on the Yanks' part? Why on earth were they pitching to Ortiz with a base available in the 14th with Mientkiewicz on deck? Are you telling me that the smart money is on facing Ortiz with guys on first and second rather than Minky with the bases loaded? If so, the smart money is very, very dumb.

Meanwhile, in just under three hours, we get to go through the emotional wringer at least once more, as they do it all over again in the Bronx unless the weather decides not to cooperate for the second time this series. I'm not sure who benefits from a rainout, but I know this: If the mound is at all slippery, if mud is going to be a factor, that hurts Curt more than it hurts anyone else. The key is who gets hurt more by either scenario. I think we benefit as much as they do from a day of rest. Our bullpen is as weary as theirs, and a day off might even mean that we have a shot at having an almost-rested starter go on Thursday if it comes to that. Then again, does it matter? Both teams are in the same position. If it is rainy, so be it. If it is raw, everyone will deal. If there is a day off, everyone will rest. No sense reading too much into this, though if they do not play I am not sure how I'll make it another 24 hours.

About Schilling: We cannot, cannot, cannot expect him to shut them down. Indeed, we need to expect him to get hit around a bit. That is the reality. What we need is for the guys to see him as a spark and to get out there and go after Lieber from the first pitch. By that I do not mean overly aggressive—they have to get him deep into counts, they have to foul balls, off, and they need to get damned hits. Schilling is an inspiration now, but on the mound we have to expect him as a placeholder. He is going to serve the role of a rested fourth or fifth starter. He is a guy we can have some faith in, but let's not expect him to carry us. Let's keep in mind that Willis Reed scored on his first 2 shots in those 1970 finals against the Lakers, and then was ineffective for the rest of the game. Reed is a symbol, just as Schilling has to be a symbol. The guys need to pick him up, and that starts with Damon and works its way down.

I think it goes without saying, but oh yes, we believe. Damn right we believe.

Wednesday, October 20, 2004

We believe.

It had to come down to this, didn't it? For all of my disavowals of fate and destiny and curses and ghosts, this is what was supposed to happen. After the most supreme test of faith, which we passed, after three heart stopping games, which we survived, after being reminded of those ghosts and goblins and the omnipresent forces of the past, which we denied, the fact is that there had to be a game seven, some how, some way. There had to be a final confrontation between us and our tormentors. There had to be an epic storyline. These playoffs were geared toward this clash. It is what everybody outside of Minnesota and Anaheim wanted.

We believe.

Everyone talked about Curt Schilling and what this might mean. How long could he go? How long would his tattered ankle hold up? What sort of stuff would he have? He answered these questions pretty damned well, going seven innings, giving up a solo home run, and departing with a 4-1 lead in a performance that far surpassed Willis Reed or the over-hyped Michael Jordan flu game in immensity, performance, and obstacles overcome. As I said yesterday, I'd have been happy with five innings, a surmountable handful of runs, and a huge psychic victory. Instead, on a night when we could only muster four runs, Schill was our workhorse. And it is even more remarkable once one discovers what precisely he overcame. The talk the last few days has been all about finding shoes or a brace that would work, some wonder of technology and duct tape, medical science and voodoo. But in this balance, Schill never found a comfort zone. So according to Dr. Bill Morgan this morning, what they did was actually sew his flesh to cartilage in order to provide a barrier that kept the tendon out of its groove, since it slipped out on every pitch and it was the slippage back to its normal slot that caused excruciating pain. That was why his sock had blood on it last night, which we saw on innumerable close-ups and chalked up to seepage from a shot. They sewed flesh to cartilage, unsewed it last night, and if they go on . . . well, let's not go that far yet. Schilling had his date with destiny. He carried us. Which is why . . .

We believe.

For those who believe in the forces of fate or history or the ghosts of Yankee Stadium, last night must have been an exorcism. We lose those games. Bellhorn's home run that the umps initially called a double? That call never gets overturned. It did last night—correctly, as the ball clearly bounced off a fan's chest about two feet above the wall. Instead of a two-run double that made it 3-1, Belli got to trot the rest of the way, giving us an extra run that would prove vital. Then in the eighth A-Rod tried to cheat his way onto base. His perfidy, blatantly swatting the ball out of Arroyo's glove on a play in front of first that would have otherwise been a clear fielder's choice, would have been rewarded in the past. The call, initially that A-Rod was safe and that Jeter had scored when the ball was knocked out of Bronson's glove, would have remained, a seeming example of how evil can sometimes overcome good. Instead, after huddling, the umpires again made the right call, ruling that A-Rod had obviously cheated, that he was out, and that Jeter had to return to first. Two calls that always go against the Sox, two calls that required umpires to huddle, two calls that they reversed rightly. The prehensile slackjawed mouth-breathing troglodytes in the Toilet Bowl howled madly, threw things onto the field despite their lack of opposable thumbs, and caused the game to be halted while riot police ringed the field, but justice prevailed.

We believe.

These games have been lots of things. But for a Sox fan, it may initially shock some to know that they have not been especially enjoyable. How could they be? When every pitch can mean the end of the season, when the tension is enough to open up ulcers, when the games play themselves out so excruciatingly, how could any sane person enjoy this? Of course there have been moments of rapture, but rapture born as much of relief and release as of unadulterated joy. This is our lot. We can derive pleasure from the process after the fact, but coming back from a three games to none hole tends to absorb frivolous sentiments such as joy.

We believe.

There were not going to be any easy games. The Yankees and their fans had to know this even with that seemingly insurmountable lead. We had to know it even as the comeback went from irrational dreamscape to tangible reality. And so last night's events were not surprising. The Yankees rallied for a run off of Bronson Arroyo when Derek Jeter drove in Miguel Cairo, who had doubled. A-Fraud tried to cheat, but instead was nailed, with the resultant brouhaha giving Arroyo a chance to settle down a bit and retire the rest of the side. It was 4-2 going into the ninth, and our bats were silenced. Keith Foulke came out in the bottom of the ninth, and there was no way it could go 1-2-3. As Rob had been saying for a few innings at that point (once a superstition takes hold, you cannot stop it—we talked between every half inning, getting off the phone as the first batter came to the plate), there was no way that the Yankees would not have the winning run up at the plate at some point in the ninth. Rob buys into fate and destiny and all of that claptrap far more than I, but we both knew that whether it was destiny or simply parity, he was right. And it proved to be so. Foulke walked two guys and eventually faced Tony Clark with two outs. In a tense at bat (aren't they all when these teams are in the ninth inning?) Foulke struck out Clark. We were on our way to game seven. In a situation in which the Yankees have so often found a way to win, we faced them down and took the victory.

We believe.

And so this is it. Whether through predestiny or the simple fact that for two years these two have been separated by a sliver, it had to come down to this. Game 7, Yankee Stadium, both teams weary, neither putting an ace on the mound, neither team even having a starter with something resembling full rest. We will throw D-Lowe and Waker, likely in that order (If Francona's first guess last night holds), and then everyone is eligible. Might we see Pedro on the mound in the ninth in the Toilet Bowl? Absolutely. Could Foulke possibly be asked to summon up another inning? Might Ramiro Mendoza or Curtis Leskanic play a huge role? Anything is possible now. The Yankees' pitching is in equal disarray. And of course at the plate and in the field anyone might be the difference maker. Manny has been nearly silent all series. Ortiz has been the hero this week. Either might have the crucial plate appearance. Maybe Johnny Damon or Doug Mientkiewicz or Trot or Tek or Belli or Roberts or Mueller or Millar. Maybe the Idiots will be able to do it one more time. Maybe they can make history, and in so doing, rewrite some.

We believe.

It had to come down to this. I do not know if it is fate or simply faith that has brought us to this point. I do not know if it is destiny or drive. I do not know if it is talismans or talent. At this point I can no longer say. It is out of my hands. It is out of our hands.

We believe.

Thursday, October 21, 2004

Four more wins.

That is what it is going to take. Four more victories, whether by overwhelming knockout or knock-down, drag-out fight.

Do not get me wrong—pathetic though it may seem to someone who is not a passionate sports fan, last night was one of the greatest of my life, even though for most of it, it wasn't. Only a Red Sox fan can understand being almost violently nauseous with a seven-run lead in the bottom of the ninth inning. Only a Red Sox fan can understand why I was screaming at Tito Francona and my television when he took Derek Lowe out for Pedro (the stupidest and most inexplicable decision by a human being in my lifetime). Only a Red Sox fan can understand why, after a night of screaming and yelling and entreating and pleading, I could only sink to my knees, prostrate before whatever it is that makes me do this to myself, and weep just a little bit.

Only a Red Sox fan can know.

I may well have succumbed to convulsions or paroxysms or an

aneurysm last night had we not taken a solid lead and run with it from the first inning on. Another Dale Sveum moment, in which he ran Johnny Damon into a (close) out at home plate despite the fact that Manny's single was to shallow right and Jesus H. Damon had not yet reached third when Matsui gathered up the ball, might have been the felling blow, except that seconds later Ortiz jacked a home run to put us up 2-0 and spot us a lead that we would never relinquish.

The rest is something of a blur. In the second Johnny came in with the bases loaded and smashed the first offering of Kevin brown's replacement, Javier Vazquez, into the right field bleachers to make it 6-0. No one in Red Sox Nation felt entirely comfortable, but at the same time, with the belief that we all have developed in this team, we knew that things were going to be different from the past, even if we did not dare articulate it. And believe me, in the stream of phone calls between my friends and me, especially my half-inning by half-inning updates with Rob and my regular calls with Pep, we did everything to skirt the obvious: That we were about to slay the monster and put all of the talk, the curse talk, the ghost talk, the Babe Ruth talk, to rest.

And none of it would have happened without Derek Lowe. We all knew that he would have a role to play in this series, and most of us suspected that Sunday night's quality start was not the end of that calling. He simply had the best pitching performance of a Red Sox starter since, since, well, since I do not know when. He went six innings and gave up one hit and one run. His sinkerball was nasty, cutting the corners and virtually unhittable. He looked like a guy with redemption on his mind. Or a contract. Or simply a World Series ring. Whatever it was, he was masterful, and I was murderous when it was clear that Pedro was not simply throwing to get his side work in between starts.

Of course Pedro came in, to the inevitable "Who's Your Daddy" chants, and he was all over the place. He gave up two runs, and while toward the end he was showing flashes of 1999 (97 mph fastballs—we'd best see those on Saturday night, or my homicidal rage may re-emerge), he never ought to have been out there no matter what reason Tito gives—and we have not yet heard one.

But this is not a Sox team to be daunted. And once the Pedro experiment ended, mercifully after an inning, our relief corps got it done again—Timlin pitching for five outs, with Embree coming on to induce the grounder to Pokey that sent Red Sox Nation into a collective celebration that probably will not subside until Saturday night.

And there is Saturday night. It was glorious to win the American League. And yes, it was all the better to have done it against the Yankees, who allowed the Red Sox to stage the greatest comeback in sports history. But this is not about the Yankees, even if beating them in their house makes it all the better. This is about the Red Sox. And let there be no mistake about it, it is also about us, the fans, Red Sox Nation. But while we will all celebrate and dance and walk around like zombies, albeit like zombies with perma-grin, there is still a job to do. Tonight we will watch the Cards and Astros hopefully bash the hell out of one another (I'd like an order of extra innings with extra relief pitchers please). We will bask in one of the greatest victories of our life, and surely the greatest Sox victory we have ever seen. But the guys definitely know, as we all do, that there are four more wins to get.

As for what it means to have beaten the Yankees, I'll let an email that Rob sent me before the game yesterday sum it up:

> I have to say, I'm not nervous at all. I've transcended it. I'm excited. I'm ready to go. Let's get it on. Like I said, I've taken the approach that it's house money. The Yanks own us. They've owned us for 85 years. If they win tonight, they own us for 86. What's the difference? We've got nothing to lose. But they do—we are putting our chips on the table in an attempt to win something huge. We made 56,000 NY fans shut up for a while last night. We can make millions of them shut up forever tonight. What's not to be excited about? This is how it has to be—I said before the series started that I wanted to win it in the fashion where we run up big numbers, hit batters and give the finger to everyone in the stadium before we leave . . . This is bigger than that. You NY fans want to talk about how long it's been since we won the World Series? You want to talk about how close we've been? You want to talk about our big chokes? Well, here you go, ... the biggest choke in sports history. You think

it's been fun reliving the curse every year? Well get ready to relive the biggest choke in sports history every time a team goes down 3-0. Knicks get down 3-0 to the Pistons in the playoffs? Here come the highlights of the Sox. Rangers get down 3-0 to the Flyers? Here come the Sox highlights. Hell, the Padres in 2025 get down 3-0 to the Dodgers? Here comes the Sox highlight. This is not a situation to fear. This is a situation to embrace. The one good thing I remember Pitino saying was on opening night of his first season when the C's took a decent lead over the world champion Bulls into the fourth quarter and the Bulls started coming back, he called a timeout and said "stop staring at the clock and wishing it would get to zero—you are about to beat the world champions on opening night-go out and play and enjoy it." If we take that approach tonight, we'll win.

This series is about redemption. I said it before. For things that happened this series, this year and last year and forever. Schilling got it. Bellhorn got it. Foulke got it. Wakefield got it. Lowe got it. Arroyo got it. I don't know what Ortiz needed redemption for, but whatever it was, he got it. Tonight, a few more guys get it. We win this game the way we've won so many others—with Damon getting on base and moving along, with Manny driving in runs and with Pedro coming in to pitch the last five innings and get the win. It's going to happen and when it does the Red Sox and all their fans get redemption. F Kevin Brown. F getting runs off him. F the whole Yankees team and F the whole city of New York. As Mikey said in the Goonies when everyone wanted to ride up the bucket in the wishing well and go home, "it's our time right now—out there, it's been their time, but right now, it's our time."

I'll be nervous come game time. I'll do the routine. I'll bring out the thunderstick if needed. But I'm going to enjoy the hell out of his. We have a chance to take the greatest franchise in the history of American sports and pin on them the most embarrassing loss in this history of American sports. Embrace it. Enjoy the moment. It's finally our time.

I'm out--will talk to you later tonight.

And yes, we still believe.

Sunday, October 24, 2004

It is far better to win ugly than it is to lose pretty. This is a good thing, because last night we won ugly. It was probably a fun game for the disinterested fan to watch—11-9 games usually are. And it was good for Sox fans to see the guys face some adversity and continue to put the pressure on the Cards. Every time they scored to make it close or tie it up, we put runs on the board. It must have been frustrating for Cardinals' fans. One thing is for sure – neither of these lineups will give pitchers much breathing room. To win this thing, we have to expect a lot of 11-9-type games.

I watched the first Red Sox World Series game in 18 years with my buddy Tom at a hotel in Nashville. Just a handful of hours after the Sox beat the Yankees, after two hours of sleep, I had to get up and catch a plane to Nashville for a conference at Tennessee Tech in Cookeville, some 80 miles west of Music City. Tom was also giving a paper there, so we met for a weekend of debauchery. Just a few hours after last night's win, on three hours of sleep, I had to get up for an early flight back.

Given the gravity of the game and the fact that we kept letting the Cardinals get back into it, I was remarkably sane throughout. The Yankees' series probably inured me to the fear of losing the first game, at least to some degree, though I must admit there were a few occasions when I wondered if we had not left something back in the Bronx. But we got the win, even if Waker did not pitch well, even if the defense fell apart, even if Manny made not only two fielding errors within moments of one another in the 8th inning but also made a baserunning gaffe that almost cost us, even if we gave up leads of 4-0, 7-2, and 9-7. (Rob did use the Thunderstick in the 8th, which means he kept his streak alive).

Game two is tonight. Schilling will take the mound with his jerry-rigged ankle. If he can resemble the guy who pitched last week, or is anything close to his regular season performance, we should be in great shape. The Cardinals simply do not have a number one starter who strikes fear into anyone's heart. They have serviceable pitchers. Woody Williams saw last night what happens to serviceable pitchers against the Red Sox. Matt Morris has never scared me. And while the Jeff Suppan storyline will be one that Fox will surely play up, whatever chip he has on his shoulder from being left off of last year's playoff roster when he was with the Sox is not going to change the fact that he has to try to get our hitters out consistently while facing off against Pedro.

Tonight's is a big game, because St. Louis is tough at home, we are weaker on the road (though the Yankees might wonder about that) and getting a jump on a team in a short series is always preferable. A strong outing from Schilling and a cleaner style of baseball, with fewer errors and dumb mistakes should get us that second win. Three more to go . . .

Monday, October 25, 2004

OK, Derek, don't get too worked up yet. Don't start talking about a lifetime as a Sox fan and being on the brink and what this all feels like. DO NOT, I repeat, do not, start wondering what a Boston victory parade will be like, or how it will feel to finally have done it, or what Dan Shaughnessy or Bob Ryan or Peter Gammons or for that matter Buster Olney will have to say. And for the love of God, do not start looking at the list of free agents on the roster and whom we will sign and whom we will not and in any case what do you think the odds of repeating are?

I've got just one compound word to discourage thinking about anything beyond the glories of last night and the possibilities for tomorrow: Nineteen-eighty-six. 1986. There. How's that for a buzzkill, a major bummer, a serious reality check? In 1986 we won the first two games of the World Series against the Mets, and we all know how that ended. Now as always I do not believe in fate or curses or any of that nonsense. But I do believe in the possible. I do believe that the Cardinals did not win 105 games out of sheer luck. I do believe that going to St. Louis will make this a very different series. I do believe that a 2-0 deficit is not insurmountable, a 2-0 lead not bulletproof.

There. I've said all of the right things. In cliché form: Don't count your chickens, don't let your eyes get too big for your belly, don't put the cart before the horse. I am a Sox fan, so I know the history. I know what can happen. I know that what is possible and what is unlikely are one and the same. I know these things. I've lived these things.

Still ... how can we not be at least a little bit giddy right now? We have a 2-0 lead against the Cardinals in a series in which we have not even played all that well. We have had consecutive games with four errors after being nearly flawless in the ten preceding postseason games. Two nights ago it was Manny, last night Bill Mueller, who looked as if the baseball was an ex-girlfriend whose eyes he was not trying to meet. And yet last night we won more convincingly than the night before, 6-2, and we took it over from the get-go and never seriously allowed the Cardinals to compete. The bats were working, with Varitek driving in two with an early triple, Bellhorn driving in two with a double in the fourth, and Cabrera driving in—yes—two with a single off the Monster in the 6th. All three big hits came with two outs.

But if that is enough to make a fan feel happy about a two-game advantage in a series that many felt had letdown written all over it, what about Curt Schilling's performance? He did it again. On an ankle almost literally held together by spit and bailer twine (on the farm when I was a kid my grandmother used to work magic with bailer twine) and more than a little hope and imagination, Schilling had another dominant performance. He went six innings, giving up one unearned run on four hits and one walk. We are witnessing one of those special events in sports and Curt Schilling, against all odds, is bringing it to us. My guess is that there will be a lot of young men born in July, 2005 with names like "Curt Schilling Johnson" and "Schilling Curt Smith." Hell, I'm about to get a dog, and while I usually prefer to name pets after historical figures, you have to figure that he or she will bear a name reflective of this Red Sox team.

The Sox are absolutely rolling. But of course the series switches to Busch Stadium tomorrow night. They get their home crowd, a sea of good Midwesterners wearing red, applauding the fundamentals, and saying things like "shucks, dad, I sure wish that our pitchers could figure a way to get out these pesky Red Sox hitters," and "me too, son, me too. Want a Vanilla Coke?" And in that environment, with the crowd behind them, and the last at-bats, and the ability to play their brand of baseball, and with no designated hitter (meaning David Ortiz will play first base and Millar will come off the bench to provide pop when we need it), at least some advantage shifts to the Redbirds.

Then again, we have shut down the middle of their vaunted lineup for most of these two games. Our guys are highly unlikely to feel intimidated by the loyal fans of St. Louis given our recent experiences in the Bronx. (Johnny Damon: "Did that guy just call me a 'dastardly rapscallion'?" Kevin Millar: "Yeah, I think he did." Manny: "We have a game tonight?"). And while Pedro seems to have lost a step or two, especially in light of the "Who's your Daddy" nonsense in the Bronx, I have to say, I feel pretty good about Pedro facing off against Jeff Suppan. Pedro knows a good hunk of his legacy rests with tomorrow's start. Jeff Suppan realizes that he could not make the Red Sox' playoff roster last year. I could be very wrong on this one, but I believe that the Red Sox can hit Jeff Suppan. I believe they can hit him very hard indeed.

There are no guarantees. But we have five potential games left in the season, and we need to win two of those to win the World Series. Two of those games, if they prove necessary, will be in Fenway Park. We have been jumping out to leads, pummeling their pitching, and getting solid relief, especially last night when Embree and Foulke were lights out and Timlin gave up one run in what was at the time a 6-1 ballgame. We have all been through too much to start popping corks and popping off. We feel good.

Two more wins. And of course we believe. Not that it matters, but others are starting to too.

Tuesday, October 26, 2004

Two days have rarely seemed to have taken so long. And in two days the mind can play tricks on you. Especially when the mind has accomplices.

Off days are killers in a series like this largely because the media can frame a story however they want to and make it seem legitimate. The Cards are invincible at home! The Sox lose pop without the DH! The Sox defense is horrible and with Ortiz it will be worse! Pedro is in decline! And of course variations on the curse quackery.

First, the Cards won 105 damned games, meaning that much of the time they have been invincible just about everywhere. They also had the best road record in baseball. See where that got them? We can play fine in St. Louis, and the only advantage they'll have against our merry little band of idiots is that they get to bat last.

This is not insignificant, but when we enter the bottom of the ninth with a three run lead all it will mean is that Foulke will strike them out to end the game at the bottom of the ninth rather than the top. Whoop-dee-freakin' doo.

Yes, the Sox lose pop without the DH. And the Cards lose the extra hitter they got in Fenway. I've seen their pitchers' batting numbers. This is a wash for both teams. Oooooh—but with the DH gone some pull out the old double switch argument. National League fans hitch their entire belief in their league's strategic superiority on the double switch. I hate to drop this bomb on the good fans of the Senior Circuit: The double switch is not that fucking hard. Tito managed for four years in the National League, and with guys like Roberts and Youks and now Millar on the bench, I think we can figure out the cosmic mysteries of the double switch. (Anyone want to place a bet on the over/under on times Tim McCarver evokes this sanctified bit of piffle in the next three days? I say at least 4). I still say our lineup will be ready to rake, and as a karmic bonus, I cannot wait for Pedro to bloop a Texas Leaguer for a single, or to draw a walk, and to score a run.

As for the defense, David Ortiz started 34 games at first this year, or more than 20% of our total games. This is his natural position in the field. I recall him making a few scoops on throws that showed that he has quick hands. I also recall that there was a time when Millar-Ortiz at first was really a wash, with Millar offering a slight upgrade. This fear of our defensive misplays is way overstated. Our defense's performance was quite clearly an outlier, with one guy making multiple errors in each of the first two games. Need I remind people of the results of the series so far? If needed when the game matters, we can bring in Minky. We will not lose this game because of Ortiz being at first. We may win because he jacks a ball 475 feet off of Jeff Suppan, who had a great vantage point in last year's playoffs when his ass was nailed to the bench because we had eleven pitchers in whom we had greater faith than him.

Pedro's numbers against everyone but the Yankees have still been quite stellar, and once you get him out of the AL East, where they have seen him 20 times each the last few years, he approaches those rarefied heights of the glory years. Do I expect the Pedro of 2000 to walk out there tonight? No. But I expect the best of the

Pedro of the last three years. I expect him to go 7. I expect to have the lead. I expect to see the radar gun hit 97 once or twice. I expect him to out-pitch Suppan. I expect him to get the win. I expect him to take his place in this series. Pedro is the least of our worries. Perhaps the ones who should be worrying about him are the guys in the Cardinals' clubhouse, who so far have not lived up to their vaunted billing.

Basically, I expect all of this talk about the coming Cards resurgence to be put to rest when they take the field for game three. We hope that is tonight, but if rain delays it until tomorrow (and it seems about 50/50 that a delay or even postponement will happen) so be it. That will leave more room for speculation. And another day for the guys to get rest and enjoy the experience and for Schill to get a bit healthier and Pedro to visualize the most important game of his career and St. Louis to think about being down two games to zero.

We'll ignore the curse nonsense. At this point that's talk for charlatans and fools.

Believe!!! Two more wins . . .

Wednesday, October 27, 2004

Is this the day? Is this the day we have all been waiting for? Is this the night when the Boston Red Sox win the World Series? I get chills thinking about it. We've been waiting for this moment for all our lives.

It should by now be obvious, but I loathe the whole idea of the curse, the whole defeatist-voodoo-wikken-eye-of-newt mentality of it all. But I have come to realize something. The very idea of the curse was never about the Red Sox. It was about us. It was about being a Red Sox fan and wanting so much for this team to win, and yearning so much to feel the joy that other teams have felt in October, which lesser teams and lesser fans got to experience, that when we continued to fail we needed an explanation. It's like Billy talking to Jules after she finally loses it in St. Elmo's Fire. He explains to her what that strange and mythical eponymous fire was—it wasn't real, it was an illusion that sailors made up, something to get them by on their journeys. That is what the curse is. It was something that allowed some fans to grasp on to the failures of something they so wanted to succeed. Thus the Red Sox did not need the mythical curse, certain fans did. Well, for those who believed in curses. It really was broken on Wednesday night when the Sox blasted open the doors and won. In four straight games the Sox came in and believed in themselves and in so doing brought the rest of us along with them. They did not need St. Elmo's Fire. They did not need curses.

So now listen to Red Sox fans. Where we have always been preternaturally cautious, most of us are having a hard time containing ourselves. We talk about "when" and then quickly correct ourselves and say "if." But our hearts are not in it. We no longer think that horrible things are going to happen. We no longer believe in mystical forces that will snatch defeat from the jaws of victory. We no longer are burdened by a past that makes us believe that we are destined to relive past failures. And even those of us who never believed in curses have come to realize how fatalistic we have been, how much the past has affected the way we live out the present.

But that all ended last week. In taking those last four games from the Yankees, in staging the most epic and significant comeback in sports history, in watching the other guys fail, in watching our guys get it right, in watching kismet bounce a few our way, the Red Sox, and all of us in Red Sox Nation, shed a burden almost entirely of our own making. That it never existed does not mean that in a sense the curse was not real. But now it is gone. It is vanquished. I do not know how it is going to happen. I do not know what path it will take. I do not know how much anguish we'll have to confront.

But the Red Sox are going to win the World Series.

Last night the Sox won 4-1, and truth be told, I am not certain I've ever been more spot-on in predictions as I was in yesterday's diary, right down to the circumstances of Foulke's appearance and Pedro's outing. Pedro guaranteed his place in Valhalla with an epic seven inning, three hit appearance in which he gave up no runs. Manny blasted a four bagger and in the same inning made a throw to the plate to nail the potential game tying run that erased whatever mistakes he made the other night. We got a 4-0 lead and save for a solo Larry Walker shot in the 8th off of Foulke, never looked back. Foulke nailed the door shut. Somehow we survived the almighty National League Stadium and that ferocious style of play. Somehow we were able to field the ball cleanly (Ortiz not only fielded his position but made one huge play when that savvy National League baserunning guile failed the Cardinals. Suppan neglected to go home from third on a ground ball to right and instead got nailed when Ortiz made a perfect throw back to third). Somehow we overcame the treacherousness of substituting guys in a league without the designated hitter. We are up three games to none, and standing between us and the World Series title is today's Cardinals' starter, Jason Marquis.

I remember back in high school when I played football we used to have rituals before our games. Newport High School played scrappy, competitive football that mobilized an entire community. Given the level of our competition we were pretty good, but in the larger view, we were just a bunch of undersized kids playing a game. But back then, back in high school where everything is so raw and it all means everything, those Saturday afternoons seemed like the most important thing in the world. Before every game, about 15 minutes or so before we all went out to the field, right before coach came in to give his last fiery speech, the locker room would get really quiet. We had a mix tape that we listened to, with lots of Van Halen and AC/DC and the like. The last song on the mix was Phil Collins' "In the Air Tonight." I want to make it perfectly clear – Phil Collins is an insipid little gasbag. But with that one song, which I believe first played on Miami Vice, he hit magic.

As with all rituals, most people from without, especially 16 years later, would look back and cringe. And maybe this is all incredibly sophomoric. But at that moment, when Phil Collins sang "I've been waiting for this moment for all my life, hold on, hold on, hold on" and our testosterone surged and our fists clenched and our hearts raced and our bellies churned, life was never more vivid, more alive, more urgent. With the slow build of the guitars and the heart-thump backbeat and the crescendos and desperate lyrics, we were young men prepared to take the burdens of the world, or at least our little New Hampshire town, on our shoulder pads. Anything was possible. There was no cynicism. There was no irony. There was just the bittersweet vine of life and we grabbed on for all that we had.

I've been thinking about that song, that time, a lot lately. The Red Sox were good then, too, just not quite good enough. It was soon after 1986; the wounds of Bill Buckner and Mookie Wilson and Ray Knight and Bob Stanley still festered. I'm a lot older now. And so much in my life has changed. But I remember that kid in the locker room. I've been waiting for this moment for all my life. The Red Sox are going to win the World Series. Hold on, hold on, hold on . . .

Thursday, October 28, 2004

(9:59 am): So this is what pure unadulterated joy feels like.

(10:13 am): (An email I sent to myself this morning at 4:12):

First impressions:

We did it.

We finally did it.

When I was a little kid I spent the bulk of my time at my grandparent's house, which is where my Dad ran our dairy farm. And that is where I used to watch Red Sox games. It was a time before cable, and all of the Sox games were on channel 38 from Boston.

My grandfather was the hardest worker I've ever known. He'd put in a full week at the lumber yard, and then would come home and work until nightfall on the farm—milking cows, repairing fences, fixing tractors, or whatever else it took. He was a man who expected dinner on the table at 5:30, after which he'd go out for a few more hours to feed and clean the stalls, do some milking with my dad, and when he'd come in inevitably I'd be watching the Sox.
He always said the same thing. My grandfather was a salty old New Englander. He said exactly what he felt. Always. (That's where I got it from, folks). And every time he'd come in, see me watching the game, worshipful of my heroes in

double-knits, and he'd say a variation on the same thing: "Jesus Christ, these goddamnedsonovabitchin' dummies always lose." Of course then he'd always sit down in his recliner and he'd watch the game with me. When they'd win, I'd get some variation on "Well, those dummies got it right this time." When things didn't go well, "I told you, those goddamnedsonovabitchin dummies would lose."

But not so deep below the surface he always wanted them to win. (He said the same thing when the Pats were on. Or the Bruins. Or the Celtics. Or, to be honest, when I was playing football for the Newport High School Tigers. The man was an equal opportunity curmudgeon.)

God, I loved my grandfather.

Then after I had graduated from college and had also gotten my MA, I won a fellowship to South Africa. My biggest worry was that something would happen to Papa, and I would not be there for him. I made it through most of the year, and it happened. The heart that had not failed him when he had a massive heart attack when I was in high school got to him when he tried to bring his beloved dog Goldie to be put away. He died putting Goldie in the van. By the time I would have gotten back to the States, Papa would have already been buried, so I stayed in South Africa, and it broke my heart.

So now I think of him. Oh, I can imagine the string of profanities he would have strung together when the Sox fell down 0-3 to the hated Yankees. (Papa was, it can be said, no fan of anything related to the very idea of New York). But he would have known that I was watching. And he would have chided me (if by "chided" we mean calling me a goddamnedsonovabitchindummy) for believing. But he'd have watched too. Because underneath it all he believed. He wanted to believe. He just did not want anyone to know it.

We won tonight, Papa. We won. I have cried almost all night. I'm a goddamnedsonovabitchindummy. But they finally did it.

They finally did it.

(2:40 pm): There is no rational reason why the performance of a baseball team should make me this happy. Of course for all of the pain and suffering they've put me, us, through, I guess maybe we've earned some elation.

It is still difficult even to discuss the game rationally. The Sox took an almost immediate lead when Damon led off the game with a solo home run to right field. By the third inning, after a Trot Nixon double (he had a hell of a game, a hell of a series) drove in two runs, it was 3-0. That was it. That was the score that would bring the first World Championship to Boston in 86 years (the last one was 1918, in case the media was unsuccessful at bludgeoning you with that info the last few years). The reason that score could hold up was because Derek Lowe had yet another lights out performance. The guy who was so erratic that Tito left him out of the rotation to start the Anaheim series ended up getting the win in all three clinching victories in the postseason. Methinks Mr. Lowe earned himself a lot of money in the last three weeks. In any case, D-Lowe was masterful, matching the outings by Pedro and Schill by going 7 innings, giving up three hits, and allowing no earned runs. (Between the three of them, in this World Series sweep, Schilling, Pedro, and Lowe pitched twenty innings of shutout baseball.) At one point he retired 13 straight Cardinals. Arroyo, Embree, and Foulke closed it out, with Arroyo allowing a walk to the second batter he faced before Embree shut the door in the 8th. In the ninth Foulke came out, gave up a single up the middle to Pujols, one of only two Cardinals (Larry Walker being the other) who rose to the occasion of the World Series. He induced a fly ball to Gabe Kaplar, who had taken over for Trot in right field. One out. He then struck out Jim Edmonds. Two out. The Red Sox were one out away from that elusive prize.

One out away. That is a phrase that has haunted and tortured and vexed us since game 6 in 1986. We were one out away then, too. But this is not that team. I'll never forget the play that ended this game, this series, this season, that drought. Edgar Renteria, a truly talented player whom I had seen when he played for the Marlins' Triple A affiliate, the Knights, in Charlotte, when I lived in the Queen City, bounced a tapper back to Foulke, who gloved the ball, took a few steps, soft-tossed it underhanded to Doug, who secured it, made sure he was on the bag, and then let loose with a scream and a jump. Pandemonium ensued.

We swept the Cardinals to win the World Series. We never trailed for even a half an inning in the entire series, something previously accomplished by only three other teams, the 1989 A's, the 1966 Orioles, and the 1964 Dodgers (not for nothing, but that last one came against the Yanks, by the way).

And finally I got to see it. The Red Sox mobbed the field after the last game of the season. There were no horrific errors. There were no last inning rallies. There were no boneheaded manager's decisions. There were no reasons for recriminations. There was just pure, unadulterated joy. Foulke jumped into 'Tek's arms, the guys mobbed the field, the Sox fans in attendance went crazy with joy. (Our fans at times drowned out the vaunted Cards fans just as they had the cro-magnons in the Bronx and the brie-eaters in Anaheim. In all three cities, "Let's Go Red Sox!" cheers were audible throughout the games.) I'd waited my entire life for this scene, and it was all that I had hoped.

As for me? It is hard to describe what it was like. I watched almost all of the playoff games alone or with a select number of friends. Last night I watched the game alone at home, except for when my friend and colleague Jaime stopped by for an inning or so at the mid-point of the game. I wanted it that way. As I learned when I nearly got thrown out of Vette's, people around here could not understand what it meant to me. I did not want to be drunk, and I wanted the moment, when it came, to be mine, at least for a few minutes. I allowed the tears to stream down my cheeks. I stood and watched them celebrate. I let out a shout or a yelp or a barbaric yawp. I basked. I opened a bottle of champagne. I savored that moment. I've said it before as a sort of idle speculation, and I can confirm it now: It might seem sad or pathetic to those who don't, can't, or won't understand what this means, but that might have been the most purely happy I have ever been in my life. And if you do understand, you know exactly what I mean, what it means.

And then the phone calls started coming. And in between my cell phone ringing ("Take Me Out to the Ball Game" is my ring tone) I made calls. I talked to my dad, my Stepfather, my Mom's answering machine, my buddy Josh. Rob and I did our usual conversations every half inning during the game, and we agreed that we'd talk later, which we did, after everyone had gotten to us who wanted to in the wake of the game.

I was basically up all night. It wasn't crazy or chaotic. I did not have to wake anyone up to bail me out of jail. I did not run naked through the streets of Odessa. I did not go to the university and let out a Tarzanian scream. I did a lot of crying. I did a lot of smiling. I did a lot of remembering. I did a lot of laughing. And I smiled and I cried and I remembered and I laughed, I laughed and remembered and smiled and cried. I did get a couple of restive hours of sleep, but once I woke up it was more of the same. I've been on campus all day, worthless as all get-out, enjoying the visits from colleagues and students and people I swear I've never seen before, responding to emails, reading everything I can get my hands on.

I'm still not ready to talk about what it all means. I'm still walking on clouds. I'm still enjoying the idea of the 2004 World Champion Boston Red Sox. They won. We won. We did it. We believed. We deserve this.

Sunday, October 31, 2004

Today was supposed to be the day. Game 7 of the 2004 World Series was scheduled for October 31, Halloween night. When I started this diary, I fully anticipated that the long, draining, marvelous journey would end tonight, one way or the other. When I first started out, I perhaps romantically thought that it would come down to a Cubs-Sox matchup. It really never crossed my mind that if the Sox made it this far it would not go the full seven—that is simply the Red Sox way. Instead, here I sit four days after the Red Sox won the 2004 World Series.

So after all of this time, after all of this hoping and wishing and yearning, what does it all mean? How will this change my life, the life of Sox fans everywhere? How will it impact the Red Sox, their place in American sports?

It takes a particular kind of obsessive to write a daily diary about a baseball team. Or to be a member of a chat board devoted to all things Red Sox, as so many are. Or to live and die a little with every pitch, as I always have. And so the answer to these questions is both simple and complicated: On the one hand, obviously a great deal changes, but everything that changes is stuff that we all wanted to change. Red Sox fans love our team, and we have done so for all of our lives unconditionally. That will not change. Ever. But no longer will chants about Bill Buckner or 1918 or "Who's Your Daddy?" faze us. Indeed, no longer will most of them reasonably exist. That phase is done. That there was not a curse does not mean that there was not a heavy, heavy burden that each of us carried like a yoke. So in that sense there is relief, and with relief has come release.

Yet at the same time, there has been a perpetuation of a vacuous and stupid myth about Red Sox fans. The myth is that we somehow found our identity in our suffering, that to be a Red Sox fan was to embrace anguish and pain, to revel in painful losses even as we appeared devastated. This is stupid on so many levels that it baffles the imagination. It also presents a two-dimensional view of Red Sox fans. Sportsguy has said this on a number of occasions and I have been saying and writing it for years, but the reality is that all we have wanted as Red Sox fans was the chance to win.

The Boston Red Sox are one of the great, historic, respected franchises in all of sports. Red Sox fans do not need to get their identity from losing. We have maybe the greatest old ballpark in the world in a city teeming with history and significance. We have a roster of all-time greats that few can match. We have had great teams in the past. We have a fan base that is second to none in terms of passion, devotion, and commitment. The Red Sox and their fans never, ever, ever defined themselves as losers. Most of us are also Patriots and Celtics and Bruins fans, and there are very few cities that can match the total number of championships that we have in the four major team sports. The Sox are certainly far and away the team closest to the hearts of New Englanders. There is no doubt about that. But there are not a lot of Red Sox fans of a certain age who were not also fans of the Bird or Cowens or Russell Celtics. The same fans who rooted for Carl Yastrzemski fell in love with Bobby Orr. Kids whose first Red Sox hero was Nomar also love Tom Brady. This idea of Red Sox fans as curmudgeonly losers is stupid because it was always factually, demonstrably wrong. The same fans of the Red Sox are fans of the greatest franchise in the history of the NBA and of the team currently dominating the NFL.

Concomitant with this silly trope was the idea that the Red Sox would become just another franchise if somehow the team climbed the mountain and won the World Series. This has been a favorite of Dan Shaughnessy over the years. But it too is wrong. It is laughable that the Red Sox will become less special or less important now that they have won it all. It is counterintuitive to argue that a World Series win makes the Red Sox just another team. The Red Sox are a great, historic, vital franchise that now has won a World Championship and can now reclaim its rightful place alongside the great winning franchises in baseball history. Despite the drought that began in 1918 and ended last Wednesday, the fact remains that the Red Sox have won six World series titles, a number surpassed by only three other franchises, all historic clubs in their own right (Yankees, Cardinals, A's). And while we are tied at six with the Dodgers, we really should be able to claim seven, since in 1904 the Giants refused to play us in the still-new championship format. These are facts that have been overlooked in all of the blather about 1918.

So what does it all mean for me? Mostly it just makes me really, really happy. As I've often said before there is something irrational about being a sports fan. But whatever reason lies behind it, the Red Sox are a team I have followed since as long as I can remember, and for all of that time all I wanted was a World Series title. This year they finally delivered. If others perceive me as being somehow less of a fan because we have won, that is their own problem. But for the next few months I can revel in this. I can buy the t-shirts and hats and World Series programs and pennants and commemorative editions of magazines. I can put the posters on the wall and make sure that everyone back home sends me copies of the Globe.

When it is all said and done, maybe being just another fan of just another team is even ok. Maybe I am just another fan, albeit more knowledgeable and passionate and obsessed than most.

And as another fan, I'll start asking myself the one question that most fans ask at the end of a season: Do I think they can do it next year?

And the answer will be simple: Yes. I think they can do it AGAIN next year.

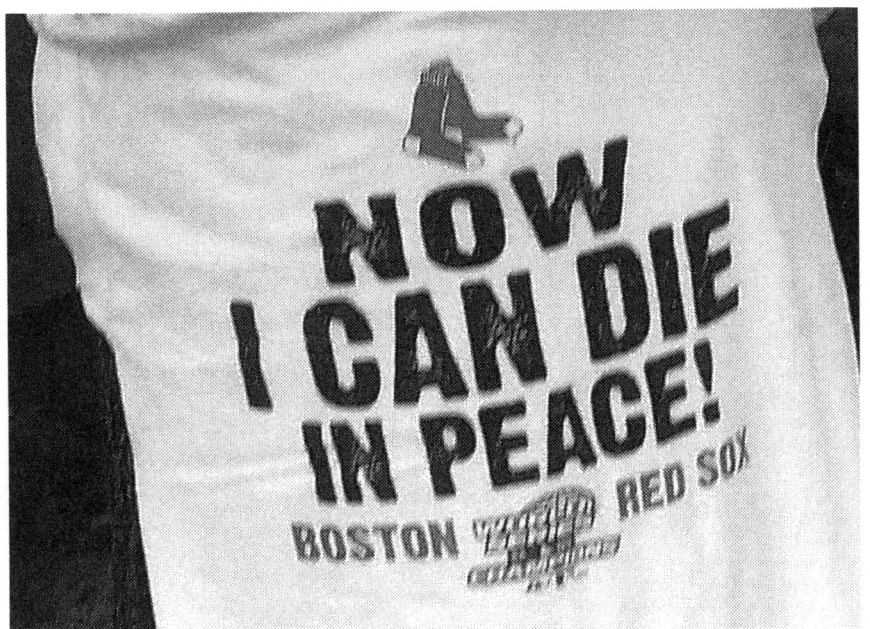

10

August 2005 (Epilogue)

Monday, August 1, 2005
Yesterday the Sox played maybe their most emotionally fraught game of the season. In many ways I think it might be akin to the July 24 game last year when Tek jacked A-Rod and it set in motion the events of the rest of the season. To make a long saga short, for the past few days the rumors were that Manny was on his way out via a trade because his antics, "Manny being Manny" had gotten to be too much, especially after the supposedly refused to enter a game last week despite the fact that we were injury-depleted. It seemed for a while that Manny was on his way to join Pedro in Queens and that we were going to get Mike Cameron and Aubrey Huff in a three team deal also involving the Devil Rays. Things heated up substantially when Tito announced that he was sitting Manny to allow the sometimes petulant slugger to "clear his head."

Fast forward to yesterday afternoon. The trade deadline was 4:00 in the east and much like last year, Sox fans kept their ears to the ground awaiting word of deals big (anything involving Manny) and slightly less big (everything else, but most rumors centered on us trading Mueller for JC Romero, a reliever for the Twins). When the deadline came and went, it was apparent that we had stood pat, and that Theo's moves in the last couple of weeks were going to have to suffice. In the meantime, the Sox, who entered the afternoon on a four-game winning streak, still had to finish off a taut game against Minnesota. It was tied 3-3 in the 8th, Ortiz was intentionally walked, and out stepped many as a pinch hitter. By all accounts Fenway was electric, as loud and ecstatic as anyone there could recall. And as if it had been scripted, many knocked a single that drove in what would prove to be the game-winning run as Fenway erupted.

In the eight months since that glorious night in St. Louis, my suspicions have been confirmed: Not much has changed despite the fact that everything has changed. Winning the World Series meant that a historic weight was lifted, a monkey came from off our backs, a yoke was removed, and any other cliché that evokes the end of a burden. In that sense, we entered a brave world unfamiliar to all of us. At the same time, we are still passionate fans and the Red Sox put us through a wide array of emotions, not all of them good. I write this from England, where I am spending the summer as a fellow at the Rothermere American Institute at the University of Oxford. I spend a disproportionate amount of my time trying to compensate for the five hour time lag between here and Boston so that I can keep on top of every tidbit of information about them. When they win, I am happy; when they lose I am pissed, frustrated or just plain annoyed. I am not alone. The fact is, our emotional investment in this team did not wane once that ball nestled in Doug Mientkiewicz' glove, or after that splendid cathartic parade through the streets and rivers of Boston. Why would it have? This is where so many people had it so very wrong – Red Sox fans never identified with losing and certainly did not take any sort of pleasure from it. The Red Sox, almost always tantalizingly good, finally were good enough last year, and fans have been able to savor it. But that does not mean that we do not want to win it all this year, and that throughout the offseason the comings (Edgar Renteria, Matt Clement) and goings (Pedro, D-Lowe, etc.) did not effect us, or that we did not spend most of the Hot Stove League wondering if we could not repeat.

This year's team is good. They are in first place, two-and-a-half games up on the Yankees. But they have some weaknesses, and the injury bug has bitten them hard this season, with Schill just now coming back (as our closer!) and with Foulke, who was ineffective when he was healthy, on the shelf for at least another few weeks after knee surgery that he ought to have had last winter. Trot is now out. Wade Miller, another offseason acquisition, missed his last start. But as games like yesterday's prove, they still have that same tenacity, and they still are never going to quit. It would really be nice to punctuate this season with an AL East title, our first since 1995. And we still believe that they can win the World Series. Again. That they can repeat as champions. And that feels really nice to write, even eight months after the events of last October. We still bleed red. And we still believe. That was never going to change.

www.ingramcontent.com/pod-product-compliance
Lightning Source LLC
Chambersburg PA
CBHW032102090426
42743CB00007B/212